The
South
Atlantic
Quarterly
Winter 2003
Volume 102
Number 1

D1220312

Dear Karl —

I have a few copies of this,
and thought you might like to have
the whole issue. Thank you
again for your stimulating discussions
of your work, and of your
generous response to my essay.

All my best,
Wai Chee

Visit Duke University Press's Web site at www.dukeupress.edu.

Subscriptions. Direct all orders to Duke University Press, Journals Fulfillment, 905 W. Main St., Suite 18B, Durham, NC 27701. Annual subscription rates: institutions, $120; e-only institutions, $108; individuals, $35; students, $21. Add $16 for foreign subscriptions. Back volumes (institutions): $120. Single issues: institutions, $30; individuals, $12. For more information, contact Duke University Press Journals at 888-387-5687 (toll-free in the U.S. and Canada) or 919-687-3602; subscriptions@dukeupress.edu.

Permissions. Photocopies for course or research use that are supplied to the end user at no cost may be made without explicit permission or fee. Photocopies that are provided to the end user for a fee may not be made without payment of permission fees to Duke University Press. Address requests for permission to republish copyrighted material to Permissions Coordinator, Duke University Press, 905 W. Main St., Suite 18B, Durham, NC 27701; permissions@dukeupress.edu.

Advertisements. Direct inquiries about advertising to Journals Advertising Specialist, Duke University Press, 905 W. Main St., Suite 18B, Durham, NC 27701; journals_advertising@dukeupress.edu.

Distribution. The journal is distributed by Ubiquity Distributors, 607 DeGraw St., Brooklyn, NY 11217; phone: 718-875-5491; fax: 718-875-8047.

The *South Atlantic Quarterly* is indexed in *Abstracts of English Studies, Academic Abstracts, Academic Index, America: History and Life, American Bibliography of Slavic and East European Studies, American Humanities Index, Arts and Humanities Citation Index, Book Review Index, CERDIC, Children's Book Review Index (1965–), Current Contents, Historical Abstracts, Humanities Index, Index to Book Reviews in the Humanities, LCR, Middle East: Abstract and Index, MLA Bibliography, PAIS,* and *Social Science Source.*

The *South Atlantic Quarterly* is published, at $120 for institutions and $35 for individuals, by Duke University Press, 905 W. Main St., Suite 18B, Durham, NC 27701. Periodicals postage paid at Durham, NC, and additional mailing offices. Postmaster: Send address changes to *South Atlantic Quarterly*, Box 90660, Duke University Press, Durham, NC 27708-0660.

Copyright © 2003 by Duke University Press

ISSN 0038-2876

Afterlives of Romanticism

SPECIAL ISSUE EDITORS: IAN BAUCOM AND
JENNIFER KENNEDY

The
South
Atlantic
Quarterly
Winter 2003
Volume 102
Number 1

Ian Baucom

A "Stranger's Near Approach": Afterlives of Romanticism

> A small shed had been added to my grandmother's house years ago. Some boards were laid across the joists at the top, and between these boards and the roof was a very small garret, never occupied by anything but rats and mice. . . . To this hole I was conveyed as soon as I entered the house. The air was stifling; the darkness total.
> —Harriet Jacobs, *Incidents in the Life of a Slave Girl*

I am not and cannot pretend to be a Romanticist and so cannot claim to know in any detail the discrete rules of scholarly competence that govern the field, the subdisciplinary bylaws that hold membership in this, as in any, intellectual community minimally conditional on some shared experiences of reading. Nor am I interested, here, in adding an item to the list of texts that all good, self-respecting Romanticists should know. Rather, it is precisely because, whatever my ignorance of the current state of the Romanticist contract, I feel fairly sure that a knowledge of Harriet Jacobs's *Incidents in the Life of a Slave Girl* is not obligatory in the field that I want to start with it.[1] There is the matter of dates to begin with. Originally published in 1860, Jacobs's text

The *South Atlantic Quarterly* 102:1, Winter 2003.
Copyright © 2003 by Duke University Press.

(written under the pseudonym Linda Brent) falls a few good decades outside the historical moment with which Romanticism is usually associated and that, generally, allows it to designate not only a shared (if never quite agreed on) set of ideological, epistemological, or aesthetic protocols but a reasonably stable period concept. And then, too, there is the problem of genre or mode. As Valerie Smith has argued, the primary influence on Jacobs's text would appear to be the domestic, sentimental novel (whose situationally compromised but virtuous heroine, as Smith further suggests, both provides a model for the narrative of sexual menace at the heart of *Incidents* and proves itself radically inadequate to the experiences of sexual violence Jacobs reveals to be definitive of the life of the "slave girl").[2] And if there is a generic allegiance to something other than the sentimental novel in the passage I cite it would certainly seem to be to the Gothic, though again, even gothic terror seems flippant in relation to the racial terror that drove Jacobs, in the "incident" she here relates, to go into hiding from her predatory master, Dr. Flint, in the garret of her grandmother's shed. But Romantic*ist* I nevertheless want to argue this chapter from the *Incidents* is, though I probably would not have noticed it if I had not been struck, first, by how frequently, if variously, the texts I *am* supposed to know ("postcolonial," "diasporic," "postmodern") wander into seemingly "Romantic" territory, and, subsequently, in the process of editing this collection, by registering for the first time the allusion that frames this chapter of Jacobs's text. The chapter is entitled "The Loophole of Retreat," and, as Kevis Goodman's contribution to this collection reminds us, that phrase is not original to Jacobs but occurs in one of the more famous lines from William Cowper's 1785 poem *The Task* ("'Tis pleasant through the loopholes of retreat / To peep at such a world.")[3]

What are we to make of this repetition? The phrase is unusual enough that it seems unlikely that both Cowper and Jacobs (and more to the point, Jacobs, writing three-quarters of a century after Cowper) would have generated it at random. Had Jacobs read *The Task* prior to writing *Incidents*? I cannot answer definitively. Certainly, as someone whose education had familiarized her with the conventions of eighteenth- and nineteenth-century English literature she could be expected to have known of Cowper, whose collaboration with John Newton on the *Olney Hymns* together with his 1793 poem "The Negro's Complaint" (which, set to music and multiply reproduced in pamphlet form, became the virtual ballad of the Abolition movement in England) had made him (together with Robert Southey and Anna Letitia Barbauld) one of the most celebrated English poets to have addressed the problem of transatlantic slavery. *The Task*, too, is not devoid of interest in, and protest against, the peculiar institution ("Slaves cannot breathe in England; if their lungs / Receive our air, that moment they are free, / They touch our country, and their shackles fall"), and on the basis of this circumstantial and allusive evidence I find it hard to believe that Jacobs could not have had Cowper in mind when she published her chapter on her garret confinement under that odd phrase. But if Jacobs was thinking of Cowper, possibly even paying tribute to him, what might it have meant for her to be thinking of his "loopholes of retreat" rather than, for instance, that celebrated line from "The Negro's Complaint": "Still in thought as free as ever"?[4] Or what might it have meant for her, perhaps, to be thinking of both poems, to have found that the condition of being "Still in thought" and "free as ever" (which, legally, through this point in her life meant "never") was coincident with finding a Romantic "loophole" through which to "peep" at the "world"? What, indeed, might such a determination to "retreat" not only into the protected space of her grandmother's garret but, belatedly, into a Romantic habit of worldly spectation betoken both for Jacobs's text and for the worldly "afterlife" of Romanticism beyond its designated historical period and outside its customary archive of texts?

———

This is an introduction to a collection and not an essay within it, so I will not indulge myself by attempting to offer anything like comprehensive answers to these questions. Rather—though I will return briefly to Jacobs's text and its Cowper pretext at the conclusion to this introduction—what I want to note is that it is questions of this *sort* that have inspired the collection at hand. Jacobs is not alone; nor is Cowper the only "Romantic" to survive the moment that produced him; nor is the deferred or long-distance rewriting of one or other recognizably Romantic figure the only way in which, over the course of the past two centuries, Romantic ideologies, epistemologies, and aesthetics have been rendered globally vagrant, historically untimely, perversely resistant to the "numerical determinism," as Wai Chee Dimock here puts it, of the "Newtonian" period concepts by which we make sense of history. The essays in this collection are, of course, not the first to notice this Romantic unwillingness to honor conventional unities of time and place; nor, in many instances, is this the first thing the collection's contributors have had to say about this phenomenon. In the early 1990s, thanks in large part to David Simpson and Alan Liu, it became if not quite a commonplace then certainly an influential strand of critical thought to identify the postmodern (with its various devotions to the anecdote, the local, the locale, the detail, the nontotalizing, the singular, and the politics of melancholy) as, among many other things, a belated or neo-Romanticism.[5] More recently, James Chandler has reminded us—or, for many of us, taught us—that our very conception of the "contemporary" has a Romantic provenance, as does historicism, our dominant method for constructing and making sense of present and historical "moments" and the political events, social dynamics, and aesthetic artifacts such contemporaneities are understood to encompass.[6] If, as Chandler's work suggests, contemporary understandings of the "contemporary" are Romantically noncontemporaneous with themselves, then so too, Mary Poovey has suggested, are contemporary understandings of fact, system, and epistemology. As she notes in the concluding chapter of her magisterial *A History of the Modern Fact*, "Whether it takes the form of Ferdinand de Saussure's claim that signs are arbitrary, Jacques Lacan's definition of the ego as lack, Jean Baudrillard's fascination with simulation's ability to end all original reference, or Slavoj Žižek's celebration of the 'meaningless traces' that thrust meaning production onto analysis itself, the postmodernist conviction that the systems of knowledge humans create constitute the only source of meaning is [not only] gradually displacing both the problem of induction and all the variants of the modern fact" but is formally repetitive of the counterinductive and hence countermodern epistemology "adumbrated by the romantic poets' turn away from phenomenal particulars and toward the mind that contemplates those things."[7]

This last point, needless to say, constitutes not only a synthetic characterization of postmodern modes of knowledge production but an equally generalized typification of a Romantic conception of knowledge. In either case, Poovey's departicularized Romanticism and her autoreferential and counterinductive (Romantic) postmodernism appear to be the very antithesis of, say, Liu's hyperdetailed Romanticism and transcendently detailed (if equally Romantic) postmodernism. The point, of course, is not that either Liu or Poovey has it right while the other does not, or even that the internal heterogeneity of both the Romantic and the postmodern render both excessively susceptible to selective transcoding in one another's select key-terms, but, rather, that the very heterogeneity of these two objects of study, and the ease with which that heterogeneity allows two deeply informed scholars to apparently say the same thing (that the postmodern is a belated or neo-Romanticism) while in fact meaning two very different things (that the postmodern is Romantic by virtue of its hyperparticularism; that the postmodern is Romantic by virtue of its disinterest in empirical particulars) should lead us to suggest that the original statement ("The postmodern is a belated or neo-Romanticism") is not *an* answer to *a* question ("What is postmodernism?") but an invitation to ask a series of others. Perhaps not so much, What *is* Romanticism? as, How many *are* there? Where have they traveled over the long history of modernity? Where are they now? How are they now? How did they get from there to here? and, What, now, are we to make of them and of a now that seems not so much contradictorily as multiply Romantic?

Multiple Romanticisms; multiple modernities; multiple postmodernities: the essays that follow engage and transcode such multiplicities—as they also pose or answer such questions as I have framed—in a variety of ways that I do not wish to impoverish by summary. So, instead, as a means of learning from them rather than advertising them, let me return by way of four passages drawn from my customary archive to the questions I put to Jacobs's *Incidents*. Each of the passages I have in mind touches in some or other way on what, following Robert Farris Thompson and Paul Gilroy, we have taken to calling the black Atlantic. But other than sharing that very broad and very diverse rubric, they appear to have nothing else in common. The question I want now to ask of them (and implicitly also to put to both the Romanticist and non-Romanticist readers of this collection) is whether we have something to learn of them by reimagining them as, also, commonly Romantic and thus expressive of the value Romantic specialists and nonspecialists alike might find in attending to the untimely, vagrant, and worldly afterlives and other-lives of what is not, after all, an exclusively European late-eighteenth- and early-nineteenth-century phenomenon.

The four passages come in pairs: the first two address the common Romantic topos of cognitive indolence, the second two are broadly elegiac. Here are the first two—one, again, from Jacobs (from the concluding paragraph of "The Loophole of Retreat": she recalls peering through a hole she has bored in the wall of the garret), the other from the title story of the South African writer Njabulo Ndebele's 1983 collection *Fools and Other Stories.*

> O, those long gloomy days, with no object for my eye to rest upon, and no thoughts to occupy my mind, except the dreary past and the uncertain future! I was thankful when there came a day sufficiently mild for me to wrap myself up and sit at the loophole to watch the passers by. Southerners have the habit of stopping and talking in the streets, and I heard many conversations not intended to meet my ears. I heard slave-hunters planning how to catch some poor fugitive. . . . Very rarely did any one suggest that I might be in the vicinity. Had the least suspicion rested on my grandmother's house, it would have been burned to the ground. But it was the last place they thought of. Yet there was no place, where slavery existed, that could have afforded me so good a place of concealment.[8]

> I was awakened, late in the afternoon, by a light knock on the door. I slowly awoke from a long uncertainty about whether I had been awake or asleep. Since I had told myself it was the day for thinking, I had willed myself to think: but my mind had been unable to focus on any specific thing. I had willed without direction. And I had become aware that I did not really know how to think; how to induce the mind to work; that it was really possible to be dedicated without any real aims to be conscious of. . . . Thinking about thinking, I *had* been thinking. I had smiled and then closed my eyes and tried to think about something concrete. . . . For such a long time. Was I thinking or not? Was I asleep or awake? It was the light knock at the door that brought me to full consciousness.
>
> There was a little boy at the door. He must have been about seven years old, and he wore only a dirty pair of black trousers. . . . As I looked at him, it struck me suddenly that he was the thing I should have been thinking of. As he stood at the door, he seemed such a large part of the world just behind him, for he was bigger than it, and had blotted most of it out with his body. His presence there seemed to be the beginning of questions.[9]

And here are the next two—the first, from the epilogue to the Martini-quan novelist Patrick Chamoiseau's *Texaco* (1998), recounts the narrator's final visit to the "Doum" (a thickly vegetated section of Fort-de-France's shantytown that the text associates with indigenous magic and vernacular folk wisdom) in search of a "Mentoh," a sort of living embodiment, and organic intellectual, of the folk tradition of the slave past; the second is from the dedication to Jacques Derrida's *Specters of Marx*.

> Penetrating the Doum, I found it deserted. Abandoned. I had been in so many places of Power, that I had acquired an immediate intuition for them. In my daily life, I detected around me so many cultural ruins in our mute countryside, so many gradual mummifications in the land all around, that I could at any point, before a hutch, a spot, a landscape, a river mouth, perceive a historical presence, stricken with staggering wear and tear. The Doum was dead: nothing could be done. . . .The Mentohs had always mustered our collective imaginings. They had imprinted upon them a convergence—a coherence. Out of the scattering of Carib, African, European, Chinese, Indian, Levantine . . . , they fixed the fibers for a good rope. . . . The disappearance of our Mentohs was revealing (oh silent pain) the domination of our spirit by new means unknown to traditional resistance. The boot, the sword, the rifle, or the banking powers of Occidental Being were no longer a threat to the peoples, the erosion of differences was.[10]

One name for another, a part for the whole: the historic violence of Apartheid can always be rendered as a metonymy. In its past as well as in its present. By diverse paths (condensation, displacement, expression, or representation), one can always decipher through its singularity so many other kinds of violence going on in the world. At once part, cause, effect, example, what is happening there translates what *takes place* here, always here, wherever one is and wherever one looks, closest to home. Infinite responsibility, therefore, no rest allowed for any form of good conscience.

But one should never speak of the assassination of a man as a figure, not even an exemplary figure in the logic of an emblem, a rhetoric of the flag or of martyrdom. A man's life, as unique as his death, will always be more than a paradigm and something other than a symbol. And this is precisely what a proper name should always name. . . . Allow me to salute Chris Hani and to dedicate this lecture to him.[11]

Let me begin at the end, with Derrida and Chris Hani, the assassinated South African communist leader whom Derrida invokes, recognizes, salutes at the beginning of *Specters of Marx*, and who, thus, is in some senses the text's first and most abiding specter, the African ghost who most haunts and "figures" Derrida's late-twentieth-century "state[ment] of the debt," his "work of mourning," his conjuring of a "new international." I do not doubt the sincerity of Derrida's salute, but it also cannot have escaped most readers that that salutation, that desire at once to honor and to speak with or to the dead man ("The more life there is, the graver the specter of the other becomes, the heavier in its imposition. And the more the living have to answer for it. *To answer for the dead, to respond to the dead.* To correspond and have it out with obsessive haunting. . . . nothing is more serious and nothing is more true) is at once strategically useful, rather askance both to the argument of *Specters* and to the spirit of Derrida's larger enterprise, and oddly reminiscent of the desire that frames two of the now canonical elaborations of contemporary historicist thought: Stephen Greenblatt's *Shakespearean Negotiations* ("I began with the desire to speak with the dead") and Fredric Jameson's *The Political Unconscious* (which identifies its project, and that of a more encompassing materialist historiography, with the determination to "give us an adequate account of the essential *mystery* of the past, which, like Tiresias drinking the blood, is momentarily returned to life and warmth [by the historicist operation] and allowed once more to speak, and deliver its long-forgotten message in surroundings utterly alien to it").[12] Derrida, Jameson, Greenblatt: there are, of course, any number of other trios one could assemble as representative of the major currents of contemporary critical thought, but these three will do quite nicely, at least as three of the more currently influential members of the masculine elegiac tradition.

To identify Greenblatt, Jameson, and Derrida as elegists is, of course, a little willful. But perhaps only a little. Alan Liu has elsewhere suggested that in its untiring exhumations of the "lost object" of history, new historicism assumes a "habit (matched by that of Jameson mourning the loss of 'cognitive mapping' and Habermas the loss of 'lifeworld') [that] is the flip side of mania in Freud's schema: a mourning so existential as to be comparable to melancholia."[13] And Walter Benn-Michaels, in a characteristically gadflyish essay, has detected in both the "new historicism" and deconstruction something very much like an elegiac conjuring ("For you who never was there") of the lost historical past.[14] It is not, though, Thomas Gray and his brother elegists that I ultimately want to suggest haunt Greenblatt, Jameson, and Derrida but another set of Romantic precursors that ghosts their work and makes its presence so forcefully present in Derrida's salute to Chris Hani. Not Gray, then, but Sir Walter Scott; and not elegy but eighteenth-century sensibility discourse, Smithian sentiment theory, the historical novel, and the Romantic politics of friendship. For eighteenth-century sensibility (like, I am suggesting, the sentimental politics of late-twentieth-century deconstruction and historicism, both Marxist and "new") is partially, as Julie Ellison has argued, a masculine politics of recognition (of suffering nobility), but it is also a mode of worldly interestedness in global systems of inequality and a reimagining of global politics as an invitation to geopolitical friendship.[15] Sensibility is also, as Ian Duncan has previously indicated and as he suggests again in his contribution to this collection, foundational to the emergence of the historical novel (at least as Scott framed that genre of Romantic discourse) and, as Chandler has further detailed, thus, also, genealogically dispositive (if not determinative) of a contemporary historicism that traces itself through Jameson's reception of Lukacs and Lukacs's reception of Scott back to the work of Adam Smith. But still: Jameson and Adam Smith? Derrida and Sir Walter Scott? What truly odd nightmares of past generations to prey like ghosts on the minds of the living.

In any absolute sense of one-to-one correspondences the questions certainly invite a no. But also, in a more conversational, epistolary, or call-and-response sense of correspondence, a yes. For if history always repeats itself with a difference, it also repeats itself. By which I mean that it endures, that, as Jameson himself has argued (as, indeed, is virtually the central methodological argument of *The Political Unconscious*), the present is always nonsynchronous with itself, always still working out at the level of genre, if nothing else, the unresolved ideological contradictions of prior ages.[16] That this is the case, that the present is irredeemably haunted, that the life of the present is always, also, a living out of the afterlife of the not-in-fact-past "past" is, of course, not a conviction original to the postmodern or to Derrida (even if his *Specters of Marx* is our most elaborate recent exploration of that proposition). It is, rather, a paradigmatically Romantic article of faith. Indeed, as Thomas Pfau's and Wai Chee Dimock's contributions to this collection remind us, to speak of the "afterlives of Romanticism" is to risk an entirely Romantic tautology. One might as well say the afterlife of the afterlife-ly or, in Derridean parlance, to speak of the haunting of the haunted, the reapparition of the reapparent, the appearance as if (and only *as if*) for the first time of that which reappears.

Paying his debts to Marx (or, at least, demanding that we see him thus indebted) is Derrida thus also revealing a debt to a lyric mode of Romantic historical consciousness in which, as Pfau has it, the subject is always "the unwitting vessel of its own past"? Unwittingly vesseling that lyric Romantic past is Derrida, in his very Marxianism, further indebted to the Romantic wing of the Scottish Enlightenment? Marx himself certainly wrestled with Adam Smith, and if for many of us it seems as if he won the battle with the political economist it remains unclear whether he, and those, like Jameson and Derrida, who count themselves as in some or other way faithful to his "spirit," was or have been entirely able to throw off the more sympathetic influence of the theorist of *Moral Sentiments* and his novelistic inheritors. I do not want to push the suggestion too far. But still there is the matter of that entirely anomalous and utterly representative dedication, that decisively indecisive masterpiece of "undecidability/decision" in which Derrida allows himself to read Chris Hani's death as simultaneously singular and exemplary, simultaneously figurative and properly nominative. "Infinite responsibility" indeed. An infinite responsibility, in this case, simultaneously entertained and not deferred. Derrida risks the proper name. For which I can do nothing but applaud him while also wondering whether this is not the one thing a programmatically antiontologizing fidelity to the "specter" of Marx cannot permit itself? Standing over Hani's grave, Derrida, it occurs to me, salutes a friend only to rebuke himself for betraying, with that salute, the spirit of his epistemological convictions. Is *this* Romantic? Think perhaps not so much of Wordsworth on his return from France as of Edward Waverly, that prototypically undecided representative of the historical novel, whose typically romance posture (as Duncan has sketched it) is further representative of what Chandler calls the Romantic "type": the belated historical spectator who stands sympathetic witness to scenes of historical suffering; registers his friendship with the vanquished; provisionally reverses Marx's injunction to "let the dead bury the dead" by determining, instead, "to let the living revive the dead";[17] but then, ultimately, finding himself unable to sustain a fully melancholy devotion to the irreducible singularity and unexchangeability of the slain, moves mournfully and undecidedly on.

Hence my curiosity about the proper name, that brief moment in which

Derrida's idiom shifts from the register of Romantic mourning into a full-blown (if swiftly vanishing) articulation of Romantic melancholy. But why this vanishing? Why is the proper name, having been attached to an assassinated African politician who had proven himself, after his own fashion, faithful to the spirit of Marx and to the attempt to institute a communist state in some "actually existing" form, then withdrawn when it comes to the question of anything else that assumes the form of the "actually existing," anything that is not either spectrally coming-again or spectrally to-come? Why, having served to attach the antispeculative speculations of Derrida's lecture to a recognizable scene of historical suffering and an entirely "salutary" geopolitics of friendship must the ontic proper name of the revolutionary, or what Derrida also calls the "proper content" of revolutionary history, then be so elaborately deconjured? ("Everything is concentrated therefore in the question of this 'content' . . . the *proper* content, the appropriate content. . . . By all logic, one ought to recognize it by nothing other than the [spectral] excess of this untimely disidentification, therefore by nothing that is. By nothing that is presently identifiable.") Is the decisively proper—the *proper* name, the *proper* content—such a threat to difference and *différance* alike?[18] Is the infinite responsibility of *différance* simply, in the last instance, ethically prior to any singular, melancholy, or named political commitment, anything that would dare specify its content? Is *différance* responsibility? Is difference? And, if so, to what does it respond and correspond? To Romanticism, as I have been suggesting? But if so, to which one? For again, like Marx's specters, there are many, certainly at least two in what I have thus far sketched: a mournful and a melancholy Romanticism, both of which seem to haunt Derrida's salutary address and what I am tempted to call his axially Atlantic (rather than transatlantic or circum-Atlantic) Franco-African political theater *of* address. Hani's shade, after all, is not the only African ghost to haunt *Specters*: the Algerian dead and the North African immigrant are there too. And perhaps it is that very multiplicity of the African living and dead with whom Derrida is entering into correspondence that suggests to him that responsibility (and correspondsibility) is restless difference; and that might suggest to us that in this moment of its geopolitical afterlife, so too is Romanticism.

Though that should come as no surprise. For to regard Romanticism as the safeguard, the preserve, the refuge of difference in the face of a homogenizing, dedifferentiating, and synchronizing modernity is to put an entirely familiar gloss on the phenomenon (one that, it might be noted, both informs Michael Lowy and Robert Sayre's recent *Romanticism against the Tide of Modernity*—a revisionary account that treats Romanticism less as an aesthetic movement or a period concept than as a long-durational counter-discourse on and of modernity, a melancholy weltanschauung "co-extensive with capitalism itself"—and, as Lowy and Sayre and Pfau point out, helps to explain Romanticism's otherwise puzzling reactionary-to-revolutionary ideological range).[19] But if Romanticism is thus, arguably, difference, is difference Romantic? And in what way? The passage I have cited from Chamoiseau's *Texaco* provides some clues. Like Derrida's "dedication" it is, after its own fashion, broadly elegiac. But what it mourns is not a man but a concept, indeed the concept of difference itself: "The disappearance of our Mentohs was revealing (oh silent pain) the domination of our spirit by new means unknown to traditional resistance. The boot, the sword, the rifle, or the banking powers of Occidental Being were no longer a threat to the peoples, the erosion of differences was." But this is not just any difference, it is a determinate difference, a creole difference. Though again, in one of the countless ironies of history, this creole difference is itself the product of a historical dedifferentiation, a braiding or roping together of differences ("Carib, African, European, Chinese, Indian, Levantine . . .") in one common cord and (to add one melancholy twist to this now cross-Atlantic strand of Romanticism) under one common proper name: *creolite*, as Chamoiseau identifies it in his coauthored manifesto *Éloge de la créolité*.[20]

But if, in the impulse to the proper name, Derrida might detect a melancholy will-to-ontologize in this vagrant and belated Romanticism, then creolite also signifies something else. As Edouard Glissant, Chamoiseau's chief philosophical influence, indicates, creolite is also apprehensible as an entirely antimelancholy "transversality." Though in the very process of defining this transversality and attempting to dissociate it from one of the key concepts of Romanticism, Glissant reveals that transversality/creolite has, in fact, entered into a long-distance and long-durational Romantic correspondence: "And so transversality, and not the universal transcendence of the sublime, has come to light. It took us a long time to learn this. We are the roots of a cross-cultural relationship. . . . We thereby live, we have the good fortune of living, this shared process of cultural mutation, this convergence that frees us from uniformity."[21] Creolite-transversality/the sublime: countermode and mode, if we are to believe Glissant, of the modern. But how "counter" is *this* creolite and the transverse difference it makes and safeguards? What, indeed, is it counter to? If the answer is Kant, and that sublimely disinterested philosophical discourse on and of modernity, and that sublimely empty, homogeneous, and globe-traversing theory of the cosmopolitan and the contemporary Foucault has detected in Kant's postrevolutionary historical writings, then creolite is certainly countersublime.[22] But if creolite's sublime interlocutor is not Kant but Wordsworth, then the difference creolite fashions, guards, and names is a decidedly Romantic and sublime countermodernity.

This, certainly, will have been apparent to anyone who has even a glancing familiarity with Wordsworth on reading the first sentences from the *Texaco* passage I have cited:

> Penetrating the Doum, I found it deserted. Abandoned. I had been in so many places of Power, that I had acquired an immediate intuition for them. In my daily life, I detected around me so many cultural ruins in our mute countryside, so many gradual mummifications in the land all around, that I could at any point, before a hutch, a spot, a landscape, a river mouth, perceive a historical presence, stricken with staggering wear and tear.

Penetrating the Doum, Chamoiseau's narrator, like Wordsworth on his traipses round England's commons and heaths, discovers in the "cultural ruins" of his mute countryside, in these "stricken" "spots" in the landscape, nevertheless eloquent "historical presences." This might as well be "Michael" or "The Ruined Cottage." Certainly it adopts an entirely Wordsworthian reading habit, that same "strange discipline" of reading the "spot of time" not only as a personal *lieux-de-memoire* but as a collective historical monument to (the erosion of) a customary cultural habitus that Wordsworth identified as the project of his postrevolutionary verse in the "Reconciling Addendum" to "The Ruined Cottage."[23] Where Wordsworth's "strange discipline" locates and seeks to safeguard the ruins of rural Englishness and to train the poet's readers to detect such presences and so to preserve them in the experience of reading (if nowhere else), Chamoiseau discovers the stricken remains of creolite but bequeaths to his readers a common power of recollecting lost difference.

That recollection is also, as Glissant suggests, re-creation and recollection, that the stricken scenes of historical memory and the worn monuments to a historical strickenness might imply not only melancholy but the birth of a collectivity only increases the imaginative and sentimental sublimity of such sites of memory. To be sure, the creole sublime is neither universal nor transcendent. It is, as Glissant avers, rooted and locally or regionally transverse, constitutive not of "the human race at large and all at once" (as Kant has it) but of what Benedict Anderson calls a "bound" (rather than an "unbound") seriality, a nontotalizing but still (re)collective mode of inhabiting difference.[24] If this too is Romantic, if, indeed, this is the Romantic difference creolite makes and belatedly recollects for postmodernity, then it is, nevertheless, a historically situated rather than a historically nostalgic Romanticism. Or, perhaps, it is a situational nostalgia that by the very specificity and limit of its arena of address reminds us that romantic anticapitalism or Romantic countermodernity is not necessarily nostalgic, precisely because it exists not merely to recollect prior (lost) historical struggles but to collect the energy by which to engage and possibly counter the ongoing advance of a still unevenly developed and not yet universally distributed Enlightenment modernity. Wordsworthian or creole, proper or spectral, Romanticism thus appears and reappears on the contested margins of modernity to remind us that like the ghost, or like Romanticism itself, modernity is also unfinished business.

I have been suggesting that creolite, like Romanticism, is countermodern. Let me now revise that opinion. Creolite, like Romanticism, is not countermodern, it is paradigmatically modern, paradigmatic of modernity's internal countermodernity, paradigmatic, perhaps, of what Jürgen Habermas calls "Romantic Modernity."[25] This is so in any number of ways, but just two that I want to stress, the first of which Srinivas Aravamudan's "Colonial Logic of Late Romanticism" makes clear. The "where" of Aravamudan's late Romanticism (or, as he also calls it, of a "supplementary" or "prosthetic," phantom-limb Romanticism) is not Caribbean but Indian. But what he discovers in the "Guru English" of late-nineteenth- and early-twentieth-century Indian Romanticism is also true of Chamoiseau's and Glissant's creolite: it is simultaneously a practice of, or an elegy for, difference, and a cosmopolitanism, perhaps even, as Glissant notes of creolite in *The Poetics of Relation*, one of the dominant forms of a contemporary cosmopolitanism. Metissage; hybridity; creolite; Aravamudan's "Guru English": these are as cosmopolitan as is currently gets. Reduced to a slogan, the postmodern (as Jameson puts it in the work that stands as Aravamudan's allusive intertext) is that in which "difference relates." To which we can imagine Glissant responding: as it is that in which "relation differs." Either way, as Aravamudan demonstrates, if the related differences of the globally sub-altern variants of a late Romanticism engage and contest the modern at the level of what Partha Chatterjee calls the problematic (if, that is, they reverse modernity's core market of values by determining to value rather than to exchange or annul difference) they nevertheless risk doing so in such a way as to confirm modernity's cosmopolitan thematic, fashioning for the present a comprehensively global relationship of related differences.[26] There is, after all, no more global, no more universal, no more cosmopolitan token of cultural value, now, than the adulterated coin of mixed difference. And this too is Romanticism, a Romanticism gone global, a cosmopolitan Romanticism.

But if Romantic difference is thus apprehensible as the future rather than the antithesis of Enlightenment cosmopolitanism, then there is another way in which the Romantic, the creole, and the circum-Atlantic slave past, constitutive of the difference creolite properly names, are paradigmatically and long-durationally modern. The subtitle of Gilroy's *The Black Atlantic* is *Modernity and Double Consciousness*. While there is a vast argument in that subtitle there is only one point I wish to draw from it, the point with which Gilroy concludes his text. The condition of the slave, Gilroy suggests, is not only to be "in but not of" modernity. The transatlantic experience of enslave-ment is also, in its most intense, accelerated, and brutalizing form, the con-dition *of* modernity. As a way of naming the transition from a customary, "traditional," largely rural and agrarian habitus (what Pierre Nora calls an "environment of memory") to the mechanized, the hyperbureacratized, the instrumentalized, and the devernacularized, modernity, Gilroy argues, is nowhere more evident, nowhere more rapid, and nowhere more totalizing than in the experience of Africans drawn into the capital machinery of the Atlantic world system ("It is being suggested that the concentrated inten-sity of the slave experience is something that marked out blacks as the first truly modern people").[27]

The wide range of slavery-derived metaphors used for describing the con-dition of modern industrial labor in eighteenth- and nineteenth-century social theory is, on this account, more and less than gratuitous. For while the analogies between, say, slavery and wage-slavery do not hold in any num-ber of crucial ways, such figures do capture the fundamental experience of dispossession and alienation common to both the industrial laborer and the plantation slave. And to the extent that Romanticism devotes its energies to protesting, and finding some space of retreat from, such experiences of dispossession, to the extent, that is, that it offers at least an imaginative refuge from the hegemony of modern European and circum-Atlantic capital, it is both in and paradigmatically of modernity. But what sort of retreat does Romanticism provide the dispossessed and their sentimental and vicariously dispossessed allies? The melancholy of lost difference for one. But that, clearly, is not all. And in concluding I want to consider at least one other "loophole of retreat" that Romanticism recurrently writes into the long code of modernity.

Recall that line from "The Negro's Complaint": "Still in thought as free as ever." Cowper's "still" is, obviously enough, a pun, betokening, like Keats's "still," both a state of continuity and one of quietude. If some form of mental freedom endures despite the experience of enslavement, the line thus suggests, it persists as a quietness of thought, or indeed as a quieting or stilling of thought, a calm turning of thought in upon itself, what Cowper in *The Task* calls "quiescence." And if this begins to sound very much like Poovey's description of the Romantic poet's "turn away from phenomenal particulars [the empirical particulars, in this instance, of the slave condition] and toward the mind that contemplates those things" (if not quite like the antimaterial turn Celeste Langan finds in both a Coleridgean theory of poetic speech and certain *virtually* "pathological" modes of postmodern countercommunication) then, as Kevis Goodman's essay indicates, such an inward-turning quietness or quietude of thought does not necessarily imply a political or historical quietism. Or it certainly does not for Cowper, whose "loopholes of retreat" imply a loophole onto the world cut out of just such a turning in of thought upon itself. As Goodman points out, the "loophole" lines gloss a passage in *The Task* in which Cowper, like the slave in his "Negro's Complaint," encounters his own stilled mind, thinking on itself:

> Not undelightful is an hour to me
> So spent in parlour twilight; such a gloom
> Suits well the thoughtfull or unthinking mind,
>
> . . . .
>
> . . . I am conscious, and confess
> Fearless, a soul that does not always think.
> Me oft has fancy ludicrous and wild

Sooth'd with a waking dream of houses, tow'rs,
Trees, churches, and strange visages express'd
In the red cinders . . .

. . . .

Nor less amus'd have I quiescent watch'd
The sooty films that play upon the bars,
Pendulous and foreboding, in the view
Of superstition prophesying still
Though still deceiv'd, some stranger's near approach.
'Tis thus the understanding takes repose
In indolent vacuity of thought,

. . . .

Thus oft reclined at ease, I lose an hour
At evening, till at length the freezing blast
That sweeps the bolted shutter, summons home
The recollected powers, and snapping short
The glassy threads with which the fancy weaves
Her brittle toys, restores me to myself.[28]

Turned by the gloom in upon itself, the poet's mind encounters both its
own "indolent vacuity of thought," its "unthinking" thoughtfulness, and, as
Goodman stresses, a world outside that presses in on the "bars," window, or
"loophole" of this retreat in the form of a "stranger's near approach." Turning in upon itself, in other words, the "indolent" mind of Romanticism here
finds a space from within which to open itself out onto the world: and not
just any world but a world of approaching strangers, a nonfamiliar, non-
insular, nonsolipsistic world of others at the window. But what strangers?
For Cowper, Goodman argues, the approaching strangers are the subjects of
empire brought to the poet's attention by the newspapers he was addicted to
reading. And if "the mind that contemplates these things" is that stranger's
mind? If the eye peeping out through the "loophole of retreat" is the eye of
a slave or of a colonial subject? What will he or she see? Or, as a still more
basic question: Does that subject, that stranger, even have access to such
a retreat, such a space of unthinking thoughtfulness, such a "parlour" of
indolence?

As has been repeatedly observed, and as Michael Hanchard has made particularly clear, black experiences of disenfranchisement across and throughout the spaces of the British empire and the transatlantic diaspora have regu-

larly been predicated not only on the denial of civil or political rights but on an extensive, sometimes a total appropriation of the black subject's time. Denied possession of their own bodies, slaves, and to a lesser extent colonial subjects, and, to an almost equal extent, black South Africans under apartheid, were also not allowed to own their "own" time. The "struggle for the appropriation of time," particularly "'free time' . . . time that was not accounted for" thus becomes, Hanchard argues, one of the characteristic forms of political struggle in the making of what he calls an alternate "Afro-Modernity," much as such struggles, by E. P. Thompson's account, became a central component of the political consciousness of the eighteenth- and nineteenth-century English working class.[29] Indolence—an extent or "spot" of free time, the opportunity to find oneself "still in thought"—thus looks very different for the working-class wage laborer, the slave, or the apartheid-era black South African than it might for Cowper at his Olney retreat. Or perhaps I should say it means something different, for at least in the two examples I have provided, the "spot of (free) time" in apartheid South Africa and Jacobs's indolent and gloomy retreat from "where slavery existed," *look* remarkably like Cowper's retreat into "parlour twilight."

In the South African case, the teacher who is the central character of Ndebele's *Fools* has spent a day of quiet civil disobedience, at the advice of a young student radical, marking the "Day of the Covenant" (the Nationalist government's commemoration of a nineteenth-century Boer victory over a Zulu army) by retiring to his bedroom for a "day of thinking." But like Cowper his mind proves vacant of all but a consciousness of the luxury of its own purposeless activity and a fanciful cinema of impressions, until he, too, is brought back to the world by the approach of a stranger: "Since I had told myself it was the day for thinking, I had willed myself to think: but my mind had been unable to focus on any specific thing. I had willed without direction. And I had become aware that I did not really know how to think; how to induce the mind to work; that it was really possible to be dedicated without any real aims to be conscious of. . . . Thinking about thinking, I *had* been thinking. I had smiled and then closed my eyes and tried to think about something concrete. Nothing came but colours: red, white, blue, green, and black flashing across the screen of my closed eyes. For such a long time. Was I thinking or not? Was I asleep or awake? It was the light knock at the door that brought me to full consciousness."

The structural parallel is almost exact, though Ndeble's character seems both relaxed and troubled by his indolent vacuity of thought, or perhaps simply more impatient for his free time also to be the time of the "stranger's near approach." That stranger does, of course, materialize, though not in the form of a long-distance other but in the guise of a child ("the thing I should have been thinking of") whose slight frame, like the shadowy outline of Cowper's stranger, nevertheless manages to embody "such a large part of the world just behind him, for he was bigger than it, and had blotted most of it out with his body. His presence there seemed to be the beginning of questions." What those questions are, and what their answers might be, I do not have space here to address, so let me mention just one of the questions that boy brings with him as he brings the world into the space of the room: the question of the "child." It is the teacher's troubled conviction that children are, and should remain, strangers; strangers, that is, to the world of adults, particularly the adult worlds of sexuality and politics. That conviction is troubled because as an educator his task is to prepare children for the adult world, a generally commended vocational calling but one, in apartheid South Africa, that seems to him like an exercise in cruelty, a project of issuing children into an adult world that will have no place for them and in which they will increasingly be forced to live as the race-strangers they do not yet understand themselves to be. Complicit in depriving the children of the political innocence he wants to preserve (but which his activist foil informs him is nothing but an indulgent, romantic fantasy), the teacher is also complicit with a sexual betrayal of childhood "innocence." Years earlier, he had slept with one of his students, a young girl he had known since her early childhood and whom he now torments himself for not keeping a sexual stranger to himself. That children are and should remain strangers to the world of adults is, of course, as the political activist in Ndebele's story contends, a Romantic notion, indeed, as Frances Ferguson indicates in her essay in this collection, one of the chief and more enduring articles of Romantic and Romantically liberal faith over the long history of modernity. That the Romantic child is still with us; that these are the representational strangers most commonly in our midst; that there is a Romantic politics whose task is to think the difference children make; that this is a matter of interest not only for a European intellectual elite but for the global subaltern, for those such as Ndebele's black South Africans who must find some retreat from apartheid, some spot of free time in which to be still in thought if they are to be able to recollect what, in addition to national politics, they (we) "should be thinking of"; that all these are also ways in which Romanticism marks its life and afterlives seems evident and, to me at least, not at all an entirely unwelcome disruption of period unities.

Harriet Jacobs was also thinking of children in her retreat. Indeed, as she indicates, she bored her hole through the wall of her grandmother's garret, cut out that loophole in her retreat, chiefly in the hope of catching sight or hearing the voices of her children, who were living with her grandmother in the house across the yard. The tactic worked. She saw and heard her children. But letting in that world of children also let in the wider world outside, while also casting her mind back on the gloomily majestic range of its own cramped indolence. Looking for and brooding on her children, Jacobs also broods, with typical understatement and appropriately pragmatic anxiety, on her mind's own grandeur of historical survey ("O, those long gloomy days, with no object for my eye to rest upon, and no thoughts to occupy my mind, except the dreary past and the uncertain future!"). But engloomed, like Cowper, within its own universe-in-a-nutshell space of cognitive retreat, Jacobs's mind, like Cowper's, also finds in gloomy retreat the occasion for qualified intellectual delight.

The light admitted through her borehole, Jacobs indicates, was not only sufficient to allow her to look out but adequate to permit her to read within ("My eyes had become accustomed to the dim light, and by holding my book or work in a certain position near the aperture I contrived to read").[30] I do not know what book Jacobs was reading by her loophole of retreat, but I like to think that the words illumined on the page were Cowper's words; that it was while reading *The Task* that she set herself the task of entering into a delayed and long-distance Romantic correspondence and of casting for us the reflective, ghostly afterlight of her reading on Cowper's text; that peeping from one loophole of retreat to another she could imagine Cowper as the stranger making his nearer approach to her gloomy confinement while she became the stranger more nearly approaching Cowper's window on history. However fanciful the conceit, it occurs to me that it is precisely of such historical "fanc[ies] ludicrous and wild" that Cowper's own loophole was made and that, whether or not she was reading Cowper in her grandmother's garret, such a Romantic loophole of retreat was indeed, one of "the last places" in which her pursuers would have thought—or we her belated readers have thought—to find an enslaved black woman, "still in thought" and "free as ever." If for Jacobs, a century and a half ago, there were indeed "no" or few "[other] places, where slavery existed, that could have afforded . . . so good a place of concealment," then for us, now, it is perhaps time to start examining this and other such places in which, over the course of the past two centuries, Romanticism has gone into such cannily recreational (and recreational) hiding. The essays that follow do not exhaust that task. But their presence here suggests, at the very least, the beginning, again, of questions.

Notes

1 Harriet Jacobs, *Incidents in the Life of a Slave Girl* (New York: Oxford University Press, 1988), 173.

2 See Valerie Smith's introduction to Jacobs, *Incidents in the Life of a Slave Girl.*

3 William Cowper, *The Task*, in *The Poems of William Cowper*, ed. John D. Baird and Charles Ryskamp, 3 vols. (Oxford: Clarendon Press, 1995), 2:4.88–89.

4 Ibid., 2:4.88–89. William Cowper, "The Negro's Complaint," in *Verse*, vol. 4 of *Slavery, Abolition, and Emancipation: Writings in the British Romantic Period*, ed. Alan Richardson (London, Pickering and Chatto, 1999), 75:9.

5 See David Simpson, *The Academic Postmodern and the Rule of Literature: A Report on Half-Knowledge* (Chicago: University of Chicago Press, 1995); Alan Liu, "Local Transcendence: Cultural Criticism, Postmodernism, and the Romanticism of Detail," *Representations* 32 (Fall 1990): 75–113; and Alan Liu, "The New Historicism and the Work of Mourning," *Studies in Romanticism* 35 (1996): 553–66.

6 See James Chandler, *England in 1819: The Politics of Literary Culture and the Case of Romantic Historicism* (Chicago: University of Chicago Press, 1998).

7 Mary Poovey, *A History of the Modern Fact: Problems of Knowledge in the Sciences of Wealth and Society* (Chicago: University of Chicago Press, 1998), 327.

8 Jacobs, *Incidents in the Life of a Slave Girl*, 177–78.

9 Njabulo Ndebele, *Fools and Other Stories* (London: Readers International, 1983), 263–64.

10 Patrick Chamoiseau, *Texaco*, trans. Rose-Myriam Rejouis and Val Vinokurov (New York: Vintage International, 1998), 386–87.

11 Jacques Derrida, *Specters of Marx: The State of the Debt, the Work of Mourning, and the New International*, trans. Peggy Kamuf (New York: Routledge, 1994), xv–xvi.

12 Ibid., 109, emphasis in original; Stephen Greenblatt, *Shakespearean Negotiations* (Berkeley: University of California Press, 1988), 1; Fredric Jameson, *The Political Unconscious: Narrative As a Socially Symbolic Act* (Ithaca: Cornell University Press, 1981), 19.

13 Liu, "The New Historicism," 560.

14 Walter Benn Michaels, "'For You Who Never Was There': Slavery and the New Historicism, Deconstruction and the Holocaust," *Narrative* 4 (1996): 1–16.

15 See Julie Ellison, *Cato's Tears and the Making of Anglo-American Emotion* (Chicago: University of Chicago Press, 1999).

16 The argument is made throughout *The Political Unconscious* but is particularly clear in the following passage: "What this model implies is that in its emergent, strong form a genre is essentially a sociosymbolic message, or in other terms, that form is imma-

nently and intrinsically an ideology in its own right. When such forms are reappropriated and refashioned in quite different social and cultural contexts, this message persists and must be functionally reckoned into the new form. . . . The ideology of form itself, thus sedimented, persists into the later, more complex structure. The notion of the text as a synchronic unity of structurally contradictory or heterogeneous elements, generic patterns and discourses (what we may call, following Ernst Bloch, the *Ungleichzeitigkeit* or synchronic 'uneven development' within a single textual structure) now suggests that even Frye's notion of displacement can be rewritten as a conflict between the older deep-structural form and the contemporary materials and generic systems in which it seeks to inscribe and to reassert itself" (141).

17   Chandler, *England in 1819*, 167.

18   Derrida, *Specters of Marx*, 115.

19   Michael Lowy and Robert Sayre, *Romanticism against the Tide of Modernity*, trans. Catherine Porter (Durham: Duke University Press, 2001).

20   Jean Bernabé, Patrick Chamoiseau, and Raphaël Confiant, *Éloge de la créolité* (Paris: Gallimard/Presses Universitaires Créoles, 1989).

21   Edouard Glissant, *Caribbean Discourses: Selected Essays*, trans. J. Michael Dash (Charlottesville: University of Virginia Press, 1989), 66–67.

22   See Michel Foucault, "Kant on Enlightenment and Revolution," trans. Colin Gordon, *Economy and Society* 15.1 (February 1986): 88–96; and "What Is Enlightenment?" trans. Catherine Porter, in *The Foucault Reader*, ed. Paul Rabinow (New York: Pantheon Books, 1984), 32–50.

23   William Wordsworth, "Reconciling Addendum" to "The Ruined Cottage," in *The Poetical Works of William Wordsworth*, ed. Ernest de Selincourt and Helen Darbishire (Oxford: Clarendon Press, 1940–49), 5:400.

24   The phrase comes from Kant's essay "An Old Question Raised Again: Is the Human Race Constantly Progressing?" (in *Kant on History*, ed. Lewis White Beck [New York: Liberal Arts Press, 1963]) and follows his discussion of the French Revolution as a sublime sign of that progress: "This event consists neither in momentous deeds nor crimes committed by men whereby what was great among men is made small or what was small is made great, nor in ancient splendid political structures which vanish as if by magic while others come forth in their place as if from the depths of the earth. No, nothing of the sort. It is simply the mode of thinking of the spectators which reveals itself in this game of great revolutions, and manifests such a universal yet disinterested sympathy for the players on one side against those on the other. . . . Owing to its universality, this mode of thinking demonstrates a character of *the human race at large and all at once*: owing to its disinterestedness, a moral character of humanity, a least in its predisposition, a character which not only permits people to hope for progress toward the better, but is already progress insofar as its capacity is sufficient for the present" (143–44, 147).

25   See Jürgen Habermas, "Modernity: An Incomplete Project," in *The Anti-Aesthetic: Essays on Postmodern Culture*, ed. Hal Foster (Seattle: Bay Press, 1983), 3–15.

26   See Partha Chatterjee, "The Thematic and The Problematic," chap. 2 in *Nationalist Thought and the Colonial World: A Derivative Discourse* (Minneapolis: University of Min-

nesota Press, 1986), 36–53; Edouard Glissant, *Poetics of Relation*, trans. Betsy Wing (Ann Arbor: University of Michigan Press, 1997).

27   Paul Gilroy, *The Black Atlantic: Modernity and Double Consciousness* (Cambridge: Harvard University Press, 1993), 221; Pierre Nora, "Between Memory and History: *Les Lieux de Memoire*," trans. Marc Roudebush, *Representations* 26 (Spring 1989): 7–25.

28   Cowper, *The Task*, 4.278–80, 4.277–79.

29   Michael Hanchard, "Afro-Modernity: Temporality, Politics, and the African Diaspora," in *Alternative Modernities*, ed. Dilip Parameshwar Gaonkar (Durham: Duke University Press, 2001), 282, 283.

30   Jacobs, *Incidents*, 175.

Kevis Goodman

The Loophole in the Retreat:
The Culture of News and the Early Life
of Romantic Self-Consciousness

"Tis pleasant through the loopholes of retreat /
To peep at such a world": we are so accustomed
to thinking of William Cowper as a figure of
retirement that the "loophole" in these famous
lines from *The Task* (1785) has often been read
in its twentieth-century sense, as an escape
or retreat—an "out," as in tax law—as if the
phrase presents a mere redundancy, a retreat
consisting of retreat.[1] Yet in its original sense
(from fortification) a loophole is more precisely
an aperture, channel, or passageway, and it is
thus that Cowper uses it here to describe the
newspaper, which he was not only addicted to
reading but also fond of turning into verse. Recognized in his own day as the coauthor of an
influential collection of congregational hymns,
Cowper inhabits and animates both sides of the
suggestive metaphor borrowed from Hegel by
Benedict Anderson to describe the daily reading
of the news:

> The obsolescence of the newspaper on the mor-
> row of its printing . . . creates this extraor-
> dinary mass ceremony: the almost precisely
> simultaneous consumption ("imagining") of

The *South Atlantic Quarterly* 102:1, Winter 2003.
Copyright © 2003 by Duke University Press.

the newspaper-as-fiction. We know that particular morning and evening editions will overwhelmingly be consumed between this hour
and that, only on this day, not that. . . . The significance of this mass
ceremony—Hegel observed that newspapers serve the modern man
as a substitute for morning prayers—is paradoxical. It is performed
in silent privacy, in the lair of the skull. Yet each communicant is
well aware that the ceremony he performs is being replicated simultaneously by thousands (or millions) of others.[2]

The retreat has an "out"—that "of" is possessive, and not merely descriptive.

   Where Anderson's interest lies in the newspaper's role in the imagining
of national communities, my own purpose is to develop this passage's brief
intuition of the historical and collective subjectivity engaged by the news
as a permeable, open circuit of awareness. The "lair of the skull" is here
no fine and private place, like Marvell's grave, or the Cartesian ego, but a
curiously crowded haunt. As Raymond Williams suggested in several formulations of his elusive signature phrase, "structures of feeling," much of
what we call "private, idiosyncratic, and even isolating" may be a misrecog-
nition of social experience "in process." For Williams, the treatment of the
social field as "past, in the sense that it is always formed," or always "precipitated," meant that we turn by default to find other terms for the immanent
(though *not* unmediated) perception of any moment as a seething mix of
unsettled elements. If the terms of analysis, "the known relationships, institutions, formations, positions," are fixed and explicit, then "all that escapes
from the fixed and the explicit and the known is grasped and defined as the
personal[,] this, here, now, alive, active 'subjective,'" rather than recognized
as social experience "in solution." "Feeling"—by which Williams usually
meant unpleasurable sensations of "disturbance, blockage, tension, emotional trouble"—yields evidence, a sensitive measurement, of the uncertainty principle of history-on-the-move.[3]

   This essay explores the possibility that certain modes of affect that have
seemed hallmarks of early Romantic self-consciousness offer significant
sites of engagement with a historical presentness not—or not yet—available
to thought or direct articulation, as well as registers of an expanding international structure of relations whose reach exceeds any individual grasp
but which, like the Althusserian absent cause, is the precondition of any
individual's subject's sense of "this, here, [and] now."[4] As a form of social

experience in process, the "subjectivity" we see engaged by the newspaper in *The Task* offers a loophole indeed—a channel through which the flux of Cowper's "now" can pass. My argument therefore implicitly queries the periodization assumed in most accounts of the distinctiveness of our own postmodern culture of information, as, for instance, in Mark Poster's generally nuanced differentiation between an earlier stage of "written exchanges mediated by print" and "electronically mediated exchange": "in the print stage the self is constructed as an agent centered in rational/imaginary autonomy," whereas in the "electronic state the self is decentered, dispersed, and multiplied in continuous instability."[5] No reader of Cowper's *Task* or, for that matter, of the rhizomatic consciousnesses of much later eighteenth-century verse through Wordsworth's *Prelude* ("I seem / Two consciousnesses—conscious of myself, / And of some other being") will find constructed there such a substantial self. Without losing Cowper's historical specificity, but without assuming that the problems of our own media culture are unique when in fact they have a long and intricate prehistory, I try to reconceive the problem of Romantic self-consciousness by focusing on a condition that Cowper—in a passage that would strongly influence Coleridge—calls "indolent vacuity of thought," and that emerges in *The Task* as an involuntary mode of knowledge responsive to the pressure of an eventful present. This paradoxically full but nonideational vacancy, I argue, presents us with a pivot, historical and affective, between the perceived "overload" within the later-eighteenth-century culture of information and Romantic aesthetic perception.

News and the "Not Yet" History

The reading of the news provides an opportune site for examining the pressure of ongoing presentness because, as our dismissive colloquial coinage ("That's history!" or "She's history!") suggests, what is news is precisely what is *not yet*—although some of it may become—history. Far more than our papers today, with their regular sections and tables of contents, the *Morning Chronicle*—one of the newspapers that we know Cowper was reading and making into poetry during the fall of 1783—exhibits an extraordinary collision of undifferentiated items. The front page for September 30, 1783, for instance, displays the following array: at top left, theatrical intelligence from Drury Lane and Sadler's Wells; below that an advertisement for the "great Wonderful Wonders" of the conjurer Gustavus Katterfelto, who does make it into *The Task* ("Katterfelto with his hair on end / At his own wonders, wond'ring for his bread" [4.86–87]); then, slightly to the left, a notice for an anatomy lesson performed by one Mr. Sheldon and another for "Carter's Medicine for Dropsy"; moving right, a letter about the Poor Laws; and last, furthest to the right and bottom, the text of the treaty between Great Britain and that fledgling entity about to be recognized: the United States of America. While it is obvious to us which of this material would persist in the main headings of historical narrative—as well as what would become a footnote (poor Katterfelto "with his hair on end") and what, like Mr. Sheldon and Dr. Carter, would vanish altogether—to the contemporary onlooker, the future course of such a differentiation into the *grand récits* and minor happenings would not have been certain.

It was this "chaos of confused matter promiscuously jumbled together," in the words of one 1757 commentator, that so struck later-eighteenth-century reading audiences.[6] George Crabbe, writing his own poem on the newspaper in the same year that Cowper's *Task* was published, satirized "that variety of dissociating articles which are huddled together in our Daily Papers"; these staged, as Crabbe noted critically, a deliberate narrative incoherence such that readers (and poets writing about the news) "cannot slide from theme to theme in an easy and graceful succession; but, on quitting one thought, there will be an unavoidable hiatus, and in general an awkward transition into that which follows."[7] This antinarrative tendency was in part a function of the multiple columns and several possible points of entry, and it was intensified by the eminence given to "foreign intelligence" from Europe, the Americas, India, and beyond, since editors could not wait for confirmation before going to print, and later posts often superseded or contradicted earlier ones.[8] And if the newspaper worked to counter narrative continuity and coherence, it also worked (notwithstanding its uses to the later historian) against memory and against what Walter Benjamin would call transmissible experience (*Erfahrung*). "When you have once perused the four pages of unconnected occurrences, and miscellaneous advertisements," wrote one contributor to the *London Magazine* in 1766, "the abrupt transitions from article to article, without the smallest connection between one paragraph and another, overload and confuse the memory so much that, when you are questioned, you can never give a tolerable account of what you have been reading."[9] Where some, like Crabbe, found the inchoate array of discrete and discontinuous items appalling, others felt an exciting frisson. A letter sent to the editor of the *London Magazine* in 1780 — and suggestively signed "W.C." — offers a more tolerant, amused appreciation.

> It has been often observed, that there is not so inconsistent, so incoherent, so heterogeneous, although so useful and agreeable a thing, as a publick News-paper: the very ludicrous contrast in advertisements, the contradictory substance of foreign and domestick paragraphs, the opposite opinions and observations of contending essayists, with premature deaths, spurious marriages, births, bankruptcies, &c &c. form a fund of entertainment for a world, of which it is in itself no bad epitome.[10]

The verifiable William Cowper wrote William Unwin in similar terms in 1782, referring to a page of the *Morning Chronicle* published two days earlier: "What a medley are our public prints. Half the page filled with the ruin of the country, and the other half with the vices and pleasures of it! Here an Island taken, and there a new comedy, here an Empire lost, and there an Italian Opera, or the Duke of Gloucester's rout on a Sunday!" (*Letters* 2:33). And he kept on reading, avidly.

The "dissociating articles" of newspaper prose rendered contemporary reality as pliant, the moment as unstable or metamorphic and therefore, or so it seemed, open to intervention. Readers could quickly become writers, and vice versa; consumers and advertisers also changed roles. If, as Crabbe put it, "here, compressed within a single sheet, / Great things and small, the mean and mighty meet" ("The Newspaper," 245–46), just how they were to meet appeared open to a playful negotiation, thanks to the distinctive layout of the newsprint (usually four folio pages of four columns each). The entry from the *London Magazine* of 1766 cited earlier offered the following "improvement of the newspapers," and one can find in other accounts variations on this method: "After we read the Public Advertiser in the old trite vulgar way i.e. each column by itself *downwards*, we next read two columns together *onwards*; and by this *new method* found much more entertainment than in the *common* way of reading, with a greater variety of articles curiously blended, or strikingly contrasted." Then come three pages of examples, of which the following "improvements" on the usual way of reading are representative:

Yesterday Dr. Jones preached at St. James's,
and performed it with ease in less than sixteen minutes.

The sword of state was carried———
before Sir John Fielding, and committed to Newgate.

There was a numerous and brilliant court;
a down-look, and cast with one eye.

Last night, the princess royal was baptised;
Mary, alias Moll Hacket, alias Black Moll. . . .

At noon, her R.H. the princess dowager was
married to Mr Jenkins, an eminent taylor. . . .

Sunday a poor woman was suddenly taken in labour,
the contents of which have not yet transpired [Etc.].[11]

Although this is all in fun—only in print do princess dowagers marry
tailors—the turn from vertical reading by column to horizontal scanning
anticipates, in peculiarly literal form, the conceptual terms used by Terry
Eagleton, Jon Klancher, and other scholars of the eighteenth-century public sphere. In Eagleton's words, "Cultural discourse and the realm of social
power are closely related but not homologous: the former cuts across the
latter and suspends the distinctions of the latter, . . . temporarily transposing its 'vertical' gradations onto a horizontal plane."[12] Of course, as Eagleton
and Klancher intimate, not too much should be made of the radical or leveling potential of the newspaper in and of itself; for while it makes apparent
the dissonances and inequities within the social realm, it does not necessarily create the expectation that these will be altered, let alone guarantee
the opportunity for such change. Yet there does emerge, in the accounts of
contemporary news practitioner-readers, an important illusion of the mal-
leability of the present. By inserting one's own advertisement ("'Tis this
which makes all Europe's business known, / Yet here a private man may
place his own" ["The Newspaper," 247–48]), by subscribing to a publication
or a petition, or just by dying, one might make news. And by responding to
the implicit demand to join together those dissociating articles—that is, to
articulate them (in one of the several contemporary senses of the word)—
even a reader could "make" history.

In trying to render the newspaper's teeming presentness, and the resulting sense of ongoing history as a flexible, absorbing, or oppressive "now," I am not claiming that a paper like the *Morning Chronicle* offered some sort of pristine contact between the subject and the reality in which he or she was immersed, an accusation frequently (and I think wrongly) leveled at Raymond Williams. Although the news is relatively undifferentiated in comparison with historiographical narrative, it too undergoes a process of selection—even the *New York Times*, with all the modern advantages of cheap paper and the advanced printing technology that permits variously sized editions, advertises its contents as "All the news that's fit to print." Something presumably does not fit, or is not "fit," for publication. While less carefully organized and packaged, the late-eighteenth-century press operated under considerable restraints, some similar, others different. These included the confines of space, since both the Stamp Duty on paper and the capacity of each printing unit limited most daily newspapers to four folio pages, no matter the volume of incoming correspondence, although weeklies and monthlies had more flexibility. There were also strong commercial considerations (paid advertising, in part to offset the cost of publication, in part because of the appeal of the goods advertised) and political partisanship vied with what was at best a nascent ideal of journalistic objectivity.

Yet I would stress that where it fell short of transmitting "reality" to the moment, the newspaper created a significant reality effect. Its very busyness or "hypermediacy"—the separate columns, differently sized types, and several points of entry; the various possible combinations and recombinations of its "dissociating articles" as well as the ephemerality of their "intelligence"—all generated the illusion of immediacy. The paradox of the newspaper, as Richard Terdiman nicely observes, is that in it "form *denies form*."[13] The paper thus testified obliquely to the contradictions and complexities of ongoing events not by mapping them faithfully but by miming them with its own incoherences or dissociations.[14] As the 1766 *London Magazine* entry cited above suggests by observing that the overloaded and confused memory cannot "give a tolerable account of what" it has read, the sense of presentness created by the news is less cognitive—following Fredric Jameson, we might say that it resists cognitive mapping—than it is sensory and affective. This consciousness we might call a virtual historicity, and we will see that it includes the desire for—but also desire's counterpart, an anxiety about— historical participation.

Articulating the News

With the spread of daily print publication all readers are potentially writers, of course, but some engage in the habit more sedulously than others. Cowper, as I have noted, had his own, peculiar way of making news—he translated its prose "articles" into verse, reassembling them in his poetry, most famously in the form of a long sequence of Book 4 of *The Task* (16– 119). In an excellent recent treatment of this curious kind of remediation, Julie Ellison has argued that the newspaper appealed to Cowper because it offered the fragile author a therapeutic exercise in the "management of variety." Essential to such an enterprise, Ellison nicely shows, is the newspaper reader-cum-poet's capacity to map the global cacophony presented by the news, and figured as undifferentiated noise on the page, into space.[15] "Here," writes Cowper, his use of deictics in this passage pointing at once to specific news items, traced by his editors to editions of the *Morning Chronicle* and the *General Evening Post* from 1783 to 1784, and self-mockingly to the page of *The Task* as a rival print medium of information:

> Here rills of oily eloquence in soft
> Meanders lubricate the course they take;
> The modest speaker is asham'd and griev'd
> T'engross a moment's notice, and yet begs,
> Begs a propitious ear for his poor thoughts,
> However trivial all that he conceives.
> Sweet bashfulness! It claims at least this praise,
> The dearth of information and good sense
> That it foretells always comes to pass.
> Cataracts of declamation thunder here,
> There forests of no-meaning spread the page
> In which all comprehension wanders lost;
> While fields of pleasantry amuse us there
> With merry descants on a nation's woes.
> (4.64–77)

If successful, the reader that Cowper desires to cultivate—in himself as well as in those who read the news in (and through) his verses—apprehends, instead of Crabbe's "dissociating articles" in print, the picturesque landscape of a prospect piece, complete with rills, cataracts, forests, and fields.

Such spatial or perspectival reshaping of the flat nonsense of sound inserts a saving distance between the noise of the world and the reader, who is now able to "see the stir / Of the great Babel and not feel the crowd. / To hear the roar she sends through all her gates / At a safe distance, where the dying sound / Falls a soft murmur on th'uninjured ear" (*Task* 4.89–93).[16]

More specifically, *The Task* seeks to turn the noise of the present into *conversation*, the "divine Chit-chat" for which Coleridge and others would soon praise its author. In his own poem entitled "Conversation," Cowper's epithet for the practice ("sacred interpreter of human thought") drew on Henry Fielding's earlier definition and etymology, which had developed the pun on *vertere* (to turn) and con*versation* (as a way of revolving ideas in discussion). For Fielding, "the primitive and literal Sense of this Word is . . . to *Turn round together*; and . . . we intend by it, that reciprocal Interchange of Ideas, by which Truth is examined, Things are, in a manner, *turned round*, and sifted, and all our Knowledge communicated to each other."[17] In *The Task*, the longing for just such a dream of orderly apprehension informs the momentary, Lucretian perspective on the newspaper:

> Thus sitting and surveying thus at ease
> The globe and its concerns, I seem advanc'd
> To some secure and more than mortal height,
> That lib'rates and exempts me from them all.
> It *turns* submitted to my view, *turns* round
> With all its generations; I behold the tumult and am still.
> (*Task* 4.94–100; emphases added)

By adopting a version of *georgic* for his speaking *versus*, Cowper exploits Fielding's etymological pun to its fullest. The intentional "task" of this georgic of the news, we might say, is to "articulate" those dissociating articles of prose in both senses of that verb at once. To utter them as if in well-cultivated conversation amounts, or so the poet hopes, to joining or jointing them together—to constructing the nation, indeed the globe, in the image of what David Hume called "the conversable world."[18] This, in its double sense as the fashionable world that converses and, more significantly, as a nicely "sifted," genteel understanding of the world, is a far-ranging cognitive ideal as much as a matter of decorum.

That is the *hope*. Yet, as the poet pithily observes, "to talk is not always to converse," and *The Task* as a whole, or at any length, reads as a desperate attempt to keep up the conversation — any conversation.[19] In the passage just cited, the potentially vertiginous image of the turning globe (as opposed, for example, to a rural or urban prospect available to a fixed view) is not incidental; the later-eighteenth-century newspapers, which put a premium on "foreign intelligence," testified to a newly far-flung global reality, one that seemed particularly uncertain in Britain during the early 1780s, with the loss of America and with the sharp controversies about the management of the East India Company. With its advertisements for exotic "nectareous essences, Olympian dews" (*Task* 4.84), moreover, the newsprint offered a confused reminder of the dependence of any individual, bodily existence on far-flung conditions; this is a contradiction that Jameson describes by remarking that "the truth" of any local "experience no longer coincides with the place in which it takes place . . . [but] lies, rather, in India or Jamaica or Hong Kong; it is bound up with the whole colonial system" and is therefore not fully "conceptualizable" for most people.[20] Yet what is not available as a concept — in Hume's terms, what is not a "conversable" truth — is not therefore beyond the poem's representation. I turn, then, to the poem's animation of what might be called the "unconversable world," something like the Althusserian cause, a structure immanent in its effects. Where a more properly Althusserian critic might turn to the overall structure, however, I want to bring into focus an effect that rarely comes under Althusserian scrutiny: the presence of the structure in a peculiar kind of affect.

The Unconversable World: Waiting for Strangers

Cowper had hoped that *The Task* would be read as a whole piece, writing that "if the work cannot boast a regular plan (in which respect however I do not think it altogether indefensible) it may yet boast, that the reflections are naturally suggested always by the preceding passage" (*Letters* 2:285). Yet the passage that follows the newspaper sequence has proved especially attractive to the excerpting practice of anthologists. Also to those of poets: in his lyric "Frost at Midnight" (1798), Samuel Coleridge would preserve Cowper's lines largely intact, but significantly moved some distance from its worldly context. Before returning briefly to Coleridge, let us consider Cowper's passage (which the argument to *Task* 4 called "A Brown Study") back into its original setting:

Not undelightful is an hour to me
So spent in parlour twilight; such a gloom
Suits well the thoughtfull or unthinking mind,

. . . .

. . . I am conscious, and confess
Fearless, a soul that does not always think.
Me oft has fancy ludicrous and wild
Sooth'd with a waking dream of houses, tow'rs,
Trees, churches, and strange visages express'd
In the red cinders, while with poring eye
I gaz'd, myself creating what I saw.
Nor less amus'd have I quiescent watch'd
The sooty films that play upon the bars,
Pendulous, and foreboding, in the view
Of superstition prophesying still
Though still deceiv'd, some stranger's near approach.
'Tis thus the understanding takes repose
In indolent vacuity of thought,
And sleeps and is refresh'd. Meanwhile the face
Conceals the mood lethargic with a mask
Of deep deliberation, as the man
Were task'd to his full strength, absorb'd and lost.
Thus oft reclined at ease, I lose an hour
At evening, till at length the freezing blast
That sweeps the bolted shutter, summons home
The recollected powers, and snapping short
The glassy threads with which the fancy weaves
Her brittle toys, restores me to myself.
(*Task* 4.277–79, 284–307)

With the lines, "I am conscious, and confess / Fearless, a soul that does not always think" (284–85), Cowper plunges into the unfinished debate in Lockean and post-Lockean philosophy concerning the relationship of consciousness to thought and the basis of personal identity. In the *Essay Concerning Human Understanding*, Locke had insisted that all ideation is conscious: it is impossible for a man to think without being "conscious to himself, That he thinks"; "consciousness," which depends on physical embodiment, "is inseparable from thinking, and . . . essential to it."[21] It is, however, possible not to think at all: as Locke writes in the lines that Cowper quotes roughly, "I confess my self, to have one of those dull Souls, that doth not perceive itself always to contemplate *Ideas*, nor can conceive it any more necessary for the *Soul always to think*" (*Essay* 2.1.10). Just what happens in those gaps or syncopes of thought is not Locke's concern; since it is not possible for him that one might be conscious without thinking, he mentions the unconsciousness of sleep and leaves it at that, hoping (wrongly, as his successors made clear) to have located in consciousness a continuous principle of "self."[22]

Cowper cites Locke, but in order to probe the very vacant spaces in thinking that the *Essay* had suggested but not explored, to imagine at some length the "unthinking mind" (279) that is not the sleeping mind. His innovation, as Marshall Brown has suggested in an important, extended reading of *The Task*, is the way he renders "the divorce of consciousness from attention."[23] Yet I would part from Brown's conclusion—which separates the passage from its context and makes Cowper a more imminent Kant than perhaps he is—that here, for the first time, "consciousness becomes autonomous, independent of the world in which the conscious being lives." For while that may at some level be Cowper's hope, what is striking is how much this "unthinking" consciousness that eludes the Lockean idea—this "indolent vacuity of [i.e., in] thought" (297)—in fact offers a curious reprise or précis of some of the most worldly moments of the poem, including the newspaper sequence that precedes it. Within the rifts of identity or personhood move other persons: Cowper's unthinking of the Lockean idea coincides with a moment in which the poem's pattern of figuration is acutely open to context, so that the affective consciousness represented is not a recess or retreat but an aperture, a medium—that loophole—through which the world's strangeness enters.

In the brown study, the physiognomical sign or figure for the "vacuity of thought" and remission of Lockean identity is "a mask / Of deep deliberation" (299–300), which makes of the first-person speaker a third person, that seemingly "task'd" man of lines 300–301. The speaker suddenly seems foreign or at least inscrutable to his domestic circle, where, of course, strangers are promptly multiplied: the masked, tasked man apprehends "some stranger's near approach" (295) presaged in that sooty film (292), which also contains, among other things, "strange visages" (288; the film would be anthropomorphized fully by Coleridge as a "fluttering stranger"). Moreover, the "fancy ludicrous" and "poring eye" activated during this seeming deliberation are recurrent, almost compulsive figures throughout *The Task*.[24] We should recognize them, to begin with, as versions of the fancy and "peering eye" that have been engaged by the newspaper in the passage that precedes the brown study. Of the newspaper correspondent (or the subject of his "foreign intelligence"), Cowper writes:

> He travels and I too. I tread his deck,
> Ascend his topmast, through his peering eyes
> Discover countries, with a kindred heart
> Suffer his woes and share in his escapes
> While fancy, like the finger of a clock,
> Runs the great circuit and is still at home.
> (*Task* 4.114–19)

If the newspaper here places the reader on the topmast without quite removing him from the sofa, the brown study immediately following enacts a similar but inverted chiasmus. There, as we just saw, under the sway of "fancy ludicrous" the "I" becomes "he" (the "task'd" man) until the shutter, swept by the wind, "summons home / The recollected powers, and . . . restores me to myself" (304–7). This second exchange absents the "I" altogether, but rather than putting him on the ship instead brings the stranger in. The result is that the space between *The Task*'s reader and the world—in the landscape topography fashioned out of newsprint, in the more attenuated "finger of a clock"—suddenly contracts, so that, for a moment, it is as if not only the newspaper itself but a foreign intelligence has entered the home.

When I suggest that Cowper's Englishman engaged in sofa-travel has so absented himself that he resembles a stranger in his home, I am not using that vocabulary just for effect. The "poring eye" and "fancy ludicrous" associate him with the several haunted, profoundly un-Lucretian spectators roaming the poem, each of them dispossessed or vagrant subjects touched by the effects of imperial expansion or exploration. There is the "fancy . . . delusive" of Crazy Kate, whose transoceanic stare follows a lost lover, a sailor, "through foaming waves / To distant shores" (see *Task* 1.539–44). Staring back toward Britain across a similar, watery waste is the strange figure of "gentle Omai," the South Seas visitor first brought to England in 1774, who in *Task* 1 provides the most extended instance of these wishful, anxious gazers. Omai was returned in 1776 on Captain Cook's final voyage to Tahiti and did not long survive his artificial repatriation, but since the news of his death had not yet reached Britain by 1784, Cowper imagines Omai in the poem's present, standing on the shores of his native island. Out of place in what was once his home, but ambivalent about another capture, he gazes out to sea. The speaker asks:

> And have thy joys
> Lost nothing by comparison with ours?
>
> . . . .
>
> Methinks I see thee straying on the beach,
> And asking of the surge that bathes thy foot
> If it ever has wash'd our distant shore,
> I see thee weep, and thine are honest tears,
> A patriot's for his country. Thou art sad
> At thought of her forlorn and abject state,
> From which no pow'r of thine can raise her up.
> Thus fancy paints thee, and though apt to err,
> Perhaps errs little when she paints thee thus.
> She tells me too that duly every morn
> Thou climbst the mountain top, with eager eye
> Exploring far and wide the watr'y waste
> For sight of ship from England. Ev'ry speck
> Seen in the dim horizon turns thee pale
> With conflict of contending hopes and fears.
>
> . . . .
>
> Alas, expect it not.
> (*Task* 1.647–48, 654–68, 672)

At first glance, Omai appears as an exfoliation of ideal Englishness, a "patriot" weeping over his country's internal corruptions: the poet, groping for an understanding of an inaccessible other, supplies a version of himself, so that Omai appears here as a mirror image of the weepy speaker gazing out at him; the erring fancy of the "I" meets Omai's similarly deluded fancy returning across a horizontal, watery space. Yet if we look more closely, such a complacent image of sentimental patriotism seems troubled by the visage "pale / With conflict of contending hopes and fears" (667–68) and that "eager eye" futilely scanning the horizon for moving specks. Like Kate earlier in the poem, like the speaker later in his brown study, Omai is also waiting, expectantly, for—"some stranger's near approach." Or, as in the uncanny logic of the superstition that intrigued Cowper and Coleridge, he is anticipating a stranger who may be a friend. Kate, Omai, and the speaker by the hearth are all in the impossibly frozen situation of apprehending something without knowing when, who, or what it will be.

For my purposes, Omai offers an interesting way of interpreting this recurrent figure, not because he provides the comforting ballast of a historical referent (the rumors that constitute the English account are remarkably weightless), but because, as one of the biggest and most confused public events of his time, he provides an opportunity for seeing how an incoherent "article" of news enters into contemporary public consciousness and representation, including poetic representation, which tries, unsuccessfully, to make sense of it. From the moment of his arrival, Omai had been followed avidly by the newspapers, which offered vastly conflicting accounts of his parade of visits to Court, Parliament, and Cambridge, his smallpox inoculation, his taste in food, his manner of speaking.[25] Ritual and reportage fumbled to fill the void of understanding, attempting to grapple with open questions about the consequences of British expansion and exploration overseas, the newest phase of which was inaugurated by the opening of the South Seas in the 1770s. What is Englishness and what will it be in a quickly expanding empire? To what extent is—and should—any life lived at home be ineradicably intertwined with far-flung existences, among which this visitor from the South Pacific offered just one, unusually visible, example? What burdens are carried by such incompletely known, but extensive, interdependencies? This is, in the terms I introduced earlier, an anxious uncertainty about the boundaries of the "conversable world" in both senses of Hume's resonant phrase: not only the world made up of polite conversationalists but also the world as knowable at all. Does the "globe . . . tur[n] submitted to view"—as we have seen Cowper briefly fantasizing in the newspaper sequence? Or is it no longer possible to comprehend a global reality that can be—as Fielding hoped it could—"turned round, sifted, and . . . communicated to each other"? It is not accidental that the question most often renewed with respect to Omai concerned the visitor's skills of communication and conversation. He was reported either to speak quite poorly or else remarkably well, as in the *London Chronicle*'s improbable report that "Omiah, the native of Otaheite, we are informed can read and write English well enough to hold a correspondence," a rumor whose next sentence makes clear the proximity between conversation and other more intimate minglings, "It is still said he is going to be married to a young Lady of about 22 years of age, who will go with him to his own country."[26]

Interspersed among other news that had nothing to do with him, Omai was thus an instance of what the *London Magazine* entry cited earlier calls "the contradictory substance of foreign and domestick paragraphs"—but one in which the possibility and the contradiction of positing substance distinctively "foreign" or "domestic" was precisely the issue. Although he was returned by Captain Cook in 1776—left on Huahine with a stock of goats, horses, and European clothes—such uncertainties about the implication of transoceanic expansion did not much abate but took a new, even more unanswerable form: What happened to Omai, once reinstalled in his native context with a measure of English culture (plus livestock, gratuitous clothes)? The posthumous publication of Cook's official *Voyage to the Pacific Ocean* in 1784 and the sally of rival, spurious accounts of Omai's return that between 1781 and 1784 preceded and sought to scoop the authorized version did much to keep the question alive but little to answer it, since Cook had died before reaching England and no one successfully followed his path back until 1789.[27] All the *General Evening Post* could do—as late as 1784 and while Cowper was still working on *The Task*—was to reprint portions of Cook's narrative of the return voyage in an attempt to "satisfy our readers who will no doubt be anxious with regard to the fate of Omai."[28] We can now see that Cowper's representation of Omai in *Task* 1 is attempting to perform the same work as the *General Evening Post*: to satisfy an anxiety both personal and collective about the fate of this enigmatic, briefly befriended stranger—token of the new fluidity of relations across space—by trying to fill in the interstices of what the press could render only as "dissociating articles," both because of the dearth in intelligence and because of the narrative incoherence we have seen described by Crabbe.

Recall Fredric Jameson's account (cited earlier) of the contradiction, under imperialism, of any lived experience and the structures (social and economic) that inflect that experience with the force of an absent cause, immanent in its effects: a full account of any such experience can no longer be rendered from the home "in which it takes place . . . [but] lies, rather, in India or Jamaica or Hong Kong." "Yet," Jameson continues, "this absent cause can find figures through which to express itself in distorted or symbolic ways."[29] In this regard Jameson's Althusserian understanding of history is close to the formulation of Williams, defending his position that "there are cases where the structure of feeling . . . tangible in a particular set of works is undoubtedly an articulation of an area of experience which lies beyond them." One recognizes such moments, Williams claimed, with the appearance of a "semantic figure" or new kind of work that "produces a sudden shock of recognition."[30] Mindful of the impact that it had on its readers, I would suggest that the peering, poring, scanning eye that collapses space by dwelling intently on such distant objects felt as almost-but-not-quite present—as the brown study puts it, the stranger in "*near* approach"—offers just such a figure, although it is in certain respects misleading to say that it "articulates" an experience, since it is a figure of expressive inarticulateness, and of the limits of lived experience. A gesture shot through with contradiction, since it is both desire and apprehension for both stranger and friend, this immersed stare marks the point at which the conversable world's attempts at polite articulation (in both senses of the word that designated the acts of joining and uttering) come up against a world system too large to sustain them, a system that introduces and imbricates "strangers" among "friends."

As such, the expectant, fixed stare of fear and desire offers the antithesis of the mobile, visual "command," the "equal, wide survey," that John Barrell has so nicely explicated in Thomson, Dyer, and eighteenth-century georgic-topographical verse—and which the transformation of the newspaper into landscape attempts to accomplish.[31] It qualifies, although it does not refute, Suvir Kaul's contention that the author of the long poem in the eighteenth century, Cowper included, "imagined poetry to be a unique and privileged literary form for the enunciation of a puissant (and plastic) vocabulary of nation, particularly one of a Britain proving itself (in fits and starts, to be sure) great at home and abroad."[32] For it acknowledges (as may Kaul's own penchant for parenthesis) a teeming historical present that is not, cannot be, enunciated in the anthems of empire, for it is not "conversable" in the various senses of that term.

However, what interests me in particular is not just the fact of this darker apprehension of historicity but the occasion of its involuntary return in the poem. What the brown study in *Task* 4 with its Janus-faced speaker helps us understand is that fixation on that pending strangeness and "indolent vacuity of thought" are the two faces of each other. In attempting to specify their relationship we could call the vacuity of thought a protective defense against those imminent strangers or, less figuratively, the as-yet-unknown implications of overseas intimacy dramatized so pathologically in the baffled coverage of Omai's visit and more mundanely in any issue of the daily news. It is, after all, an "*indolent* vacuity of thought," and indolence in one of its incarnations is boredom—that state often associated with the eighteenth century and described nicely by Adam Phillips as a state of "suspended animation." Boredom, Phillips writes, "makes tolerable the impossible experience of waiting for something without knowing what it could be," the terrible fixity of desiring an object and fearing that desire at the same time.[33] Yet the significance of that vacuity of thought is more than just a defense, or, if it is one, we need to recognize that it admits the threat it parries—it is loophole and shield at once. For I have been suggesting that this lapse in Lockean ideation and identity, this interstitial moment of unthinking consciousness that is both described in the brown study and enacted by the pattern of figure in the poem more generally, is the *condition* for the entry of ongoing history's absent but immanent force. This apperception *cannot* enter as idea or articulation (direct narrative statement, recognition of explicit structure) because it is not—not yet or not acceptable as—one. But its potent sign or effect is the peculiar affect of muted risk, that register of waiting "with conflict of contending hopes and fears." For that reason it would be precisely the wrong question to ask whether Cowper "intends" the poring eye and mask of the speaker to recall Omai and other staring spectators: to put the question in those terms is to miss Williams's and Jameson's separate insights about the work that figure can do in excess of intention, particularly when the history one is part of lies beyond lived experience and sense perception. It is to miss the critique of the Lockean idea that Cowper's poem itself mounts.

The Flicker of History: Cowper and Walter Benjamin

Acedia, Walter Benjamin wrote in the "Theses on the Philosophy of History," "despairs of grasping and holding the genuine historical image as it flares up briefly."[34] Since Benjamin offers a sustained meditation on the relationship between a culture of news or of information (a later development on the continent) and involuntary consciousness as a distinctively open, historical medium, he provides an important frame of reference for Cowper's flickering film of fire. Taking aim at the "dissociating articles" of news very much as we have seen Crabbe and others doing, Benjamin argues in his essay on Baudelaire that with their "lack of connection between the individual news elements," "newspapers constitute one of the many evidences" of modern man's "inability to assimilate the data of the world around him by way of experience" (*Erfahrung*, or collective "tradition," passed between generations). Not solely the newspaper itself but more generally the "replacement of the older narration by information, of information by sensation, reflects the increasing atrophy of experience." Yet just because the news, with its privileging of the "happening" isolated from narrative tradition, eludes *Erfahrung*, it is not therefore unavailable. Its content becomes available in a different way: in the form of *Erlebnis*, the lived event or "happening," which "tend[s] to remain in a certain hour of one's life" and is therefore subject to compulsive recurrence, or "involuntary memory."[35]

Although Benjamin seems to expect this shocklike encounter to "sterilize the incident for poetic yield," the achievement of Baudelaire, he argues, is to make poetry out of such fragmentary lived moments, which stand like blank spaces in the calendar, dropped from tradition. Baudelaire "envisioned blank spaces which he filled in with his poems," Benjamin writes enigmatically: "His work cannot be categorized as historical, like anyone else's, but it intended to be so and understood itself as such." Baudelairean lyric is *peculiarly* historical (historical not "like anyone else's"), that is, because of its capacity both to parry and to lodge within it "heterogeneous, conspicuous fragments," resistant to chronological connection with other days; such heterogenous articles, nonetheless, are "the fragments of genuine historical experience." Despite all his poignant plaints for lost *Erfahrung*, Benjamin does not nostalgically hope for its restoration, and in his later work he began to look forward to a dialectically recovered likeness of *Erlebnis*, as in the "Theses," with their flame image and their emphasis on the "time of the now . . . blasted out of the continuum of history."[36]

Short of making William Cowper into a Benjaminian historical materialist (which he certainly was not) or into Baudelaire (with whom he did indeed have certain social and splenetic affinities), I hope to have suggested a similar, complex relationship between his poetry and the news, or, more aptly, the sense of the historical present that is fostered by a nascent news culture. At a level that differs quite sharply from all the overt statements for or against empire, and for or against the imperiled condition of Britain in 1784 (and *The Task* contains many, of each kind), Cowper's poetry is more interestingly and involuntarily "historical"—although not just "like anyone else's"—for the ways it captures, lodged in the interstices of thought, those figures and flickering recognitions of historicity that do not answer to the pleasure principle of narration and cannot be assimilated into polite conversation. Benjamin's understanding of the way such recognitions "tend to remain in a certain hour of one's life" helps us interpret Cowper's insight into the temporal quality of Fancy both in the brown study passage and in the newspaper sequence leading up to it. Under the sway of fancy, as we have seen, the poet in his reverie "lose[s] an hour / At evening" (*Task* 4.302–3); as he reads the newspaper just before that—and now we can return to the most striking aspect of the passage discussed earlier—"fancy, like the finger of a clock, / Runs the great circuit and is still at home" (4.118–19). Cowper, I think, invokes the image of a clock that goes around and around not as a reminder of chronology, as one might expect, but for its relative stasis; it cannot mark progression as can a calendar, but rather the hours, over and over again.

Cowper, it must be interjected at this point, however, was writing not lyric but a version of georgic, whereas historiography was, for Benjamin (and Benjamin's Baudelaire), distinctively lyrical and antinarrative. It was Coleridge who would make lyric out of *The Task*, fifteen years later in "Frost at Midnight," and now we can see that he did so precisely by excising the "indolent vacuity of thought" sequence from its narrative surroundings, moving what "Frost at Midnight" renders as "the interspersed vacancies / And momentary pauses of the thought" ("Frost," 46–47) far from the newspaper's "map of busy life" (*Task* 4.55). The memory that flares up in response to Coleridge's "film, which fluttered on the grate, . . . the sole unquiet thing" (15–16) is involuntary but personal, the dream "of my sweet birth-place" (28)—a phrase that would in turn migrate one year later into the opening of the 1799 *Prelude*.[37] The stranger that materializes in Coleridge's poem reassuringly becomes "townsman, or aunt, or sister more beloved" (42); the thematization of historical strangeness and the actuality of strangers is muted. What is so interesting about Cowper's choice not to separate consciousness from the world of information that imprints it—which in modal terms appears in the choice not to submerge the georgic in lyric—is that *The Task* thereby makes palpable the connection between the pressure of historical presentness and sensory consciousness that is less discernible in "greater Romantic lyric." This is not merely a point about literary history or the genealogy of form, although it is not uninteresting as such. More provocatively, it begins to suggest a curious relationship between the eighteenth-century culture (and perceived overload) of news, the georgic attempt to offer a rival medium of knowledge, and Romantic *aisthesis*—which in Kant's *Critique of Judgment* also takes as one of its images "the sight of the changing shape of fire on the hearth" as contemplated by the fancying subject.[38] That relationship now needs attention.

"Vacuity of Thought": Between Acedia and Aisthesis

At this point a skeptical questioner might rightly ask whether I am giving too much credence to Cowper's claim that textual contiguity in *The Task*—in this case, the poem's juxtaposition of the newspaper's national and international map with the "vacuity of thought" that comes right after it—articulates a significant *cultural* connection. While association may indeed be the organizational principle of the baggy, paratactical monster that is *The Task*, on what basis can one claim that this particular one transcends the train of thought, the idiosyncratic and "ludicrous" imagination, of William Cowper? In fact, this association was not Cowper's isolated quirk but had a wider currency. At the same time that the problem of "vacuities of thought" was vexing moral philosophical and early psychological discourse with the fault lines and fictionality of any integrated "personal identity," vacant spaces were making news in a neighboring arena—within the numbers of the periodical press which, from *The Spectator* on, offered a kind of paraphilosophical symposium, a university without walls, or with different ones. The concerns grouped under such frequently employed phrases as "vacant of thought," "vacuity of the mind," "interstitial vacancies," or "the blanks of society" took, in journalistic discussions, a slightly different but no less anxious turn, displaying worries about what kind of characters magazine and newspaper writing both catered to and constructed.

In one of its contemporary senses, a vacancy was a temporary interval of leisure or unoccupied time. Addressing men and women affluent enough to have such freedom, periodical publications made it their work to recommend, as Addison wrote, "certain Methods for filling up their empty Spaces of Life."[39] No one was more worried about the productive management of free time than Samuel Johnson, who kept an equally stern eye on his own wayward propensities for melancholic idling, and the Rambler accordingly advised a strict regimen of improving hobbies: "He that should steadily and resolutely assign to any science or language those interstitial vacancies which intervene in the most crouded variety of diversion or employment, would find every day new irradiations of knowledge."[40] But this sense of vacancy as vacation was active alongside another, which designated not a certain kind of free time but a certain kind of empty mind. "There is a Creature," Steele wrote in *The Spectator*, "who has all the Organs of Speech, a tollerable good Capacity for conceiving what is said to it, together with a pretty proper Behaviour in all the Occurrences of Common Life; but naturally very vacant of Thought in it self, and therefore forced to apply it self to foreign Assistances" (2:386). To these "Blanks of Society," as they were frequently called, the periodical and newswriter happily offered such assistance: "It is incredible to think how empty I have in this Time observed some Part of the Species to be," Addison wrote, "what mere Blanks they are when they first come abroad in the Morning, how utterly they are at a Stand till they are set a going by some Paragraph in the Newspaper" (*Spectator* 1:18). To this "set of Men . . . altogether unfurnished with Ideas," Addison added several days later, "I must likewise lay Claim" (*Spectator* 1:46).

These dicta of Mr. Spectator begin to suggest the complex dialectic taking shape between the news as a cultural phenomenon and vacuity of mind as a social as well as psychological problem, as well as the rivalry between the periodical essayist and the news writer. Although the idle man could turn to the papers to "fill the vacuity of his mind with the news of the day," as *The Idler* put it, the phenomena of "news" also tended to empty the same minds it was designed to fill. Johnson himself, seeking in part to distinguish himself from the daily hack, provides a particularly trenchant diagnosis of this circular movement of effects, criticizing the "rivulets of intelligence" that streamed from the daily newspaper as "information sufficient to elate vanity, and stiffen obstinacy, but too little to enlarge the mind into complete skill for full comprehension."[41] Such foreshortened comprehension was exacerbated by two seemingly contradictory aspects of news writing, according to Johnson: its tendency to encourage "reading without the fatigue of close attention" (*Yale* 2:95), but also its redundancy, which paradoxically caused rather than spared mental exhaustion. "The tale of the morning paper is told again in the evening, and the narratives of the evening are bought again in the morning," and so even "the most eager peruser of news is tired before he has completed his labour"; the result, Johnson grimly concludes, is that "journals are daily multiplied without increase of knowledge" (*Yale* 2:23). As a playful remedy, Johnson in the person of the Idler proposed the slowing down, or gradation, of the news: if all news writers agreed to confederate, "the morning and evening authors might divide an event between them; a single action, and that not of much importance, might be gradually discovered so as to vary a whole week with joy, anxiety, and conjecture." If the news could be rendered in slow motion it might give more time for thought, or so the fictional example of such slow-motion news provided (at some length) suggests. What the Idler does not acknowledge, although Johnson knows it perfectly well, is that any event, presented ever so gradually, over time, stops being "news."

The Idler in 1758 thus corroborates the contributor to the *London Magazine* of 1766 cited in the first section of this essay, who noted that the "abrupt transitions from article to article, without the smallest connection between one paragraph and another, overload and confuse the memory." Johnson, however, provides the more sophisticated social analysis, free of any hint of technological determinism, which has been nicely criticized in our own times by Michael Warner for its artificial separation of the logic of print technology from the culture of which it is a part.[42] News does not cause the overload by itself, Johnson recognizes; rather, news writers are only "necessary in a nation where much wealth produces much leisure, and one part of the people has nothing to do but to observe the lives and fortunes of the other" (*Yale* 2:22).

Both world spectator and "castaway" of history, representing himself both as the consumer of the "rich repast" proffered from around the globe in the newspaper advertisements of *Task* 4 and as the assiduous producer of the poem-as-luxury item, that famous cucumber of *Task* 3, William Cowper, like Johnson, is poised uneasily in both of these worlds. What is distinctive about *The Task* is the way that, while Cowper is well versed in Lockean philosophical psychology and immersed in contemporary discussions about the effects of newspaper reading (he could easily be our "W.C.," quoted earlier), he nonetheless tilts both discourses about vacancies within thought in a new direction—one decisive in retrospect, as it turned out, because of the influence of his poem on the next generation of writers. Johnson had construed mental "vacuity" in the most negative terms, as an unproductivity verging on spiritual sloth, or *acedia*. Cowper, prone as he was to cyclical melancholy and loss of faith, is by no means free of such associations, but in the brown study passage and *The Task* at large, we see him uncertainly edging this state toward a creative "repose" (4.296), a movement glossed by his revision of the *Georgics*'s phrase, *studiis florentem ignoblis oti* (studious of the arts of inglorious ease) (4.564), as *The Task*'s "studious of laborious ease, / Not slothful" (3.251). "Laborious ease" might cause us to assimilate Cowper's revision of the torpid indolence of *The Spectator*'s empty-headed "Blanks of society," Johnson's melancholic idler, or Locke's sleeper, to the "majestic indolence" of aesthetic experience that Willard Spiegelman has recently traced in Romantic poetry and philosophy. Kant, as Spiegelman points out, describes the poet as "conducting the free play of the imagination as if it were a serious business of the understanding."[43] But Cowper's "indolent vacuity of thought" is not (yet) Kantian free play either. Far more unstable, weaving precariously "brittle toys" (*Task* 4.307), it may be play of sorts — ludic or ludicrous, but, as we have seen, it is not free. That image of the "bars" hemming in the "sooty flames" might stand nicely for the embeddedness, textual and cultural, of this interstitial consciousness, a vacuity replete with contemporaneity's "dissociating articles" and news.

Spiegelman surveys the historical and qualitative shift whereby a pathological torpor or *acedia* gradually became the more genial recreation of aesthetic suspension or wise passiveness; he does not seek to account for its cause. Of course, just "what caused" such a notable epistemic and semantic drift is overdetermined, but the example of Cowper points to one form a partial answer might take. At the position of pivot between the emptiness of *acedia* and the fullness of aesthetic experience, Cowper's teeming vacuity of thought, I have tried to suggest, is an unlikely, involuntary mode of knowledge that responds to the pressure of an eventful and information-laden present, one shaped by technological and territorial extension. The relationship between the late-eighteenth-century culture of news and the affective, proto-aesthetic consciousness that starts to emerge out of the georgic attempt to offer a rival medium of information is not just the "displacement" or "negation" of contemporaneity by the "self," as in the forceful historicist arguments of the later 1980s and 1990s. Instead, it defines this consciousness as the heir, a crucial if residual carrier, of a world of information-in-flux, that teeming historical presentness that is "not yet" fully formed as knowledge but presses insistently, insinuating itself at the level of recurrent figure. This genealogy might remind us as well of the ele-

ment of external risk and historical inundation that intervenes at the genesis of full-fledged account of aesthetic perception.[44] To render my argument
in the most provocative or playful terms: I am turning the tables on our
plaint that the postmodern condition of information supersedes a Romantic
idea of the literary and asking whether the reverse is not also true. Recalling the impulse of so many biblical and postbiblical accounts to provide
a narrative of the events leading up to Genesis 1:1's "In the beginning," I
have proposed that if, according to a narrative of the genesis of Kantian or
Schillerian aesthetics, "in the beginning" was the first free play of the imagination, then "before the beginning" but strongly contributing to it was—
the news.

Notes

1 Cowper, *The Task* 4.88–89. All quotations from *The Task* are cited by book and line from
  The Task and Other Poems, ed. James Sambrook (London: Longman, 1994). Citations of
  the letters are from *The Letters and Prose Writings of William Cowper*, ed. James King and
  Charles Ryskamp, 5 vols. (Oxford: Clarendon, 1979–86).

2 Benedict Anderson, *Imagined Communities: Reflections on the Origin and Spread of Nationalism*, rev. ed. (London and New York: Verso, 1991), 35.

3 Raymond Williams, *Marxism and Literature* (New York: Oxford University Press, 1977),
  128–29, 133–34. The chemical language, as well as helpful elaborations of Williams's formulation, are offered in Williams's response to the interviewers from the *New Left Review*:
  see Williams, *Politics and Letters: Interviews with the New Left Review* (London: NLB, 1979),
  156–74; quotation from 167.
      Williams was more frequently criticized than celebrated for his use of the terms "feel-
  ing" and "experience"—open as such terms are to accusations of foundationalism and
  other idealizations—but those who have charged him with positing experience "as a pristine contact between the subject and the reality in which this subject is immersed" (*Politics and Letters*, 167), or those who have accused him of making experience a foundational
  authority, read Williams incorrectly or partially. For "feeling" was for him never the property of isolated (let alone pristine) subjects; it is just misunderstood as such because analytic categories cannot accommodate the flux of events. Nor was it an authentic realm of
  experience prior to or outside language. An expert on nineteenth- and twentieth-century
  media, Williams recognized that "means of communication" are always "means of production" (as in the title of a late essay), and he insisted from *The Long Revolution* on that
  "there is no natural seeing and therefore there cannot be a direct and unmediated contact
  with reality" (see ibid.). But he also understood that all articulations have their interference, their static or their silence. He groped, in a wayward, occasional, even baffled way,
  to give such dissonances some meaning, to find for them a referent that is not merely
  personal—that exists whether or not it gets signified, whether or not it enters the realm of
  any individual perception, although we may sometimes identify it there. For that reason,
  although his work is usually regarded as antithetical to the Marxism of Louis Althusser,

I suggest in a later section that Williams's talk of collective disturbances, blockages, tensions, troubles, and other sensory symptoms is not incompatible with the Althusserian notion of history as an "absent cause" immanent in its effects, except that Williams often has in view a different field of effects.

4   My work here is indebted not only to Williams's phrasing but also to Alan Liu's Althusserian formulation: "History is the absence that is the very possibility of the 'here and now.' . . . If there 'is' no history, then the relevant problem becomes the knowledge or *sense* of history in the full sense" (*Wordsworth: The Sense of History* [Stanford: Stanford University Press, 1989], 39). In Liu's magisterial book, from which I have learned volumes, I think it is fair to say that "history" steals the show from "sense," so that the term is not scrutinized in its "full sense." To do so would be to examine the Lockean heritage—as well as the aporias in Locke's thought—and such is the investigation this essay seeks to inaugurate.

5   Mark Poster, *The Mode of Information: Poststructuralism and Social Context* (Chicago: University of Chicago Press, 1990), 6.

6   Entry dated April 11, 1757, printed in *London Magazine* 26 (April 1757): 160.

7   Preface to "The Newspaper: A Poem," in George Crabbe, *The Complete Poetical Works*, ed. Norma Dalyrmple-Champneys, 3 vols. (Oxford: Clarendon, 1988), 1:179.

8   See Jeremy Black, *The English Press in the Eighteenth Century* (London: Croom Helm, 1987). Other helpful discussions of the eighteenth-century British press include Lucyle Werkmeister, *The London Daily Press* (Lincoln: University of Nebraska Press, 1963), as well as portions of J. Paul Hunter, *Before Novels: The Cultural Contexts of Eighteenth-Century English Fiction* (New York: W. W. Norton, 1990); Lennard Davis, *Factual Fictions: The Origins of the English Novel* (New York: Columbia University Press, 1983); and Paul Langford, *A Polite and Commercial People: England 1727–1783* (Oxford: Clarendon, 1989).

9   Printed in *London Magazine* 35 (December 1766): 638.

10   *London Magazine* 49 (August 1780): 354.

11   *London Magazine* 35: 639–40.

12   Terry Eagleton, *The Function of Criticism: From the "Spectator" to Post-Structuralism* (London: Verso, 1984), 10; also quoted by Jon Klancher, *The Making of English Reading Audiences, 1790–1832* (Madison: University of Wisconsin Press, 1987), 23.

13   Richard Terdiman, *Discourse/Counter-Discourse: The Theory and Practice of Symbolic Resistance in Nineteenth-Century France* (Ithaca: Cornell University Press, 1985), 122.

14   Relevant to the relationship that I am describing here is Jay David Bolter and Richard Grusin's observation about the logic of immediacy and hypermediacy in digital media: "Transparent digital applications seek to get to the real by bravely denying the fact of mediation; digital hypermedia seek the real by multiplying mediation so as to create a feeling of fullness, a satiety of experience, which can be taken as reality" (*Remediation: Understanding New Media* [Cambridge: MIT Press, 2000], 53). As they make clear, the phenomena Bolter and Grusin are investigating have a long prehistory, and their citation of Jacques Derrida's account of Immanuel Kant's third *Critique* is apposite, both for their purposes and for mine. Derrida defines "true mimesis" in Kant as follows: It "is not the representation of one thing by another . . . the reproduction of a product of nature by a product of art. It is not the relation of two products but of two productions. . . . The artist

does not imitate things in nature . . . but the acts of *natura naturans*, the operations of the *physis*" ("Economimesis," *Diacritics* 11 [1981]: 9). The newspaper's "as if," in other words, mimes that aspect of presentness that resists known historical categories and structures because the terms that will describe it are not yet fully formed or known.

15 Julie Ellison, "News, Blues, and Cowper's Busy World," *Modern Language Quarterly* 62.3 (2001): 219–37, especially 226–33 (quotations from 235, 226, respectively).

16 Ibid., 232.

17 Henry Fielding, "An Essay on Conversation," in *Miscellanies*, ed. Henry Knight Miller, 3 vols. (Oxford: Clarendon, 1972–97), 1:120.

18 See David Hume, "Of Essay Writing," in *Essays, Moral, Political, and Literary* (London: Oxford University Press, 1966), 568.

19 Here I quote from Cowper's own poem entitled "Conversation" (line 8). See William Cowper, *The Poems of William Cowper*, ed. John D. Baird and Charles Ryskamp, 3 vols. (Oxford: Clarendon, 1995), 1:354.

20 Fredric Jameson, "Cognitive Mapping," in *Marxism and the Interpretation of Culture*, ed. Cary Nelson and Lawrence Grossberg (Urbana and Chicago: University of Illinois Press), 349.

21 John Locke, *An Essay Concerning Human Understanding*, ed. Peter H. Nidditch (Oxford: Clarendon Press, 1975), 2.1.1, 2.27.9.

22 So Thomas Reid, writing in the same year as the publication of *The Task*, protested that "if personal identity consisted in consciousness, it would certainly follow, that *no man is the same person any two moments of his life.*" Reid is quoted, and the larger controversy is discussed, by Christopher Fox, *Locke and the Scriblerians: Identity and Consciousness in Early Eighteenth-Century Britain* (Berkeley and Los Angeles: University of California Press, 1988); quotation from 10.

23 Marshall Brown, *Preromanticism* (Stanford: Stanford University Press, 1991), 69.

24 Ellison's work is especially pertinent for any discussion of the role of Fancy in imperial or topographical verse of the eighteenth century: in addition to "News, Blues, and Cowper's Busy World," see her *Cato's Tears and the Making of Anglo-American Emotion* (Chicago: University of Chicago Press, 1999), especially chap. 4. Where Ellison understands Fancy primarily as a mode of subjective "mastery and escape" (*Cato's Tears*, 100), I place more stress than she does—although her account is a finely dialectical one—on Fancy's involuntary and intersubjective engagement and movements.

25 See, for example, the following issues of the *General Evening Post* and the *Morning Chronicle*: *General Evening Post*, July 14–16, 1774, July 19–21, 1774, July 21–23, 1774, July 26–28, 1774, August 6–9, 1774, August 9–11, 1774; *Morning Chronicle*, July 16, 1774, July 26, 1774, July 29, 1774, August 5, 1774, August 8, 1774, November 9, 1774, etc. Articles or accounts are also frequent in the *London Magazine* for 1774–76.

26 *London Magazine* 20–22 (April 1775): 382.

27 See E. H. McCormick, *Omai: Pacific Envoy* (Auckland, NZ: Auckland University Press, 1977), especially 261–94. For a more panoramic study of the opening of the South Pacific, see Bernard Smith, *European Vision and the South Pacific* (New Haven: Yale University Press, 1985).

28 *General Evening Post*, September 23–25, 1784; see also September 25–28, 1784.

29 Jameson, "Cognitive Mapping," 350.

30 Williams, *Politics and Letters*, 164.

31 John Barrell, *English Literature in History, 1730–80: An Equal, Wide Survey* (London: Hutchinson, 1983).

32 Suvir Kaul, *Poems of Nation, Anthems of Empire: English Verse in the Long Eighteenth-Century* (Charlottesville: University of Virginia Press, 2000), 5.

33 Adam Phillips, "On Being Bored," in *Kissing, Tickling, and Being Bored: Essays on the Unexamined Life* (Cambridge: Harvard University Press, 1993), 77 and 68–78 more generally. Patricia M. Spacks gives Phillips's psychoanalytic insights historical specificity by arguing that while something like boredom may have existed earlier by a different name, boredom was in the eighteenth century "a new concept, if not necessarily a new event" (*Boredom: The Literary History of a State of Mind* [Chicago; University of Chicago Press, 1995], 28).

34 Walter Benjamin, "Theses on the Philosophy of History," in *Illuminations*, ed. Hannah Arendt, trans. Harry Zohn (New York: Schocken, 1968), 256.

35 Benjamin, "On Some Motifs in Baudelaire," in *Illuminations*, 158–59, 159, 163.

36 Ibid., 162; Benjamin, "Theses," 261.

37 "Frost at Midnight" is cited by line from *The Oxford Authors: Samuel Taylor Coleridge* (New York: Oxford University Press, 1992), 87–89.

38 Kant writes: "Beautiful objects are to be distinguished from beautiful views of objects. . . . In the latter case taste appears, not so much in what the imagination apprehends in this field, as in the impulse it thus gets to fiction, i.e. in the peculiar fancies with which the mind entertains itself, while it is continually being aroused by the variety which strikes the eye. An illustration is afforded, e.g. by the sight of the changing shape of a fire on the hearth or of a rippling brook; neither of these has beauty, but they bring with them a charm for the imagination because they entertain it in free play" (*Critique of Judgment*, trans. J. H. Bernard [New York: Hafner Press, 1951], 81).

39 Addison, *The Spectator*, ed. Douglas F. Bond, 5 vols. (Oxford: Clarendon, 1965), 1:395.

40 Johnson, *Rambler* 108, in *The Yale Edition of the Works of Samuel Johnson*, ed. W. J. Bate and Albrecht B. Strauss (New Haven: Yale University Press, 1969), 4:212.

41 Johnson, *Idler* 7, in *The Yale Edition of the Works of Samuel Johnson*, ed. W. J. Bate, John M. Bullitt, and L. F. Powell (New Haven: Yale University Press, 1963), 2:23.

42 Michael Warner, *Letters of the Republic: Publication and the Public Sphere in Eighteenth-Century America* (Cambridge: Harvard University Press, 1990), 5–7, and chap. 1 more generally.

43 Willard Spiegelman, *Majestic Indolence: English Poetry and the Work of Art* (New York: Oxford University Press, 1995).

44 "To analyze the element of *comfort* in beauty, without false emphasis," Kenneth Burke reminds us with characteristic pragmatism, "we must be . . . more 'dialectical,' in that we include also, as an important aspect of the recipe, the element of *discomfort*" (*The Philosophy of Literary Form* [Berkeley and Los Angeles: University of California Press, 1973], 61.

Thomas Pfau

Conjuring History: Lyric Cliché, Conservative Fantasy, and Traumatic Awakening in German Romanticism

> *Schläft ein Lied in allen Dingen,*
> *Die da träumen fort und fort,*
> *Und die Welt hebt an zu singen,*
> *Triffst du nur das Zauberwort.*
>
> [Song slumbering in all things
> That dream forever on and on,
> The world leaps into song,
> If only you divine the magic word.]
> —Joseph von Eichendorff, "Wünschelrute"

The ambiguity of the . . . revelation of the past does not depend so much on the vacillation of its content between the Imaginary and the Real, for it locates itself in both. Nor is it exactly error or falsehood. The point is that it presents us with the birth of Truth in the Word, and thereby brings us up against the reality of what is neither true nor false. . . . For the Truth of this revelation lies in the present Word which testifies to it in contemporary reality and which grounds it in the name of that reality. Yet in that reality, it is only the Word which bears witness to that portion of the powers of the past which has been thrust aside at each crossroads where the event has made its choice. . . . [Historical anamnesis] is not a question of reality, but of Truth, because the effect of a full Word is to reorder the past contingent events by conferring on them the

The *South Atlantic Quarterly* 102:1, Winter 2003.
Copyright © 2003 by Duke University Press.

> necessities to come, just as they are constituted by the
> little liberty through which the subject makes them
> present.
> —Jacques Lacan, *Speech and Language*
> *in Psychoanalysis*

Heeding the call of German Romanticism's programmatic declarations rather than that of its momentous history, readers have long construed that epoch as the very apotheosis of aesthetic autonomy or, if critical of that value, as succumbing to strictly theoretical contradictions.[1] Except for obligatory, token references to the threat of the French Revolution and the pervasive disorder of the Napoleonic era, criticism has generally proven reluctant to relate the period's artistic or theoretical output to its momentous history. Just how to configure aesthetic production and the experience of historical change has long proven elusive, if hotly debated business.[2] My aim in the following pages is to sketch and exemplify how to read literature as a critical medium for historical cognition, which is to say, to approach literature as maintaining a dialectic (rather than evasive, reactive, or otherwise secondary) relation to history. To help set the stage, we may recall Theodor Adorno's prescient warning against a historicism that deems literature generically incapable of historical cognition and, with its rich methodological armature, purports to redeem literature from its canny, if unconscious obfuscation of ideological positions. Early in his *Aesthetic Theory*, Adorno thus remarks on something both profound and enigmatic that lies at the heart of all claims for aesthetic autonomy. By way of qualifying his earlier optical metaphor ("There is no aesthetic refraction without something being refracted"), Adorno observes:

> The communication of artworks with what is external to them, with the world from which they blissfully or unhappily seal themselves off, occurs through noncommunication; precisely thereby they prove themselves refracted. . . . Even the most sublime artwork takes up a determinate attitude to empirical reality by stepping outside of the constraining spell it casts, not once and for all, but rather ever and again, concretely, unconsciously polemical toward this spell at each historical moment. That artworks as windowless monads "represent" what they themselves are not can scarcely be understood except in that their own dynamic, their immanent historicity as a dialectic of nature and

its domination, not only is of the same essence as the dialectic external to them but resembles it without imitating it. . . . Art's double character as both autonomous and *fait social* is incessantly reproduced at the level of autonomy. It is by virtue of this relation to the empirical that artworks recuperate, neutralized, what once was literally and directly experienced in life and what was expulsed by spirit. Artworks participate in enlightenment because they do not lie: they do not feign the literalness of what speaks out of them. They are as real as answers to the puzzle externally posed to them. Their own tension is binding in relation to the tension external to them.[3]

Most salient about this passage is Adorno's claim that the artwork's recalcitrant, quasi-autistic relationship to the "tension" permeating what is "external" to it ought to be understood not as a defensive and escapist maneuver but, rather, as borne of the deeper awareness of history itself as a welter of chaotic, traumatizing forces. In forgoing the complacency of the "literal" (of language as "communication"), art draws closer to understanding history as profoundly enigmatic. Whatever history may turn out to be, it is never just "context"; nor is it a ready-to-purchase truth vis-à-vis some putative aesthetic ideology.[4] To sharpen these as yet rather abstract remarks, I propose to scrutinize the rhetorical organization of the lyric—which, following Hegel, I here posit as the exemplary form of Romantic art—to the point where it becomes legible as an affective response to a historical situation whose urgency and complexity strikes the expressive subject with belated, traumatic force. Yet doing so constitutes but a first step. For beyond approaching literary form as the symptomatic encryption of a historical tension seeking poetic release, we must also remain alert to the enabling, generative power of cultural forms. To take that crucial second step—one frequently ignored, even disparaged by Romantic historicism—is to recognize historical cognition (rather than the vaunted "evasion of history") as a salient, indeed motivating force within Romantic aesthetic production.

Meanwhile, the transition from the rhetorical analysis of a specific poetic idiom to historical cognition—or, in Kenneth Burke's nomenclature, from a grammar of symbols to a grammar of motives—amounts to but a first step in a more complex itinerary. For the dialectic of literature and history, form and function, remains in turn susceptible to, indeed demands, integration into a larger and forever evolving history of human relations. In what follows, I approach the Romantic lyric as a dialectical form struggling to articulate its speaker's and audience's belated and hence precarious cognitive relationship to their own historical moment. Rather than striving for historical "truth" intentionally, the lyric word, untrammeled by the banal certitudes of communication and "events," divulges its historical import with a clarity at once belated, serendipitous, yet also inescapable. In just that way, Jacques Lacan situates "the birth of Truth in the Word . . . which bears witness to that portion of the powers of the past which has been thrust aside at each crossroads where the event has made its choice." In what follows, then, I argue that the Romantic lyric mediates, rather than occludes, historical consciousness. It does so out of the recognition that history can only ever be known as a moment of "depth" unexpectedly and inescapably opening up amid the surface order of waking, quotidian life. Indeed, like the symptom in post-Freudian psychoanalysis, Romanticism can only think the subject as a type of inwardness (*Innerlichkeit*) that bears nearly eponymous affinity to the spontaneity of remembrance (*Erinnerung*). In other words, Romanticism can postulate the affective depth of its subjects only by historicizing them, a process that begins, in Germany no less than in England, with a comprehensive recovery and advocacy of "ancient" folk culture.[5] The latter forms part of the late-eighteenth-century European "invention of tradition," to borrow Eric Hobsbawm and Terence Ranger's phrase, and it is dialectically related to the repudiation of sentimental literature.

Chronologically, the mobilization of folk culture as a strategic resource for an aesthetic and political "rebirth" of Germany coincides precisely with the collapse of the old Reich in 1806, and its "ground zero" is the intellectual circle of Romantics at Heidelberg. Among those preeminently associated with the Heidelberg school, Ludwig Achim von Arnim offers a prefatory account of his and Clemens Brentano's epoch-making collection of German folk poetry, *Des Knaben Wunderhorn* (1806–8), whose intent often resembles Wordsworth's slightly earlier defense of his poetics in the preface to *Lyrical Ballads* (1800–2). In von Arnim's view, sentimentalism and the allegedly mannered forms of writing associated with a late-eighteenth-century system of literary patronage are nothing but "illness and annihilation" [*Krankheit und Vernichtung*]—a mere "imitation . . . of feeling" [*das Nachahmen . . . des Gefühls*].[6] By contrast, the "authentic tone" [*wahrer Ton*] of folk poetry is posited as a vital resource for an eventual German national community, a project that pivots on attuning a collective reading-audience to memories at once imperiled yet magically preserved in the archetypal form of the *Volkslied*: "Dear God! Where are the old trees under which even yesterday we found rest, the ancient signs of firm borders; what has happened, is happening to them? Almost forgotten by the people, we make painful contact with their roots" [*O mein Gott, wo sind die alten Bäume, unter denen wir noch gestern ruhten, die uralten Zeichen fester Grenzen, was ist damit geschehen, was geschieht? Fast vergessen sind sie schon unter dem Volke, schmerzlich stoßen wir uns an ihren Wurzeln*]. Not surprisingly, perhaps, this programmatic cultivation of Romantic interiority through the resurrection of once-spontaneous literary forms, of again hearing "people sing who were no singers" [*was ich von Leuten singen hörte, die nicht Sänger waren*], entails a formalization of folksong itself.[7] Thus the *Volkslied* is postulated as the spontaneous expression of a timeless naiveté—that is, of an affect impervious to time-as-difference (Hegel's *absolute Unruhe*) but, instead, supported by time as *in*difference (Bergson's *durée*).[8] Upon closer inspection, however, this postulated "naïveté" constitutes no original value but, rather, bespeaks the Romantics' will to think the lyric's (supposedly) intuitive foundations in explicit disjunction from historical time. Hence von Arnim also laments the disappearance of "ancient forests" irretrievably leveled by the economic forces of modernity. If the "ancient signs" of folk culture have been "almost forgotten," their recovery is said to pivot on the kind of archival industry, philological technique, and aesthetic reflections belatedly furnished by the editors of the *Wunderhorn* collection. In short, immediacy and spontaneity alone no longer guarantee cultural value. Conceived only ex post facto from the alienated perspective of modernity, folk culture's naïveté is here formalized and institutionalized as an "ancient" wisdom encrypted in linguistic artifacts whose integrity can no longer be produced but, instead, can be recovered only through serendipitous encounters on the order of what Proust was to name *mémoire involontaire*.[9]

In what follows, I seek to explore more closely the peculiar efficacy of the Romantic lyric as a lucid form of mediation—both by representing for its initial readers their own agonistic modernity (in thematic, topical form) and to reflect that audience for itself as a proto-national community defined by its shared cultural avocation. This the lyric effects transferentially, that is, by (unconsciously) projecting visions of social and cultural health into a hypostatized past and recovering such values through sophisticated literary forms and institutions concerned with allowing an embattled community to awaken to its cultural "memories." As remains to be seen, the high-Romantic lyric conceives its subjects to be uneasily perched on the threshold between a state of pure presence, consciously experienced and widely cherished as middle-class inwardness (*Innerlichkeit*), and unsolicited yet insistent fragments of recollection (*Erinnerung*) that point back to an antecedent trauma to which lyric writing and reading respond with a formal concision whose searching relation to the past we must not misconstrue as a defensive aestheticism. Approached as a richly speculative, textual strategy, Romanticism's reflexive transposition of folk culture into high lyric art—its conditional recovery of a lost organic presence through contingent moments of recollection, song into text—is anything but naïvely teleological or didactic in intent. Far from proclaiming the outright recovery and reinstatement of medieval folk culture, writers like Wordsworth in England, or von Arnim, Brentano, Joseph Görres, Friedrich Creuzer, and Joseph von Eichendorff in Germany premise their literary productivity on a moment of inspiration ("spontaneous overflow of powerful feelings . . . recollected in tranquility").[10] Inasmuch as the formulation promises the containment of subconscious turmoil within the studied, textual affect of repose, the latter remains but the printed image, and hence the trace, of a negative whose insistent claims the writer's expressive locutions sought to contain (though never disavow outright) and, in so doing, continually reproduced. This dialectic also shapes the language of high-Romantic lyricism. Here, too, we note a quasi-schizophrenic split between the quotidian and the magical, the blandly descriptive and flashes of conjury. The lyric word stands in the service of both, politics and revelation; at once a record of local-material ephemera (Wordsworth's "real language of man") and a holograph capable of unveiling the supersensible depths encrypted in history's fleeting detail; indeed, it appears the only repository for a notion of the supersensible that is not opposed to but distilled from historical experience.

Rather than abridging historical awareness, this basic schema—first proposed by the ballad revival of the late eighteenth century and, by 1815, fully amalgamated either with the more speculative form of the lyric or the more discursive genre of the historical novel—constitutes a powerful strategy of historical cognition in its own right. Forgoing historicism's gluttonously accumulative and naïvely leveling faith in history's material concreteness and transparency, the Romantic lyric cultivates a richly dialectical relation to historical process strikingly prescient of Walter Benjamin's unique rewriting of historical materialism as a type of critique bent on "the salvation of phenomena" by the "idea." For von Arnim and Brentano no less than for Benjamin, the critical reconstruction of phenomena is not aimed at a "totality" but, instead, aims to cultivate a historical fact to the point where "its innermost structure appears to be so essential as to reveal it as an origin." In order for the idea to establish a rapport between concrete phenomena and truth, it must locate within the former the unique quality of *Intentionslosigkeit* (lack of intentionality). The goal of literary-historical study, in Benjamin's words—and they could well have been Brentano's—is "not therefore one of intention and knowledge, but rather a total immersion and absorption in [truth]." Above all, "the state of being, beyond all phenomenality, to which this power belongs, is that of the name." In close proximity to Plato's ideas—which, Benjamin argues, "might be considered . . . nothing but deified words and verbal concepts"—poetic language presents its subject with the uncanny and unsuspected ("intentionless") authority of "almost forgotten" memories whose claims prove both arresting and unsettling.[11] In Brentano's and von Arnim's programmatic statements about *Des Knaben Wunderhorn*, the ancient memories miraculously preserved in, and suddenly again conjured up by, the poetic word also rekindle the conflict between the collective truth of the past (the "people" [*Volk*]) and the dispersed knowledge of modern individuals (the "public").[12]

Reiterating what David Wellbery has analyzed as Goethe's and Herder's myth of "primordial orality," von Arnim conjures up the image of artless songs woven into the fabric of quotidian existence, say, of miners and chimney sweeps.[13] Only later, von Arnim notes, did he understand "that their songs had already achieved what [artificial] songs strive for in vain, namely, that one tone should resonate in many people and unite them all" [*Später sah ich den Grund ein, daß in diesen schon erfüllt, wonach jene vergebens streben, auf daß ein Ton in vielen nachhalle und alle verbinde*]. In the lucid encryption of lyric form, itself "bound" up with the objective materiality of text and book, Romanticism mediates a complex and conflict-laden historical situation, and it typically does so by staging that situation as a hermeneutic crisis provoked by the unsuspected resurgence of ancient meanings within the damaged psyche of the modern subject. If Benjamin tells us that "historical knowledge should treat of awakening . . . and nothing else," the "greater Romantic lyric" anticipates and fulfills that exigency with uncanny precision.[14]

This very enjambment of heuristic and archival matter, of a traumatic awakening triggered by the deceptively innocent memories embodied in folk culture, prompts Romantic authors such as Brentano and von Arnim (or Wordsworth in England) to characterize their literary productions as "experiments." In appealing to a deep interiority that springs from the modern subject's abrupt encounter with archaic forces slumbering within its quotidian, obliquely poetic language, Romantic writing claims for itself a strong hermeneutic role. Not surprisingly, Freud was quick to acknowledge and capitalize on the apparent correlation between the inscrutable efficacy of Romanticism's articulate forms and his own theory of the unconscious's "delayed" (*nachträglich*) efficacy. Indeed, Freud's decision to credit Romanticism with having first mapped, at the level of literary practice, those psychological substrata that he himself sought to reclaim through and for his new theoretical discipline, is little less than shrewd. Still, subsequent generations of readers have pointed out with growing precision how Romanticism—rather than being a folksy or embryonic precursor for modern psychoanalysis—developed a highly reflexive and programmatic grasp of the modern subject as the unwitting vessel of its own past.[15] This already reflexive tendency in Romantic writing—evident in the work of Novalis, Freidrich Schlegel, Brentano, and von Arnim—suggests a deep-rooted epistemological mission intrinsic to Romantic cultural production. For these writers, the poetic word was imbued with the unsettling power of projecting the past into the present regardless of the modern subject's conscious intentions or avowed beliefs. As an insistent, albeit "intentionless" function silently shaping the modern subject's conscious existence, the past functions in ways structurally cognate with a specific dynamic of the Freudian unconscious. Alluding to his first encounter with the outline of folk poetry, von Arnim conjures up the revealing image of "a firm foundation shimmering through from beneath the waves, old streets and piazzas of a submerged city" [*als ich dieses feste Fundament noch unter den Wellen, die alten Straßen und Plätze der versunkenen Stadt noch durchschimmern sah*].[16] Von Arnim's figuration of the past as a virtual agency forcing the subject to receive previously unwitnessed memory fragments joins up with Freud's conception of "trauma" whose distinctive symptomatic feature of "repetition compulsion" is said to respond to a past so catastrophic at the time of its original occurrence as to have precluded its conscious assimilation by the subject.

At first glance, my conjunction of Romantic lyricism with concepts of traumatic awakening would seem to credit the cultural matter professᴇ￼ remembered with a degree of authenticity that a number of recent and highly accomplished critics have justly called into question. One recalls Susan Stewart's account of the late-eighteenth-century ballad, an example of what she names "distressed genres," and distinguished by its tendency to "rescue forms that seem to be disappearing—that is, to effect a kind of archeology of speech forms . . . [and] to place such specimen as curiosities, characterized by fragmentation and exoticism, against the contemporary."[17] More recently, Katie Trumpener has remarked on "a long history of pseudodocumentary fictions framed, in their prefaces, by pseudoeditorial authenticating devices." Thus she reads the literary archetype for this practice, James Macpherson's *Ossian* poems, as "a new way of conceiving the unevenness of character, and of textuality, as historical testimony, as an inadvertent record of historical upheavals and endurance, survivals and extinction. This model understands witnesses to history, whether human or textual, as inherently passive, mute on the subject of their sufferings." By contrast, "the broader Ossianic tradition—and the Ossian controversy itself—makes available a rather different model, in which the representatives of the old order loudly challenge the representatives of the new; their way of life may be doomed, but they will go down fighting."[18] And yet, as Trumpener's last statement affirms, the urgency and consequent capacity of such cultural memories for awakening modern subjects to their own, alienated condition, resides not in their de facto authenticity (if such could ever be authoritatively established) but, on the contrary, in the widespread endorsement of their authentic appearance. In accord with Freud's shrewd distinction between memories dating from and those relating to childhood, "authenticity" thus must be read as self-conscious fiction—a "fantasy" in Slavoj Žižek's definition—and hence an effect performatively wrought by specific literary, figural means. In other words, the archival ethos that proclaims them to be fragments of folk culture serendipitously recovered in and for the present is itself the effect wrought by an imaginative, literary writing whose fictitious nature that ethos subsequently neutralizes by the sheer gravitas of philological work on cultural "traditions" miraculously preserved or recovered (yet never actually produced). In this manner, the late-eighteenth-century archival cult of authenticity—seizing upon ballad, romance, and eventually the historical novel and what M. H. Abrams long ago christened the greater Romantic lyric as its generic lynchpins—brings about the larger collective fantasy of a timeless social order and, as remains to be seen, the genesis of Romantic conservatism. These genres add a crucial new dimension to such ideological dreamwork, that of an adventitious, albeit belated awakening. In these forms, aesthetic inventiveness is naturalized inasmuch as it conceives of itself, and professes itself to be, an awakening to a deeper historical truth slumbering within its thematic surfeit; thus literary topos is quietly transfigured into cultural value, and *inventio* becomes *traditio*. Consequently, the acutely "literary" quality of reconstituted fragments of (a putatively vanishing) folk culture does not threaten to expose such materials as "inauthentic." On the contrary, their "literary" presentation crucially instances and affirms their broader social value as fragments of a collective memory, something that nonliterary discourse with its different standards of authenticity and verification would be hard pressed to do.

In the high-Romantic lyric, past experience continues to determine a priori and trace a fortiori the conscious history of its subject with oblique but unrelenting tenacity. Subjected to an inscrutable, because never consciously experienced, causality, the conscious subject is obliged, in Freud's words, "to *repeat* the . . . material as a contemporary experience instead of . . . *remembering* it as something belonging to the past," and it typically does so with "unwished-for exactitude."[19] As Cathy Caruth has recently argued, Freud's theory of trauma allows us "to recognize the possibility of a history that is no longer straightforwardly referential (that is, no longer based on simple models of experience and reference)." The formal eloquence of literature, she points out, may itself be taken as a "parable of trauma" and, indeed, as "a parable of psychoanalytic theory itself as it listens to a voice that it cannot fully know but to which it nonetheless bears witness." Caruth's argument amounts to a new prescription for close, scrupulous reading of the literary text, and for an insistent listening to literature's characteristic tonal mix of vocal urgency and textual reticence, a dynamic of which the hybrid genre of the ballad is a particularly apt expression. I agree with Caruth that to approach the text as "an address that remains enigmatic yet demands a listening and a response" may indeed allow "*history* . . . [to] arise *where immediate understanding* may not."[20] Caruth's account unfolds Benjamin's insistent reminder that "the presentation of history [must] begin with awakening; in fact, it should treat of nothing else."[21]

Like Freud's controversial account of the traumatic origins of Judaism, the literary production of the Heidelberg Romantics (Creuzer, von Arnim,

Brentano, and, for a brief but significant period, Eichendorff) centers on the involuntary remembrance of a catastrophe that had suddenly erased an entire, seemingly timeless economic, cultural, and spiritual order. Time and again, these writings tell of their protagonists' "traumatic departure" from some phantasmagoric order of time and place. Exodus here is realized as a narrative of progressive disillusionment that continues to point back at an instance of catastrophic *méconnaissance* in the protagonist's past—and formal concision of lyric writing furnishes a self-consciously fantasized vantage point from which "history can be grasped only in the very inaccessibility of its occurrence."[22] To conceive the disruptive impact of a contingent memory within the structure of conscious experience in terms no less explicit than Freud's archeological metaphors is to locate poetry within a broad disciplinary and programmatic context. In the case of the Heidelberg Romantics—von Arnim, Brentano, Görres, Creuzer—the reflexive power of the poetic word establishes an implicit rapport between the contingent moment of its own production and the vast historical aura of its linguistic materials. Or, as Kevin Newmark has recently argued, poetry oscillates "between the punctual defensiveness of the consciousness that produces it and the retentive duration of the memory it serves to replace." Referring to Walter Benjamin's account of "Some Motifs in Baudelaire," Newmark proceeds to argue that at issue in the symbolist lyric is the

> fundamental question of the *historical* relationship between tradition and modernity. When the formal patterns of continuity that are presumed to have been grounded in traditional experience by the assimilation of consciousness to memory are disturbed by the truly alien experience of modernity, the coherence of subjective experience is itself displaced in unexpected ways. Consciousness and memory, whatever their relationship in some more or less mythic past, are no longer able to function as associative elements within the same system of individual and collective identity. According to this model, then, modernity would itself be structured like a historical "accident" that has at some prior moment befallen and disrupted the homogeneous structure of experience. And the traces of this accident manifest themselves whenever consciousness . . . can no longer be made compatible with memory.

Insofar as the Romantic lyric articulates the modernity of its subject as a recurrent tension between consciousness and memory, it is bound to stage the intrusion of the latter as an unexpected, haunting intervention. On New-mark's definition, the lyric would be one such "place where the wholly unex-pected and accidental can happen to the subject."[23] Still, the past obtrudes on consciousness not only as something that has not yet been consciously known. Rather, what Newmark refers to as "the homogeneous structure of experience"—with all its deceptive coherence and authority as socially valid knowledge—could only constitute itself because and insofar as it had not acknowledged its dialectical other: the past.

≡≡≡≡

More than any other German Romantic writer, Joseph von Eichendorff (1788–1857) centers his lyrics on this irruption of past memories into the patterns of quotidian, conscious existence—a strategy calculated to inten-sify not only our perception of psychological depth as "recollection" (*Erin-nerung*) but also our sense of a nontranscendable covenant between subject and history. To be sure, the past sings and "murmurs" (*rauschen*) every-where in Eichendorff's writings. Yet the poetry also suspends that uncon-scious dynamic between the subject's belated awakening to a strictly nega-tive knowledge—of one's having failed to develop a timely grasp of the past when it was still "event" [*Ereignis*]—and a mystification of that very awakening as a purely natural revelation. As we read in Eichendorff's "Liebe in der Fremde" [Love in a foreign world]: *Erinnernd rührt sich in den Bäu-men / Ein heimlich Flüstern überall* [The covert whisper of memory bestirs itself / Everywhere in the trees].[24] In what follows, I explore first how the Romantic subject's traumatic awakening to its own disorienting modernity is being contained in lyric form and, in a subsequent move, how Eichen-dorff's distinctive affiliation of lyricism and memory relates to the emer-gence of Romantic conservatism (*Altkonservatismus*). Indeed, late in his career, Eichendorff came to be associated with this (often misunderstood) movement. Similarly, and at a rather early point (1806), von Arnim already remarks how the "whirlwind of innovation, the lightening-quick presump-tion of being able to fashion paradise on earth" [*in diesem Wirbelwind des Neuen, in diesem vermeinten urschnellen Paradiesgebären auf Erden*], of the French Revolution had virtually extinguished all folksong.[25] At least from the moment of Prussia's utter defeat, the culture of Romantic lyricism begins to edge progressively closer to the discourse of conservatism. Both languages are preoccupied with a traumatic disjunction of past and present, memory and experience.

If the *ideologeme* of early conservatism marks the outer limits of my inquiry into the operation of traumatic affect in Romantic writing—that is, beyond its historical motif (*Erinnerung*) and its psychological effect (*Innerlichkeit*)—the evidence for these larger claims must ultimately always be found in the literary text. A reading of an early Eichendorff poem may help us develop a sharper outlook on what Karl Mannheim calls the *tensio* of thought toward "contents surviving from the past."[26] The first lyric is entitled "Vesper" [Evening meal]. Though it was included in Eichendorff's play *Ezzelin von Romano* (1828), it was first published in his 1837 collection (*Gedichte*).

Die Abendglocken klangen	The evening bells sounded
Schon durch das stille Tal,	Already through the quiet vale,
Da saßen wir zusammen	While above we sat in communion
Da droben wohl hundertmal.	Well-nigh a hundred times.
Und unten war's so stille	Down below a calm pervaded
Im Lande weit und breit,	the whole land far and wide,
Nur über uns die Linde	And only the lime tree above us
Rauscht' durch die Einsamkeit.	Rustled through this solitude.
Was gehen die Glocken heute	Why will the bells ring today
Als ob ich weinen müßt?	As if I should have to cry?
Die Glocken, die bedeuten,	The bells that tell
Daß meine Lieb gestorben ist!	Of my love which has died!
Ich wollt, ich läg begraben,	I wish I lay already entombed,
Und über mir rauschte weit	And each evening far above
Die Linde jeden Abend	The lime tree rustling would
Von der alten, schönen Zeit![27]	Speak of the dear old time!

The four stanzas break down into two halves, each marked by the concluding, archetypal image of the rustling lime tree. The overall coherence of the lyric is insured by its temporal dimension, initially brought into focus through the notion of a recursive, potentially empty event: "While above we sat in communion / Well-nigh a hundred times." In contrast with such routine sociability, the concluding image of the tree's "rustling" points to a rupture between the rhythm of the quotidian present and "the dear old time." This phrase or, rather, cliché constitutes Eichendorff's veritable poetic signature. Here, as elsewhere, it establishes the ideal of an end to all time—a hypothetical future kept at bay by a poetic voice wishing for its own annihilation and interment (*Ich wollt, ich läg begraben*) in the immaculate temporal order of the past. Indeed, the peal of the church bell that resonates through the ominously "quiet vale" positions the voice at the threshold between empirical perception and metaphysical intuition. Gauging the spatial depth of the valley, the faint, distant peal of church bells prefigures the concluding, funereal vision. More important, though, it exhorts the voice to specify the nature of its "loss." The local and particular dimension of affect, bereavement at the loss of a beloved (*Die Glocken, die bedeuten, / Daß meine Lieb gestorben ist*), enters only in hypothetical form. Significantly, though, the loss of *die Lieb* may refer both to a beloved and to the capacity to love. Thus the scene of evening oscillates bewilderingly between an intensification of affect (loss of the beloved) and its complete erosion (the incapacity to feel love). Twice in this short lyric, we thus have affective states bracketed by subjunctive constructions: *Als ob ich weinen müßt* and *Ich wollt, ich läg begraben*. This hypothetical notation of affect as the last bastion of authentic subjectivity—if not as the subject's de facto awakening to the knowledge of its atrophied interiority—proves truly defining of early-nineteenth-century lyric writing.

Meanwhile, the distant sonority of the bells also serves as the emblem of a specifically lyric form of attentiveness. Just as the spatial depth of the "land far and wide" [*Lande weit und breit*] is gauged only through the migration of sound, the peal of the bells also gives rise to a fundamental subjective self-awareness. We recall how, in the *Logical Investigations*, the colloquialism of attentiveness (*Aufmerksamkeit*) is suddenly introduced as the pivotal condition allowing so-called intentional acts to be promoted to objective status and hence to become accessible to an "inner perception." In short, without the (irreducible) operation of *Aufmerksamkeit*, consciousness itself would remain but a contingent signified by its own (supposedly "intentional") relation to particular "material" contents. Yet it could never arrive at a coherent representation of their quality and, consequently, could never become conscious of itself as a cognitive agency.[28] This same sense of "attentiveness"—a belated calling-away of the subject from its mundane "contents" and so awakening it to its inscrutable historical situatedness—is enacted in Eichendorff's lyrics. Time and again, the subject is subtly extricated from its precarious absorption in the mythical coherence of appearances, beliefs, and objectives. Rather than merely symbolizing a vague "mood" or outright mystical state of affect, Eichendorff's spatial and aural figurations always point toward a rupture in the fabric of human time. Far from indulging in the myth of a purely affective, timeless interiority, a poem like "Vesper" effectively encodes—in the image of the bell tolling—the imminent passing of that self-enclosed dream world. If a desire for total immersion in this imagistic world takes us into the poem, the lyric's excessive accommodation of that desire—a kind of hypersimulation to be explored in further detail— effectively compels us to awaken to its status as a text-based fantasy.[29] If Eichendorff's characteristic choice of the subjunctive has already qualified affect as dangerously mesmerizing and wholly self-privileging, the subtle yet insistent call for the subject to awaken centers on a symbol of death.

To be sure, we may be tempted to frame the entire lyric within an opposition between the empty, repetitive time of social existence (*Da saßen wir zusammen / Da droben wohl hundertmal*) and an absolution from all temporality marked by the bells' distant sonority. Yet to proceed in this manner is to ignore that a phrase as overtly clichéd as "the dear old time" has been carefully framed in a subjunctive syntax, thereby alerting us to interpretive pitfalls that lurk beneath clichés encountered in lyric writing. To escape from empirical, social time is to express a desire for transcendence that can only take the textual form of a paradox: to escape to a state of being that could only be realized as nonbeing. Thus the epistemological collision of two worlds characteristic of all traumatic awakening finds objective, lyric expression in an interference between image and grammar, between the banal certitude of the poetic cliché and the prevarication of the subjunctive. Indeed, even the lyric image resonates with such tension by alternately ensnaring its readers in inauthentic clichés or consigning them to the epistemological vagaries of an anxious and disorienting modernity where experience and memory are no longer aligned. And the suspicion that Eichendorff's poetry might be little more than an array of clichés skillfully deployed dates back a long way,[30] something echoed by Adorno's remark that "when one first hears many of Eichendorff's lines . . . they sound like quotations, quotations learned by heart from God's primer." Richard Alewyn expands on this point by offering a short catalogue of what Adorno had called the "stage-prop quality of the linguistic elements" in Eichendorff's poetry.[31] For Alewyn, these lyrics

> operate altogether in the external world of visible and audible things, which is one of the reasons why they appear so 'slight.' At the same

time, Eichendorff is certainly no 'realist.' His poetry contributes little to our knowledge of some straightforward reality. It has often been remarked with how narrow a segment of life and world he seems to content himself. With even greater annoyance—though scarcely attuned to the true scope of the matter—readers have responded to the fact that the same motifs recur in endless repetition. Forever we have forests rustling [*rauschen*], nightingales singing, fountains murmuring, rivers shimmering. Time and again, light reflexes and harmonies from summits, from down below, or from among the treetops waft over to us or enter through the window. All this is pushed to the point of formulaic rigor.[32]

Alewyn's characterization is at once accurate and, as he himself concedes, in need of further reflection. For the presence of images as overtly schematic as Eichendorff's confounds the plausible attitude of an "empathetic reception" (reading as "empathetic practice," which Wilhelm Dilthey was later to elaborate as the aesthetics of *Einfühlung*) by alerting the audience to the lyric's citation-like quality. To do so is to press, within the form of the lyric itself, the question of literariness—of what shall count as "literary value" and the purposes to which it appears so obliquely committed. As it turns out, this very question, "Does a specific poem belong to the order of invention or citation?" correlates with the subject's epistemological condition: Can it grasp (*begreifen*) experience by means of autonomous categories of rationality, or is it at the mercy of an "almost forgotten" past, at once unfathomable and inescapable? Clichés disconcert because of their conspicuous enjambment of form and cognition. They no longer communicate referentially but, instead, appear bent on dismantling the audience's faith in stable referential connections between affect and form, interiority and expression, pathos and its communicability. The cliché stages the subject's troubled awakening to those depths of its language that are not "expressive." Beneath its placid, seemingly unruffled rapport with inherited rhetorical models, the cliché unmasks (allegorizes) an earlier period's excessive faith in linguistic mastery over the contingent world of perception and intuitions. It is Romantic allegory *sensu strictu*—that is, a language reflecting its historically overdetermined and materially exhausted artifactual constitution. Hence, its baroque mournfulness, so powerfully at work throughout Eichendorff's lyric oeuvre, resides in its imperceptible ability to estrange us from any residual faith in a (supposedly inalienable) affective rapport (*Einfühlung*) between self and world. By disarticulating the myth of a language wholly self-sufficient and untrammeled by any contingencies of perception, the poetic cliché effectively subverts the mimetic principle on which its over-confident surface representations continue to be predicated.

We will have further occasion to consider whether this unsettling proximity of poetry to outright citation or cliché may indeed constitute the underlying aesthetic and ideological signature of European writing during the era of the Regency in Britain and the *Restauration* in Germany. For the time being, it remains imperative to listen to the peculiar idiom of Eichendorff's lyrics and so close in on their construction of a specific affective economy. At first, the voice that constitutes itself so unmistakably in these poems seems to relate to a curiously nonspecific past with an attitude of deep nostalgic longing. Yet as one slows down the reading of this poetry, a peculiar reversal of cause and effect, image and referent, affect and expression can be found to occur. Rather than presenting itself as the timeless and unimpeachable source of writing, affect here seems to emerge as an epiphenomenon of eerily familiar stylistic patterns. Indeed, Eichendorff's lyrics seem bent on rehearsing for us what Paul de Man had long ago described as moments of interference between the referential or expressive function of language and its performative ability to conjure being in the form of textual simulacra.[33] Almost imperceptibly, the lyric's official faith in a symbolic coincidence of word and referent begins to shift and decompose because techniques mobilized for the representation of affect work, in effect, too well. That is, the poetic cliché hastens the demise of the mimetic principle, for it lays bare how that principle works to begin with. Here we see *in actu* what Adorno meant when he said that the artwork is "not only of the same essence as the dialectic external to [it] but . . . resembles it without imitating it."[34] Thus the excessive "fit" of word and referent in Eichendorff's lyrics disrupts the reader's initial assumption that to read is to enter a domain of quasi-sensory perception. Asked to witness the operation of *Vorstellung*, we effectively become aware of mimesis as an effect of hypersimulation. If "mimesis [is] the presentation of an ideal reality" [*Darstellung eines ideell Wirklichen*], David Wellbery argues, then the "simulacrum [asserts] the reality of the presentation" itself [*Wirklichkeit der Darstellung*]. Thus Eichendorff's lyrics ought to be approached not as "mood-based [*Stimmungslyrik*] in any conventional sense but as thematizations of the lyric medium." Wellbery convincingly locates Eichendorff's poems "perched on the threshold between two worlds," that of an unconscious, dreamlike immersion in the principle of mimesis and that of an awakening to the medial character of the lyric image as simulacrum—its reflexive detachment from all faith in mimetic and expressive technique.[35]

Yet rather than extending this observation into a more sweeping conception of literary language and its supposedly intrinsic aporias, as Paul de Man proposed it some twenty years ago, my aim here is somewhat broader in scope. To begin with, moments of rhetorical instability ought to be grasped—albeit with a caution that befits all speculative proceedings—as symptomatic condensations of a larger historical tension. Indeed, it is only on the basis of a deeper affinity between formal-aesthetic and historical processes that we can begin to grasp Romanticism as a specific phase in the historical evolution of affect—not as an autonomous fact—but as the object of aesthetic creativity and, thereupon, interpretive-disciplinary attention. Above all, we find the period conceding interiority to its post-Enlightenment subjects only in supplemental form. Rather than collapsing inwardness into a purely imaginary order—a quasi-maternal and allegedly unimpeachable source of pure affect—post-Waterloo Romanticism stages the inwardness of its subjects as a progressive awakening to the insoluble dilemma of their traumatic history. A strictly literary-historical narrative could identify Eichendorff's lyrics as the second stage in an epistemological crisis, first apparent in the way that Goethe's lyrics struggle to name and thus affirm an absolute source and origin for all expressive and creative acts. Indeed, for quite some time readers have been remarking on the Romantic lyric's formal-rhetorical antagonisms, such as its subject's deeply personal investment in affective experiences (melancholy, indolence, longing, dejection, etc.) that seem oddly generic and are rendered in curiously mannered images, or the paradox of escapist desires not concealed but curiously accented in lyric speech. Such tensions, it may be said, prove not so much symptomatic of the Romantic lyric as they are constitutive of it. That is, far from being mere rhetorical accidents randomly vitiating the expressive agenda of a given poem, these tensions are rehearsed by the text and for an audience whose longing for a state of pure inwardness the text is calculated to qualify rather than indulge.

For as Eichendorff repeatedly stresses, the social and cultural crisis of the central European aristocracy and gentry around 1815—its atrophied historical mission and legitimacy—stemmed from their failure to heed the urgent call of the past. Given the historical failure of the gentry and, especially, the aristocracy, the sudden defeat of regionally differentiated cultural, political, and economic practices, first by Napoleon and then (at least partially) by Karl Freiherr vom Stein's and Karl August von Hardenberg's ambitious reforms, seemed just retribution. And yet, characterized above all by a pervasive loss of history, modernity seems the very antithesis of an *altkonservativ* order, even as the latter breaks with the often crudely Machiavellian politics of post-Napoleonic *Reaktion*, such as the Viennese aristocracy or the East Prussian landed nobility (*Junker*). Any "ideal loyalty" has been displaced by "monetary forces" (*Die Stelle der idealen Treue wurde sofort von der materiellen Geldkraft eingenommen*).[36] Eichendorff thus feels caught between a phantasmagorical past whose resources and once-legitimate order had been squandered long before by the upper echelons of society, and a modernity similarly largely shaped by the basest craving for economic and political ascendancy among anonymous, competitive individuals. The resulting sense of historical abjection is acutely felt in "On a Stronghold" [*Auf einer Burg*], a poem memorably set to music by Robert Schumann in 1840.

Eingeschlafen auf der Lauer	Gone to sleep while keeping watch
Oben ist der alte Ritter;	Sits up there the ancient knight;
Drüber gehen Regenschauer,	Over yonder rain is falling,
Und der Wald rauscht durch das	And woods rustle through the
Gitter.	trellis.
Eingewachsen Bart und Haare,	Inward grown his beard and hair,
Und versteinert Brust und Krause,	Turned to stone his breast and ruffle,
Sitzt er viele hundert Jahre	He sits for many hundred years
Oben in der stillen Klause.	Aloft in the noiseless cell.
Draußen ist es still und friedlich,	Outside it is still and peaceful,
Alle sind ins Tal gezogen,	All have moved into the vale,
Waldesvögel einsam singen	Little woodbirds sing all forlorn
In den leeren Fensterbogen.	In the empty window arches.
Eine Hochzeit fährt da unten	Far below a wedding glides along
Auf dem Rhein im Sonnenscheine,	Bathed by sunlight on the Rhine;
Musikanten spielen munter,	Musicians play oh so gaily,
Und die schöne Braut die weinet.[37]	And the lovely bride is weeping.

With its ironic opening (*Eingeschlafen auf der Lauer*), the lyric swiftly establishes its overarching focus on the inexorable and inscrutable nature of historical change. The calcified feudal body of the knight who fell asleep on his
watch furnishes us with a schoolbook example of Romantic allegory. Rendered wholly impersonal, even generic by the passage of time and by the
advent of change for which his faltering vigilance was no match, the once
individual knight has been utterly transformed by the fluctuations of historical time. To the speaker's archeological gaze, *der alte Ritter* is no longer
the representative of a coherent social formation. Indeed, it is only now that
he is conceived in fully calcified and involuntarily statuesque form that the
knight successfully embodies a feudal order whose historical mission, it
seems, can be articulated only from the vanishing point of the postrevolutionary lyric. "Inward grown" and "turned to stone" [*Eingewachsen . . . und
versteinert*], the feudal body illustrates what de Man has called the "rediscovery of an allegorical tradition beyond the sensualistic analogism of the
eighteenth century." For the lyric allows us to grasp the knight's representative character only as something accidental and, perhaps, serendipitous.
As de Man continues, "the prevalence of allegory always corresponds to the
unveiling of an authentically temporal destiny. This unveiling takes place
in a subject that has sought refuge against the impact of time in a natural world to which, in truth, it bears no resemblance." The ability of the
feudal body to represent its authentic "destiny" thus requires its estrangement, its vivid (almost tactile) transfiguration from a flesh-and-blood individual into an accidental monument. As de Man further notes, "the meaning" of allegory can "consist only in the *repetition* . . . of a previous sign
with which it can never coincide."[38] Hence the knight's two bodies—the
"real" and evidently deluded individual and his accidental preservation in
etiolated, statuesque form—reflect the ultimate ineluctability of historical
time, a fact that can be illustrated only by means of a visible discontinuity
between two embodied states. In the third stanza, this fundamental evacua-
tion of determinate (human) meaning from the passage of historical time
is captured in the empty windows occupied only by the natural, asemantic
chatter of birds.

Yet how does the voice of Eichendorff's lyric modernity position itself
vis-à-vis this disconcerting conception of historical change as inherently
unknowable and hence uncontestable by any individual or community,
however intently vigilant (*Lauer*) these may have been? What does it mean

to grasp history only a posteriori, as a failure to "see in time" and, more specifically here, as the traumatic demise of a social order that cannot be reconstituted but only mourned wherever we happen upon its stony debris? Pivoting around the conspicuous muteness of their principal catalyst—with the *versteinert* knight holding the same function as the admonitory "heap of unhewn stone" in Wordsworth's "Michael" or Keats's Saturn, "quiet as a stone," Eichendorff's lyrics at once precipitate the Romantic subject's traumatic recognition of its irremediable historical estrangement even as they formally attenuate that "shock" in a faintly aestheticized scene of "mourning."[39] Thus the location where the feudal order met its unanticipated demise has been evacuated—*Alle sind ins Tal gezogen*—and now figures as the objective site of the modern subject's belated and insistently mournful recollections (*Erinnerung*).

The last stanza features that quintessential Romantic image, a wedding ceremony observed from afar, and it projects continuity for a now modern society that is buoyantly committed to its quotidian rituals and pursuits, though also arrested by inexplicable flashes of grief that occur without warning. Thus the image of a bride basking in the distant sunlight "far below" is momentarily disrupted by the unsettling acuity of the speaker's vision as he captures her apparent state of mourning: *Und die schöne Braut die weinet*. Far from a recuperation of modernity, the wedding yields tears that portend (at the level of affect) a knowledge already available in statuesque form in the castle above: the logic of historical time as an inexorable and nonteleological progression of betrayal, sudden change, and *méconnaissance*.[40] This indictment of his own times as trivializing and vulgarizing poetry by forcibly conjoining it with politics would appear the very hallmark of a staunch Catholic conservative. Indeed, a casual reading of the section entitled "Geistliche Gedichte" in Eichendorff's 1837 collection of his lyrics would seem to exemplify "the familiar romantic finale," as Nietzsche had put it, the "break, breakdown, return and collapse before an old faith, before *the* old god."[41]

The remainder of this essay, however, is less concerned with proving or disproving this popular (if also facile) position than with probing its epistemological assumptions and aesthetic consequences. What is the nature of Romantic conservatism, a term first coined by Chateaubriand's journal

Le Conservateur in 1818 and soon popular throughout central Europe? Is it merely an antimodern reaction formation, a transparently regressive form of behavior—or of writing? Already this ambivalent suspension of conservatism between a purely affective, unselfconscious disposition and a distinctive rhetorical practice, however, hints at the existence of a critical problem. For the apparent eagerness of contemporary criticism in the humanities to uncover and brand certain thought-formations or strategies of writing as "conservative"—and in so doing presume that it has also discredited them— leaves the actual nature of conservatism unexamined and thus undecided. Is the recursive temporal structure of *Erinnerung* as it resonates in many of Eichendorff's titles ("Erinnerung," "Rückblick," "Letzte Heimkehr," "Vergebner Ärger," "Verlorne Liebe," "Trennung," "Abschied," etc.) merely an expression of a nostalgic longing, a desire for something as implausible as an outright reversal of historical time? Against this hypothesis speak Eichendorff's self-conscious and explicitly hypothetical acts of lyric introspection. Particularly the highly reflexive formalization of interiority as a holograph of spontaneous memory (*Erinnerung*), historically conditioned anxiety, and utopian, para-religious longing strongly militates against interpreting conservatism as a case of naïve and unqualified nostalgia. Nor, it would seem, is the phenomenon of Romantic conservatism fully captured by Hegel's speculative thesis of the bureaucratic nation-state as a world-historical force that has preserved and contained the past in institutional form. For the Protestant "can-do" spirit of Hegel's historical inventory-taking appears ultimately geared toward enhancing the authority of the Prussian nation-state, and as such seems notably impatient with the mythical or Catholic figurations of Joseph Görres or the later work of Friedrich Schlegel. What, then, are we to understand as the ideological place of Romantic conservatism, and how are its affective, rhetorical, and cognitive spheres to be demarcated from one another?

In what may seem counterintuitive and startling, I propose to understand Romantic conservatism in close proximity to postmodernism. Doing so means, first of all, to discriminate sharply between the ideational character of Romantic conservatism and its practical, quotidian counterpart— the politics of reaction. Standing in sharp and self-conscious antithesis to the politics of the *Reaktion*, Romantic conservatism seeks less to indulge the antimodern prejudices that are undoubtedly part of it than to articulate an organic vision that combines diverse elements of a precapitalist and even a preschismatic social formation. Hence, Romantic *Altkonserva-tismus* must be distinguished from the period's established politics of restoration and reaction. For conservatism encompasses prima facie an aesthetic, and often stridently anticapitalist, program.[42] At the same time, it appears less to be directed toward some future utopia than to stress the persistence of History in a holistic sense. While the past is ultimately irretrievable in any objective sense, it proves nonetheless inescapable. That is, Romantic conservatism does not actually seek to implement its peculiar cultural vision of an implicitly Catholic and genially stratified, precapitalist society. It does not purport to reverse the flow of historical time. Rather, the past is conjured up—in the medial form of a Platonic allegory—as a system of values conceivable only from the shadowy (because irreducibly rhetorical) perspective of the modern, abject individual. Rather than capturing incidental empirical matter, *Erinnerung* amounts to a self-conscious "fantasy." Fully aware of its terminal confinement in the cave of modernity, conservative thought embraces history and tradition as something mesmerizing—not despite but because of the fact that they have been irretrievably lost and that, indeed, they had never been consciously experienced to begin with.[43] As Slavoj Žižek notes, "The psychoanalytic notion of fantasy cannot be reduced to that of a fantasy scenario which obfuscates the true horror of a situation." If fantasy "conceals" the "horror of the Real," it also, and "at the same time . . . creates what it purports to conceal, its 'repressed' point of reference."[44] Furthermore, if we are to accept Žižek's definition of "fantasy [as] the primordial form of *narrative*, which serves to occult some original deadlock," Romantic conservatism can certainly be interpreted as a narrative of just this kind. For it is above all a bourgeois, not a feudal phenomenon.[45] As the successor of a feudal age that alternately missed or squandered its historical opportunities, the proto-bourgeois subjects of the modern, bureaucratic, and capitalist nation-state continue to be haunted by the revolutionary trauma to which, in effect, they owe their very existence. Forever distraught over the loss of a simpler and happier past, the "sadder and wiser" ideology of Romantic conservatism could only consolidate itself in dialectical relation to the very modernity whose cultural and social ramifications it continues to deplore. Speaking of conservatism as a "historical-dynamic structural complex," Karl Mannheim has elaborated the curious emergence of this ideology. Rather than falling back on realist or "nominalist" models, according to which conservatism was either received as an already finished (quasi-"metaphysical") construct or was generated by supposedly autonomous individuals, Mannheim interprets conservatism as a fundamentally dynamic type of "retroaction." In this view, conservatism is intimately "bound up with the actual existence and destinies of human groups and appearing as their product." Having achieved its conceptual integrity only "in relation to [a] particular course of experience," the "stylistic design" of conservative thought is necessarily something "historically embedded." Like Freud's concept of "retroaction" (*Nachträglichkeit*), Romantic "conservatism" thus involves a partial compensation for, and a partial reenactment of a pervasive traumatic disruption for which the French Revolution, Napoleon's radical reorganization of the central European landscape, and the economic and ideological depression of the post-Waterloo era constitute successive phases. As evidenced by the persistence of figural and textual metaphors in its formulation, earlynineteenth-century *Altkonservatismus* can be understood as responding to its historically specific experience of modernity by developing a nearly selfconscious ideological fantasy. Insofar as its intellectual program unfolds in synchrony with such historical disruptions, conservative thought "may well be nothing more than [its] conceptual effect." The distinctive characteristic of conservatism, meanwhile, lies in the fact that here "past and trauma are treated as if they were one and the same (factical)."[46] Seen as the development of a "traditionalism [that has] become self-reflective," Romantic conservatism bespeaks its proponents' awareness of their "authentically temporal destiny" (de Man's phrase).[47] Like a more mature embodiment of Friedrich Schlegel's concept of irony, the conservative knows that his is an irremediable allegorical condition, one in which the certainty of temporal change can no longer be absorbed by the ingenuity of any politics, liberal, nationalist, or reactionary.[48] Indeed, with its logic of "retroaction" (*Nachträglichkeit*) Romantic conservatism appears strikingly prescient of at least one criterion repeatedly invoked to define postmodernism: that of a fundamentally "posthistorical" era. Moreover, though arguably at a more intuitive level, Romantic conservatism also seems to know of a profound (if ultimately ineluctable) relation between the languages of theory and fantasy, politics and aesthetics. Hence, as Fredric Jameson points out, it looks "for breaks, for events rather than new holds, for the telltale instant after which it is no longer the same, . . . for shifts and irrevocable changes in the *representation* of things and why they change." It only "clocks the variations themselves, and knows only too well that the contents are just more images." As Jameson elaborates later on:

> Cultural production is . . . driven back inside a mental space which is no longer that of the old monadic subject but rather that of some degraded collective "objective spirit": it can no longer gaze directly on some putative real world, at some reconstruction of a past history which was once itself a present; rather, as in Plato's cave, it must trace our mental images of that past upon its confining walls. . . . It is a realism that is meant to derive from the shock of grasping that confinement and slowly becoming aware of a new and original historical situation in which we are condemned to seek History by way of our own pop images and simulacra of that history, which itself remains forever out of reach.[49]

As we have already seen, Eichendorff's oeuvre is shot through with "pop images" or clichés simulating an irrecuperable history and articulating conservatism as a strictly virtual, aesthetic fantasy. To be sure, it is tempting to read Eichendorff's political prose—specifically his late treatise on the *Folgen von der Aufhebung der Landeshoheit Bischöfe und der Klöster in Deutschland*— as straightforward conservative propaganda. What else could be meant by his patriotic *laudatio* to the "German tendency, one of more profoundly inward character, that venerates its own while respecting everything sacred and showing consideration for all tradition" [*die deutsche Richtung, tiefsinniger nach innen gekehrt, und sich selber ehrend achtet . . . alles Heilige, berücksichtigt alles Herkömmliche*]?[50] And what would better exemplify the "mythical transcendence" that Karl Mannheim identifies as a salient characteristic of Romantic conservatism than the following passage in which Eichendorff juxtaposes post-Waterloo European politics with its "well-adjusted palaces that impress on us a certain ennobling feeling of order and security" to the inchoate political landscape of Restoration Germany.[51] The latter resembles

> *eine fröhliche Aussicht vom Berge ins Freie, schroffe Felsen, Ströme, Wälder und Saaten in buntem Gemisch bis in die unermessene blaue Ferne hinaus, wo Himmel und Erde einander rätselfhaft berühren, jede einzelne Erscheinung . . . als ein Ganzes für sich bestehend, jeder Bach und Strom seine eigene Bahn zum ewigen Meere suchend, alle zusammen doch in einem Farbenton jene blühende Tiefe bildend, welche, wenn sie auch das blöde Auge*

mit ihrem Reichtum verwirrt, das Herz mit einem unvergänglichen Natur-gefühl wunderbar erhebt und erlabt.

a lovely view from the mountain[s] into the boundless space, precipi-tous cliffs, rivers, a colorful mish-mash of forests and states, out into the immeasurable cerulean distance, where heaven and earth myste-riously touch, every single appearance . . . as a whole for itself, every stream and river searching for its own path to the eternal ocean, and yet all together building in a colorful tone the blossoming profundity, which, though it may confound the naked eye with its opulence, won-derfully exalts and refreshes the heart with an imperishable feeling of nature.[52]

Because of its overtly clichéd presentation (*Darstellung*), Eichendorff's pas-sage does not so much indulge in aesthetic mythmaking as it rehearses for us that very process. For what better way to exemplify the mythical structure of conservatism and draw attention to the metaphysical desire underlying the entire passage than with a citation of German Romanticism's arché-text or (if a pun be permitted) architect: Novalis. Surely, the reference to "the immeasurable cerulean distance, where heaven and earth miraculously touch" [*die unermessene blaue Ferne hinaus, wo Himmel und Erde einander rätselhaft berühren*] constitutes a pointed reference to *Heinrich von Ofter-dingen*, the text that, for a generation, defined Romantic longing. Particu-larly with reference to Novalis's romance, where the phrase *blaue Ferne* recurs no less than four times, such citation is a distinctly self-conscious form of repetition, and Eichendorff's specular notation not only reenacts the impossible nostalgia of early Romanticism: it also recalls the widely quoted image in one of his best-known poems, "Mondnacht": "It was as though heaven had / Quietly kissed the earth" [*Es war, als hätt der Him-mel / Die Erde still geküßt.*] Suspended between its own, inscrutable affec-tive origins and an expressive language that proves overtly allusive of an earlier text, Eichendorff's "old-germanic" (*altgermanisch*) political commu-nity constitutes an exemplary instance of Freudian "retroaction" (*Nach-träglichkeit*). It renders an ideological fantasy in an overtly allegorical (that is, self-consciously textual) form. Not surprisingly, Eichendorff's essay pro-ceeds to demur the hegemony of the "understanding" (*Verstand*) in Protes-tant culture, advocating instead the liberation of "fantasy" (*Phantasie*) from the constraints of "stale sentimentalism or outright political madness."[53] In the modality of lyric form—the smaller-scale image of an agonistic modernity inhabited by the writer and his projected audience—fantasy simulates original creation as involuntary recollection. As Adorno puts it, "Through fantasy, as recollection, genius continuously restores original creation—not as the creator of its reality but by the reintegration of its given elements in an image. . . . Through recollection, fantasy transforms the traces of the collapse of a sinful creation into a sign of hope for one that is whole and without sin and whose image it forms out of ruins." In his early attempt at formulating an aesthetic theory, Adorno stresses the miniature-character of the aesthetic vis-à-vis creation itself ("Fantasy imitates creation through miniaturization"), a speculative thesis borne out by Romantic lyric writing in particular. Moreover, the discrepancy in scale between the magnitude of a ruined creation and its "reintegration" in a dialectical, rather than Platonic, "domain of the image" (*Bilderreich*) stands in strict correlation with temporal discontinuity. Adorno quotes Kierkegaard: "Art consists in producing an enjoyment which never actually becomes present, but always has an element of the past in it, so that it is present in the past. This has already been expressed in the word: posthumous [*nachgelassen*]."[54]

Given its twofold sense as *nachgelassen*—that is, as self-consciously "posthumous" at the level of both form (creation as simulation) and historical time—Eichendorff's conservatism proves *nachträglich* in a more complex sense even than Freud's own usage of that term.[55] For a conservative aesthetic—taking the term in its strong, reflexive sense—represents its disaffected subjects not merely as "belated," since doing so would assume a basic continuity between history and the present, between the plenitude of times past and the conscious impoverishment of the here-and-now. A reflection of this kind would still be, in essence, a type of (epistemological and political) *Reaktion* and thus would bear all the customary traits of a delusional formation. True to the rich semantics of *Nachträglichkeit*, however, Eichendorff's stress on conservatism's "retroactive" or allegorical status (also a motive for his late project of translating Calderón) takes history to be by definition a missed experience.[56] As such, it can be recovered only through the (truly necessary) fantasy of a specular, mythical "depth" (*jene blühende Tiefe*). Like Proust's *mémoire involontaire*, the insights of conservative thought appear legitimate and authoritative only if their serendipitous occurrence is construed as a sign of (metaphysical) providence. Yet, as our last reading will show, Eichendorff's writings typically do not take that leap.

The final text by Eichendorff to be considered here, and unquestionably one of his most distinctive and memorable lyrics, is entitled "Mondnacht." In its "humble irrationality" this poem exemplifies the challenge of Eichendorff and, more generally, of the deeply engrained mystical strain in Romantic writing for a contemporary audience.

Es war, als hätt der Himmel	It was as though heaven had
Die Erde still geküßt,	Quietly kissed the earth,
Daß sie im Blütenschimmer	That amidst shimmering blossoms
Von ihm nun träumen müßt.	She must now dream of him.
Die Luft ging durch die Felder,	The air passed over the fields,
Die Ähren wogten sacht,	Grain stalks gently yielded,
Es rauschten leis die Wälder,	The forests rustled softly,
So sternklar war die Nacht.	So translucent was the starlit night.
Und meine Seele spannte	And my soul widely
Weit ihre Flügel aus,	Extended its wings,
Flog durch die stillen Lande,	Passed over the silent lands,
Als flöge sie nach Haus.[57]	As though it was bound for home.

One must, above all, overcome one's "lazy unwillingness to muster up the energetic receptivity the poem requires."[58] How, then, are we to read a lyric that whose imagery is carefully poised at the threshold between naïvely empirical mimesis and a self-conscious textuality reminiscent of baroque *topoi*. At a strictly formal level, such oscillation between mystical longing and allegorical distance can be located in the poem's conditional syntax—sustained from the very opening (*"Es war, als hätt . . ."*) through the last line (*"Als flöge sie . . ."*). Taken as a whole, the vision of "Mondnacht" appears decidedly qualified, a fantasy attenuated by *allegoresis* rather than a desire condensed into symbolism. Thus the opening image of the *Brautkuss* whereby heaven and earth are reconciled—far from overcoming the split between fecund perceptions and transcendent truths—only widens it.[59] For the image of reconciliation proves itself a purely literary device, a baroque topos (archetype, commonplace, or perhaps cliché?). Likewise, the subsequent construction of an analogy between cornfields and treetops animated by a breeze and the soul spreading its figural wings for flight never allows us to forget that we are witnessing a rhetorical operation. Weary of any mimetic commerce with such overworked terms as history or nature, and governed by "the ruling Baroque metaphor of life as a dream," the poem "strip[s] the allegorical world book down to a few root words, its radical lexemes."[60] And yet, Eichendorff in this poem anticipates Walter Benjamin's remarks about the "contemplative calm" of earlier, baroque allegory. Indeed, it is tempting to read "Mondnacht" strictly as an expression of baroque Stoicism—in the vein of the *Nulla in mundo pax sincera* so memorably set to music by Vivaldi (RV 630). Still, such a reading must take care not to reduce Stoic and allegorical language to a mere commonplace or cliché. On the contrary, the allegorical topos of the *Brautkuss* explores what Benjamin refers to as "the chasm between pictorial being and significance [*bildlichem Sein und Bedeuten*] where we find nothing of the flouting indifference that characterizes the deceptively similar intention of the sign."[61] Hence, the poem's capacity to hint at the elusive metaphysical kinship between perception and knowledge pivots on qualifying its own voice as intrinsically unreal and chimerical. Yet such qualities do not betoken indifference, even less an evasion of the sublime discontinuities of history. Far from it, a surreal imagery reveals the poem's reflexive self-awareness as irremediably textual (allegorical). Recognizing both the impossibility of transcending or "knowing" history, the lyric holds in an equilibrium the two dominant conceptual strains of German Romanticism: mysticism and historicism. It does so by placing the lyric voices—taken as both a spiritual and an intellectual agency—in an overtly phantasmagoric relation to the temporal forces of history. The latter can be encountered only by chance, not by design. Because the "knowledge" of history can come only in the form of an involuntary (and belated) memory act (*mémoire involontaire* or *Erinnerung*), one can easily be deceived by the poem's seemingly incidental, naturalistic images. Yet the insistently conditional syntax and the persistence of allegorical topoi prevent any mimetic conflation of imagery with perception and, consequently, any reading of the overall poem as a symbolic revelation.

In Eichendorff no less than in Blake or Wordsworth, revelation does not mark the end of temporal knowledge but, instead, signals the emergence of a deeper, quasi-Stoic form of historical awareness: that of a traumatic belatedness.[62] Like the interiority of a subject traumatized by the apparent and definitive collapse of history as a stable field of reference, "the meaning constituted by the allegorical sign can . . . consist only in the *repetition* of a previous sign with which it can never coincide."[63] Hence, Eichendorff's deceptively simple opening ("*Es war, als hätt der Himmel / Die Erde still geküßt"*) dwells on the inscrutability of an affective state (*Stimmung*) that, from the very start, is presented as incommensurable with any empirical perception. Heaven and earth embrace only in the virtual domain of an expressly conditional syntax. Such a union is further qualified as a fantasy of, rather than desire for, affective fulfillment inasmuch as the lyric captures it as a received literary topos. Because its utopian character can no longer be denied, the paradise of inwardness can be properly expressed only in a terminally self-alienated literary language. The Romantic traumatized voice rediscovers itself in and as a baroque topos; lyric utterance finds itself transmuted into the involuntary memory of a purely literary citation.[64]

Yet if the self-demystification of allegorical topoi risks the outright demotion of nature and history (through the image) to mere clichés, the vestige of this operation—that is, the figural world of lyric writing—still exhibits traces of the totality whose disappearance it confirms. In his remarkable account of shifting conceptions of figural language, Erich Auerbach notes that "beside the opposition between *figura* and fulfillment or truth, there appears another, between *figura* and *historia. Historia* or *littera* is the literal sense or the event related; *figura* is the same literal meaning or event in reference to the fulfillment cloaked in it, and this fulfillment itself is *veritas*, so that *figura* becomes a middle term between *littera-historia* and *veritas*." Presaging the French symbolists, Eichendorff's radical figural enjambment of such terms as heaven and earth, soul and wings ("*Und meine Seele spannte / Weit ihre Flügel aus*") unfolds with just enough self-conscious literariness and artificiality as to keep the magical pretensions of Christian symbolism at bay. Whereas "the symbol must possess magic power, . . . *figura*, on the other hand, must always be historical," Auerbach notes, for "it is a product of late cultures, far more indirect, complex, and charged with [literary] history. Indeed, seen from this point of view, it has something vastly old about it: a great culture had to reach its culmination and indeed show signs of old age, before an interpretive tradition could produced something on the order of figural prophecy."[65]

We now can articulate the complex affinity between the formal-literary character of Eichendorff's poetry and the fantasy-structure of Romantic conservatism, when approached as a matter of ideation rather than quotidian politics. Both view the *punctum* of perception and the self-identity of a "feeling" as shot through with a temporal dimension, a past whose significance for the present and the future proves irresistible, if also incalculable. Notwithstanding its naturalist veneer, Eichendorff's image of a breeze sweeping over cornstalks and treetops, as well as its analogue of the soul (in Greek, *Pneuma* [breath, wind, soul]) spreading its wings for flight reveals, upon closer inspection, an acutely temporal dimension. Suspended (in Auerbach's phrase) between *littera-historia* and *veritas*, Eichendorff's mystical *figurae* of natural and spiritual animation harbor intimations of unrest, of potentially cataclysmic historical change. A passage in Eichendorff's historical prose restates the mystical tranquility of "Mondnacht" almost verbatim, though now the explosive historical forces seething just below the surface (or beyond the horizon) of Romantic nature writing are impossible to ignore:

> *Dazwischen tönte vom Hofe herüber immerfort der Lärm der Sperlinge, die sich in der Linde tummelten, das Gollern der Truthähne, der einförmige Takt der Drescher und all jene wunderliche Musik des ländlichen Stillebens, die den Landbürtigen in der Fremde, wie das Alphorn den Schweizer oft unversehens in Heimweh versenkt. In den Tälern unten aber schlugen die Kornfelder leise Wellen überall eine fast unheimlich schwüle Gewitterstille, und niemand merkte oder beachtete es, daß das Wetter von Westen bereits aufstieg und einzelne Blitze schon über dem dunklen Waldeskranze prophetisch hin und her zuckten."*

Intermittently, from across the farmstead there wafted the noise of starlings frolicking in the trees, the gobbling of turkeys, the monotonous rhythm of the harvesters, and all the magical sonority of rural, peaceful life that, like the Alpine horns for the Swiss, leaves the traveler unexpectedly *submerged in a state of profound longing* [*Heimweh*]. Down below in the valleys *the cornfields pulsated quietly*, an ominously humid atmosphere presaged thunderstorms, and nobody noticed or took heed that heavy weather was on the rise in the West and some initial lightening was already prophetically flashing above the bluff of trees in the distance.[66]

Like its historical and ideological kin, the language of *Altkonservatismus*, Eichendorff's oeuvre derives its stylistic charisma and literary authority from one central and recurrent figural operation. It is that of presenting the symbolic-mystical and the allegoric-historical, Revelation and History, in a state of conditional suspension. Are we to read the breeze that momentarily animates the cornfield expectantly (as a symbol of incipient revelation) or anxiously (as a scene of unpremeditated and unfathomable, traumatic memory)? In the end, truth (*veritas*) is not so much captured by awakening to it as in the continuous rhetorical enactment of such awakening itself. *Figura*, in Eichendorff, is a condition—not merely a technique—to which the (poetic) form of the voice gives the indispensable (if necessarily textual) substance. We note how the prose text introduces both the "prophetic" (*prophetisch*) and the "nostalgic" (*Heimweh*) as affective qualities at once unpremeditated and inescapable (*unversehens*). With revolutionary terrors having cast all of European culture and politics in a permanently surreal light, the music of repose (*Musik des ländlichen Stillebens*) is not mimetically there. Rather, like von Arnim's "ancient signs of firm boundaries" [*uralten Zeichen fester Grenzen*], such an idyll manifests, in appropriately allegorical form, how the Romantic subject has been permanently cut adrift from its imagined affective and political moorings. Inasmuch as this estrangement also entails a traumatic awakening to History as the nontranscendable horizon of European culture, the oblique volatility of the lyric image mediates such awakening in particularly apt form. Perched on the fluid continuum that includes topos, cliché, and revelation, Eichendorff's images serve both as the cause and the medium for this awakening. Far more articulately and honestly than his prosaic conservative fellow writers, his poetry enacts Coleridge's programmatic characterization of poetry as "a rationalized dream dealing [about?] to manifold Forms our own Feelings, that never perhaps were attached by us to our own personal selves."[67]

Notes

1   Even within the contemporary critical landscape and its often vociferous political dis-agreements, this basic paradigm of a purely "theoretical" accounting for Romanticism and the consequent reaffirmation of theory as untrammeled by the rough-and-tumble world of material politics holds true. Thus Manfred Frank's *Einführung in die Frühromantische Ästhetik* (Frankfurt: Suhrkamp, 1989) maintains a strictly text-immanent, exegetical perspective on aesthetic theory. More oddly yet, Hans-Georg Gadamer's famous pronouncement concerning the "historicity of all understanding" in the second part of *Truth and Method* (trans. John Cummings [New York: Continuum, 1975]) confines its own application of that insight to the late-nineteenth-century writers (Dilthey, Yorck, Ranke) who had first formulated it, while leaving previous aesthetic theory (Kant, Schiller, Schlegel) untouched by historical considerations simply because these writers had declared such matter to be incommensurate with aesthetic cognition. Other instances of preemptive identification with the aesthetic as a purely theoretical, not historical event—even, or perhaps especially, where the critic dissents from Idealist and Romantic aesthetics on logical, conceptual grounds—include Ernst Behler, *German Romantic Literary Theory*

(Cambridge: Cambridge University Press, 1993); Philippe Lacoue-Labarthe and Jean-Luc Nancy, *The Literary Absolute: The Theory of Literature in German Romanticism* (Albany: SUNY Press, 1988); and Azade Seyhan, *Representation and Its Discontents: The Critical Legacy of German Romanticism* (Berkeley: University of California Press, 1992).

2   For a discussion of problems intrinsic to contemporary Romantic Historicism, see James Chandler, *England in 1819* (Chicago: University of Chicago Press, 1998), 3–93; Steven Cole, "Evading Politics: The Poverty of Historicizing Romanticism," *Studies in Romanticism* 34.1 (1995): 29–49; Alan Liu, "Local Transcendence: Cultural Criticism, Postmodernism, and the Romanticism of Detail," *Representations* 32 (1990): 75–113; and my own "Reading beyond Redemption," in *Lessons of Romanticism*, ed. Thomas Pfau and Robert F. Gleckner (Durham: Duke University Press, 1998).

3   Theodor W. Adorno, *Aesthetic Theory*, trans. Robert Hullot-Kentor (Minneapolis: University of Minnesota Press, 1997), 5.

4   Terry Eagleton, whose book title I am echoing here, largely reconstitutes Adorno's insights in the lesser key of individual case-studies (Kant, Schiller, Schopenhauer, etc.). See his opening assertion that "the mystery of the aesthetic object is that each of its sensuous parts, while appearing wholly autonomous, incarnates the 'law' of totality." See also his subsequent remarks on the split personality of the aesthetic as both, an "emancipatory force" and as "internalized repression." *Ideology of the Aesthetic* (Oxford: Basil Blackwell, 1990), 25, 28.

5   For a discussion of English folk culture as the product of various literary and philological strategies dedicated to its "recovery," see Katie Trumpener, *Bardic Nationalism* (Princeton: Princeton University Press, 1997) and Eric Hobsbawm and Terence Ranger, *The Invention of Tradition* (Cambridge: Cambridge University Press, 1983), specifically the essays by Trevor-Roper and Prys Morgan.

6   The remarks are found in von Arnim's important postscript, entitled "Von Volksliedern," to *Des Knaben Wunderhorn*, which he and Clemens Brentano first published in 1806. See volume 6 (ed. Heinz Rölleke) of Brentano, *Werke*, ed. Jürgen Behrens, Wolfgang Frühwald (Stuttgart: Kohlhammer, 1975), 407.

7   Ibid., 409; my translation.

8   On the concept of time, see Manfred Frank, *Zeitbewußtsein* (Pfullingen: Neske, 1990).

9   As Walter Benjamin first noted, Proust's concept is itself an expression of the historical forces of modernity with its characteristic dispersion of economic causality and its erosion of conscious agency. For in this new psychological dynamic, the contingent and the personal converge without advance warning: "Man's inner concerns do not have their issueless private character by nature. They do so only when he is increasingly unable to assimilate the data of the world around him by experience." Such "atrophy of experience," Benjamin argues, accounts for the replacement of "older narration by information, of information by sensation." *Illuminations*, ed. Hannah Arendt, trans. Harry Zohn (New York: Schocken, 1968), 158–59. Knowledge has now ceased to operate through direct lines of oral narrative transmission. Instead, it is realized through the affective simulacra of memory, such as sympathy, nostalgia, and similarly oblique forms of "sensation." As a result of this development, Benjamin argues, knowledge has become a matter of contingency, of flashes of awareness triggered seemingly at random. What Proust calls

mémoire involontaire is thus "part of the inventory of the individual who is isolated in many ways." When taken "in the strict sense of the word," Proust notes, "experience" names the moment when "certain contents of the individual past combine with material of the collective past" (ibid.). Not surprisingly, Benjamin extends his reflections on Proust's notion of an "involuntary memory" into a discussion of Freud's theory of trauma (ibid., 160–63). Benjamin reinforces the point, noting that "experience is indeed a matter of tradition, in collective existence as well as private life." However, as such it depends less on "facts firmly anchored in memory than [on] a convergence in memory of accumulated and frequently unconscious data" (ibid., 157).

10 William Wordsworth, *Lyrical Ballads and Other Poems, 1797–1800*, ed. James Butler and Sharon Green (Ithaca: Cornell University Press, 1992), 756.

11 Walter Benjamin, *Origin of German Tragic Drama*, trans. John Osborne (New York: Verso, 1998), 47, 36. In "convolute" N of *The Arcades Project*, Benjamin reiterates and sharpens his conception of historical knowledge. For not only does "the historical index of . . . images" locate them in "a particular time; it says, above all, that they attain to legibility only at a particular time." The time of historical knowledge, *Jetztzeit*, is a moment of sheer serendipity: "Each 'now' is the now of a particular recognizability. In it, truth is charged to the bursting point with time. (This point of explosion, and nothing else, is the death of *intentio*, which thus coincides with the birth of authentic historical time, the time of truth.)" (*Arcades Project*, trans. Howard Eiland and Kevin McLaughlin [Cambridge: Harvard University Press, 1999], 463).

12 In England, Wordsworth's sharp discrimination between the "people" and the "public" in his 1800 and 1815 prefaces echoes Burke's earlier antithesis and is shortly afterward taken up by William Hazlitt. See his "What Is the People?" in *Selected Writings of William Hazlitt*, ed. Duncan Wu (London: Pickering and Chatto, 1998), 4:241–60. The absence of firm geopolitical boundaries in Germany, at least until 1815 and, in many ways, until 1871, may account for the, if anything, more urgent symbolic struggle over the idea of a cohesive national polity and its shared cultural endowment. For a detailed account of dialectic between German culture and politics between 1815 and 1840, see James Sheehan, *German History, 1770–1866* (Oxford: Oxford University Press, 1989), and Thomas Nipperdey, *German History from Napoleon to Bismarck, 1800–1866*, trans. Michael Nolan (Princeton: Princeton University Press, 1996).

13 See David Wellbery, *The Specular Moment* (Stanford: Stanford University Press, 1996), 187–284.

14 Von Arnim, "Von Volksliedern," 409. On the "strong" hermeneutic role of Romantic texts, see Tilottama Rajan, *The Supplement of Reading* (Ithaca: Cornell University Press, 1990), 15–100; on Schleiermacher's foundational arguments in this regard, see my "Immediacy and the Text: Friedrich Schleiermacher's Theory of Style and Interpretation," *Journal of the History of Ideas* 51.1 (1990): 51–73.

15 For more on Romanticism's mediation, see, for example, Thomas Weiskel, *The Romantic Sublime* (Baltimore: The Johns Hopkins University Press, 1976); Geoffrey Hartman, "The Poetics of Prophecy," in *The Unremarkable Wordsworth* (Minneapolis: University of Minnesota Press, 1986); and Rainer Nägele, *Reading after Freud: Essays on Goethe, Hölderlin, Habermas, Nietzsche, Brecht, Celan, and Freud* (New York: Columbia University Press,

1987). See below the comments by Fredric Jameson cited in note 49; Benjamin, *Arcades Project*, 464.

16 Von Arnim, "Von Volksliedern," 410–11.

17 Susan Stewart, *Crimes of Writing* (Durham: Duke University Press, 1991), 103. Building on Stewart's thesis, I have argued elsewhere how the redefinition of literature as an unwitting archeology of cultural meanings contributes to the formation of a new type of middle-class readership that embraces the reading process as a collaborative extension of the Romantic paradigm of authorship as a socially responsible remembering; see Thomas Pfau, *Wordsworth's Profession* (Stanford: Stanford University Press, 1997), 208–46.

18 Trumpener, *Bardic Nationalism*, 111, 117.

19 Sigmund Freud, *Beyond the Pleasure Principle*, in *The Standard Edition of the Complete Psychological Works of Sigmund Freud*, ed. James Strachey (London: Hogarth, 1953–74), 18:7–66.

20 Cathy Caruth, *Unclaimed Experience* (Baltimore: The Johns Hopkins University Press, 1996), 11, 9.

21 Benjamin, *Arcades Project*, 464.

22 Caruth, *Unclaimed Experience*, 15, 18.

23 Kevin Newmark, "Traumatic Poetry: Charles Baudelaire and the Shock of Laughter," in *Trauma: Explorations in Memory*, ed. Cathy Caruth (Baltimore: The Johns Hopkins University Press, 1995), 238–39.

24 Joseph von Eichendorff, *Neue Gesamtausgabe*, ed. Gerhart Baumann, 4 vols. (Stuttgart: Cotta, 1958), 1:72.

25 Von Arnim, "Von Volksliedern," 408.

26 Karl Mannheim, *Conservatism: A Contribution to the Sociology of Knowledge*, trans. David Kettler and Volker Meja (London: Routledge and Kegan Paul, 1986), 100.

27 Eichendorff, *Neue Gesamtausgabe*, 1:250.

28 See Husserl, *Logical Investigations* (Tübingen: Niemeyer, 1980), vol. 2, sec. 22, vol. 5, sec. 19.

29 Oskar Seidlin notes that the quintessentially "transfixed" (*verzaubert*) disposition of the subject in Eichendorff "ought indeed to be understood in its proper sense: the state of hypnotic fixation on oneself, an immersion in one's own interiority, a dreaming imprisonment and brooding. . . . What Eichendorff's landscape requires . . . is a sudden act of awakening, a quick rending of the oppressive veil; and precisely that will happen time and again in Eichendorff's work." Seidlin links this feature of rupture (*An-Bruch*) to a preoccupation with time. "Through the medium of a visible landscape Eichendorff time and again mediates temporal perspectives" [*Durch das Medium sichtbarer Landschaft vermittelt Eichendorff immer wieder die Perspektiven der Zeit*]. Seidlin, "Eichendorffs Symbolische Landschaft," in *Eichendorff Heute*, ed. Paul Stöcklein (Darmstadt: Wissenschaftliche, 1966), 237–38, 236. Similarly, James Rolleston notes how "Eichendorff's images are deliberately unstable, oscillating ceaselessly between an almost naïve claim to contingent immediacy and an erosion of that claim through a skeptical interpretive narrative" (*Narratives of Ecstasy* [Detroit: Wayne State University Press, 1987], 39).

30 See Reinhard H. Thum, "Cliché and Stereotype," *Philological Quarterly* 62.4 (1983): 435–57, and some of the early, largely dismissive accounts of Eichendorff cited in that essay

(Richarda Huch, Gisela Jahn, René Wehrli). A more astute interpretation of the prevalent *literarhistorische Klischeevorstellungen* and *formelhafte Sprachelemente* in Eichendorff's oeuvre can be found in Klaus Dieter Krabiel, *Tradition und Bewegung: Zum sprachlichen Verfahren Eichendorffs* (Stuttgart: Kohlhammer, 1973), 45–47.

31 Theodor Adorno, *Notes to Literature* (New York: Columbia University Press, 1991), 1:57, 70.

32 Richard Alewyn, "Ein Wort über Eichendorff," in Stöcklein, *Eichendorff Heute*, 7–18; my translation. A similar, albeit much earlier discussion of this oddly formulaic yet elusive style can be found in a review of Eichendorff's 1835 novel, *Dichter und ihre Gesellen*, by the contemporary, left-oriented playwright Karl Gutzkow. See his *Schriften* (Frankfurt: Zwietansendeins, 1998), 2:863–68.

33 See Paul de Man, "Semiology and Rhetoric," in *Allegories of Reading* (New Haven: Yale University Press), 3–19.

34 Adorno, *Aesthetic Theory*, 5.

35 David Wellbery, "Verzauberung: Das Simulakrum in der romantischen Lyrik," in *Mimesis und Simulation*, ed Andreas Kablitz and Gerhard Neumann (Freiburg: Rombach, 1998), 452, 460, 458; my translations.

36 Eichendorff, *Neue Gesamtausgabe*, 1:899.

37 Ibid., 64. See also Eichendorff's closely related poem "Der Geist," in ibid., 143.

38 Paul de Man, "The Rhetoric of Temporality," in *Blindness and Insight* (Minneapolis: University of Minnesota Press, 1983), 205–7.

39 Caruth, *Unclaimed Experience*, 100. For Benjamin, sculpted stones are the material reflex (*Sinnbild*) of cultural matter recognized to be afflicted by the inexorable passage of historical time. Like John Ruskin before him, Benjamin interprets sculpted stone as the unwitting expressive disclosure of a melancholic state; see *Origin of German Tragic Drama*, 154–55.

40 Robert Schumann appears to have had a keen understanding of this dynamic when setting this lyric to music. For Adorno, Schumann's setting of the poem "is distinguished by its bold dissonances . . . which result from the collision of the melodic line and the chorale-like ties in the accompaniment, which moves step-wise; it is as though the modernity of this harmonization were an attempt to protect the poem from aging" (Adorno, *Notes to Literature*, 77).

41 Friedrich Nietzsche, *Birth of Tragedy*, trans. Shaun Whiteside (Harmondsworth: Penguin, 1993), 11.

42 As Karl Mannheim argues, the common assumption that a critique of capitalism originated only with the proletarian socialist movement ought to be revised. "There are many indications that this criticism was initiated by the 'right-wing opposition'" to which such anticapitalist tendencies were an integral part of its larger "experiential reaction against Enlightenment thinking." Mannheim, *Conservatism*, 67, 65. See also Alfred Riemen, "Die reaktionären Revolutionäre? Oder Romantischer Antikapitalismus," *Aurora: Jahrbuch der Eichendorff Gesellschaft* 33 (1973): 77–86.

43 The memorable and much-quoted opening of Eichendorff's *Der Adel und die Revolution* bears recalling here: *"Sehr alte Leute wissen sich wohl noch einigermaßen der sogenannten guten alten Zeit zu erinnern. Sie war aber eigentlich weder gut noch alt, sondern nur noch*

eine Karikatur des alten Guten. Das Schwert war zum Galanteriedegen, der Helm zur Zip-felperücke, aus dem Burgherrn ein pensionierter Husarenoberst geworden, der auf seinem öden Landsitz, von welchem seine Vorfahren einst die vorüberziehenden Kaufleute gebrandschatzt hatten, nun seinerseits von den Industriellen belagert und immer enger eingeschlossen wurde. Es war mit einem Wort die mürb und müde gewordene Ritterzeit, die sich puderte, um den bedeutenden Schimmel der Haare zu verkleiden; einem alten Gecken vergleichbar, der noch immer selbstzufrieden die Schönen umtänzelt, und nicht begreifen kann und höchst empfindlich darüber ist, daß ihn die Welt nicht mehr für jung halten will" [Only people of very advanced age can still recall the so-called dear old time. In fact, that time was neither dear nor old; rather, it was merely a caricature of old nobility. The sword had become a gallant's foil, the helmet had turned into a powdered wig, the lord of the manor had become a retired colonel of the hussars who now found himself besieged and encircled by industrialists on the very estate from whence in former times his ancestors had plundered and torched merchants passing through. In so many words, the age in question was that of an enfeebled and fatigued chivalry, now generously powdered so as to cover its rot. It could be compared to an aged lecher who continues to dance with young, beautiful people and is unable to comprehend, indeed, waxes indignant, that the world no longer considers him young] (Eichendorff, *Neue Gesamtausgabe*, 1:898; my translation).

44 Slavoj Žižek, *The Plague of Fantasies* (New York: Verso, 1997), 7.

45 As Helga Grebing has argued, conservatism is a bourgeois phenomenon, not a feudal one: "Conservatism originates not as an ahistorical, retrospective form of opposition to bourgeois society. Rather, it emerges from the ideological needs of that society insofar as it furnishes bourgeois society with a strategy to counteract those emancipatory characteristics that are at once intrinsic to it and appear to imply the bourgeoisie's ongoing transformation in the future. The historical moment for this genesis of conservatism is thus the transition from an old, dissolving mode of production toward a new, capitalist one. As regards both, its mode of origination and its further development, conservatism can thus not be understood as legitimating precapitalist, feudal modes of production *per se*." Helga Grebing, *Aktuelle Theorien über Faschismus und Konservatismus: Eine Kritik* (Stuttgart: Kohlhammer, 1974), 26–27; my translation.

46 Angelika Rauch, "Post-Traumatic Hermeneutics: Melancholia in the Wake of Trauma," *diacritics* (Winter 1998): 111–20; quotations from 113.

47 Mannheim, *Conservatism*, 88.

48 It bears remembering that Friedrich Schlegel himself emerged as one of the preeminent conservatives of the later Romantic period. His conversion to Catholicism and subsequent ascent as a major intellectual presence in Vienna—where he also promoted Eichendorff's literary fortunes—follow a familiar trajectory of conversion and the gradual formulation of an antimodern metaphysics.

49 Fredric Jameson, *Postmodernism* (Durham: Duke University Press, 1991), ix, 25.

50 Eichendorff, *Neue Gesamtausgabe*, 4:1155; my translation.

51 Mannheim, *Conservatism*, 56.

52 Eichendorff, *Neue Gesamtausgabe*, 4:1155–56; my translation.

53 Ibid., 4:1160; my translation. Consistent with Eichendorff's self-consciously deployed notion of "fantasy," J. G. A. Pocock remarks that "a tradition," which, "in its simplest form,

may be thought of as an indefinite series of repetitions of an action," does not so much require an original reference-point as the fiction of one: "It may well be that it is the assumption, rather than the factual information, of previous performance that is operative; each action provides the grounds for assuming that it had a predecessor." Later in the same essay, Pocock persuasively distinguishes between tradition as "stress[ing] either the continuity of the process of transmission, or the creative and charismatic origin of what is transmitted. The two are conceptually distinct, . . . but they are dialectically related, and are often—perhaps normally—found together within the same tradition. A distinction may be drawn between traditions which conserve highly specific and significant images of the creative actions with which they began and of which they are in some way the continuation, and traditions which depict themselves as sheer continuity of usage or transmission and conserve little or no account of their beginnings" (*Politics, Language, and Time* [Chicago: University of Chicago Press, 1971], 237, 244).

54 Theodor Adorno, *Kierkegaard: Construction of the Aesthetic*, ed. and trans. Robert Hullot-Kentor (Minneapolis: University of Minnesota Press, 1989), 139). See also the German text, Adorno, *Gesammelte Schriften*, ed. Rolf Tiedemann (Darmstadt: Wissenschaftliche, 1998), 2:197–98. Adorno's phrase *"Die Kunst ist, einen Genuß hervorzubringen"* fuses a definition and a colloquialism: "Art consists in producing an enjoyment" and "The trick is to produce an enjoyment."

55 For Freud's usage of *Nachträglichkeit*, see especially his 1918 case history of the Wolf-Man ("From the History of an Infantile Neurosis") where, in a long footnote, Freud comments how "the patient under analysis, at an age of over twenty-five years, was lending words to the impressions and impulses of his fourth year which he would never have found at that time." Freud, *Three Case Histories* (New York: Macmillan, 1963), 231–32n. While such delayed eloquence may "seem comic and incredible," Freud defends his patient's substitution of his "present ego into the situation which is so long past" as "legitimate" (*mit Recht*). It is simply a case of "deferred action" (Strachey's translation of *Nachträglichkeit*). Freud's unusual eagerness to justify a moment of substitution that, in point of fact, eclipses no less than "three [intervening] periods of time" [*Zeitphasen*], reflects his professional objective of translating preverbal affect into intelligible propositions. Inasmuch as psychoanalysis renders all preconscious suffering intelligible, medical "cure," and methodological self-legitimation go hand in hand. Not surprisingly, most of Freud's key-concepts—such as repression, the unconscious, displacement, and indeed *Nachträglichkeit*—effectively presuppose the entire terminological edifice of psychoanalysis to be in place already. In ways that cannot be taken up in full detail here, *Nachträglichkeit* thus constitutes not only a key concept of the unconscious as a "missed" or previously "unclaimed" experience. It also reveals that, within the architectonics of Freudian thought, any key concept is by definition always in(tro)duced "retroactively," part of an intellectual economy in which dissent and falsification are preempted by the on the grounds of an anterior agency (the unconscious) that can only be caught in its necessarily belated effects, but never *in actu*.

56 See Slavoj Žižek's characterization of history as the "supreme example of [the] paradoxical coincidence of emergence and loss. . . . On the one hand, pre-capitalist societies allegedly

do not yet know history proper; they are 'circular,' 'closed,' caught in a repetitive move-ment predetermined by tradition—so history must emerge *afterwards*, with the decay of 'closed' organic societies. On the other hand, the opposite cliché tells us that capitalism itself is no longer historical; it is rootless, with no tradition of its own, and therefore para-sitical on previous traditions, a universal order which (like modern science) can thrive everywhere" (*Plague of Fantasies*, 13). Here as elsewhere, however, Žižek's precariously generalizing tone leaves it unclear what authority these ostensibly "clichéd" positions hold within his account.

57 Eichendorff, *Neue Gesamtausgabe*, 1:286; my translation.

58 Adorno, *Notes to Literature*, 57.

59 Gerald Gillespie briefly cites a poem by Friedrich von Logau (1605–55), eminent and prolific author of countless epigrammatic, aphoristic, and sententious poems, among them his *Two-hundred Rhymed German Proverbs* (1638) and his magnum opus, the *Three-thousand German Epigrams* [*Deutscher Sinn-Getichte Drey Tausend*] (1654). Logau's "May" ["Der Mai"], centers on the image of the nuptial kiss wedding earth to heaven: "*Dieser Monat ist ein Kuß, den der Himmel gibt der Erde, / Daß sie, jetzund seine Braut, künftig eine Mutter werde*" [This month is a kiss that heaven places on earth's forehead / That she may become his bride now and a mother in the future]. Cited in Gillespie, "Hieroglyphics of Finality in Eichendorff's Lyrics," *German Life and Letters* 42.3 (1989): 203–18; quotation from 209. Eichendorff's work corroborates Paul de Man's contention that "truly modern poetry" requires an "imagery that is both symbol and allegory, that represents objects in nature but is actually taken from purely literary sources" (*Blindness and Insight*, 171).

60 Gillespie, "Hieroglyphics of Finality," 209, 204.

61 Walter Benjamin, *Ursprung des deutschen Trauerspiels* (Frankfurt: Suhrkamp, 1982), 144; my translation.

62 Echoing Adorno's apprehension of readers complacent enough to construe Eichendorff's allegorical landscape as imbued with metaphysical consolation, de Man cautions against the desire to "understand the relationship between mimesis and allegory as a genetic pro-cess, forcing into a pattern of continuity what that which is, by definition, the negation of all continuity" (*Blindness and Insight*, 185–86).

63 Ibid., 207.

64 Walther Killy notes how, in the age of baroque literature, "literary practice transmutes the topical principle of *inventio* for arguments into an inventory of fixed turns of phrase. Cognitive principles are transformed into verbal cues" [*In der literarischen Praxis wird aus dem topischen Auffindungsprinzip für Argumente häufig eine Sammlung von feststehenden Redewendungen, allgemeinen Erwägungen, traditionellen Behauptungen, berühmten Aus-sprüchen usw. Aus dem Denkprinzip wird das Stichwort*] (Walther Killy, *Literaturlexikon*, 15 vols. [Gütersloh: Mohn, 1988–93], 14:436). Ernst Robert Curtius, notwithstanding his formidable erudition in medieval and early modern rhetorical convention, often appears uncertain about whether a given topos ought to be approached as a moral commonplace, rhetorical cliché, or as the expression of archetypal, and enduring (substantive) contents. See Ernst Robert Curtius, *European Literature and the Latin Middle Ages*, trans. Willard R. Trask (Princeton: Princeton University Press, 1967), chap. 5, secs. 2, 3, 6.

65 Erich Auerbach, "Figura," trans. Ralph Manheim, in Auerbach, *Scenes from the Drama of European Literature* (Minneapolis: University of Minnesota Press, 1984), 47, 57.

66 Eichendorff, *Neue Gesamtausgabe*, 1:903; translation mine, emphases mine.

67 Samuel Taylor Coleridge, *Notebooks*, vol., 2, ed. Kathleen Coburn (Princeton: Princeton University Press, 1961), entry 2086.

Ian Duncan

Authenticity Effects: The Work of Fiction in Romantic Scotland

The *Private Memoirs and Confessions of a Justified Sinner: Written by Himself: With a Detail of Curious Traditionary Facts, and Other Evidence, by the Editor* was published anonymously in London in 1824. Figure 1 reproduces the frontispiece and title page of the book. The frontispiece is a facsimile extract from a manuscript journal, corresponding to page 366 of the printed text, which turns out to be the penultimate entry in the "Private Memoirs and Confessions of a Sinner." In the book's concluding section, the anonymous editor gives an account of the discovery of the manuscript. He reprints an "extract from an authentic letter, published in *Blackwood's Magazine for August*, 1823," describing the exhumation of the corpse of an eighteenth-century suicide at a remote location in the Scottish Borders.[1] The letter is signed "JAMES HOGG": a figure well known to contemporary readers as "the Ettrick Shepherd," the author of traditional Scottish ballads, lyrics, and tales and, over the past few years, some more contentious forays into the metropolitan genres of novel and metrical romance. Hogg's letter can indeed be found printed, under the title "A Scots Mummy,"

The *South Atlantic Quarterly* 102:1, Winter 2003.
Copyright © 2003 by Duke University Press.

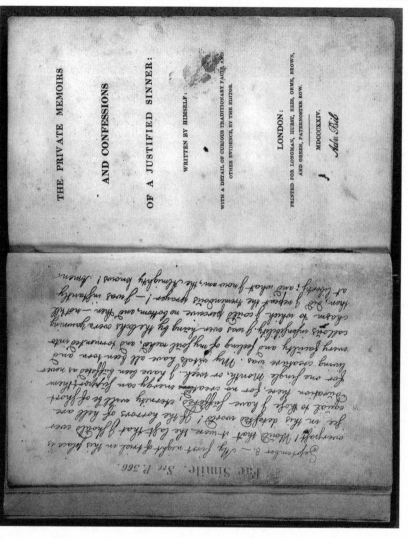

Figure 1. Frontispiece and title page from James Hogg, *Private Memoirs and Confessions of a Justified Sinner* (London: Longman, 1824). Reproduced by permission of the Trustees of the National Library of Scotland.

in the August 1823 number of *Blackwood's Edinburgh Magazine*, to which he was a frequent contributor.[2] The editor of the *Confessions of a Justified Sinner* comments: "It bears the stamp of authenticity in every line; yet, so often had I been hoaxed by the ingenious fancies displayed in that Magazine, that when this relation met my eye, I did not believe it" (169).

A literary friend of the editor's—who seems to be none other than John Gibson Lockhart, a leading *Blackwood's* contributor and the son-in-law of Sir Walter Scott—assures him that Hogg's letter is indeed "authentic." They organize an expedition to investigate the Scots mummy and track down the Ettrick Shepherd at a local market, where he is busy trading livestock. Speaking in Border Scots, Hogg brusquely refuses to cooperate with the literary gentlemen: "Od bless ye, lad! I hae ither matters to mind. I hae a' thae paulies to sell, an' a' yon Highland stotts down on the green every ane; an' then I hae ten scores o' yowes to buy after, an' if I canna first sell my ain stock, I canna buy nae ither body's. I hae mair ado than I can manage the day, foreby ganging to houk up hunder-year-auld banes" (170). The editor and his party hire another guide, eventually find the grave (it turns out Hogg's letter gave misleading directions), and reopen it. The upper body has disintegrated after the previous exhumation; as the literati inspect the lower half, marveling at its intact state, it too crumbles into shreds. Among the relics they bring back is a sodden roll of printed and manuscript pages: the text of the "Private Memoirs and Confessions of a Sinner" we have been reading.

Contemporary readers were soon in a position to know that the *Private Memoirs and Confessions of a Justified Sinner* was written by Hogg, despite his rather careful attempts to keep his authorship a secret. (Hogg planted clues that it was the work of a Glasgow or west-country author, only to have his identity leaked by his colleagues in *Blackwood's*.)[3] Hogg's novel presents us with a combination of effects that seems unprecedented even in the era of radical literary innovation and experimentation we call Romanticism. Here is a work of fiction that goes to unusual lengths to reproduce authenticating devices, in the form of documentary evidence—the manuscript facsimile, the letter in *Blackwood's*—and at the same time to conceal the identity of its author: who then appears as a character in his own book, only to announce his refusal to have anything to do with the work of literary production.

Hogg combines modern conventions of literary production, *authentication* and *anonymity*, which enjoyed high-denomination currency in post-

Enlightenment Edinburgh. Anonymity, the signature of "Nobody" that marked the potent volatility of writing in eighteenth-century commercial society, was installed as the trope of a professionalized author-function in the *Edinburgh Review* from 1802 and deployed by Scott in an elaborate, serial "anonymity game" in the Waverley novels from 1814.[4] Beginning in 1817 *Blackwood's Magazine* systematically mystified the identities of its editors and contributors in a set of ciphers and pseudonyms that cloaked their often libelous interventions in the bitter cultural politics of the postwar era. Hogg himself had achieved notoriety as both subject and object of *Blackwood's* "hoaxes": in an effective reversal of anonymity, other authors took over his Ettrick Shepherd persona and made it the mouthpiece for organic nationalist fantasies.[5] Thus, by the early 1820s anonymity had become the site of a politicized, vexed, and dangerous rather than neutral or transcendent cultural authority.

The authenticating apparatus of documentation and editorial commentary is a convention of antiquarian writing. Mined for satire by the Augustan wits, the rhetoric of antiquarianism had its legitimacy renewed in the genres of Enlightenment romance revival, such as collections of "ancient poetry," ballads, and other premodern literary and vernacular forms. Susan Stewart interprets what she calls an "eighteenth-century crisis in authenticity" as a reaction-formation of the economic modernization of literary production in Great Britain.[6] As "literature" becomes an abstracted and commodified object (a printed book for sale), it must recuperate what Stewart calls its "contexts," an alienated world of organic relations of production, which it does by representing itself as a trace or relic of lost, precapitalist origins. This recuperation takes place as a formal dynamic internal to the literary object: hence the series of eighteenth-century scandals in which a literary original turns out to be an invention, a writing grounded on nothing but its own act of writing. Stewart suggests that the novel—the modern, commodified, disenchanted literary genre par excellence—stands in an antithetical relation to the poetic project of a nostalgic simulation of origins and eventually subsumes it. The mimetic and heteroglossic technology of novelistic realism, presumably, displaces those attenuated shades of "context" within its more robustly secular, metonymic domain.[7]

Scott's historical novels took up with a vengeance the authenticating devices of romance revival—editorial frames, antiquarian commentary, the citation of documentary sources—to establish the technical repertoire of what Fiona Robertson has called "fictions of authenticity."[8] Far from withering away under the inexorable rise of the novel, authenticity gains a heightened categorical prominence through the tropes of authorial anonymity and self-representation deployed in Hogg's *Confessions of a Justified Sinner*. These issues are highlighted in a novel "By the Author of Waverley" published in the same month, June 1824, as the *Confessions of a Justified Sinner*. Scott's *Redgauntlet: A Tale of the Eighteenth Century* shares with Hogg's masterpiece a striking set of formal and thematic properties.[9] Both novels feature a division of the protagonist and an associated thematics of reflexive doubling and political-ideological excess ("fanaticism"). In an extension of the fissile principle, both novels present themselves as a heterogeneous collection of stories, languages, documents, and genres, including letters, journals, editorial narratives, renditions of popular speech, and inset oral tales of Scottish "folklore." Each insists upon its condition as a book, an artifact that grants a sheerly material unity to a miscellany of styles and sources by the circumstance of their being bound together.

Their extreme degree of formal self-reflexivity has encouraged recent critics of these novels to read them through a late-twentieth-century, more or less postmodernist vocabulary.[10] Such accounts tend to overlook the knotty question of historical specificity, drawn tighter by the novels' almost identical time and place of production: June 1824, Edinburgh and its cultural hinterland, the Scottish Borders. "Possible links between the composition of *Redgauntlet* and *Confessions of a Justified Sinner* are frustratingly obscure," notes Robertson, in a discussion of the novels' shared thematic preoccupation with "ripping up auld stories."[11] Although Hogg and Scott were working in close institutional and personal proximity, it seems fairly certain that with these two works, despite their former intimacy (as recently as 1821 Scott had insisted on changes at proof stage to Hogg's *The Three Perils of Man*), neither author knew what the other was doing.[12] The coincidence presents a problem of explanatory specificity that neither the traditional terms of influence (locked into a positivist scheme of causality) nor intertextuality (too vague and free-floating) can account for; while the kind of discursive, technical, or institutional history favored by some recent scholars evokes a necessary rather than sufficient causality that has too little to say about the difference between the works at hand.

One way to begin thinking about the question is to interpret the rhetoric of reflexivity—the signature of an aesthetic that Jerome McGann has called (regarding Scott) "Romantic Postmodernity"—as a local and temporal rather than universal effect.[13] Both novels, that is, position themselves as "post-" in relation to a locally legible, indeed prominent discourse of modernity. The tropes of reflexivity appear at a much earlier moment of the English novel, in the first decade of the eighteenth century: in the very era of the historical opening of modernity, as these authors would have understood it, and of the formation of the novel as modernity's typical genre.[14] The recurrence of these devices a century later, in Scottish "tales of the eighteenth century," marks a historicizing difference rather than the blindness of anachronism. Anachronism, as James Chandler has shown, is itself a historicizing trope, developed in Scottish Enlightenment theorizations of uneven development.[15] The rhetoric of reflexivity, that is, now articulates a metahistorical doubling: history squared. Both novels set themselves in critical, retrospective relation to the ten-year-old Scottish tradition of national historical romance (initiated with *Waverley*, 1814) to which they belong, and to its topic, the era of modernization, the hundred years from the Treaty of Union to the wars with Revolutionary and Napoleonic France—an era distinguished, in turn, by the rise of the Scottish Enlightenment human sciences, which abstracted modernity into written discourse as a scientific, historical, and philosophical category. Jerome Christensen has recently suggested that British intellectuals viewed the end of the Napoleonic wars as an epoch comparable to the end of the cold war in our time— an "end of history" characterized by a closing of alternative political possibilities and the triumph of a liberal ideology of "normal change."[16] Certainly Scott's novels (at least some of them) perform a complex act of closure, of looking back, at an era of modernization—national and world-historical— that has reached its period. In that strictly technical sense, we might say that Scott's and Hogg's novels are "postmodern": they situate themselves on the far threshold of an identifiable historical stage of modernity, constituted by the literary genres and discourses that make it intelligible. If the Scottish historical novel narrates—and so performs—a dialectical closure of modernity, in which historical conflict yields to civil society,[17] what follows that closure? What will the end or aftermath of the historical novel look like?

Such self-positioning is more explicit in *Redgauntlet*, as it reflects back on the great sequence of "Scotch novels" of the first five years of Scott's career as a novelist, from *Waverley* to the third series of *Tales of My Landlord* (1819). In the five years since, beginning with *Ivanhoe*, Scott had turned from writing novels about the making of modern Scotland—tales of the long eighteenth century—to "romances" with decisively premodern British and Continental settings.[18] (That last five years had also seen a proliferation of works of Scottish fiction by a host of imitators and rivals, among them Hogg.) *Redgauntlet* performs its retrospect through a conspicuous revision of, in particular, the Jacobite and family plots of *Waverley* and *Rob Roy*. Like those works, *Redgauntlet* insistently thematizes its status as a "historical romance," a compound of fiction and history, with a difference that has been made much of in recent criticism:[19] the historical event narrated in *Redgauntlet*, the secret return of Charles Edward Stuart for a last Jacobite rising in the summer of 1765, never took place. It is Scott's invention.

Unusually for Scott, the editorial frame of *Redgauntlet* identifies itself at the close rather than opening of the novel, in the form of a "Conclusion, by Dr Dryasdust, in a Letter to the Author of Waverley" (378–80). Dr Dryasdust, an antiquarian persona invoked in earlier Waverley novels, reports several examples of what the title page of the *Confessions of a Justified Sinner* calls "traditionary facts and other evidence": an article in the *Whitehall Gazette*, a marriage contract in a family archive, the oral testimonies of an Edinburgh street porter and a Jacobite priest. This evidence, however, flaunts its unreliability, its invented or fictive character, as it wraps up the novel's plots, emptying them into burlesque (the obsessive litigant who drops dead in court of a "perplexity fit") or generating a parodic, or maybe utopian, variant of the story we have been reading: instead of joining modern civil society, the feudal heir recedes into the folkloric world that has come to his rescue. Scott's editorial frame executes a set of strategies apparently opposite to Hogg's. It insists upon its fictional status, it makes urbane mockery of the structure of authentication, and it keeps the biographical figure of the author out of sight—even as Scott's identity as "the Author of *Waverley*" was pretty widely known by 1824.

If the original of the Author of *Waverley*, let's call him Walter Scott, is not visible in his own text (in either the fiction or the apparatus), where might we find him? Lockhart's great biography of Scott, published a dozen years after *Redgauntlet*, awards that novel a privileged place in the Scott canon.[20] Developing a strategy initiated by Scott himself in the editorial apparatus of the collected edition of his works,[21] Lockhart casts *Redgauntlet* as the most autobiographical of the Waverley novels ("it contains perhaps more of the author's personal experiences than any other of them, or even than all the rest put together"), featuring characters (including the author's father), events (his first love affair), and other details drawn from Scott's childhood and youth.[22] Lockhart's detection of this vein of autobiographical reference proved so decisive that later biographers have followed suit, basing much of their information about Scott's early life on the evidence of the novel. Indeed, *The Life of Scott* institutes the circular logic that sustains modern literary biography, whereby the works generate the meaning of the life that is supposed to be their explanatory ground.

Scott's and Hogg's novels, then, represent themselves as occupying very different relations to the Romantic source topoi of *authenticity* (denoting a cultural-historical origin behind the text) and of the *author* (a personal origin behind the text). In *Redgauntlet*, Scott's topical apparatus insinuates itself, until the last few pages, largely through allusion to the prior canon of Waverley novels, while the author is likewise absorbed into a purely conventional figure—until his presence "behind" the text, guaranteed by never being named, becomes visible, after Scott's death, on the plane of biographical reference: after the novel, chronologically, but also, etiologically, before it. Literary biography establishes the tradition according to which the author is the origin of the work, subsuming other cultural, historical, and documentary sources, which are flagged within the text as his own inventions. Fictionality guarantees, as it is guaranteed by, the invisible, informing "real presence" of the author. In the *Confessions of a Justified Sinner*, however, James Hogg not only is named but makes a formal appearance in the editorial frame. At the same time, this James Hogg—the Ettrick Shepherd who rebuffs the literati and holds fast to his georgic world—cannot be the same person as the nameless, alienated author of the book we are reading. "The Author" does not occupy the station of an origin anterior to the novel's thematic of a metaphysically disastrous doubling and splitting: he is himself subject to it, penned within, rather than transcending, the field of literary effects.

───────

The appearance of a work of fiction in mock-antiquarian disguise, as a found manuscript translated and edited for modern readers, is a venerable convention, dating back (at least) to the great prototype of modern romance, *Don Quixote*.[23] Horace Walpole reinvented it in the mid-1760s in *The Castle of Otranto*, where he made the historicizing feint—crucial for Scott—of invoking a premodern register of cultural difference.[24] The device is also the cornerstone of a specifically Scottish tradition of modern national literary representation. The "authenticity effect"[25] that advertises a problematic, unstable boundary between history and fiction, evidence and invention, textual surface and ontological depth, may be called the foundational trope of this Scottish tradition. Nor is the appearance of the author as a character in his own novel entirely without precedent. Although a "so-and-so de Saavedra" is mentioned in an inset tale in the first part of *Don Quixote*, a more definitive instance occurs in Smollett's *Expedition of Humphry Clinker* (1771), one of the seminal works of modern Scottish fiction. *Humphry Clinker* traces a sentimental journey around the United Kingdom, from Wales (standing for "British" origins), through the corrupt metropolitan core of Bath and London, up to Scotland, and finally back home. In London one of the characters attends a luncheon for indigent authors given by a certain "S——": Smollett himself, the author of the book we are reading. "S——" is represented as stolidly ordinary, showing none of "the outward signs of authorship"; at the same time he is able to live by his writing, free from "patronage" or "dependence." His very blankness, the lack of "characteristic" features, is the mark of this author's proto-professional integrity and strength. Yet he occupies an ambiguous relation to the discourse of satire that defines metropolitan corruption: his very inclusion in the diegesis (as literally a "character," a cipher, "S——") erodes any certainty that he can stand outside its conditions. This is not the last we hear of him. On the banks of Loch Lomond, "the Arcadia of Scotland," the party visits the author's birthplace, and a poem by "Dr Smollett" is cited in the text. Physically absent, he may be given his name and title, in his capacity as author. The poem celebrates Smollett's birthplace as a "Pure stream"—literally (in the novel's topographical allegory) a source, unsullied and transparent. But the author of *Humphry Clinker* remains a figure divided: between the name at home in the Highlands and the "S——" who accommodates fools and knaves in London.[26]

Humphry Clinker alludes several times to the literary event that founded an invention of Scottish cultural origins on a scandalously disputed authenticity: the publication, in the early 1760s, of James Macpherson's translations of the ancient heroic poetry of the Gaelic Highlands. *Fingal, Temora*, and the other "Poems of Ossian" effectively inaugurate the romance-revival tradition of works of historical fiction supported by an antiquarian apparatus, with the crucial difference that in this case the authentication was meant to be taken literally. Not least among the achievements of Macpherson's epic, highlighted rather than canceled by the controversy over authenticity, was its representation of a psycho-phenomenological condition of Scottish cultural modernity. A series of radical disjunctions in political and social history, culminating in the 1707 Union, made possible the appearance of modernity as a discursive category in Scotland, in the form of a breach, a "Great Divide," between the ancestral nation and the present. If modernity could positively constitute the theme of Enlightenment philosophical history, the recovery of national origins from the far side of the breach would always be vulnerable to denunciation as a hoax, a fabrication, an act of fiction. Hence the modern conceptual pressure upon "tradition": What could reliably connect the present with a lost past? Samuel Johnson challenged Macpherson to exhibit the manuscript originals of the Ossian poems, and Macpherson's prevarication encouraged the verdict that he had faked them. If (as now seems clear) Macpherson based his texts on extant oral traditions as well as manuscript remains, he lacked an adequate theorization of oral tradition in a modern culture aggressively committed to the authenticity of the written word and so found himself unable to mount a defense against (especially) Johnson's denigration of orality. The Ossian affair has been read as expressing a critical relation between literary culture and a vanishing (or occluded) oral origins.[27] It also brings into focus a categorical crisis in the material forms of writing as the medium—the sublime substance—of a modern national culture: in the relation between printed text, a mechanically reproduced and multiplied commodity, and manuscript, the trace of an authentic, unrepeatable act of creation. This is the crisis to which the frontispiece of the *Confessions of a Justified Sinner* alludes. A printed simulation of manuscript (the ghost of an original hand) confronts a title page that flaunts the rhetoric of print culture, with its signature of mass production and bureaucratic abstraction.

Hogg's authenticity effects thus address not only, not even primarily, a residual, metaphysical nostalgia for orality but an emergent, modern idealization of writing as a transfigured mode or medium of industrial production: one that closes the circuit of the human by guaranteeing, at one end, the purposeful labor of an individual author and, at the other, the corporate identity of a national culture. In one of those technical histories mentioned earlier, Clifford Siskin argues that this sublime circuit of writing, folding author, reader, and nation into a unified organic formation, comes decisively together in Romanticism under the disciplinary title of "Literature." According to Siskin (and, in an analogous argument, to Friedrich Kittler), the Romantic emergence of "Literature" marks the historical point at which the modern technology of writing is at once industrialized (turned into machinery) and naturalized (phantasmatically reattached to the body).[28] Nothing less than the primary technology through which modernization realizes itself as a "project," writing is made to seem an organic extension or function of human life. This naturalization takes place, crucially, in the Romantic-era novel, which identifies literacy with developmental narratives of individual and national subject-formation.

In many ways the novels of Scott rehearse this very process: binding together the plots of personal, historical, and literary development, installing by example a national cultural formation.[29] At the same time, the variety of fictions by Scottish authors opens up a set of vital critical disturbances in a cultural historiography that can too easily (in less careful hands) reproduce the smooth, homogenizing narrative of hegemony that it exposes. It thus makes a crucial difference to read them as products of a Scottish, not just an English or even British, literary history: not least because "writing," "English," and "literature" occupied historically very different relations for authors and readers in modern Scotland. The novels of Scott, notoriously, alienate post-Victorian readers through their resistance to naturalization at the level of style, in part because those readers have absorbed the achievement of Scott's contemporary, Jane Austen, who perfected the stylistic technique of naturalization in free indirect discourse. Scott's English clings with a rigorous heaviness to the page, severed from the lively imitation of Scots speech and thus from a homological bonding of speaking, writing, and consciousness. Readers continue to read, that is, the burden of historical and institutional mediations—constituting the practice of literacy and the object of literature—that made English the language of an imperial political economy in Scotland.[30] Writing, as English, continues to bear an excess (manifest in the work of reading) that keeps visible the machinery of a "national" subject-formation that abstracts its users from a vernacular (organic) community. The gap between speech and literacy remains evident, generative in its very openness rather than through a naturalizing closure. Penny Fielding has analyzed the structural contradictions of the figure of orality, posited by Scottish Romantic writing as at once its abject other (popular illiteracy, symptom of modern social fragmentation) and lost origin (fantasia of an organic ancestral culture). Orality, that is, keeps reflecting back the aporia that constitutes the metaphysical and sociohistorical substance of writing.[31] Articulating this aporia, making it visible as the principle that at once drives and limits narrativity, Scott's and Hogg's novels, *Redgauntlet* and *Confessions of a Justified Sinner*, project functionally contrasting abstractions of their own work of writing: in the respective figures of fiction and textuality.

Stewart argues that figures of origin can receive authentication only through more writing, further textual production, in the form of those editorial and documentary supplements.[32] Johnson's critique of Ossian exposed the circularity of such logic—the (at best) prematurity of its claim on cultural origins. The native proponents of Ossian, he sneered, "remember names, and perhaps some proverbial sentiments; and, having no distinct ideas, coin a resemblance without an original."[33] The strong solution to such a critique was to insist on the act of invention that coins a resemblance *as* an original. It would be Scott's solution. The first of Scott's verse-romances, *The Lay of the Last Minstrel*, and his first novel, *Waverley*, are allusively steeped in Ossian, which they swallow whole (scandal and all) by insisting upon their status as inventions, as works of fiction, even as they pedantically invoke historical evidence and traditional sources. The effect is amplified in the more elaborate antiquarian framework of the late "Magnum Opus" edition: "In Scott's notably fluid stratagems of authenticity and fictionality, source becomes story just as surely as, in the increasingly referential world of the first-edition frames, story becomes source."[34] The self-referencing rhetoric of fiction subsumes (but does not cancel) the burden of historical reference, perfecting a paradoxical logic of authentication.

Scott's highly sophisticated romance epistemology develops a still more consequential precedent in eighteenth-century Scottish writing: the moral philosophy of David Hume (and of Hume's disciple, Adam Smith). Hume's deconstruction of the metaphysical grounds of understanding exposes the fictional status of the cognitive relations that inform our knowledge of the world and of ourselves. A "grammar of the imagination," in Susan Manning's phrase, produces the figures of cause and effect, of temporal and spatial continuity, through a logic of customary associations.[35] The revelation need not, however, condemn us to a melancholy solipsism, since we take part in a collective fiction of "common life," sustained by transactions of linguistic, economic, and sympathetic exchange, which regulate individual excesses of fancy and reason. In the absence of a metaphysical basis of causality, the associative grammar that sustains empirical effects is anchored in "nature," represented by the human body. Hume posits a universal psychological structure, fixed in the body, that Smith makes the ground for his explorations of the social regime of exchange. As Smith makes clear (in *The Theory of Moral Sentiments*), the techniques of this social subject-formation are techniques specific to literacy, involving rigorously reflexive acts of reading and composing an imagined self through an imagined other.

In the wake of the Ossian scandal, the modern nation could be recovered and circulated as a fiction, founded not in metaphysical properties, in causal connections, but in the shared associations—articulated in aesthetic categories, sustained through acts of exchange—of its participating subjects: in other words, a reading public. This is the epochal invention of Scott's historical romances, far more consequential than the ideological reduction of those romances by his Tory allies and protégés in *Blackwood's Magazine*. The Nation as Romance assumed garish colors in the political spectacle that crowned civic life in postwar Edinburgh, the tartan-festooned state visit of George IV in August 1822. Critics have always liked to denounce "the King's Jaunt" as an obnoxious travesty—the iconographic investiture of the British monarchy, as well as of Scotland's postnational identity, with a bogus, retro-Jacobite Highland pageantry. More recent commentators have attended to the deliberation with which Scott stages a disenchanted, thoroughly textualized figure of sovereignty in a modern commercial culture.[36] Their analyses bring a salutary complication to the gesture of ideological exposé with which the royal visit is usually dismissed—as though it is enough to reiterate the inauthenticity of an occasion of which inauthenticity was the point. Slavoj Žižek reminds us that *"ideology is not an illusion"*: Scott's pageant exerted symbolic power precisely through the conspicuousness of its fictional devices. Seeing that it is only a show, the public is invited freely to take part, rather than coerced into believing in something "real."[37]

In other words, the viewer's (and the reader's) assent to the representation takes place as an assent to—a recognition of—its fictional character. Such representations already assume their own demystification as a condition of access to them. In proffering the authenticity effect as the very device that yields the recognition of fictionality, Scott invokes a quintessentially modern, liberal ideology of reception, which relies upon recognition

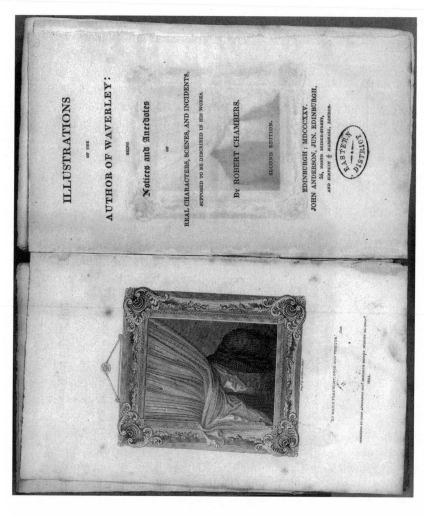

Figure 2. Frontispiece and title page from Robert Chambers, *Illustrations of the Author of Waverley*, 2nd ed. (Edinburgh: John Anderson, 1825). Reproduced by permission of the Trustees of the National Library of Scotland.

and consensus and participation, rather than requiring a "primitive," naïve or fetishistic, subjectivity of belief. (Hence both Scott's and Hogg's invocation in these novels of "fanaticism" as the antithetical subjectivity of civil society.) Benedict Anderson and other nationalism theorists have tended to posit a more or less unified reading public at this era of its inception, constituting the subjective field of the nation as an "imagined community." Other commentators (such as Jon Klancher) have described the fragmentation of the Romantic-era reading public along lines of political, religious, class, and gender difference in the periodicals that called it into being.[38] Victorian critics cite the novel, beginning with Scott, as the strong form that absorbs and regulates those differences to produce a unified figure of the nation.[39] Scott's novels, however, mark this unified national reading public as itself a fiction, a provisional and experimental construct, as they continue to invoke a divided readership. To put it crudely: the novels appeal to those who see through the fiction (of national cohesion, of historical progress, of liberal participation) as well as those who do not, who are in thrall to its illusions and accept it all as "real." Rather like the Straussian formula for management of a liberal democracy, the novels invoke an elite readership, encoded in their dense texture of literary and historical allusion, and a naïve or popular readership that does not get all that, that identifies with the characters and reads for the plot. Crucially, however, this distinction reflects a rhetorical or temporal difference within the same subjectivity of reading more than it does actual, objectively different audiences. The "naïve reader" is a figure projected by these texts for our own indulgence, an aspect of ourselves, as we are doubled and divided between mental states of enlightened freedom and a primitive, irrational bondage. This structural doubling and division of the reader within the work of fiction necessarily destabilizes a specific ideological content, as Scott's reception history shows.[40]

Contemporary accounts of George IV's visit invoke Scott himself as the authentic presence in the scene: the Author of *Waverley*, whose works constitute Scotland's genuine and lasting "national monument." Scott was the sovereign's true shadow in a modern, postabsolutist, and postnational age, poised equivocally between competing fictions of democracy and legitimacy—insofar as he was sovereignty's author too.[41] The frontispiece of Robert Chambers's *Illustrations of the Author of Waverley* (Figure 2) follows Scott's own self-representation, in the novel prefaces of the early 1820s, of "the Eidolon, or representative vision, of the AUTHOR OF WAVERLEY," a figure as "closely veiled and wimpled" as the hermaphrodite Nature of Spenser's *Mutabilitie* Cantoes.[42] The difference between this veiled eidolon and its eighteenth-century precursors lies in the allusion to a celebrity whose identity has already been made public and is now occluded: astute readers might have recognized the bust behind the veil from Sir Henry Raeburn's 1808 portrait of Scott the minstrel, whose signed productions preceded those of the Author of *Waverley*. The "Great Unknown" does not denote, in other words, a merely anonymous persona, a blank, but a known name's public reclamation of private cover—that "lair of the skull"[43] which is the secret site of imagination for author as well as for reader, behind the material apparatus of the production, circulation, and reception of printed books. The veiled eidolon, his anonymity founded on his fame, crucially precedes the modern, Victorian cult of the author, which offers instead a miraculous meta-biographical proliferation of Scott's visage, as though to make up for the years behind the veil.

Jonah Siegel argues that the screen of anonymity covering Scott represented the guarantee of his ultimate, larger-than-biographical presence in a culture steeped in his inventions: heralding a distinctively nineteenth-century rerouting of a threatened originality onto the figure of the artist.[44] What remains obscure is the relationship between the numinous presence of this veiled author and the modern condition of his works in an age of industrial production, grounded upon their own, quasi-automatic fictiveness (those stories that keep on coming), rather than in any organic connection to reality. It is a fictiveness, I have been suggesting, sustained and regulated by the social, consensual medium of a national reading public that recognizes and accepts the currency of fictional conventions, as the stock of an intimate human image—the face behind the veil—we hope may be our own.

Lockhart's authentication of an autobiographical presence in *Redgauntlet* gives body to the phantom of an original presence guaranteed by the veil of anonymity. It helps us read the strategy by which *Redgauntlet* revisits the topoi of Scott's earlier Scottish novels in order to reaffirm, with unprecedented virtuosity, their aesthetic and ideological principles: that history, nationality, and legitimacy are fictional constructions, which we fully possess in knowing them as such. Our recognition of their fictive status authenticates, in other words, our own privileged condition as liberal subjects, who give ourselves willingly to the discipline of illusion. The editorial conclusion of *Redgauntlet* enacts a terminal recession of the narrative into the condition of fiction, which it represents, hauntingly, as an essence of storytelling that at once precedes and outlasts the novelistic. Dr Dryasdust quotes one of his oral sources: "'Willie, and a friend he had, they called Robin the Rambler, gae them warning, by playing tunes such as, "the Campbells are coming," and the like, whereby they got timeous warning to take the wing.' I need not point out to your acuteness [*adds Dryasdust*] that this seems to refer to some inaccurate account of the transactions in which you seem so much interested" (379). Oral tradition vindicates itself with this "inaccurate account," in which the feudal heir is absorbed into the Burnsian persona of "Rob the Rambler," instead of joining modern civil society, and popular minstrelsy comes to the rescue of the Jacobite conspirators. For rather than an "inaccurate account" this is surely a variant, a distinctive feature of oral tradition. Roberto Calasso makes a distinction between myth, kept alive in a culture by the proliferation of "variants," and "the novel, *a narrative deprived of variants*," which "attempts to recover them by making the single text to which it is entrusted more dense, more detailed"—the familiar novelistic effects of heteroglossia, a referentially saturated social and historical mimesis, and so on.[45] *Redgauntlet* ends with a glimpse of narrative paradise in the dissolution—the release—of its characters and plots into the unreliable but also, therefore, unconditional realm of popular tradition, which represents not so much an earlier historical stage as a pure, frictionless economy of storytelling, endowing the printed trace with a marvelous buoyancy. The novel draws upon this economy to entertain the very possibilities it is ostensibly, programmatically, shutting down; or rather, its pages provide the only place where we may catch the echoes and shadows of those possibilities, not so much shut down as subject to perpetual deferral. This at once melancholic and utopian domain is modern rather than ancient, in that it corresponds to the perpetual, profit-coining circulation of Scott's own tales in a culture (a reading public) that they themselves constitute: fiction as inexhaustible surplus, cultural production as the redemptive double of an industrial political economy.

Such a conclusion is quite remote from that of *The Private Memoirs and Confessions of a Justified Sinner*, which leaves its reader with a baffling dissolution into the terminal literary condition not of fiction as a transfigured mode of production but of textuality, troped as a negative production of waste matter. Robert Wringhim, the Justified Sinner, is unable to inhabit history as though it were a fiction. He is possessed by fanaticism, Scott's (Humean) term for a fatal relation to history unmediated by aesthetic reflection. Robert is raised by a Calvinist stepfather whose authoritarian interpretation of the Word yields to the more thoroughly despotic and phantasmatic patronage of the Devil himself, called Gil-Martin. Robert's sense of his identity, his destiny, is that above all it is written down: "written in the book of life" (69). In the antinarrative structure of predestinarian theology beginnings and ends are already scripted, finished, closed: "I was now a justified person, adopted among the number of God's children—my name written in the Lamb's book of life, and . . . no bypast transgression, nor any future act of my own, or of any other man, could be instrumental in altering the decree" (79). No variants are possible here.[46]

We are not surprised to learn that Gil-Martin is a reader of the book—the text of which provokes extraordinary sensations irrespective of its legibility: "I came up to him and addressed him, but he was so intent on his book, that, though I spoke, he lifted not his eyes. I looked on the book also, and still it seemed a Bible, having columns, chapters, and verses; but it was in a language of which I was wholly ignorant, and all intersected with red lines, and verses. A sensation resembling a stroke of electricity came over me, on first casting my eyes on that mysterious book, and I stood motionless" (85). Indeed illegibility is the point—the effect of writing viewed from outside itself. The electric shock Wringhim feels is the charge of an abstract textuality, a printed sign-system unattached to human hand or voice. The Devil's book is a text for one reader only—it does not circulate in an exchange economy, it does not constitute a "culture." It is as though, in a blinding glimpse, Hogg's novel divines its own fate: a book of the damned, outcast from literary tradition, unreadable until an appropriately infernal later century.

Hogg figures the condition of an unregenerate, material textuality through tropes of doubling and splitting that proliferate beyond their narrative or even allegorical occasion. In detecting these figural patterns—that is, in remarking certain details, repetitions, and connections—the reader becomes aware, foremost, of the presence of the pattern itself: the wovenness of Hogg's fiction, the status of the *Confessions of a Justified Sinner* as a text. One of the more intricate of these figural patterns plays upon the etymon *texere* (to weave); a more concise example of this textual work of language, producing its meanings by doubling and splitting, is the apparently gratuitous generation of the devil's name, Gil-Martin, out of the name of Wringhim's schoolboy nemesis, M'Gill.[47] At the purely lexical level the logic rehearses the narrative doubling of the antagonistic brothers (Robert and George) within the divided family, followed by the phantasmal appearance of Robert's "second self," Gil-Martin.

Robert's relationship to Gil-Martin, virtuoso of the "cameleon art of changing...appearance" (86), articulates a diabolical parody of the Scottish Enlightenment technique of modern subject formation through imaginary sympathetic exchange. In Gil-Martin's own account, it is a practice at once natural and hyperdisciplinary:

> "My countenance changes with my studies and sensations," said he. "It is a natural peculiarity in me, over which I have not full control. If I contemplate a man's features seriously, mine own gradually assume the very same appearance and character. And what is more, by contemplating a face minutely, I not only attain the same likeness, but, with the likeness, I attain the very same ideas as well as the same mode of arranging them, so that, you see, by looking at a person attentively, I by degrees assume his likeness, and by assuming his likeness I attain to the possession of his most secret thoughts." (86)

Gil-Martin's confession, relentlessly parsing the Smithian logic of sympathy, exposes its textual basis as well as a political fantasy of Enlightenment despotism. As it converts depth to surface, likeness to sameness, inside to outside, subject to object in the impulse to hermeneutic mastery, his act of reading obliterates the ontological distinctions that the liberal programs of literacy are invoked to secure.

Alongside the misery of the sinner's end, Hogg's authenticity effects iterate, then, not the fictional status of what we have been reading—the editor complains that he cannot understand whether this is a fable, an allegory, the ravings of a lunatic, or some other kind of writing (165, 174–75)—but its material condition as a text. With the scenario of a document unearthed from a grave, Hogg literalizes the central metaphor of modern antiquarian romance revival: the recovery of "remains," "reliques," or "fragments" of a departed, organic culture. Scott provides a striking example in the Dedicatory Epistle to *Ivanhoe*, where (alluding to the episode of the witch Erichtho in Lucan's *Pharsalia*) he compares the Scottish historical novelist's task to the necromancer's reanimation of mangled corpses on a battlefield (15).[48] In Hogg's exhumation scene, the dead may be raised only in a revoltingly literal sense: "There was one thing I could not help remarking, that in the inside of one of the shoes there was a layer of cow's dung, about one eighth of an inch thick, and in the hollow of the sole fully one fourth of an inch. It was firm, green, and fresh; and proved that he had been working in a byre" (172). The sinner's body, reduced to a lower half that dissolves into slime, and its accessory, the manuscript "wrapped so close together, and so damp, rotten, and yellow, that it seemed one solid piece" (173), partake metaphorically as well as metonymically of that dung. The Calvinist doctrinal scheme invoked in the novel casts body and text as an excremental residue, like the reprobate sinner to whom they belong, like the material world itself: God's waste products.

Confessions of a Justified Sinner predicts its own condition as an outcast text, not to be brought to life in a reader's imagination, circulated in a market, or perpetuated in a tradition, as a fierce gloss upon Hogg's failure to imitate Scott's career as a rich and distinguished author of national historical romances. Alert to this biographical resonance, commentators have nevertheless underestimated the reach of the skeptical abyss opened at the end of the novel, by implying a secure foundation in the reader's act of interpretation, or else in the traditional popular community of the author's origins.[49] But the abyss swallows author and reader as well as narrator and editor. We too, like "James Hogg," find ourselves doubled and split, without the Smithian consolation of being drafted into a society—at any rate, until the twentieth century, when the canonization of accursed books has brought *Confessions of a Justified Sinner* to a public after all.[50] We might say that Hogg's novel adumbrates a condition "outside literature"—a perspective from which literature itself becomes visible as a closed cultural system, a set of stratifying social and economic practices, a material product and "remains." But the conditions of this knowledge remain within the operations and devices of literacy itself, and of the readerly subjectivity produced by it, revolving obsessively about the figures of its own production.

Fiction, for Scott, reaffirms an authentic domain of the social and ordinary, since fiction is the medium—the imaginary commerce—through which "common life" sustains and reproduces itself. Textuality, for Hogg, represents a lethal alienation from common life in its original condition of a traditional community, which, as the medium of natural belief, cannot be recovered in the commodity form of a fiction. We are left with the brilliant paradox of a novel that articulates the radical failure of its author's career, project, and, indeed, cultural identity: yet in the mode of a terse, defiant assertion of aesthetic strength.

Notes

1   James Hogg, *The Private Memoirs and Confessions of a Justified Sinner*, ed. P. D. Garside, with an afterword by Ian Campbell (Edinburgh: Edinburgh University Press, 2001), 165.

2   [James Hogg], "A Scots Mummy," *Blackwood's Edinburgh Magazine* 14 (August 1823): 188–90.

3   See P. D. Garside's introduction, in Hogg, *Confessions of a Justified Sinner*, lxvi–lxviii.

4   Catherine Gallagher, *Nobody's Story: The Vanishing Acts of Women Writers in the Marketplace 1670–1820* (Berkeley: University of California Press, 1994); Ina Ferris, *The Achievement of Literary Authority: Gender, History, and the Waverley Novels* (Ithaca: Cornell University Press, 1991), 19–29; Jane Millgate, *Walter Scott: The Making of the Novelist* (Edinburgh: Edinburgh University Press, 1984), 107.

5   See Mark Schoenfield, "Butchering James Hogg: Romantic Identity in the Magazine Market," in *At the Limits of Romanticism: Essays in Cultural, Feminist and Materialist Criticism*, ed. Mary Favret and Nicola Watson (Bloomington: Indiana University Press, 1994), 207–24; J. H. Alexander, "Hogg in the *Noctes Ambrosianae*," *Studies in Hogg and His World* 4 (1993): 37–47.

6   Susan Stewart, *Crimes of Writing: Problems in the Containment of Representation* (Durham: Duke University Press, 1994), 35.

7   Ibid., 35–38, 68–74, 102–31.

8   In the most detailed and perceptive discussion extant, Fiona Robertson reads Scott's editorial apparatus as a Gothic convention deployed for a skeptical destabilization of the historicist certainties it ostensibly serves. "Fictions of Authenticity: The Frame Narratives and Notes of the Waverley Novels," in *Legitimate Histories: Scott, Gothic, and the Authorities of Fiction* (Oxford: Clarendon Press, 1994), 117–60. Noting the distinction between the ludic first-edition apparatus and the more sober antiquarian and personal apparatus to the late "Magnum Opus" edition, Robertson argues nevertheless that "the paratexts of the Magnum Opus continue rather than expiate the 'liberties' taken under the guise of anonymity in the first editions" (160).

9   Walter Scott, *Redgauntlet: A Tale of the Eighteenth Century*, ed. G. A. M. Wood with David Hewitt (Edinburgh: Edinburgh University Press, 1997).

10 For example, Magdalene Redekop, "Beyond Closure: Buried Alive with Hogg's *Justified Sinner*," *ELH* 52.1 (Spring 1985): 159–84; James Kerr, *Fiction against History: Scott As Story-Teller* (Cambridge: Cambridge University Press, 1989), 102–23.

11 Robertson, *Legitimate Histories*, 248.

12 See the editorial commentaries by G. A. M. Wood (in Scott, *Redgauntlet*, 381–83) and P. D. Garside (in Hogg, *Confessions of a Justified Sinner*, lv–lxvi).

13 Jerome McGann, "Walter Scott's Romantic Postmodernity," in *Scotland and the Borders*

of Romanticism, ed. Leith Davis, Ian Duncan, Janet Sorensen (Cambridge: Cambridge University Press, forthcoming).

14 See Gallagher, *Nobody's Story*, 96–131.

15 James Chandler, *England in 1819: The Politics of Literary Culture and the Case of Romantic Historicism* (Chicago: University of Chicago Press, 1998), 105–9, 127–35.

16 Jerome Christensen, *Romanticism at the End of History* (Baltimore: The Johns Hopkins University Press, 2000), 10–13.

17 Alexander Welsh, *The Hero of the Waverley Novels: With New Essays on Scott* (Princeton: Princeton University Press, 1992), 191–96; Ian Duncan, *Modern Romance and Transformations of the Novel: The Gothic, Scott, Dickens* (Cambridge: Cambridge University Press, 1992), 51–54, 87–92.

18 Walter Scott, *Ivanhoe*, ed. Ian Duncan (Oxford: Oxford University Press, 1996).

19 See, for example, H. B. De Groot, "Fiction and History: The Case of Redgauntlet," in *Scott in Carnival: Selected Papers from the Fourth International Scott Conference, Edinburgh, 1991*, ed. J. H. Alexander and David Hewitt (Aberdeen: Association for Scottish Literary Studies, 1993), 358–69; Homer O. Brown, *Institutions of the English Novel: From Defoe to Scott* (Philadelphia: University of Pennsylvania Press, 1997), 145–70.

20 John Gibson Lockhart, *The Life of Sir Walter Scott, Bart* (London: A. and C. Black, 1896).

21 Jane Millgate, *Scott's Last Edition: A Study in Publishing History* (Edinburgh: Edinburgh University Press, 1987), 111–14.

22 Lockhart, *Life of Sir Walter Scott*, 514.

23 Miguel de Cervantes Saavedra, *Don Quixote*, trans. Walter Starkie (New York: New American Library, 1964).

24 See Katie Trumpener, *Bardic Nationalism: The Romantic Novel and the British Empire* (Princeton: Princeton University Press, 1997), 109–12.

25 I borrow the term *authenticity effect* from James Buzard (*The Beaten Track: European Tourism, Literature, and the Ways to "Culture," 1800–1918* [Oxford: Oxford University Press, 1993], 172–92), who adapts it from Roland Barthes's famous *reality effect*.

26 Cervantes, *Don Quixote*, 404; Tobias Smollett, *The Expedition of Humphry Clinker*, ed. James L. Thorson (New York: Norton, 1983), 118, 230–32.

27 Samuel Johnson and James Boswell, *"A Journey to the Western Islands of Scotland" and "The Journal of a Tour to the Hebrides,"* ed. Peter Levi (Harmondsworth: Penguin, 1984), 118–19. See Trumpener, *Bardic Nationalism*, 74–76; Penny Fielding, *Writing and Orality: Nationality, Culture, and Nineteenth-Century Scottish Fiction* (Oxford: Oxford University Press, 1996), 9–10.

28 Clifford Siskin, *The Work of Writing: Literature and Social Change in Britain, 1700–1830* (Baltimore: The Johns Hopkins University Press, 1998), 172–90; Friedrich A. Kittler, *Discourse Networks 1800/1900*, trans. M. Metteer, with C. Cullens (Stanford: Stanford University Press, 1990).

29 Duncan, *Modern Romance*, 51–105; Deidre Lynch, "Gothic Libraries and National Subjects," *Studies in Romanticism* 40.1 (Spring 2001): 29–48.

30 On the leading part played by eighteenth-century Scots writers and intellectuals in the disciplinary invention of English literature and in its standardization as a national lan-

guage, see Robert Crawford, ed., *The Scottish Invention of English Literature* (Cambridge: Cambridge University Press, 1998); Janet Sorensen, *The Grammar of Empire in Eighteenth-Century British Writing* (Cambridge: Cambridge University Press, 2000); Siskin, *Work of Writing*, 79–94.

31 Fielding, *Writing and Orality*, 3–42; Fielding, "Writing at the North: Rhetoric and Dialect in Eighteenth-Century Scotland," *The Eighteenth Century* 39.1 (1998): 25–43.

32 Stewart, *Crimes of Writing*, 102–31.

33 Johnson and Boswell, *"A Journey to the Western Islands,"* 118.

34 Robertson, *Legitimate Histories*, 120.

35 For a richly detailed account of Hume's importance for "Romantic" traditions of Scottish and American writing, see Susan Manning, *Fragments of Union: Making Connections in Scottish and American Writing* (Houndsmills: Palgrave, 2002), especially 34–40. The received history of ideas, according to which Thomas Reid's "common sense" philosophy eclipsed Hume in Scotland until the twentieth century, is not entirely accurate: a controversial revival of Hume, unsettling Reid's supposed refutation of him, took place in Scotland between about 1805 and 1820, promoted by Thomas Brown, Dugald Stewart's successor in the Edinburgh Chair of Moral Philosophy. The theme of the controversy—the status of belief and the vexed relation between truth and fiction—directs us to the theoretical blueprint for Scott's combination of romance and history in Hume's *Treatise of Human Nature*.

36 Stephen Arata, "Scott's Pageants: The Example of *Kenilworth*," *Studies in Romanticism* 40.1 (Spring 2001): 99–107; Miranda Burgess, *British Fiction and the Production of Social Order, 1740–1830* (Cambridge: Cambridge University Press, 2000), 186–234; Cairns Craig, "Scott Stages the Nation," *Studies in Romanticism* 40.1 (Spring 2001): 13–28; Ian Duncan, "Edinburgh, Capital of the Nineteenth Century," in *Romantic Metropolis: Cultural Productions of the City 1770–1850*, ed. James Chandler and Kevin Gilmartin (Cambridge: Cambridge University Press, 2002).

37 Slavoj Žižek, *Tarrying with the Negative: Kant, Hegel, and the Critique of Ideology* (Durham: Duke University Press, 1993), 230.

38 See Benedict Anderson, *Imagined Communities: Reflections on the Origin and Spread of Nationalism* (London: Verso, 1983); Jon Klancher, *The Making of English Reading Audiences, 1790–1832* (Madison: University of Wisconsin Press, 1987).

39 See Harriet Martineau, *Tait's Edinburgh Magazine*, January 2, 1833, 445–60; Siskin, *Work of Writing*, 155–71.

40 On Scott and liberalism, see David Kaufmann, *The Business of Common Life: Novels and Classical Economics between Revolution and Reform* (Baltimore: The Johns Hopkins University Press, 1995), 93–137; Christensen, *Romanticism at the End of History*, 153–75. For suggestive remarks on *Redgauntlet* and state formation, see Robert P. Irvine, *Enlightenment and Romance: Gender and Agency in Smollet and Scott* (Bern: Peter Lang, 2000), 214–15; Yoon Sun Lee, "Giants in the North: *Douglas*, the Scottish Enlightenment, and Scott's *Redgauntlet*," *Studies in Romanticism* 40.1 (Spring 2001): 120.

41 See Duncan, "Edinburgh."

42 Sir Walter Scott, *The Fortunes of Nigel* (London: A. and C. Black, 1893), xv–xvi.

43 Anderson, *Imagined Communities*, 35.

44 Jonah Siegel, *Desire and Excess: The Nineteenth-Century Culture of Art* (Princeton: Princeton University Press, 2000), 93–97.

45 Roberto Calasso, *The Marriage of Cadmus and Harmony* (New York: Knopf, 1993), 281.

46 David Groves (in *James Hogg: The Growth of a Writer* [Edinburgh: Scottish Academic Press, 1988], 115) argues that the print-culture pun on "justified" is fully intended.

47 Gil-Martin is Gaelic for "fox"—the trickster-figure of Highland oral tradition. Hogg, *Confessions of a Justified Sinner*, 226.

48 See also Chandler, *England in 1819*, 168–71.

49 Gary Kelly, *English Fiction of the Romantic Period 1789–1830* (London: Longman, 1989), 261–73.

50 See Ian Campbell, "Afterword: Literary Criticism and *Confessions of a Justified Sinner*," in Hogg, *Confessions of a Justified Sinner*, 177–94.

Celeste Langan

Pathologies of Communication from Coleridge to Schreber

> As if the passive page of a book, by having an epigram or doggrel tale impressed on it, instantly assumed at once loco-motive power and a sort of ubiquity, so as to flutter and buzz in the ear of the public to the sore annoyance of the said mysterious personage.
> — S. T. Coleridge, *Biographia Literaria*

> As if we don't, all of us, all the time, have visions, as if we are never in the grip of little phrases that pop into our heads.
> — Jacques Lacan, *Third Seminar: The Psychoses*

Coleridge has for so long been charged with plagiarizing seminal texts of German philosophy that it is perhaps time to return the favor, and to contend that a book written some one hundred years after the second part of *Christabel* was composed—Daniel Paul Schreber's *Memoirs of My Nervous Illness*—is merely an extended prose footnote to Coleridge's poem.[1] Or rather, I should say, it might be annexed to *Christabel* in fulfillment of Coleridge's own intention to publish the poem "with two Essays annexed to it, on the Praeternatural—and on Metre."[2] Think of those "preternatural" issues and themes that have drawn critical attention in commentary on

The *South Atlantic Quarterly* 102:1, Winter 2003.
Copyright © 2003 by Duke University Press.

Christabel—sounds and visions of dubious origin, spiritual possession, a family curse, and, of course, a scene of transgender or homosexual seduction—and we may find their equivalent in Schreber's *Memoirs*.[3] Schreber, a distinguished German judge whose descent into psychosis is first marked by a feeling—ambiguous product of a dream or waking thought—that "it really must be rather pleasant to be a woman succumbing to intercourse" (46), develops the auditory and visual hallucinations of a paranoid schizophrenic. He conjectures that his "communication with supernatural powers," which began the day his psychiatrist, Professor Flechsig, having attempted to take spiritual possession of Schreber's soul, could no longer "look me straight in the eye" (53) (when he looked at him, so to say, askance),[4] is a consequence of a family curse: "Something had happened perhaps between earlier generations of the Schreber and Flechsig families which amounted to soul murder" (34).[5] So vivid are his hallucinations or communications that he becomes temporarily convinced that those around him are not "real human beings" but what he calls "fleeting-improvised-men" (117). His supernatural communications, moreover, take a peculiar form: voices force him to repeat their speeches, and God, not understanding the nature of human thought (having had contact only with dreamers and corpses) assumes that everything Schreber thus recites represents his own thoughts. Finally, he reports the gradual degeneration of the language of the voices into a virtual hiss—a hiss produced by what he calls "miracled birds." The strategies he develops to drown out this unwelcome noise include everything we might think of as referenced in *Christabel*'s conclusion.

> Perhaps 'tis pretty to force together
> Words so all unlike each other;
> To mutter and mock a broken charm,
> To dally with wrong that does no harm.
> Perhaps 'tis tender too and pretty
> At each wild word to feel within
> A sweet recoil of love and pity (666–72).[6]

Schreber reports distracting the birds with slant rhymes, using a metronome, and disrupting their meaningless "phrases learnt by rote" with an interjective bellow. He even attempts to counter their incessant regularity homeopathically by silently reciting ballads by Schiller and Goethe, among others, remarking that "their value as poetry naturally does not matter; however insignificant the rhymes, even obscene verses are worth their weight in gold compared to the terrible nonsense my nerves are otherwise forced to listen to" (203).

But what leads me to propose that we read the *Memoirs* in place of the two projected essays on the preternatural and meter is something more than this series, nearly systematic, of formal and thematic resonances.[7] Nor is it merely the fact that Romantic poetry—especially Byron's *Manfred*—seems to have provided Schreber with a vocabulary and an imaginary.[8] Rather, what interests me most about Schreber's account is that, except for the occasional bellow, the verbal and metrical contestations he describes do not belong to the dimension of speech. For Schreber, the preternatural communications out of which auditory and visual hallucinations emerge take place only in language—or in that peculiar medium of information structured enough like language that Schreber identifies it as a *"nerve-language."* What interests me, in short, is that Schreber's account of nerve-language is at once metrical and preternatural, in that it forms no part of "real" utterance.

For this reason, I believe that Schreber's identification of "nerve-language" with mental representation can help to clarify what is important in Coleridge's dispute with Wordsworth over the nature of poetic language. In the *Biographia*, Coleridge objects to what he describes as "an equivocation in the use of the word 'real'" in Wordsworth's account of the "real language of men."[9] Whereas Wordsworth implies that "the best objects from which the best part of language is originally derived" are "objects" in the conventional, external or referential sense, Coleridge insists that "the best part of human language, properly so called, is derived from reflection on the acts of the mind itself" (2:54). The "best part of language," in other words, is derived from thought, not from speech. He distinguishes between "discriminating sounds"—a phonemic organization of language—and this language of reflection: "It is more than probable, that many classes of the brute creation possess discriminating sounds, by which they can convey to each other notices of such objects as concern their food, shelter, or safety. Yet we hesitate to call the aggregate of such sounds a language, other than metaphorically."[10] In the unfinished *Logic*, Coleridge describes the gradual process by which a subject of language moves from "the fondness of children for rhymes" to an understanding of "the mental elements or *factors* of likeness"; an "accidence," or principles of grammar determining inflections of words, replaces an alphabet.[11] Coleridge's distinction between "sounds" and "the forms of the human mind" is clearly relevant to understand the poetic theory represented in *Christabel*, since the poem will contrast the sounds of animals—as well as the sounds of mechanisms—to the interior or mental speech of its human characters. This contrast, which Schreber's *Memoirs* also develops, helps to remind us of the larger context within which to understand the deformations of identity that both writers explore. Schreber's "unmanning," like the processes by which Geraldine and Christabel become "other," takes place *in language*. And if the "animal sounds" by which speech mediates thought suggest one form of unmanning, the forms of grammar will be seen to threaten another: the automaton. The techniques Schreber develops to resist unmanning (not simply feminization, but also bestialization and automation) are already anticipated in *Christabel*: faltering, altered, and hollow voices; whispering tongues, muttered words, and choked cries. Concentrating on the very "performance phenomena" that linguists regard as irrelevant to the question of whether a given sentence is "speakable" or "unspeakable," Coleridge derives the "best part of language"—the language of poetry—from incompetencies and pathologies of communication, because his purpose is to detach poetry from the instrumental purposes associated with speech.[12]

As a "pathological" instance of Coleridge's poetic theory, Schreber's *Memoirs* can be seen as an extended "reflection on the acts of the mind itself" that helps to establish the central premises of my argument. First, contrary to prevailing opinion that Romantic ballad experiments derive from print culture's nostalgia for orality, we witness in poems like *Christabel* the development of a kind of early information theory, a poetry concerned with probabilities rather than meanings or even affects. Reading *Christabel* in the context of the *Biographia Literaria*, which Coleridge was writing as he finally ushered his poem into print, we can see in the poem a "metrical experiment" designed to test the difference between mechanical association and genuine thought. Second, Schreber's difficulty in distinguishing between what is spoken and what is merely heard—what some would describe as his hallucinations—is, in the context of his habit of reciting ballads "silently," an unusually clarifying account of what Lacan calls "the discourse of the Other": this discourse is a *metrical* language.[13] Third, there is an underexamined equivalency between poetry and what can be described as forms of speech pathology. Poetry, as it is practiced by Coleridge and Schreber, is the very opposite of "free" speech. As conditions of constraint, both silence and stuttering (and other forms of disfluency) foreground this fact.

Linking poetry and stuttering—described by one nineteenth-century text as "frequent repetitions of initial or other elementary sounds"—may be unusual, but it is not unjustified.[14] In both, the foregrounding of sound—for example, the way in which stuttering draws attention to the phonological code, as static or "snow" reminds us that the sounds and sights we receive over the airwaves are not unmediated—threatens to overwhelm what we call the "sense." Similarly, one is as likely to notice figures of speech, neologisms, or odd locutions in the speech of stutterers as one is to find them in poems, because some stutterers, anticipating difficulty of articulation, will often use a substitute expression—for example, "a month before the month of May" instead of April (the reference is to *Christabel*, l. 21). These similarities are usually less noted than the obvious opposition that exists between conceptions of poetry as unusually eloquent speech and stuttering as a vocal defect. For we regard the techniques of the poet—sound patterns that mark or equivocate a syntactic turn or phrasal unit, parenthetical remarks, and other filled pauses, and "significantly greater variability of the timing between stressed syllables"—as acts of will and art, whereas the same techniques in the stutterer happen, we may assume from the pained expressions that sometimes accompany attempts at articulation, either against the will or as a consequence of the failure of the will adequately to dominate the mechanisms of phonation and articulation to achieve a communicative intent.[15]

In this respect, we might be said to assume that stuttering is "unmanly," in the sense Coleridge uses that word to mark the difference between poetry and prose: "The true question must be . . . and vice versa, whether in the language of a serious poem there may not be an arrangement both of words and sentences, and a use and selection of (what are called) *figures of speech*, both as to their kinds, their frequency, and their occasion, which on a subject of equal weight would be vicious and alien in correct and *manly* prose. I contend, that in both cases this unfitness of each for the place of the other frequently will and ought to exist" (*Biographia*, 2:64; my emphasis on "manly"). Of course, Coleridge rightly distinguishes the language of conversation—what speech pathologists and linguists call "free speech" situations—from that of prose; prose differs from conversation, he says, "as reading ought to differ from talking (2:60–61). The difference is a stylistic one, there being a greater "*surview*," or prospectiveness of thought, in writing. But in elaborating the distinction between poetry and prose, he clearly identifies poetry as a form of writing and therefore denies the adequacy of regarding poetry as "eloquent speech." If the language of a serious poem transmits figures of speech with greater frequency, that is a sign of its distance from, rather than proximity to, speech. If prose differs from conversation "as reading ought to differ from talking," poetry differs from prose by an even more greatly heightened stylization. "The existence of *prosaisms*, and that they detract from the merit of a poem, *must* at length be conceded, when a number of successive lines can be rendered, *even to the most delicate ear*, unrecognizable as verse, or as having even been intended for verse, simply by transcribing them as prose" (2:79; my emphasis on "even to the most delicate ear").

Coleridge differs from Wordsworth most sharply by describing these stylizations as marking not the return of poetry to the orality of conversation but its greater separation from it. Consider the terms in which Coleridge criticizes the attempt of rationalist educators to "cure" children of their habit of "*singing*" when reading aloud:

> In order to cure them of *singing*, as it is called . . . the child is made to repeat the words with his eye from off the book; and then indeed, his tones resemble talking, as far as his fears, tears, and trembling will permit. But as soon as the eye is again directed to the printed page, the spell begins anew; for an instinctive sense tells the child's feelings, that to utter its own momentary thoughts, and to recite the written thoughts of another . . . are two widely different things; and . . . so must justify different modes of enunciation. (2:61)

"Singing" here is a mode of recitation—and let us hear "citation" in that word—that works to distinguish reading aloud from speaking one's own thoughts. The rationalist educator regards singsong recitation as inappropriately imposing an automatic rhythm on prose periods but fails to recognize the greater automatism of becoming a mere conduit of another's words. Singing—the imposition of metricality here—is regarded by Coleridge as an attempt to discriminate between thought and language. Metricality represents the capacity of the subject to speak through language, rather than to be reduced to a transparent medium of language. In effect, one might say, this "singing" acts as a mark of quotation.

But if a singsong recitation registers the difference between one's own thoughts and the language of prose, we are therefore hard-pressed to imagine what mode of enunciation might adequately distinguish one's own momentary thoughts from the already-metrical language of the poem. By what means is one to put quotation marks around a poem? Perhaps the difficulty of this task is the reason the language of the poem so often seems to possess its reciters, and to have the effect, among others, of sometimes liberating stutterers from difficulties they encounter in articulation. This effect alone is enough to suggest that it is not speech that poetry represents. If the effect of singing is to derealize, and so to distinguish prose from conversation, and it is the delicate ear that distinguishes between poetry and prose, perhaps we are justified in inferring that the mode of enunciation most appropriate to reading poetry is a silent one—a delicate operation scarcely distinguishable from thought itself.

To recognize that Coleridge's delicate ear may have as little to do with organs of sensation as what Schreber calls his "mind's eye," it might be helpful to remind ourselves that the *Biographia* turns on Coleridge's rejection of materialist models of association that condemn us at once to "the despotism of outward impressions, and that of senseless and passive memory" (1:111). We may notice in this context that, despite his focus on meter as the distinctive characteristic of poetry, and general observations about the desirability of a modulation of meter in relation to the sense, Coleridge has very little to say about rhythm; this despite the fact that, at the same time that Coleridge was composing *Christabel* and prior to the publication of the *Biographia*, his erstwhile friend and correspondent John Thelwall was developing a theory of English *rhythmus* in conjunction with his speech-therapy practice. Thelwall defined "rhythmus" as

> those elementary principles, out of which arise—the facilities and harmonies of oral utterance: principles! from the neglect, the violation, or the ignorance of which, result almost all the complicated varieties of difficulty, obstruction and imperfection, in the exercise of that faculty . . . principles! which may, therefore, at the same time, loose the tongue of the stammerer, and enable the literary student to command, and the critic to comprehend, with certainty, the genuine sources of grace and mellifluence—
>
> Untwisting all the chains that ty/ The hidden soul of harmony.[16]

In his 1796 letters to Coleridge, Thelwall accuses Coleridge of too often violating these principles, criticizing "the affectation that blurs almost every one of your poems — I mean the frequent accent upon adjectives and weak words." His 1810 treatise on English prosody attributes such errors to "the habits of silent study, and silent composition, to which the literati of modern times (who know their own language only by the eye) are almost universally devoted" (*Letter to Henry Cline*, 6–7). In terms that I hope to make relevant to the two central scenes of *Christabel* (in which what is seen defies articulation), Thelwall laments the proliferation of "so many copies of verses, that look smooth and pretty upon paper, [but] are yet revolting to the ear" and that "discourage, by their ear-cracking harshness, every attempt of the reader to give them vocal utterance" (7). The suggestion here is that modern poetry represents a kind of speech pathology, being written in a language, to borrow Schreber's phrase, "never heard uttered by a human being." Elsewhere, Thelwall likewise complains that "writers sometimes present combinations to the eye, which no effort of human organs can present, with distinct and intelligible articulation," because they have failed to consider "what letters are, of necessity, *absolutely mute*."[17]

Thelwall's treatise is actually an account of his success in curing cases of stuttering, in which he anticipates many contemporary therapies such as the use of a metronome to slow down articulation, as well as contemporary research into the possibility that stuttering is induced by (and curiously, can sometimes be offset by) a "delayed auditory feedback" in hearing oneself speak. (Stuttering often decreases when speakers cannot hear themselves — as well as when they sing.) The link Thelwall develops between the silent reading of the poet and the disjunction between inner and outer speech of the stutterer is, further, tied to mental disorder, as a disease of the will.

> Every stammerer, stutterer, throttler, constipator, involuntarily confounded, and unconscious reiterator of the elements of speech (whatever attainments or failures he may, in other respects, possess) is *partially*, and to a certain extent, either idiotic, or deranged: for what but derangement can it be called, to be constantly doing a thousand things that we neither intend to do, nor are conscious of doing? nay, are the very reverse of our intention! What, but a species of idiotcy, is it, to be ignorant of the means by which the will is to influence the simplest organs of volition, and (without excuse of palsy, stricture, or organic privation), to be unable to move a lip, a tongue, or jaw? . . . to clinch

the teeth, when we are bade to open the mouth! *And roll the eyes, when we ought to move the lips! (Introductory Discourse,* 68; my emphasis)

Of course it may strain credulity to suggest that this passage, which Coleridge is unlikely ever to have read, could (a) provide a useful gloss on the two scenes of Geraldine's and of Christabel's derangement, or (b) describe the process of silent reading (to roll the eyes across the page; to exercise the power of surview, as it were). But does not the ghost of Coleridge seem to speak through Thelwall's text when the latter represents himself as unwilling to "go to the lengths I have heard ascribed to Professor Kant—I do not mean to say—that 'Speech is a faculty purely mental; and that a man might become an orator, tho he had neither teeth nor tongue, by the mere action of the mind'" (77)? And is it not possible that Coleridge was willing to go even further than Kant, and to "mean to say" that poetry, that so-called form of speech that, like stuttering, draws most attention to phonation and articulation, is "purely mental"?

≡≡≡

In the preface to *Christabel,* Coleridge asserts he has developed a "new principle" of meter. Yet, for all the critical commentary the poem has generated, virtually no critic—not even those who claim to give the poem formal consideration (not Marjorie Levinson in the *Romantic Fragment Poem,* not Susan Wolfson in *Formal Charges*)—has yet offered to explain what its formal experiment might have to do with its subject matter: hallucination, linguistic automatism and disfluency, semantic animal speech, and the metronomic regularity of clocks and bells (Margaret Russett's forthcoming essay on *Christabel,* copyright, and the invention [what I would call hallucination] of "voice" is a brilliant exception).[18] As this (re)description of *Christabel*'s narrative content might suggest, I read the poem's pronounced interest in echo and vibration as an experiment designed to test Coleridge's belief in the "voluntary" and creative power of imagination against the lingering influence of materialist (associationist) theories of subjectivity. We know from information theory that "we hear a signal against a background of noise . . . which may vary in quality from the crackling of static to a steady hiss."[19] In *Christabel,* as in Schreber's *Memoirs,* our attention tends to focus on a signal, sign, or figure of ambiguous sexuality or ambiguous sexual embrace. But unless we attend to the "noisy" conditions of this image's reception, we will not recognize the important lesson of both texts: that the mind "leaps" to produce meaning from mere information. As Noam Chomsky remarked of the "intuitive leap" of scientific discovery, "the interval in which discovery occurs remains a blank about which nothing can be said."[20] The fact that in both Coleridge's poem and Schreber's memoir the "leap" is from one medium to another—in *Christabel*, the signal frequencies of accentual meter produce a "sight"; in the *Memoirs*, (metrical) excitement of the nervous system produces a sex change—suggests how little either writer regards the poetic medium as a medium of articulated *speech*.

What is the value of reading the unholy embrace of Geraldine and Christabel—visual or figurative equivalent of the "thoughts so all unlike each other" forced together in the conclusion to part 2—as an intimation of the "information-redundancy ratio" established as the "law" of information theory by Claude Shannon's mathematical theory of communication? According to this law, the possibility of converting information into knowledge depends on the reduction of information by repetition. If you encode English text efficiently to eliminate redundancy, errors are more likely. Redundancy and encoding are techniques with obvious relevance for understanding the difference between poetry and prose; one has only to think of the "efficient" first stanza of Wordsworth's "The Last of the Flock" ("In distant countries I have been, / And yet I have not often seen / A healthy man, a man full grown, / Weep in the public roads alone") as it is "translated" by Coleridge into the language of conversation:

> I am grievously deceived, if the following less *compact* mode of commencing the same tale be not a far more faithful copy. "I have been in many parts far and near, and I don't know that I ever saw before a man crying by himself in the public road; a grown man I mean, that was neither sick nor hurt," &c. &c. (*Biographia* 2:59)

Yet this example controverts our usual assumption—that the rhyming and metrical patterns of poetry offer *greater* redundancy, *less* information, than prose. The constraints of rhyme and meter actually reduce the syntactic probabilities that govern speech. And this reduction in probability, rather than increased efficiency, is the real purpose of Coleridge's metrical experiment: to interrupt automaticity. Unlike the communication channel that pairs syllable and accent as if they were *naturally* linked, Coleridge's "new principle" *uses* accent, that "natural law" that regulates utterance as gravity regulates locomotion, to challenge that law (even as Bard Bracy will suggest that echoes and vibrations can disrupt the "custom and law" that "five and forty beads"—no more, no less—must tell between each stroke, each stress, of the matin bell [348–51]).

To suggest that Coleridge (like Schreber) understands poetry as the rhythm of *thought* is to raise the problem of how any sensory material is translated into "sense," or meaning. Information theory has little to offer in this regard; Shannon's coauthor, William Weaver, says only that "one has the vague feeling that information and meaning may prove to be something like a pair of canonically conjugate variables in quantum theory, they being subject to some joint restriction that condemns a person to the sacrifice of one as he insists on having much of the other." In Coleridge's metrical experiment, well described by Russett as that which "sophisticates the rude accentualism of balladry with a scansion based on variously combined classical feet," the reader is "enjoined to *find* the accentual regularity belied by heterogeneous metrical units." The capacity of any communication channel, we are told, "is to be described not in terms of the number of *symbols* it can transmit, but rather in terms of the *information* it transmits." But information is not meaning; it is uncertainty. "Information is, we must steadily remember, a measure of one's freedom of choice in selecting a message. The greater the freedom of choice, and hence the greater the information, the greater is the uncertainty that the message actually selected is some particular one. Thus greater freedom of choice, greater uncertainty, greater information go hand in hand." The value of *pathologies* of communication— from a "rude accentualism" that varies syllables from seven to twelve, to the sound redundancies and errors of stuttering—is to remind us that thought is in excess of the capacities of speech—that we may *think* that which we are incapable of *saying*. A poetry based on this principle suggests, however, that *language* may nonetheless allow the representation of these unspeakable thoughts.[21]

Silent Speech

As I have said, I am less interested in the thematic continuities between Schreber's *Memoirs* and Coleridge's *Christabel*—though I have several things to say about those continuities—than I am fascinated by the relevance of Schreber's analysis of the medium of his divine communication and the "noise" that interferes with it to the "new metrical principle" that Coleridge illustrates in *Christabel*. Two concepts—both of them self-acknowledged neologisms, themselves produced by the languages they describe—are central to what we may call Schreber's media theory: the "basic language" spoken by God and "learned" by the voices that he hears, and the nerve-language that is, he suggests, a universal possession. The "so-called" basic language, as Schreber describes it, is "a somewhat antiquated but nevertheless powerful German, characterized particularly by a wealth of euphemisms (for instance, reward in the reverse sense for punishment, poison for food, juice for venom, unholy for holy, etc.)" (26). (Notice, by the way, how many of these euphemisms might be described as "words of unmeant bitterness" [*Christabel*, l. 665].) We may therefore think of the "basic language" as a binary code, not unlike a computer language, that sets parameters for what Schreber calls "loud" human language along the substitutive, paradigmatic axis. Nerve-language, by contrast, has no lexical or semantic dimension.[22] Its relation to loud human language might be described as purely formal—or, better, as metrical. Schreber writes:

> Apart from normal human language there is also a kind of *nerve-language* of which, as a rule, the healthy human being is not aware. In my opinion this is best understood when one thinks of the processes by which a person tries to imprint certain words in his memory in a definite order, as for instance a child learning a poem by heart which he is going to recite at school, or a priest a sermon he is going to deliver in Church. The words are *repeated silently* (as in a *silent prayer* to which the congregation is called from the pulpit), that is to say a human being causes his nerves to vibrate in the way which corresponds to the use of the words concerned, but the real organs of speech (lips, tongue, teeth, etc.) are either not set in motion at all or only coincidentally. (55)

How are we to understand this representation of nerve-language as a kind of silent reading? Before answering this question, I suggest we register the apparent oddity of the analogy. One usually thinks of practice for recitation as involving phonation and articulation, the idea being that the contour of sounds can be a mnemonic aid supplementary to the syntactic pattern. Of course this is the logic of (a certain debased form of) poetry, as Coleridge admits in the *Biographia*.

> It is possible, that the object may be merely to facilitate the recollection of any given facts or observations by artificial arrangement; and the

composition will be a poem, merely because it is distinguished from prose by metre, or by rhyme, or by both conjointly. In this, the *lowest* sense, a man might attribute the name of a poem to the well-known enumeration of the days in the several months;

Thirty days hath September,
April, June, and November, &c.

and others of the same class and purpose. And as a particular plea- sure is found in anticipating the recurrence of sounds and quantities, all compositions that have this charm superadded, whatever be their contents *may* be entitled poems. (2:11)

What Coleridge calls a "particular pleasure" Schreber describes as "man's *automatic need* to imprint on his mind an important thought which has occurred to him. How deeply ingrained [this] is can be seen from very char- acteristic instances when in poems rhymes (refrains) recur" (155). It is the automatism implicit in the materiality of acoustic impressions that Cole- ridge anticipates and counters with a poem that dreams of silence—not only of meaningful speech but even "the ticking of the carotid pulse" that Schreber identifies as regulating nerve-language ("Hush! Beating heart of Christabel!").[23]

In his account of "nerve-language," Schreber develops a theory of ner- vous vibrations to rival Coleridge's favorite materialist, David Hartley's. It is one of the many neologisms this is dictated to Schreber by divine rays, but that he has never heard uttered by a human being.

> I did not invent the expression "forecourts of heaven," but *like all other expressions which are in inverted commas in this essay* (for instance "fleeting-improvised men," "dream-life," etc.), it only repeats the words which the voices that speak to me always applied to the processes con- cerned. These are expressions *which never would have occurred to me*, which I have never heard from human beings; they are in part of a sci- entific, and particularly medical nature, and I do not even know if they are of current use in the human science concerned. (25)

"Nerve-language," as one of the words in inverted commas, is thus at once a name in the language and of the language; it is part message, part code—but not, we notice, a form of speech. Schreber acknowledges that most people would call his communications "delusions," even referring to a contemporary textbook, Emil Kraepelin's *Clinical Psychiatry*, for a definition. But, like Coleridge disputing an equivocation in Wordsworth's use of the word *real* in relation to the language of poetry, Schreber disputes the contemporary psychiatric account of "delusion." He argues that to define reality or "sound experience" by excluding or denying "everything supernatural" is merely to repeat "the shallow 'rationalistic ideas' of the period of enlightenment of the eighteenth century, which after all are mostly considered to have been superseded, particularly by theologians and philosophers, and also in science" (83n.) In Schreber's opinion, not all phenomena that "lack objective reality" ought to be thrown into "the lumber room of things that do not exist" (83). While he hopes that proof of the influence of the divine rays will be manifested in physical evidence of his "unmanning"—his acquisition of female secondary sexual characteristics—at the time of his death, he never suggests or believes that what he calls "voices" and "pictures" are externally perceptible. Instead, he describes how they are produced internally, though not for that reason immaterially:

> I use here the expression "seeing with the mind's eye" . . . because I cannot find a more suitable one in our human language. We are used to thinking all impressions we receive from the outer world are mediated through the five senses, particularly that light and sound sensations are mediated through the eye and ear. This may be correct in normal circumstances. However . . . I receive light and sound sensations which are projected direct[ly] onto my *inner* nervous system by the rays; for their reception the external organs of seeing and hearing are not necessary. I see such events with eyes closed and where sound is concerned would hear them as in the case of the "voices," even if it were possible to seal my ears hermetically against all other sounds. (121)

The first sentence of the *Memoirs* announces clearly enough that Schreber has read as deeply in Enlightenment materialism as Coleridge had. "The human soul is contained in the nerves of the body," he writes; "the total mental life of a human being rests on their excitability by external impressions. Vibrations are thereby caused in the nerves which produce the sensations of pleasure and pain in a manner which cannot be further explained; they are able to retain the memory of impressions received (the human memory) and have also the power of moving the muscles of the body which they inhabit into any manifest activity by the exertion of their will power"

(19). This is the account of the mind-body relation that Coleridge describes and rejects in the *Biographia*. Materialist accounts of vibratory association can explain only *being acted upon*, he suggests, and not the actions of the will: "But how any affection from without can metamorphose itself into perception or will; the materialist has hitherto left, not only as incomprehensible as he found it, but has aggravated it into a comprehensible absurdity" (1:133). Claiming that all such accounts as "Hartley's hypothetical vibrations in his hypothetical ether of the nerves" falter by attempting "to render *that* an object of the sight which has no relation to sight" (1:107), Coleridge offers an example with peculiar relevance both to Schreber's practice of "picturing" (visual hallucination) and his own poem *Christabel*: "In order to explain *thinking*, as a material phenomenon, it is necessary to refine matter into a mere modification of intelligence, with the two-fold function of *appearing* and *perceiving*. Even so did [Joseph] Priestley in his controversy with [Richard] Price! He stript matter of all its material properties; substituted spiritual powers; and when we expected to find a body, behold! We had nothing but its ghost! the *apparition* of a defunct substance!" (1:136). Coleridge's rhetoric here—a scene of undressing ("stript") followed by an interjective "Behold!"—*must* remind us of the central scene of the first part of *Christabel* ("Behold! Her bosom and half her side—/ A sight to dream of, not to tell! [252–53]). The context of this repetition in the *Biographia*—Coleridge's discussion of *thought*—can be brought to bear on the "apparition" of the poem. What Coleridge describes in both cases can be read as a version of the problem identified by one of Priestley's theoretical heirs, Noam Chomsky, and put most famously by the oft-quoted question of Alan Turing: "Can machines think?"[24] Coleridge suggests that materialist attempts to reduce "mind" to "machine" fail to demonstrate by what principle "discrete and discontinuous" stimuli come to be perceived relationally, and so inevitably the "ghost in the machine" returns.

Hartley's theory of vibrations is such a ghost, according to Coleridge: an attempt "to render *that* an object of sight which has no relation to sight" (1:106). By the logic of such an analysis, all such fictions as "the mind's eye" or the "inner voice" are ghosts as well. Of course Schreber, unlike Hartley, admits as much: "I use the expression 'seeing with the mind's eye' . . . because I cannot find a more suitable one in our human language" (120n). But Coleridge seems anxious to counteract the "strong sensuous influence" that, he suggests, makes us wish to *see* invisible things. Emancipation from what he calls "the despotism of the eye" (1:107) is enabled, he says, by numerical and musical symbols, which abstract us from the realm of sensation. But curiously for a work titled *Biographia Literaria*, Coleridge fails to treat the phonetic symbol of the *letter*.

Unless, that is, we consider the peculiar account of the theory of association in the next paragraph (chapter 6) to be such a consideration. Partly translating J. G. E. Maass, Coleridge makes one notable change. He writes, "according to this system the idea or vibration a from the external object A becomes associable with the idea or vibration m from the external object M" (108). In Maass, the symbols representing the two different stimuli had been a and π. It is obvious that Coleridge wishes, by demonstrating the complex and mechanical way theories of association attempt to connect the letters a and m, to show how far they are from an adequate concept of subjectivity. The pun here is that only the "infinite I AM" can produce that connection. Letters, as it turns out, are the best medium of divine communication, misunderstood as are their operations by materialists, who hold that "the existence of an infinite spirit, of an intelligent and holy will, must on this system be mere *articulated motions of the air* . . . a God not visible, audible, or tangible, can exist only in the sounds and letters that form his name and attributes" (1:121).

Coleridge famously parodies materialism in a self-reflexive consideration of his own medium of communication: "Thus the whole universe co-operates to produce the minutest stroke of every letter, save only that I myself, and I alone, have nothing to do with it" (1:119). No doubt Coleridge did have a great deal to do with it, but we should notice here that, in the context of the composition and publication of the *Biographia* itself, the "stroke of the letter" is hardly the kind of locomotive act that exhibits the freedom of will he wishes to instantiate. The typographical character that we read—or "process"—is, after all, a representation several times removed from Coleridge himself. We know that a large part of the text was dictated to his amanuensis, John Morgan. And by what mechanism did Morgan— any amanuensis—translate the stream of speech into writing? According to linguistic and neurological research, by a "working memory" or "on-line" language processing.

> Ordinary speech produced at normal rates has significant acoustic ambiguity because of blurring of phonetic information, the absence of

pauses between words, and background sounds. Syntactic and semantic expectations, generated by prior word sequences processed in a specialized working memory, are used by human listeners normally to
"fill in the blanks" when perceiving acoustically ambiguous speech. . . .
Sequential linguistic expectations of this sort constrain dramatically
the range of alternative word interpretations. . . . As a result, streams
of speech sounds are more readily translated into correct sequences of
word percepts.[25]

This working memory seems closely related to the use of meter (that principle of probability) prior to the invention of writing, in Coleridge's account:
"Before the invention of printing, and in a still greater degree, before the
introduction of writing, metre, especially *alliterative* meter (whether alliterative at the beginning of the words, as in "Pierce Plouman," or at the
end as in rhymes) possessed an independent value as assisting the recollection, and consequently the preservation, of *any* series of truths or incidents"
(2:67). Prior to the storage systems of writing and print, meter works proba-
bilistically to aid the retention of information. The constraint it places on
alternatives seems indicated by its collusion with sound.

But it is possible for the "working memory" to get out of order,
so to speak. Far from enabling or clarifying Schreber's perception, the
"drummed in" probabilities of his working memory interfere with it. The
effects of this incessant and hyperconscious application of probabilities—
what Schreber in *Memoir* calls "compulsive thinking" and objects to as a
violation of "the human right not to think"—are quite striking. Divine communication proceeds not only by virtue of antithetical meanings but also as
"grammatically incomplete expression":

> That is to say they omitted certain words that were essential for the
> sense. In the course of time this habit degenerated into an abominable
> use of me, because a human being's nerves of mind . . . were excited
> continuously by such interrupted phrases, because they automatically
> try to find the word that is missing to make up the sense. For instance
> as one of innumerable examples, I have for years heard hundreds of
> times each day the question: "*Why do you not say it?*," the word "*aloud*"
> necessary to complete the sense being omitted, and the rays giving the
> answer as if it came from me: "Because I am stupid perhaps." (56)

Now, this example is striking not only because it conjures up the picture of Christabel reduced to limning, by a grimace and a hiss, that which she might have said aloud; or because it also might remind us of Charles Kingsley's description of "the stupidity and cruelty with which stammering children are too often treated. . . . They are even told, 'you do it on purpose!' As if they were not writing with shame every time they open their mouths. All this begets in the stammerer a habit of secresy, of feeling himself cut off from his kindred; of brooding over his thoughts, of fancying himself under a myste-rious curse, which sometimes . . . seems the possession of a demon."[26] No; what strikes the reader at first is the oddness of the allegation that the ques-tion "Why do you not say it?" is syntactically or semantically incomplete, and that "aloud" is the only satisfactory supplement. One can only assume that the necessity of this supplement is revealed to the subject who has already "said" his thoughts as it were *internally*. One could imagine instead Schreber putting pressure on the indeterminate referent of "it"—unless it were that the memory has worked overtime so as to make "it" an entirely general referent for thought itself. And this indeed seems to be the case. Though he asserts that it is "a total misunderstanding of human thinking" for the divine rays "to believe that my store of thoughts could be exhausted by being written-down" (127), Schreber's rationale—"for instance reading a book or a newspaper always stimulates new thoughts"—partly under-mines this assertion, by suggesting that the chief stimulus to thought is the already written. Of course one notes the difference that Schreber insists upon, but that the rays, measuring only his nervous vibrations, fail to dis-tinguish: the difference between the "thought" that is merely the activation of information-processing nerve centers by reading and the "thought" that describes the meaning he derives from that information. But while such "budding thoughts" as he identifies—"Now I will wash" and "This is a beau-tiful passage"—may indeed originate in a source we call the self, we can certainly register their formulaic character.

Reading Aloud

Especially in the light of Coleridge's suggestion that the invention of writing and printing significantly alters the role of meter—with the advent of print, he argues, the function of meter is not to aid memorization but rather to act as a "stimulant of the attention" (2:69)—Schreber's claim that newspapers might sufficiently "stimulate new thoughts" seems important. Friedrich Kittler puts the irony this way: "Inexhaustibility, that *signum* of great works, becomes in Schreber's destination an attribute of newspapers as well."[27] It is not hard to recognize that Schreber suffers from *over*stimulation, but what produces this overstimulation is less obvious. It would appear that, since the newspaper speaks the language of prose, the "delicate ear" of nerve-language is a redundancy. Whether we regard the excessive noise as a consequence of the newspaper's introduction of so many "prosaisms" into Schreber's nerve-language, or the nerve-language's insistence on finding "figures of speech" in the language of prose, in either case the interpenetration of the two languages — of thought and of represented speech — contributes to Schreber's "unmanning." Coleridge had suggested that, when the object that meter calls to our attention and so "intensifies" is not worthy — when the language is prosaic, in other words — the result is deeply unsettling: "There must needs be a disappointment felt; like that of leaping in the dark from the last step of a stair-case, when we had prepared our muscles for a leap of three or four" (2:66).

In this account of the unsettling effect of heightened expectations, Coleridge appears to allude to an earlier passage in the *Biographia*:

> At its utmost, it [contemporaneity, the "law" of association] is to thought the same, as the law of gravitation is to loco-motion. In every voluntary movement we first counteract gravitation, in order to avail ourselves of it. It must exist, that there may be a something to be counteracted, and which by its re-action, aids the force that is exerted to resist it. Let us consider, what it is that we do when we leap. We first resist the gravitating power by an act purely voluntary, and then by another act, voluntary in part, we yield to it in order to light on the spot, which we had previously proposed to ourselves. Now let a man watch his mind while he is composing; or, to take a more common case, while he is trying to recollect a name; and he will find the process completely analogous. (1:123–24)

Chomsky claims that springing or elastic motion has been the "hard rock" of materialism at least since the eighteenth century; here Coleridge shows why.[28] The leap is an expression of the subject's capacity to subject the laws of gravitation to the will; but it also demonstrates, as Coleridge's analogy to composition and recollection makes clear, the problem that perception poses to materialism. The "leap," representing the suspension, however temporary, of the laws of gravity, is not unlike the more muted form of will Hermann von Helmholtz discovered, for example, in the fact that, even without moving our eyes, we can focus on different areas of a stimulus, reversing figure and ground. To make the relevance of this account of subjective agency even more relevant to *Christabel*, we should notice that the two forms of activity Coleridge juxtaposes here—leaping and recollection—are "pictured" there. We need only recall that the first sign of an enigma in the poem is the following line: "The lady sprang up suddenly" (37). Thereafter, the poem thematizes the unpredictable relation between meter and syntax by foregrounding a locomotive progress that is not only an uneven "sinking" and "rising," but also characterized by disjunctions between will and act, intention and expression ("with steps they passed / That strove to be, and were not, fast" [112–13]; "we will move as if in stealth" [120]; "they passed the hall, that echoes still, / Pass as lightly as you will!" [154–55]).

What distinguishes Schreber's account of nerve-language as a pathological version of Coleridge's poetic theory is that, for Schreber, elements are not formed into meter by a "voluntary" act. He writes, "Naturally under normal . . . conditions, use of this *nerve-language* depends only on the will of the person whose nerves are concerned; no human being as such can force another to use this nerve-language. In my case, however . . . my nerves have been set in motion *from without* incessantly and without any respite" (55). The nervous excitement to which he is subjected begins with a "recurrent crackling noise" that prevents his sleep and extends to his perception of "speech" in virtually all exterior sounds, including railways and squeaking boots (213). In the face of this information overload, even the most automatic kinds of "calculations" are rendered impossible; when he tries to walk he is so weak from nervous excitement that "every little distance of a few hundred paces seemed a hazard on which I could not decide without inner anxiety" (52).

Were Coleridge to have heard of Schreber's symptoms—both his hallucinations and his locomotive disorders—he might have diagnosed him as suffering from what, in the *Biographia*, he calls a case of "light-headedness." If the integration of will and body allows the temporary flight of the leap, "light-headedness" by contrast represents a condition of absolute passivity in which the will itself seems to take permanent flight (hence perhaps the proliferation, in Schreber's delusional experience, of birds, insects, and other winged thoughts). During this flight of the will, one can speak but not think. Language itself appears to acquire a locomotive power, inscribing itself in the memory and inciting its enunciation.

A case of this kind occurred in a Catholic town in Germany a year or two before my arrival at Göttingen, and had not ceased to be a frequent subject of conversation. A young woman of four or five, and twenty, who could neither read, nor write, was seized with a nervous fever; during which, according to the asseverations of all the priests and monks of the neighborhood, she became *possessed*, and, as it appeared, by a very learned devil. She continued incessantly talking Latin, Greek, and Hebrew, in very pompous tones and with most distinct enunciation. This possession was rendered more probable by the known fact, that she was or had been an heretic. . . . Sheets full of her ravings were taken down from her own mouth, and were found to consist of sentences, coherent and intelligible each for itself, but with little or no connection with each other. (1:113)

Coleridge narrates the Enlightenment solution to the enigma she represents (an unlettered heretic who "speaks" the language of sacred texts): first the priests and monks become "secretaries to the insane" (Lacan's phrase), writing down the acoustic information of the woman's utterance in the form of sentences (the sentences of foreign languages, we notice; not the language of her "mother tongue"); then an enterprising young physician takes to source-hunting (a methodology famously applied to Coleridge's own enigmatic poems by J. L. Lowes and Arthur Hobart Nethercot).[29] Finally he learns that "the patient had been charitably taken in by an old protestant pastor at nine years old, and had remained with him some years, even till the old man's death" (ibid.). First the enigma, then the solution.

The solution to the phenomenon was soon obtained. For it appeared, that it had been the old man's custom, for years, to walk up and down a passage of his house into which the kitchen door opened, and to read to himself with a loud voice, out of his favorite books. . . . Among the books were found a collection of rabbinical writings, together with several of the Greek and Latin fathers; and the physician succeeded in identifying so many passages with those taken down at the young woman's bedside, that no doubt could remain in any rational mind concerning the true origin of the impressions made on her nervous system. (ibid.)

This solution appears to solve the problem—called "poverty of the stimulus"—of language-acquisition theory, for the pastor's habit of "reading aloud" provides an extraordinarily rich environment.[30] In such an environment, one might find a rational basis for the belief that ideas are forged out of associations, since "the authenticated case furnishes both proof and instance, that reliques of sensation may exist for an indefinite time in a latent state, in the very same order in which they were initially impressed" (1:113).

Since, however, the anecdote of the Göttingen case appears at the end of a chapter attempting to demonstrate that "Hartley's system is not tenable," we may be justified in suspecting that Coleridge's narrative is an ironizing one. We notice, for example, that the "reliques of sensation"—a memorized sound stream—in no way lead to the production of an "idea" or meaning. It is only in the recounting of this sound stream—literally, the parsing of acoustic data by means of syntactic and phonological rules—that the sound stream comes to make sense. The anecdote leads Coleridge to speculate that "all thoughts are in themselves imperishable; and, that if the intelligent faculty should be more comprehensive, it would require only a different and apportioned organization, *the body celestial* instead of *the body terrestrial*, to bring before every human soul the collective experience of its whole past existence. And this, perchance, is the dread book of judgement, in whose mysterious hieroglyphics every idle word is recorded!" (1:114). But the pathological consequences of this (ironic) associationist explanation are evident in the experience of that other delusional, Schreber, who stores this book in his brain: "Perhaps nobody but myself, not even science, knows that man retains all recollections in his memory, by virtue of lasting impressions on his nerves *as pictures* in his head. Because my inner nervous system is illuminated by rays, these pictures can be voluntarily reproduced" (209).

Recent neurolinguistic experiments have hypothesized that the auditory hallucinations that often accompany schizophrenia may also be related to what we might call the formulaic character of working memory. In a manner suggested by Roman Jakobson's discovery of the "deflation" by which a child "temporarily ceases to be able to pronounce [certain sounds] as *significative utterances*," while still retaining the capacity to produce them (for example, in imitation of animal sounds), the decoding capacities of adults seem to sharpen as they narrow the range of their serial linguistic expectations. But "exaggerated" expectations produce "word percepts . . . in the absence of any 'phonetic input,' thus simulating hallucinations." We might think of these exaggerated expectations in terms suggested by the psychoanalyst Theodor Reik's *The Third Ear*. Readers of Reik, or of Philippe Lacoue-Labarthe's account of the 'third ear' in "The Echo of the Subject," will be aware that this name for the unconscious production of organizing redundancies has little to do with physiological listening, despite the musical theme of both texts.[31] Lacan, for example, describes it thus:

> We could call this language internal, but this adjective already falsi-
> fies everything. This so-called internal monologue is entirely continu-
> ous with the external dialogue. . . . There are properly symbolic laws
> of intervals, of suspension, and of resolution, there are suspensions
> and scansions that mark the structure of every calculation, the effect of
> which is that it's precisely not in a continuous manner that this internal
> sentence, let's say, gets registered. . . .
>
> For man it is precisely a question of knowing how to get by in the
> face of this continuous modulation without becoming too preoccupied
> by it. (112)

Schreber, of course, it quite literally "preoccupied" by this third ear/voice. In time, Schreber's ear becomes so delicate that he "hears" only organizing redundancies, such that gradually, the "terrible nonsense" (rote phrases) he hears degenerates from discordant rhythms to a virtual hiss, produced by the infinite slowing down of speech, or a self-produced system of delayed auditory feedback: "To say 'But naturally' is spoken B.b.b.u.u.u.t.t.t. n.n.n.a.a.a.t.t.t.u.u.u.r.r.r.a.a.a.l.l.l.y.y.y., or "Why do you not then shit?" W.w.w.h.h.h.y.y.y. d.d.d.o.o.o . . . ; and each requires perhaps thirty to sixty seconds to be completed" (202–3).

The ironies here are multiple.[32] On one hand, of course, there is the immediate irony that the (incomplete) phrase "but naturally" should be subjected to such a process of denaturalization; here the stuttered or ditto-graphic spelling out of the words demonstrates how the media of speech and writing might be conceived as denaturalizations of thought, a parsing into "units of information" that does violence to units of meaning. Indeed, Schreber's dittography reminds one of nothing so much as John Pierce's description of how increased redundancy allows the detection of error:

We can correct as well as detect an error by transmitting each digit three times, as follows:

sent	I I I O O O I I I O O O O O O I I I I I I
received	I I I O O O I O I O O O O O O I I I I I I

$$\wedge$$
error (150)

On the other, our recognition that the words "but naturally" are not actually spoken aloud by Schreber alerts us to the possibility that what is being represented here is less the deformation of meaning than the transformation of background noise into a code that approximates meaningful speech. In both cases, however, we recognize the nonsynchrony of thought and its medium. It is as if Schreber inhabits that perceptual point–no point between figure and ground. Indeed, "but naturally" seems itself to work as a kind of anamorphosis, the "but" framing or subverting the priority of "nature." What we realize from the examples he offers is the extent to which perception itself depends on increased attention to some stimulus that is accompanied or made possible by relaxed attention, or distraction, from others. Schreber, by contrast, represents a kind of absolute willfulness (the double of light-headedness). While the second example, "Why do you not then shit?" seems to accuse Schreber of a failure of will, an incapacity to transform involuntary or "spontaneous" operations of digestion into voluntary ones, the demand itself—to make mostly unconscious bodily processes respond to thought—is the real point. What Schreber calls "the human right not to think" is threatened by the insistence on making every process an object and product of the will.

For readers of Coleridge, this representation of a kind of stuttered thought or perception may recall yet again the terms of his criticism of materialist accounts of association. Among the "ghosts" produced by materialist attempts to describe thinking is "harmony," which Coleridge regards as an effect of attentive perception that materialists unjustifiably attribute to objects themselves. He asks, "For what is harmony but a mode of relation, the very *esse* of which is *percipi*? . . . The delicious melodies of Purcell or Cimarosa might be disjointed stammerings to a hearer, whose partition of time should be a thousand times subtler than ours" (1:118). Schreber describes himself as precisely such a hearer: "A faint idea of the nervous unrest caused is perhaps the example of a Judge or a teacher listening to a mentally dull witness or a stuttering scholar, who despite all attempts cannot clearly get out what he is asked or wants to say" (202–3). Yet for our purposes it is quite striking that Schreber needs to develop a graphic—visual—representation of this "hiss" of information—as if in imitation of Coleridge's play upon the letters *a* and *m*. For this "picturing" reminds us that acoustic distortion is only Schreber's metaphor for the excitation of his nerves. The "stuttering" he describes is irreducible to a given medium. (It is linked, for example, to haplography and dittography, which cause us to type "rember" for "remember," and "criticicism" for "criticism.")

We find a similar insistence that the perception of harmony is not restricted to a given medium in one probable source-text for Coleridge's reflections, John Gough's "On the Causes of the Variety of Human Voices," published in *Memoirs of the Literary and Philosophical Society of Manchester* in 1798. Gough, whom Thelwall acknowledges as an important forebear in acoustic research, was famous not only for his contributions to the Manchester Society but also for being blind from birth. In his essay, Gough represents this disability as relevant to his acoustic researches: "The variety of voices is perhaps as great as the variety of features: and, like the countenance, it serves as a personal distinction, to which all men have recourse under certain circumstances; and those that are deprived of sight, by cultivating a more delicate sense of the modification of sound under consideration, acquire a facility in discriminating between man and man, in their intercourse with the world" (59). Gough's "more delicate" sense of hearing, which so resonates with Coleridge's allusion to the "delicate ear" that can tell prosaisms from "figures of speech," is nonetheless not as delicate as he can imagine an ear to be. The perception of sound, according to Gough, depends on a certain *in*discriminacy of sound: "The intervals that enter into the composition of the human voice, and the tones of sonorous bodies, are too small to have their tones accurately discriminated by the ear" (62); even the delicate ear of the musician perceives sound "in the same manner that the eye of a geometer contemplates his schemes as perfect, though points and lines are represented in them by dots and strokes of ink. The existence of an error is certain in both cases; but the deviation from truth is too small to be estimated by the senses" (69). It is our inability to parse with "mathematical precision" that allows us to perceive the sameness of a voice despite differences of loudness, and the difference of voices that are equally loud.

Schreber appears to possess this ability, to record even the slightest of

vibrations. Like the modern-day linguist who reduces language atomisti-
cally to a set of parameters, heuristically subjecting language at once to tele-
scopic and microscopic distortion, Schreber's nerve-language cannot tell
the difference, we might say, between Mohawk and English, between the
language of bees and "loud human language" (the reference is to Chomsky's linguistic parameters). But therefore the strategy he develops to combat the incessant chatter of his nerves must strike us with surprise. Even
as the divine rays attempt to "stroke" his nerves by giving his thoughts
verbal expression "in a rhythm corresponding to the natural movement
of human nerves" (he reports that "words of four or perhaps six syllables
accord most easily with this cadence") and as the voices attempting soul
murder choose words "in discord with this natural cadence" (132), Schreber,
like Coleridge and Bard Bracy before him, uses (ballad) meter in defense—
though in defense not of thought, but of "the human right not to think."

> I usually found committing poems to memory a successful remedy. I
> learnt a great number of poems by heart, particularly Schiller's ballads,
> long sections of Schiller's and Goethe's dramas, as well as arias from
> operas and humorous poems . . . which I then recite *in silence on the*
> *quiet* verbatim. (203; my emphasis)

Later, when even the counteractive strategy of silently recited ballad meter
proves insufficient to prevent automatic thought, Schreber resorts to pure
number: "I simply *count* 1, 2, 3, 4, etc., in the nerve-language; this gives
one a break in thinking" (273). What Schreber's audiovisual imagination
describes as the "hiss" produced by "miracled birds"—a figure that so aptly
recalls *Christabel*'s "bright green snake" coiled around the wings and neck
of a "beauteous dove" (549–54)—presents one account of the information-
encoding properties of poetry: pure voice subjected to the arbitrary constraints of the sinuous line. His counteractive strategies suggest another. In
addition to regarding pure "counting"—no longer tied to words or accents—
as relief from thought, Schreber distracts the birds from probabilities by
thinking of similar-sounding words. Like Coleridge's rhyme-enjoying children, the birds "do not understand the meaning of the words they speak; but
apparently they have a natural sensitivity for *similarity of sounds*" (192). Here
the irrationality of counting and rhyming, by their regressive or childlike
aspect, eliminates the reduction of "manliness"—subjectivity or consciousness—to communication.

Lacan identifies two "poles" in the deformation of common language that characterizes Schreber's hallucinatory delusion: the intuition and the formula, or, in a happier construction, the *enigma* and the *refrain*. I call that construction happier because it evokes so immediately a figure in the *Biographia* of immense significance, I believe, to the metrical experiment of *Christabel*. In advocating the return of poetry to "plain sense, and a genuine mother English," Coleridge criticizes contemporary literature for being "as trivial in thought, and yet enigmatic in expression, as if ECHO and SPHINX had laid their heads together to construct it" (30). Surely there is something about this figure that vibrates, as it were, with a poem that insists on the relation between an enigmatic anacoluthon—"A sight to dream of, not to tell!" and an unmeaning repetition—"passively did imitate." In the context of Schreber's double torment—an "empty babel of ever-recurring monotonous phrases in tiresome repetition; on top of this they were rendered grammatically incomplete by the omission of words and even syllables" (152), we may recognize how deeply *Christabel* is imagined as a reflection on the perceptual activity of reading.

Reading *Christabel*

To offer a conventional "reading" of *Christabel* would be to resolve, and therefore to falsify, the figure/ground problem at its center. We are struck by how often solutions proposed to the enigma of the poem take on the character of a formulaic inevitability—from the "telling" phonetic rhyme of the line to be found in several manuscript versions of the poem—"Are lean and old and foul of Hue"—to Nethercot's paradigmatic "What else could such a creature be but a vampire?" (56).[33] Put another way, such completed readings work to dissolve the embrace of Echo and Sphinx and throw into the lumber room of things that do not exist the possibility that the poem asks us to consider: that love can speak in the voice of anger, that words of bitterness can be unmeant.[34] Let us remember that the commonplace expression that so frequently accompanies ascriptions of meaning—"It sounds like you're saying *x*"—might be regarded as a hallucination of the sort Schreber uses to distract the miracled birds, fooled by the slant rhymes of "Chinesenthum" and "Jesum Christum": they "hear" in the words and sentences something that only sounds alike. As if, in their attempts to produce meaningful sentences, all users of language suffer from a kind of vocal defect. To the psychoanalytic claim, "This is what the subject meant," Lacan suggests we respond, "How do you know? What is certain is that he didn't say it" (22) — aloud, one might add.

Christabel exposes the inadequacy of usual models of reading; or rather, it suggests that, in reading, we are suspended between two forms of halluci-nation. Insofar as we have mastered the syntactic and phonological patterns of language, we can be said to hallucinate to the extent that the perception of patterns causes us to anticipate a meaning. We see or hear "what isn't there yet," so to speak; what linguists call a "phonological loop" is usually running ahead, decoding according to probabilities. As Lacan puts it, "What makes the sentence as understood different from the sentence as not understood, which doesn't prevent its being heard, is precisely what the phenomenology of delusion highlights so well, namely the anticipation of meaning."[35] This is as true of the syntactic expectations raised when we read a "garden path" sentence (wherein we incorrectly parse "the hungry dog" as a noun phrase in "The hungry dog the conscience of the rich") as it is of the semantic expec-tations that might lead us, after reading that "Sir Leoline is weak in health," to construe the ambiguous line that follows — "And may not well awakened be" (118–19) as if it clearly referred to the small probability of health being restored with consciousness rather than the equal possibility that his ill health makes it difficult to wake him. Quite obviously the greater syntac-tic irregularity of poetry — its sentences are less garden paths than "lines of sportive wood run wild," so to speak — may decrease the possibility of automatically processing some information. But the danger of relinquish-ing expectations is that of entire delirium. Lacan asks the question this way: "What happens if you pay attention solely to the saying of what you hear, to the accent, or even to the regional expressions, to whatever is literal, in registering your interlocutor's discourse?" (136). What has been called the "music" of poetry is in this sense not the perception of harmony but rather the *non*-sense of Schreber's and *Christabel's* miracled birds.

I think *Christabel* is designed to expose the homonymy and homophony between "sense" and "sense" as false. Recall that Christabel's miming reiteration of what she has seen and heard in part 1 of the poem takes place in the Baron's "presence-room." The presence-room, as Kevis Good-man reminds us in her essay "The Microscopic Eye," is Locke's metaphor for the brain.[36] Given Coleridge's intimate knowledge of Locke, this echo seems peculiarly relevant to a poem deeply concerned with the relation between mind and body, and with *meaning*, that preternatural enigma. And I would therefore propose, instead of "reading" *Christabel*, to sketch out a rather heterodox method of scanning Coleridge's poem—a kind of looking *askance*. I would point out that the first speech act, properly so called, in the poem's narrative (that is, the representation of a human speaking aloud) does not take place until lines 69–70, when Christabel, having been "praying silently," is motivated by what she hears and sees (in both cases an enigma) to speak: "Mary mother, save me now! / (Said Christabel,) And who art thou?" Imagine, and Romantic poets and critics ask us to do, that their poems are an oral form. In that case, the line "(Said Christabel,) / And who art thou?" introduces a metrical irregularity: the *speech* contains only two stresses. Now, of course this irregularity is only apparent; the meter of the poem belongs to the narration, not to the speech act that narration represents. But this is already to confuse figure and ground, since narration, or *recounting*, is what introduces metrical regularity to speech (hence the— apparently superfluous—use of parenthesis here, whereas elsewhere in the poem, the parenthesis, like the quotation mark, comes and goes in a rather random manner).

The irregularity introduced by a focus on the difference between the several layers of voice in the poem helps, I believe, to elucidate what Coleridge is after when, in the preface to the poem, he claims that according to his "new principle" of meter—counting the accents rather than the syllables— the "variation in number of syllables is not introduced wantonly or for the mere ends of convenience, but in correspondence with some transition in the nature of the imagery or passion." Thematically, of course, the poem represents these transitions in passion as preternatural occasions, where the invisible and inaudible get represented. But Coleridge also draws our attention to a formal correlative of these hallucinatory effects. Perhaps the clearest case is in the crucial conclusion to part 2, whose first ten lines are an exercise in metrical virtuosity.

Take, for example, the line "And pleasures flow in so thick and fast." I choose to conclude with this line partly because of its relation to Coleridge's definition of the "legitimate" poem in the *Biographia*.

> The reader should be carried forward, not merely or chiefly by the mechanical impulse of curiosity, or by a restless desire to arrive at a final solution; but by the pleasureable activity of the journey itself. *Like*

> *the motion of a serpent,* which the Egyptians made the emblem of intel-
> lectual power; *or like the path of sound through the air;* at every step he
> pauses and half recedes, and from the retrogressive movement collects
> the force which again carries him onward. *Precipitandus est* liber *spiritus*
> ["The *free* spirit must be hurried onward"] says Petronius Arbiter most
> happily. The epithet, *liber,* here balances the preceding verb; and it is
> not easy to conceive more meaning condensed in fewer words. (2:14)

Consider how the metrical reading of this line requires such a retrogression.
Imagine, as Coleridge does in the *Biographia,* a child reciting aloud such
lines—"the written thoughts of another," as Coleridge puts it. Even an adult
would probably begin with an iambic rhythm—and **pleas**ures **flow**—until,
that is, they encounter the "in," which requires a retrograde correction to
an anapest: and **pleas**ures flow **in.** And in fact this is the case many times
in the poem. It is not via orality, but by rereading, that the line achieves its
own pleasurable effect.

What is the source of that pleasure? Perhaps we can best understand the
pleasure of rereading, and Coleridge's "regression" to the accentual meter
he associates with the "working memory" of oral culture, by returning once
again to the information-redundancy theorem—but this time to describe
the derailing effect of what is, in a sense, a kind of Coleridgean neologism.
Describing the particular probability constraints of English, Weaver writes,

> That there are probabilities which exert a certain degree of control over
> the English language also becomes obvious if one thinks, for example,
> of that fact that in our language the dictionary contains no words what-
> soever in which the initial letter j is followed by b, c, d, f, g, j, k, l ... &c;
> so that the probability is actually zero that an initial j be followed by
> any of these letters. Similarly, anyone would agree that the probability
> is low for such a sequence of words as "Constantinople fishing nasty
> pink."(102)[37]

In a twist, however, that Coleridge would have loved, Weaver points out that
he has just written a sentence in which the improbable phrase appears. On a
par, perhaps, with Schreber's nonsense rhymes, the sequence has the same
function as well: to disrupt the automaticity of information processing, and
to induce thought. Surely it is such a sentence Coleridge has in mind as the
"best part" of language.

The language of thought is generally regarded as the proprietary characteristic of modernist narrative; of free indirect discourse, or "represented speech and thought," as Ann Banfield describes it.

> Only the language of narrative has the resources for a picture of the activities and states of the mind commensurate with the most sophisticated theories of knowledge and consciousness. Or perhaps it is more accurate to say that in language is already contained—as part of what language knows—the very distinction that philosophy seeks to make explicit between reflection, Descartes' *cogito*, the "I am thinking" whereby the subject knows that he knows, and the other conscious states which underlie it and may never be reflected upon but are the minimal required for a subject to be conscious as opposed to unconscious.[38]

Banfield's thesis is that "this distinction is only linguistically realized in the context of narrative" because "soliloquy . . . is a crude representation of actual thoughts," one that cannot adequately distinguish differences between thought and utterance. Moreover—and this is a difficulty that Schreber also faces and complains of—soliloquy and other representations of consciousness as direct speech cannot adequately distinguish between speech and citation. V. N. Voloshinov claims therefore that irony's "multivoicedness" "is bound up with the transposition of the larger prose genres into a silent register, i.e., for silent reading. Only this 'silencing' of prose could have made possible the multileveledness and voice-defying complexity of intonational structures that are so characteristic of modern literature."[39]

Yet this identification of an "interior" language of thought with prose is too automatic, I contend. It depends on an untenable identification of poetry with speech and fails to consider the possibility—confirmed by the research of cognitive science—that both rhyme and meter are categories of linguistic difference that cannot be reduced to the phonetic level (they are, for example, elements of sign language as well). In the pairing of *Christabel* with Schreber we can resist that identification of poetry with speech and draw attention to those aspects of Coleridge's metrical experiment—such as the poem's inconsistent deployment of parentheticals and quotation marks—that seem purposefully to raise the question of "who speaks."[40] In fact, we can begin to understand the Romantic revolution in poetic language not in terms of a nostalgia for the "oral" culture of the ballad but rather as an exploration of ballad meter as the sign of "narration without a narrator," as the sign of writing-as-citation rather than of speech. Apropos of Schreber's *Memoirs*, Lacan remarks, "We talk about hallucinations. Do we absolutely have the right to do so? They are not presented to us as such when we hear them recounted."[41]

Notes

1   Although Freud's "Psychoanalytic Notes on an Autobiographical Account of a Case of Paranoia (Dementia Paranoides)" (in *Standard Edition of the Complete Works of Sigmund Freud*, 24 vols., trans. and ed. James Strachey in collaboration with Anna Freud, assisted by Alix Strachey and Alan Tyson [London: Hogarth Press, 1953–74) offered the first extended consideration of Schreber, three post-Freudian accounts have been more crucial to my own thinking: Jacques Lacan, *The Psychoses 1955–1956*, trans. Russell Grigg, book 3 of *The Seminar of Jacques Lacan*, ed. Jacques-Alain Miller (New York: Norton, 1993); Friedrich Kittler, *Discourse Networks 1800/1900* (Stanford: Stanford University Press, 1990); Eric Santner, *My Own Private Germany* (Princeton: Princeton University Press, 1996).

2   E. L. Griggs, ed., *Collected Letters of Samuel Taylor Coleridge*, 6 vols. (New York: Oxford, 1956–71), 2:716.

3   Daniel Paul Schreber, *Memoirs of My Nervous Illness* [1903], trans. and ed. Ida MacAlpine and Richard A. Hunter (New York: New York Review of Books, 1980).

4   The reference is to *Christabel*, lines 583–87: "A snake's small eye blinks dull and shy; / And the lady's eyes they shrunk in her head, / Each shrunk up to a serpent's eye, / And with somewhat of malice, and more of dread, / At Christabel she looked askance!" All references to *Christabel* are from S. T. Coleridge, *Poetical Works*, ed. E. H. Coleridge (New York: Oxford University Press, 1991).

5   In a recent essay on Schreber, "Cyberpsychosis: The Feminization of the Post-Biological Body" (in *Cyberpsychology*, ed. Angel J. Gordo-López and Ian Parker [New York: Routledge, 1999]), Jill Marsden puts Schreber's allegation of the "precise catalyst" of his nervous illness well: "On Schreber's interpretation, difficulties only began to occur when his doctor, Professor Flechsig, *hacked* into his nervous system during psychiatriatic treatment"; "he further postulates that by the time Flechsig chose to *log off*, part of the latter's nerves had mysteriously migrated in a runaway schismogenetic process" (63; emphases mine).

6   In *British Romanticism and the Science of the Mind* (New York: Cambridge University Press, 2001), Alan Richardson offers a relevant reading of the final lines of the conclusion ("And what, if in a world of sin / (O sorrow and shame should this be true!) / Such giddiness of heart and brain / Comes seldom save from rage and pain / So talks as it's most used to do"): "The 'I AM' here becomes an 'it,' the coherent, unified subject yielding to a neural network of emotionally charged associations: not a conscious, controlled ego but a blind, automatic process that does the talking" (56).

7   For instance: in the same way that *Christabel* is constructed around a central absence—

the anacoluthon of lines 252–53 ("Behold! Her bosom and half her side—/ A sight to dream of, not to tell!)—so the "meaning" of Schreber's *Memoirs* has been thought to reside in the censored third chapter, in which Schreber considered "some events concerning *other members of my family*, which may possibly in some way be related to the presumed soul murder" (43). Perhaps the most "preternatural" of connections is the fact that the English equivalents of two neologisms crucial to Schreber's account—"seelenmord" and "*Gottesstrahlen*"—can be found in Coleridge: "soul murder" occurs in the "Allegoric Vision," and the latter in a letter to Thomas Poole where Coleridge suggests that the completion of *Christabel* depends on the return of "the ray divine."

8   Schreber notes, "The name Ariman occurs by the way also in Lord Byron's Manfred in connection with a soul murder" (*Memoirs*, 31).

9   S. T. Coleridge, *Biographia Literaria*, ed. James Engell and W. Jackson Bate, 1 volume in 2 parts (Princeton: Princeton University Press, 1983), 2:55. All references are to this edition.

10   See Noam Chomsky, *New Horizons in the Study of Language and Mind* (New York: Cambridge University Press, 2000), 70–73. Recently, Chomsky has suggested the relevance of the work of eighteenth-century materialists, including Joseph Priestley, to generative grammar's attempt to study language as a "natural object." Richardson's recent book, *British Romanticism*, has inaugurated a reconsideration of the relevance of these materialists to Romantic poetry. Richardson offers a helpful review of Coleridge's vexed philosophical relation to Hartley's cognitive materialism; he also reports that Coleridge coined the term *neuropathology* (43).

11   Excerpted in A. C. Goodson, ed., *On Language*, vol. 3 of *Coleridge's Writings* (New York: St. Martin's Press, 1998), 155.

12   Or at least, communication is of a signifier rather than a signified. See Jacques Lacan, "On the Possible Treatment of Psychosis," in *Écrits: A Selection*, trans. Alan Sheridan (New York: Norton, 1977), 184.

13   Goodson, *On Language*, 157.

14   James Hunt, *Stammering and Stuttering: Their Nature and Treatment* (New York: Hafner, [1861] 1967), 13.

15   Martin Duckworth, "Stuttering and Linguistics," in *Theoretical Linguistics and Disordered Language*, ed. Martin J. Ball (London: Croom Helm, 1988), 65.

16   John Thelwall, *A Letter to Henry Cline, Esq. on Imperfect Developments of the Faculties, Mental and Moral and Organic; and on the Treatment of Impediments of Speech* (London: Arch, Cornhill, 1810), 4.

17   John Thelwall, *An Introductory Discourse on the Nature and Objects of Elocutionary Science* (London: [n.p.], 1805).

18   Marjorie Levinson, *The Romantic Fragment Poem* (Chapel Hill: University of North Carolina Press, 1986); Susan Wolfson, *Formal Charges: The Shaping of Poetry in British Romanticism* (Stanford: Stanford University Press, 1999). Having just been given the opportunity to read Margaret Russett's essay, "On the Prehistory of Poetic Voice: Coleridge, *Christabel*, and Copyright" (forthcoming in *SEL* [Autumn 2003]), I have to correct this assertion. Russett argues that Coleridge gives "an unexpectedly materialist turn" to the

concept of poetic voice by associating "untranslatableness" with "that most mechanical aspect of form, meter" (mss. 4–5). I've profited from Russett's whole discussion—particularly her linking of the mastiff bitch's howls to "doggerel"—and differ only to the extent that my interest here is in the "silent reading" that I think is at the heart of Coleridge's metrical experiment, whereas Russett emphasizes reading aloud as a necessary component of his materialist conception of voice: "The Coleridgean account of meter also requires that the contemporary understanding of 'materiality' be extended, as it usually is not, to *vocalization*. Originality does not consist in the repression of sonic matter, but its mastery" (6). Still, the distinction is perhaps only between vocalization and what cognitive neurologists study as "subvocalization."

19 John H. Pierce, *An Introduction to Information Theory* (New York: Dover, 1961), 145.

20 Quoted in Ann Banfield, *Unspeakable Sentences* (Boston: Routledge and Kegan Paul, 1982), 4.

21 Claude E. Shannon and Warren Weaver, *The Mathematical Theory of Communication* (Urbana: University of Illinois Press, 1949), 117.

22 This "basic language" actually has an interesting similarity to certain forms of "loud human language" such as the "slogan," to which Ron Silliman has recently given the name "the instrumental language of an absent subject." Silliman's example is the "Thank you" that appears on certain trash containers: a demand in the form of a gratulation. Schreber's is psychiatric jargon; he writes, "Of course other people will be ready to counter with the *slogan* that I suffered from a mere 'hallucination.'" See "Afterword: Who Speaks? Ventriloquism and the Self in the Poetry Reading," in Charles Bernstein, ed., *Close Listening* (New York: Oxford University Press, 1998), 360–78. Russett, "On the Prehistory of Poetic Voice," 20; Shannon and Weaver, *Mathematical Theory of Communication*, 106, 109.

23 Since the topic of this issue of the *South Atlantic Quarterly* is "Afterlives of Romanticism," it seems appropriate to suggest that David Lynch's film *Mulholland Drive* (World/ Independent, 2001) can profitably be read as representing *Christabel*'s afterlife. Subjected to violent abduction, a beautiful woman "cannot tell" the particulars of her story, meets a virginal dreamer who is fascinated by the mysterious stranger; eventually, they participate in a lesbian embrace. But this noir or "modern Gothic" tale is itself framed by the specter of repetition automatism—Hollywood's "manufacturing" of dreams—whose most powerful representation is the scene at the nightclub "Silencio," where the emotional affect of a singer's performance is unaffected—or rather, increased—by the revelation that the song is recorded, that she is merely lip-synching ("passively did imitate").

24 Chomsky, *New Horizons*, 114. Chomsky reminds his readers that Turing formulated the question as a patent absurdity.

25 Ralph E. Hoffman, Jill Rapaport, Carolyn M. Mazure, and Donald M. Quinlan, "Selective Speech Perception Alterations in Schizophrenic Patients Reporting Hallucinated 'Voices,'" *American Journal of Psychiatry* (March 1999) 156.3: 394.

26 Hunt, *Stammering and Stuttering*, 148. Charles Kingsley, the novelist and Anglican minister associated with Christian Socialism, was himself a stammerer who sought treatment from Hunt and wrote a prefatory letter to the volume.

27 Kittler, *Discourse Networks*, 301.

28 Noam Chomsky, "The Biolinguistic Turn" (lecture delivered at the University of California at Berkeley, March 29, 2002).

29 Arthur H. Nethercot's *The Road to Tryermaine: A Study of the History, Background, and Purposes of Coleridge's "Christabel"* (Chicago: University of Chicago Press, 1939) was a monograph undertaken in conscious emulation of John Livingston Lowes's exhaustive exercise in Coleridgean source-hunting, *The Road to Xanadu* (Boston: Houghton Mifflin, [1927] 1964). Nor does the "unlettered heretic's" automatic speech contain any part of that "antiquated high German" that Schreber identified as the "basic language" of the divine rays. Despite the fact that the minister is Protestant, he seems unaccountably never to read *Luther* aloud. This may be because, elsewhere in the *Biographia*, Coleridge describes Luther's writing as a *language* unrelated to speech: "In Luther's own German writing, and eminently in his translation of the Bible, the *German* language commenced. I mean the language as it is at present *written*; that which is called the HIGH GERMAN, as contra-distinguished from the PLATT-TEUTSCH, the dialect of the flat or northern countries; and from the OBER-DEUTSCH, the language of middle and Southern Germany. The High German is indeed a *lingua communis*, not actually the language of any province, but the choice and fragrancy of all the dialects. From this cause it is at once the most copious and the most grammatical of all the European tongues.

"Within less than a century after Luther's death the German was inundated with pedantic barbarisms. A few volumes of this period I read through from motives of curiosity; for it is not easy to imagine anything more fantastic, than the very appearance of their pages. Almost every third word is a Latin word with a Germanized ending, the Latin portion always being printed in Roman letters, while in the last syllable the German character is retained" (1.211).

30 John Searle describes the logic of Chomsky's notion of linguistic competency: "The conviction that human beings were born with an innate brain capacity to acquire natural human languages . . . seemed inescapable, given that a normal infant will acquire a remarkably complex system of rules at a very early age with no systematic teaching and on the basis of impoverished and even defective stimuli. Small children pick up a highly competent knowledge of a language even though they get no formal instruction and the utterances they hear are limited and not even grammatical." "End of the Revolution," *New York Review of Books*, February 28, 2002, 33.

31 Hoffman et al., "Selective Speech Perception," 479. See Theodor Reik, *Listening with the Third Ear: The Inner Experience of a Psychoanalyst* (New York: Farrar, Strauss, 1948); Philippe Lacoue-Labarthe, "The Echo of the Subject," in *Typography: Mimesis, Philosophy, Politics* (Cambridge: Harvard University Press, 1989).

32 The ironies are only heightened by the fact that, just outside the window of my office, a mass of honeybees is swarming, their buzz seeming a close approximation of the first phrase, reminding me at once of Coleridge's claim that the German word for *fanaticism* "is derived from the swarming of bees" (*Poetical Works*, 1:30) and that Schreber's great-uncle authored *Novae species insectorum*.

33 Nethercot, *Road to Tryermaine*, 56.

34 Another criticism of Wordsworth's poetic theory in the *Biographia* appears to explain

retroactively Coleridge's equation of poetic language with "words of unmeant bitterness." Still disputing an equivocation in the word *real*, Coleridge asks how a reader or a poet is supposed to "distinguish between the language suitable to *suppressed*, and the language, which is characteristic of *indulged*, anger? Or between that of rage and that of jealousy? Is it by wandering about in search of angry or jealous people in uncultivated society, in order to copy their words?" (*Biographia* 2.82). Because "suppressed" anger might be expressed in words of "unmeant friendliness," as love might express itself in "bitter" words, the disconnect between verbal information and "meaning" is manifest.

35 Lacan, *Psychoses*, 137.

36 Kevis Goodman, "The Microscopic Eye" (unpublished manuscript).

37 Shannon and Weaver, *Mathematical Theory of Communication*, 102.

38 Ann Banfield, *Unspeakable Sentences* (Boston: Routledge and Kegan Paul, 1982), 210.

39 Cited in ibid., 222.

40 Margaret Russett's answer to this question of "who speaks" is apropos: "Christabel allegorizes poetry as the moment of error in which, like Geraldine manifesting herself from a disembodied moan, mere sound converts into something other; it is this conversion that makes possible the attribution of voice" (28).

41 Lacan, *Psychoses*, 136.

Wai Chee Dimock

Nonbiological Clock: Literary History against Newtonian Mechanics

I take as my starting point an "obituary" Einstein puts at a dramatic turn in his "Autobiographical Notes," an obituary for Newton:

> Enough of this. Newton, forgive me; you found the only way which, in your age, was just about possible for a man of highest thought and creative power. The concepts, which you created, are even today still guiding our thinking in physics, although we now know that they will have to be replaced. . . .
>
> "Is this supposed to be an obituary?" the astonished reader will likely ask. I would like to reply: essentially yes.[1]

An obituary for Newton is in order because relativistic physics is a "revolution" in Thomas Kuhn's sense: a shift in paradigm so profound that it remakes the protocol of the field from the ground up.[2] Tenets that were once ironclad are no longer so. No one would be able to say that "all of physics could be founded upon Newton's mechanics."[3]

That revolution suggests one context in which to trace the "afterlives" of Romanticism, especially of Blake. Einstein's objection to Newton,

The *South Atlantic Quarterly* 102:1, Winter 2003.
Copyright © 2003 by Duke University Press.

striking a blow that hits home, is nonetheless not the first on record. Blake's objection, not in the least temperate, has long been a salient fact in literary history. E. P. Thompson invokes it as a counter-Enlightenment, a tradition of London Dissent pitted against a mechanical psychology and epistemology; Donald Ault, Stuart Peterfreund, and Mark Lussier have made even stronger scientific claims on its behalf.[4] It would be misleading to speak of Blake as a forerunner of modern physics; it would be equally misleading to cordon him off from that development. For Blake has been transcribed, so to speak: by someone who has not read him, who is egged on only by their common opponent, and who, in turning modern physics against Newton, must do so in a language incomprehensible to the poet, perhaps abhorrent to him. Blake's battle has been fought and won by strange hands, on strange terrain.

In this essay I would like to reverse this odd development. Keeping in mind what objecting to Newton has done to the discipline of physics, I would like to ask what effects it might have on literary studies. If physics has anything to tell us, it is that Blake's arguments are worth revisiting: not for their historical interest, significant as that might be, but for what they have to say about the field of Romanticism as it now stands and as it contributes to the study of literature broadly defined.[5] What does it mean for literary critics to take Blake seriously, as physicists have taken Einstein seriously? If a quarrel with Newton has led to a paradigmatic shift in physics, a break with an once foundational ontology, how might it alter the grounds of literary studies?[6] The afterlives of Romanticism seem to me most consequential in this sense, as a diachronic challenge to what is currently normative: a noncompliance with the premises now governing the field, a noncompliance with the analytic coordinates now naturalized by practice.[7]

It is interesting to look at Newton in this light, to see what premises govern his mechanics, what coordinates "ground" his laws, laws of motion celestial and terrestrial. These laws, as mathematical formalizations, are attempts to give a "geometrical account of motion."[8] They are attempts to describe temporal phenomena—the change of location in time—in terms of measurable units in space. This measurement of time by means of space is crucial to Newton, Alexandre Koyre suggests, for the ambition of his mathematical physics is nothing less than to "subject motion to number,"[9] to harness temporal events to a quantified metric. This quantification cannot proceed on its own. It requires a prior relay: a subsuming of motion by geometry, which is to say, a subsuming of temporal difference by spatial regularities. What results, Koyre goes on to say, is a strangely "hypostatized" paradigm. Even though Newton is describing the motion of planets, the motion of earthly projectiles, such motion takes place in a geometrical space that is itself completely uniform, completely predictable, not varying from one locale to another, every unit length "equivalent and even identical." Motion here is "changeless change," in "timeless time."[10]

Quantification and spatialization go hand in hand. Newton's mathematical laws require the prior "existence of an absolute, unchanging system of coordinates."[11] This system of coordinates is indeed what he emphasizes in the General Scholium of the *Principia*:

> Absolute, true, and mathematical time, of itself, and from its own nature, flows equably without relation to anything external, and by another name is called duration. . . . Absolute space, in its own nature, without relation to anything external, remains always similar and immovable. . . . As the order of the parts of time is immutable, so also is the order of the parts of space. . . . All things are placed in time as to order of succession; and in space as to order of situation. It is from their essence or nature that they are places, and that the primary places of things should be movable, is absurd. These are therefore the absolute places.[12]

Space and time are absolute for Newton not only in the sense that they are objective and immutable but also in the sense that they are fixed numbers, expressible as "absolute places." Mathematical truth, for Newton, requires a kind of spatial determinism. Time here is thus a dependent, a derivative. It is parasitic upon and fully contained by a more primary term. To quote Newton again: "All things are placed in time as to order of succession; and in space as to order of situation. . . . These are therefore the absolute places." Not only is there a syntactic equivalence between time and space but the latter is actually the antecedent, the originating idea from which time derives its shape, as a longitudinal "order of succession," just like a latitudinal "order of situation." Space provides the mental image for time; space dictates the ontology of both.[13] Conceived in this image, time functions in exactly the same way as a spatial coordinate. It is a place, a location, a sequence of units on a calibrated line—and, for all those reasons, a container to which any event can be assigned.

Newtonian mechanics stands or falls on this image of time as a container. It is as if time were a filing cabinet, made up of an infinite number of slots. Into these slots any given event can be automatically filed away: into a century, a year, a month. Placement is key. Everything must be assigned a temporal address; that address must be locked into a numerical series; that series guarantees an identity-across-the-board at any given point. Newton spatializes time and, in the same gesture, standardizes it. His temporal axis, as an axis serially numbered, is an axis of uniform cross-sections. Events are assumed to belong together because they take place inside the same numbered slice of time. They have the same identity because they have the same serial address. What this means is that every event is permanently tied to one set of synchronic neighbors, neighbors that situate it, comprise its measure of time, dictate to it a single context, and lock it inside the presumptive unity of a chronological number.

I have been describing Newtonian mechanics, but, as is readily apparent, I have also been describing a dominant paradigm in literary studies, a synchronic historicism that bears more than a family resemblance to the numerical determinism of scientific modernity. Newton, after all, was both a physicist and a historian: the author not only of the *Principia* but also of *The Chronology of Ancient Kingdom Emended*, an attempt to "establish scientific grounds for the study of universal history," based on "a definitive measure of calculating time."[14] Mechanics has offshoots in other disciplines— in history, of course, and, I would argue, in literary studies as well. Here, numerical determinism also begins with an image of time as spatialized, serialized, homogenized. It begins, that is, with a chronological date. This date is adduced as a kind of automatic unifier, yielding up a segment of time against which the scrutinized text is mapped, and inside whose numerical borders it is firmly placed. One year, five years, ten years: these are the standard durations we use to "contextualize" a text, on the assumption that these slices of time are integral, unified not only by their standard unit lengths but, above all, by the serial numbers that mark their borders. Events are deemed pertinent to one another if they fit inside those borders, if they are bound by two serial numbers that, if not exactly consecutive, are close enough to being that, the distance between them often limited to single digits. These digits are assumed to exercise a binding force, to yield an analytic domain both necessary and sufficient, containing both the web of relations producing the text and the web of relations flowing from its presence in the world.

Newtonian literary studies—it is helpful to call it by name—takes numerical determinism and turns it into a style of historical explanation. Chronological dates have a mechanical authority here. They automatically define what counts as context, what counts as meaningful duration for historical analysis. Since the temporal axis here is effectively a numerical axis, there is only one way to register that duration, one way to figure historical causality, one way to measure the distance between two events. Events are either simultaneous or they are not; they are either far apart or close together. The distance between them is fixed by a number that never changes. The year 1325, separated from 1825 by five hundred years, is obviously not adjacent by any ruler consecutively numbered and cannot *ever* be imagined to be adjacent. Their spatial separation is taken for granted, because any point of contact would not be subject to counting, would not show up on a quantified metric. The relegation of such a date to the causally unthinkable is a stiff but quite logical price exacted by numerical determinism. Causality across five hundred years is just too messy, too anarchic. Synchrony, however, is nicely measurable and demonstrable: a unified container, expressible as an "absolute place," expressible as a numerical constant. Or so Newtonians think.

Einstein disabuses them. Relativistic physics parts ways with Newtonian mechanics on just this point: the absolute measurability of synchrony. Einstein has "difficulty with all physical statements in which the concept 'simultaneous' plays a part."[15] Rather than accepting the concept as a given, he asks whether it is an automatic fact, a fact that can be established simply by consulting a serial number. Is there such a thing as a synchronized "now," an identity-across-the-board established by a mechanical clock? Is synchrony a numerical constant that dictates an eternal relation between two temporal neighbors? Does the motion of an object make any difference to its space and time coordinates? And if so, what difference does *that* make to the concept of the simultaneous? To answer these questions, Einstein considers the phenomenal world as seen from two frames of reference in two different states of motion. Using a moving train as one frame of reference, and the railroad embankment as the other one, he asks whether the timing for two flashes of lighting can be assigned to a unified synchronic plane. Can they be seen as simultaneous in both places?

With palpable satisfaction Einstein writes: "The answer must be in the negative."[16] The two flashes of lightning A and B might be simultaneous for the observer standing still on the embankment. But, if this is the case, they would not be simultaneous for an observer on the train moving away from A toward B. Since this observer is shortening his distance to B and lengthening his distance to A, he "will see the beam of light emitted from B earlier than he will see the one emitted from A."[17] And so, "Events which are simultaneous with reference to the embankment are not simultaneous with respect to the train, and vice versa (relativity of simultaneity). Every reference-body (coordinate system) has its own particular time; unless we are told the reference-body to which the statement of time refers, there is no meaning in a statement of the time of an event."[18] Simultaneity turns out not to be a numerical constant, an eternal identity-across-the-board. Two events might be simultaneous in one frame of reference, but in a different frame they would not be. The "now" experienced in one location, then, cannot be the same as the "now" experienced in a differently moving location. These two nows cannot be unified, cannot be expressed as an unchanging serial number. Einstein, in this way, turns Newton's absolute truth into a conditional truth, specific to one set of coordinates, not generalizable beyond those coordinates. This is what he calls relativity. Of course, for Einstein, relativity is itself a mathematical concept. Its mathematics is non-Euclidean geometry, the geometry exhibited by space-time when faced with the requirement that the speed of light be invariant.[19] And, in making that invariance of speed the foundation for physics, Einstein is as committed as Newton is to mathematical formalism. Motion, under relativity, is no less subject to number, though light (rather than space-time) now stands as the numerical constant.[20]

Relativistic physics, even as it writes the obituary of classical mechanics, remains the latter's kin. It cannot challenge Newton on nonmathematical grounds. Any such challenge would have to come from the humanities, especially literature, a field shaped by extended ties stretching across irregular lengths of time, chaotic durations messing up the synchronic plane of serial numbers. "Literature," I want to suggest, has until quite recently been experienced as a universe only loosely quantified by dates: its temporal distances not strictly measured, keeping at bay the regulative power of the clock and the calendar. No loss has been greater than the replacement of that universe by one convicted in advance of synchronicity, serial by definition.[21] But there is no reason why this should go on. And no one has more to say on this score than Blake.

In book 1 of *Milton*, Blake reaches back to the seventeenth century and pulls Milton forward to the nineteenth. "Say first! what mov'd Milton, who walkd about in Eternity / One hundred years" (1:16–17).[22] Blake's arithmetic is not very precise here. Milton has actually been in eternity longer than that, having died in 1674, 132 years before 1806, the date on the title page of the poem named after him. The imprecision is the point. One hundred years, 132 years—the exact figure does not matter. Blake is not doing any actual counting, not equating time with the measurable unit length of the calendar and the clock. His numerical lexicon—"one hundred years," Los's "six thousand years of labor," the "seven days of eternity," and so on—uses the convention of numbering only to turn it on its head. Numbers here are hermetic rather than quantitative. They do not serialize time but encrypt it, expressing it as code, as Kathleen Raine suggests, as if they were "words in a sentence of complex and ambiguous grammar."[23]

This deserialization of time makes literary history possible. Milton is able to come back to the nineteenth century because he is not sequenced and contained by only one set of dates. And he is not sequenced and contained because someone in the nineteenth century is still reading him, naming a poem after him, and putting the resounding words from *Paradise Lost*— "And justify the Ways of God to men" (bk. 1, ll. 26)—on its title page, though not without a slight amendment. Blake's motto reads "*To* justify the Ways of God to Men." He quotes Milton, but not exactly, not slavishly.[24] Mechanical reproduction of a standardized text is not the point here, and perhaps never the point for Blake as an illuminator and printmaker. His hand-inscribed letters, mixing typography with calligraphy, invokes not the uniformity of typeset print but the manual variability of autograph. These letters were not even carved with an engraving tool, as Robert Essick and Joseph Viscomi point out, but traced with a quill or pen on copper plates.[25] This dissent from standardized print, like his dissent from standardized chronology, bends and stretches time, takes it outside the dictates of the mechanical.

Milton is closer to Blake than 132 years would suggest. But what exactly are the circumstances that lead to this deserialization of time? The most immediate one, Blake tells us, is "A Bards prophetic Song!" (*M* 2:22). The Bard sings of many things, beginning with Los, hammering away to create the Ages of the universe. He sings of Satan, a bright, regular, untiring creature, mechanically inclined, whose home turns out to be up above rather than down below, in charge of the movement of the planets. As the unhappy father, Los, says:

O Satan my youngest born, art thou not Prince of the Starry Hosts
And of the Wheels of Heaven, to turn the Mills day & night?
Art thou not Newtons Pantocrator weaving the Woof of Locke?
(*M* 4:9–11)

Pantocrator (*Παντοκράτωρ*)is the word for God in the Greek New Testament, a word used by Newton in his *Principia* and retained as a Greek word by Andrew Motte in his English translation, defined there as "Lord God . . . or Universal Ruler."[26] Newton's mechanics, his laws of planetary motion, would not have been possible without this pantocrator, this ruler giving him an absolute system of coordinates, "Mathematical proportion of Length Bredth Highth" (*M* 4:27). These numerical constants are the woof of Locke's empiricism, a "Philosophy of Five Senses" (*SL* 4:16). They are also the woof of something else: the "precise clock time" identified by E. P. Thompson as the work regime of industrial capitalism.[27] Satan is thus the pantocrator both within the academy and without. He presides over the mechanized time of planetary motion, and he presides over the mechanized time of the "Mills" on earth,[28] mills that count among their products both manufactured cloth and human cogs.[29] *Jerusalem* is still more emphatic on this point:

I turn my eyes to the Schools & Universities of Europe
And there behold the Loom of Locke whose Woof rages dire
Washd by the Water-wheels of Newton. black the cloth
In heavy wreathes folds over every Nation; cruel Works
Of many Wheels I view, wheel without wheel, with cogs tyrannic
Moving by compulsion each other.
(*J* 15:14–20)

The tyranny of mechanics is what brings Milton back to the nineteenth century, what forces Blake to bring him back. Anachronism is their joint defense against mechanized time, for anachronism is duration wrested from the clock, a far-flung tie that is itself a rebuke to serial numbers. The very temporal structure of *Milton* is already a protest, a form of action: "To cast off Rational Demonstration" (*M* 41:3), "To cast off Bacon, Locke & Newton" (*M* 41:5). But—and no one is more aware of this than Blake himself—that action cannot be achieved by one person alone. For anachronism can happen only when the arrow of time is relationally reversed, only when it is looped backward, looped through some antecedent figures, temporal aliens who appear out of sequence, violating the law of seriality. These aliens are still alive, even though dates pronounce them long dead. They are still alive, because their duration is no longer an individual matter. Lifted from the finite body of one person—lifted from its numerical brevity, its determinate progress from life to death—this duration has become something shapeless, nonvectorial, an unsequenced free-for-all. This, then, is Blake's image of literary history: diachronically extended, irregularly inhabited, not based on the biological individual, not governed by the unidirectional passage of a single life span.

Literary history that begins with the return of Milton to the nineteenth century can indeed go head to head with Newton on his central tenet: the seriality of time. Blake the biological individual, with his numerical brevity, is not up to the task. The nonbiological Milton has to be brought back to do the fighting, taking on Urizen, the Newtonian spirit of fallen reason, whose name derives from $o\mathring{\upsilon}\rho\iota\zeta\epsilon\iota\nu$, to limit, with the cognate form Uranus, signifying Lord of the Firmament.[30] But "fight" is probably the wrong word for what transpires between these two.

> Silent they met, and silent strove among the streams, of Arnon
> Even to Mahanaim, when with cold hand Urizen stoop'd down
> And took up water from the river Jordan: pouring on
> To Miltons brain the icy fluid from his broad cold palm.
> But Milton took of the red clay of Succoth, moulding it with care
> Between his palms: and filling up the furrows of many years
> Beginning at the feet of Urizen, and on the bones
> Creating new flesh on the Demon cold, and building him,
> As with new clay a Human form in the Valley of Beth Peor.
> (*M* 19:6–14)

In the same place, Mahanaim, where Jacob once wrestled with God (Genesis 32:2), Milton now wrestles with Urizen. Urizen is fighting in earnest. He turns the ground under Milton into freezing marble (*M* 19:4), he tries to kill off his opponent with an "icy intellectual baptism."[31] But Milton is workmanlike rather than warriorlike. He has no weapon to speak of, only red clay. This clay he molds with care, mending his opponent rather than destroying him, putting flesh on his hollows, kneading numerical laws into folds of words.

The battle with Newton is not fought on biological grounds and is not

Figure 1. William Blake, *Newton*, 1795. Color print (Watercolor, 46 x 60.1 cm). Tate Gallery, London. Used by permission of the Tate Gallery, London, Art Resource, New York.

even a fight in any conventional sense of the word. Changing the rules of combat, turning these on their head—the feet of Urizen get treated first—Milton also turns Newtonian time from a coldly sovereign ruler into something molded by human hands. This humanization of mechanics is something Blake himself has done. In his color print *Newton* (1795), the scientist is not only kept intact but deliberately idealized: not harmed, not taken apart, golden-headed, gloriously muscular (Figure 1). Newton is absorbed in his mathematical laws, his gaze fixed on his diagram, the golden compass extending from his hand and reflecting the goldenness of his head. That head and that hand have produced three triangles—one traced on the paper, one formed by the compass, and one formed by his fingers—all three elegantly geometric and eminently measurable. Blake's head and hand, meanwhile, are doing something very different. Acknowledging Newton's geometric laws and putting them in the foreground, he nonetheless concedes

nothing to their authority. The composition of the drawing as a whole literally puts these laws in their place. Fully one-third of the drawing is a black-
blue, opaque medium, presumably the "Sea of Space and Time" (*M* 15:46),
for Blake the medium of the fallen physical world, inundated by the "flood
of the five senses." Another third of the drawing is the surface on which
Newton sits, apparently a rock, but covered by some luxuriant vegetation,
ambiguously textured, with hints of two claws extending in the opposite
direction from Newton's feet. And, beginning with those feet, the body of
Newton cannot be more different from the figures he is tracing. The lines of
the triangles are clean, flat, rectilinear; the lines of the body are bursting and
bulging, ropes of muscles giving it a sinuous thickness all the more striking against the thinness of the triangles. Blake has indeed molded Newton
anew, put flesh on the Demon cold.

Mechanics does not have to be demolished, but its serial ruler does have
to be layered over by some sort of "clay" if human beings are not to freeze in
their numerical finitude. That clay cannot come from physical life. The ticking clock of the body can yield no continuity beyond its own limits. And so,
just as Blake conjures up numbers only to relieve them from the dictates of
quantification, he conjures up body parts only to relieve them from a strictly
physiological regime. Blake's left foot, for instance, is now much more than
an anatomical locomotive device. It has become a cipher, an entry point to
dimensions of space and time not computable by any biological clock.

> But Milton entering my Foot . . .
> But I knew not that it was Milton, for man cannot know
> What passes in his members till periods of Space & Time
> Reveal the secrets of Eternity: for more extensive
> Than any other earthly things, are Mans earthly lineaments.
> And all this vegetable World appeared on my left Foot,
> As a bright sandal formd immortal of precious stones & gold:
> I stooped down & bound it on to walk forward thro' Eternity.
> (*M* 21:4, 8–14)

What does it mean for Milton to have entered Blake's left foot? Why the
foot? Why should the union between these two poets take this bizarre form?
And why should there be a union to begin with?

The "Milton" that has entered Blake's foot can hardly be a biological
entity. Blake is walking with the help of this Milton, but not walking all over

him. For this incorporeal thing is a separate thing no more, not trodden under foot because it is part of the foot. It is an interesting conception of literary history. The authors here are literally "Two yet but one" (*M* 20:1). Their extension and duration are fused, fused by necessity, because the numerical finitude of any one person—Blake was seventy when he died—is not adequate to the full weight of time. As a biological individual Blake is completely under the thumb of Newton. His days are numbered. Only literary history can give him days that are not: days that stretch backward and forward, weaving in and out of other days, an indeterminate fabric. He needs these unnumbered days to be Blake, if "Blake" is to be anything other than a finite "Vegetable Body" (*M* 42:27). Still, that vegetable body is not to be cast aside: just as Urizen is not to be cast aside, Newtonian mechanics is not to be cast aside. Rather, these burdens are to be spread out, spread across time, lightened to the weight of a sandal, worn around the foot.

Blake needs the nonbiological Milton and needs himself to become nonbiological in at least one sense, to have any freedom from serial numbers. Milton, of course, has already set an example. Even though he calls his trip to the nineteenth century a trip to "Eternal Death" (*M* 14:14), that death-bearing century in fact constitutes a grim but not uninteresting condition of life for Milton. Eternity, fed by the cycle of the continually dying, is no longer equatable with terminal stasis, just as Death, enacted again and again as a reproducible process, is no longer equatable with terminal oblivion. Continual death is here the genetic condition for continual life. What Milton dramatizes—as he dies first in the seventeenth century and yet again in the nineteenth—is a looping and layering of time, a doubling and redoubling of some stubborn words, a brave detour before that taut finishing line, beyond which time no longer has consequence. Time does have consequence for Milton, even though he is biologically dead. And, even though that consequence might not be anything he wants, there is not much he can do, having already surrendered himself, become somebody else's left foot. A nonvolitional hybrid of sorts has come into the world.[32] This is Milton's lineaments in the nineteenth century, lineaments given him by others, relieving him of his previously vested form. For that form has not been perfect. In *Marriage of Heaven and Hell*, Blake has said this about *Paradise Lost*:

> Those who restrain desire, do so because theirs is weak enough to be restrained; and the restrainer or reason usurps its place & governs the unwilling.

And being restrained it by degrees becomes passive till it is only the
shadow of desire.
The history of this is written in Paradise Lost. & the Governor or
Reason is call'd Messiah.
And the original Archangel or possessor of the command of the
heavenly host, is calld the Devil or Satan and his children are call'd
Sin & Death
(*MHH* plate 5)

Blake then goes on to make the famous (and somewhat misleading) claim
that Milton is "of the Devils party without knowing it" (*MHH* plate 5). What
he means is that Milton is mostly right about the Fall of Man, except for one
thing. He has gotten the names switched around, calling things by the opposite of what they are. The true Messiah is called Satan, and Satan, the force
of prohibition, is wrongly called the Messiah. This error is not altogether
fatal, which is why Milton is still a sublime poet, why he is called upon to
wrestle with Urizen. But, for Blake, there are definite lapses in *Paradise Lost*,
such as this description of the cosmos: "They [the Constellations] as they
move / Their Starry dance in numbers they compute / Days, months, and
years, towards his all-chearing Lamp / Turn swift their various motions, or
are turnd/ By his Magnetic beam . . ." (3:579–83).

Celebrating the motion of the planets, Milton takes his measure of time
from their numerical sequence, the "numbers they compute." His chart
of universal history imposes a mechanical order upon time, Kenneth J.
Knoespel points out, much as "the coordinates of analytic geometry bring
new meaning to space."[33] Milton and Newton do sometimes see eye to eye,
worshiping the same god, the same pantocrator. That is why the poet has to
be brought back, to "die" one more time in the nineteenth century, for he
too, no less than Newton, is due for some major overhaul.[34] There can be
no textual integrity for Milton as he is fused with Blake, just as there can
be no bodily integrity. His dates are taken beyond the limits of the biological clock the better to surrender their unity. Literary history is retroactive
and utterly ruthless in wiping out the claims of the finite individual. Only in
thus wiping out can it free up a stretch of time not based on one life span.
Thus Milton: "I will go down to self annihilation and eternal death, / Lest
the Last Judgment come & find me unannihilate" (*M* 14:22–23).

Eternity as a continuum of annihilation is probably not flattering to the
bodily ego. It is what the biological clock dictates. And, oddly enough, it is

also what literary history requires. The nonbiological clock here quarrels not at all with the biological in its finitude of numbers. Still, that finitude is the goad for a contrary measure of time. Insofar as it is able to yield that contrary measure, literary history extends to human beings a duration honoring the limits of physiology but resisting its subjection to mechanics. For what literary history offers is time drawn out to irregular lengths, drawn out by the intensities and proximities of each reading, at odds with any standard timetable. Life spans are here endlessly undone and endlessly recuperated. Numerical finitude is the starting point but not the endpoint. No obituary is handed out: not to Milton, and not even to Newton.

"Time is the mercy of Eternity" (*M* 24:72) in this sense, routine annihilations notwithstanding. Kept alive by the nonbiological clock that is literary history, Newton is still at large in *Milton*, still spatializing time, as he is wont to do. These spatial units, however, are no longer the mechanical units he demands. Not uniformly slotted or serially numbered, they are individually made, made with hands, each separately crafted, adorned with bright ornaments, made for human use, and merciful to human mortality.

> But others of the Sons of Los build Moments & Minutes & Hours
> And Days & Months & Years & Ages & Periods; wondrous buildings
> And every Moment has a Couch of gold for soft repose,
> (A Moment equals a pulsation of the artery)
> And between every two Moments stands a Daughter of Beulah
> To feed the Sleepers on their Couches with maternal care.
> And every Minute has an azure Tent with silken Veils.
> And every Hour has a bright golden Gate carved with skill.
> And every Day & Night, has Walls of brass & Gates of adamant,
> Shining like precious stones & ornamented with appropriate signs:
> And every Month, a silver paved Terrace builded high:
> And every Year, invulnerable Barriers with high Towers.
> And every Age is Moated deep with Bridges of silver & gold.
> And every Seven Ages is Incircled with a Flaming Fire.
> (*M* 28:44–57)

For Blake, as for Heidegger, time is a built environment.[35] There is nothing natural about it; it is not given but made. This *unnatural* status of time is what enables human beings to dwell in it, to be sheltered by its walls, tents, couches, and to leave their mark there, a labor-intensive signature, crafted brick by brick, the most gorgeous to come from human hands. Unnatural time is something that takes the entire history of the species to emerge, now housing those human "vegetables" lying there on their couches. Only this built environment can save human beings from biology. Only this built environment can offer significant duration to a species doomed by numerical finitude. To think of literary history as a nonbiological clock is to think of time itself as neither mechanical nor even corporeal. Wrested from the lock-stepped, unidirectional flow of the life cycle, literary history is merciful and therefore not sequential, not governed by the law of serialization. Those who dwell in it are free to take what they want, in whatever order, for the raw material here—as Blake's steadily cascading sentences make clear—is nothing more than words, a lexis not sequenced, as malleable as clay, and as commonly available. The human species could not have found a better cover. Layered over by this stuff, biology is both preserved and stretched beyond its limits: "Every time less than a pulsation of the artery / Is equal in its period & value to Six Thousand Years" (*M* 28:62–63).

Time is the mercy of eternity because literary history extends to every standard life span a nonstandard duration. For Blake himself, this duration is not quite six thousand years, but it does go far beyond his biological dates, far beyond the official dates of English literary history. The number 1790, for instance—the year in which he began writing *The Marriage of Heaven and Hell*—is a number stretching back to biblical antiquity. Blake can say, without fuss and without fanfare, that "The Prophets Isaiah and Ezekiel dined with me" (*MHH* plate 12). These two—foreign nationals and temporal aliens—can be seated at the table, for literary history is not chronologically insular and (if only for that reason) also not territorially predicated. Blake's quarrel with Newton thus pits him against three instances of the serial form: the numerical chronology dictated by dates; the national chronology imposed by territorial borders;[36] and, finally, the derivational chronology imposed by a sequential ordering of word and image, of a text and its translation into a visual medium. These rejections of the serial form come to a head at the end of Blake's life—in his illustrations to the *Divine Comedy*—an undertaking that refuses to sequence the relation between the near and the far, between the domestic and the foreign, even as it refuses to sequence the relation between the verbal and the visual, between "original" text and its "subsequent" illustrations.

Blake was asked to do these Dante illustrations by John Linnell, who had already done much to relieve his poverty by commissioning a series of illustrations to the Book of Job. The work on Dante began in the fall of 1824, two or three months before Blake's sixty-seventh birthday. It ended with his death on August 12, 1827, leaving behind 102 illustrations, most of them only preliminary sketches. Blake apparently threw himself into the work. In the course of just a few weeks he learned enough Italian to read the *Divine Comedy* in the original.[37] Visiting him on December 17, 1825, Henry Crabb Robinson found him preoccupied with Dante, but with Newton also hovering in the background, his engagement with the latter apparently renewed by his intense (and intensely critical) engagement with the *Divine Comedy*. Robinson recorded these fragments of Blake's conversation:

> A few detached thoughts occur to me. "Bacon, Locke, and Newton are the three great teachers of Atheism, or of Satan's doctrine." . . .
> "Dante saw devils where I see none. I see good only."[38]

For Blake, Dante and Newton are both intellectual enemies. Both are voices of Satan: the former, for having put sinners in a punitive Hell, and the latter, for having put time behind bars. Among Blake's inscriptions to Drawing 101 is the following: "Whatever Book is for Vengeance for Sin & Whatever Book is Against the Forgiveness of Sins is not of the Father, but of Satan the Accuser & Father of Hell."[39] It is clear which "Book" he has in mind. Still, doing illustrations for that book, and bringing the Italian Father of Hell to nineteenth-century England, Blake has managed to score a point against Newton and against a nation unified behind Newton. His last letters alternated between wrestling with Newton and wrestling with Dante. On April 12, 1827, Blake wrote to George Cumberland: "I know too well that a great majority of Englishmen are fond of the Indefinite which they Measure by Newton's Doctrine of the Fluxions of an Atom . . . Certainly a happy state of Agreement to which I for One do not Agree."[40] On April 25, 1827, he wrote to John Linnell: "I go on without daring to count on Futurity, which I cannot do without doubt & Fear that ruins Activity, & are the greatest hurt to an Artist such as I am. . . . I am too much attach'd to Dante to think much of anything else."[41]

Blake dare not count on Futurity. But perhaps he need not. The presence of a fourteenth-century poet in the nineteenth century makes "counting" both impossible and ultimately beside the point. Literary history is, in this sense, both a shelter from serial numbers and a sharp reminder of their dominion. The nonbiological clock can do nothing to halt the ticking of the biological; it can, however, turn that ticking into an unsequenced continuum. This is, in fact, the story of the *Divine Comedy*, its alternate story: not of vengeance inflicted on sinners but of the fusing of two time frames, one emanating from a poet long dead, the other emanating from a poet who brings him back to life. As a poem about Virgil and Dante, the *Divine Comedy* is literary history written in defiance of dates, literary history written to deserialize time, much like Blake's *Milton*. It is this deserialization of time that brings Virgil back, across thirteen hundred years, his voice weak from long silence.[42] Virgil needs Dante to regain his voice. Needing Dante, he is always holding him tight, hugging him, as a mother would her child. In *Inferno* 23, with the devils in hot pursuit, this is what Virgil does:

> Lo duca mio di subito mi prese,
> come la madre ch'al romore è desta
> e vede presso a sè le fiamme accese
> che prende il figlio e fugge e non s'arresta,
> avendo più di lui che di sè cura,
> tanto che solo una cimicia vesta.
> (23:37–42)

Cary's translation:

> . . . Suddenly my guide
> Caught me, ev'n as a mother that from sleep
> Is by the noise arous'd, and near her sees
> The climbing fires, who snatches up her babe
> And flies ne'er pausing, careful more of him
> Than of herself, that but a single vest
> Clings round her limbs.[43]

Virgil as a "mother" to Dante is clearly interesting to Blake: this scene from *Inferno* 23 is one he chooses to illustrate (Figure 2). However, rather than producing a graphic sequel to Dante's words—rather than allowing the verbal iconography of mother and child to dictate a visual analogue—Blake comes up instead with an image markedly different, not indebted to Dante's words. This features Virgil holding Dante, to be sure, but only slightly larger, not as a mother carrying her child but as two parallel figures, both androgynous, of unspecified relation to each other, joined only by their rhythmic

Figure 2. William Blake, *Virgil and Dante Escaping from the Devils*. Fogg Art Museum, Harvard University. Used by permission of the Fogg Art Museum.

motion. The arms of these two are entwined; the right leg of each is conspicuously extended, visually echoing each other, two poets becoming one in flight.

Blake's illustrations, as Northrop Frye and W. T. J. Mitchell have pointed out, are remarkable for their *independence* from the texts they supposedly illustrate.[44] What this independence permits is deserialization on multiple fronts. In the kind of literary history Blake practices, the fourteenth-century poet enjoys no priority over his nineteenth-century reader, even though, by chronological dates, one obviously comes first. The "original" text, for that reason, also enjoys no priority over its "subsequent" visualization. Blake's images do not reproduce Dante's words; they are freely imagined, separately crafted entities of their own. Given this autonomy of the illustrator, the very sequential order of the *Divine Comedy* cannot be maintained as a numerical sequence. The cantos can be retroactively reshuffled, and this is indeed what Blake has done. The image of mother and child, left out of his illustration for *Inferno* 23, is actually projected backward and grafted upon an earlier canto, *Inferno* 19. This one features Pope Nicholas III in a fiery hole, hanging upside down by his feet, with Virgil and Dante peering at him. Virgil is once again carrying Dante, taking him down to the hole and then up again, pressing him to his breast. In Dante's text, however, there is no mention of mother and child:

> Però con ambo le braccia mi prese:
> e poi che tutto su mi s'ebbe al petto,
> rimontò per la via onde discese.
> Nè si stancò d'avermi a sè distretto,
> Si men porto sovra 'l colmo dell'arco . . .
> (19:124–28)

Cary's translation:

> . . . In both arms
> He caught, and to his bosom lifting me,
> Upward retrac'd the way of his descent.
> Nor weary of his weight he press'd me close,
> Till to the summit of the rock we came . . .[45]

In Dante's *Inferno* 19, Virgil and Dante seem to be of relatively the same size. Blake's illustration, on the other hand, dramatizes their noticeable disparity

Figure 3. William Blake, *Simoniac Pope*, 1824–1827. Illustration to "Hell," Canto 19 of Dante's *Divine Comedy* (Watercolor, 52.7 x 36.8 cm). Tate Gallery, London. Used by permission of the Tate Gallery, London, Art Resource, New York.

(Figure 3). Virgil is at least three times as big as Dante, holding him in a bear-hug, cradling him. Only Dante's head and the upper part of his body are visible to us; the rest of him vanishes, because what the pictorial composition emphasizes is the powerful arms of Virgil, thrown around Dante in a complete circle, and the powerful legs of Virgil, more than enough to support the burden he is carrying. It is Virgil who is gazing directly, frontally, and fearlessly at Pope Nicholas III. Dante's face is turned away, pressed against the figure who cradles him, looking at Nicholas III only timidly, obliquely, out of the corner of his eyes.

And for good reason. *Inferno* 19 is one of the most tricky cantos in the *Divine Comedy*. Dante's feud with the papacy is burning at a white heat here: not only has he consigned Nicholas III to eternal damnation, he is using this pope as a mouthpiece to predict the imminent arrival in hell of two other popes, Boniface VIII and Clement V, both hated by Dante, and both destined for hell.[46] Incendiary statements of this sort need a venerable supporting cast. Virgil's larger-than-life presence here is no accident for Dante, no more than Milton's larger-than-life presence is for Blake.

Taking that figure and transposing it, in a backward loop, from *Inferno* 23 to *Inferno* 19, Blake practices literary history as he has always done.[47] Here then is nonbiological time at its most merciful: stretched across nineteen hundred years, not sequenced in any fixed order, not cowed by chronological dates, not cowed by serial numbers. This is Blake's response to Newtonian mechanics. Dante, who knew nothing about Newton, had already done something similar.

Notes

Throughout this essay, I have used the following title abbreviations: *Milton* (*M*); *Marriage of Heaven and Hell* (*MHH*); *The Song of Los* (*SL*); and *Jerusalem* (*J*).

1 Albert Einstein, "Autobiographical Notes," in *Albert Einstein: Philosopher-Scientist*, ed. Paul Arthur Schilpp (La Salle, IL: Open Court, 1969), 33.

2 Thomas S. Kuhn, *The Structure of Scientific Revolutions*, 2d ed. (Chicago: University of Chicago Press, 1970).

3 Einstein, "Autobiographical Notes," 25.

4 E. P. Thompson, *Witness against the Beast: William Blake and the Moral Law* (New York: New Press, 1993); Donald D. Ault, *Visionary Physics: Blake's Response to Newton* (Chicago: University of Chicago Press, 1974); Ault, "Incommensurability and Interconnection in Blake's Anti-Newtonian Text," *Studies in Romanticism* 16 (1977): 277–303; Stuart Peterfreund, *William Blake in a Newtonian World* (Norman: University of Oklahoma Press, 1998); Mark Lussier, *Romantic Dynamics: The Poetics of Physicality* (New York:

St. Martin's Press, 2000), 82–104. For other scholarship on Blake and Newton over the past sixty years, see Jacob Bronowski, *William Blake and the Age of Revolution* (New York: Harper and Row, 1965), 135–50; Bryce J. Christensen, "The Apple in the Vortex: Newton, Blake, and Descartes," *Philosophy and Literature* 6 (1982): 147–61; F. B. Curtis, "Blake and the 'Moment of Time': An Eighteenth-Century Controversy in Mathematics," *Philological Quarterly* 51 (1972): 460–70; Mark Greenberg, "Blake's 'Science,'" *Studies in Eighteenth-Century Culture* 12 (1983): 115–30; Jean H. Hagstrum, "William Blake Rejects the Enlightenment," in *Blake*, ed. Northrop Frye (Englewood Cliffs, NJ: Prentice-Hall, 1966), 142–55; Marjorie Hope Nicolson, *Newton Demands the Muse: Newton's "Optics" and the Eighteenth Century Poets* (Princeton: Princeton University Press, 1946); Kathleen Raine, *William Blake and Tradition*, 2 vols. Bollingen series (Princeton: Princeton University Press, 1988), 53–83. For a compelling argument linking Romanticism to the biology of mind, see Karl Kroeber, *Ecological Literary Criticism: Romantic Imagination and the Biology of Mind* (New York: Columbia University Press, 1994).

5 In structuring Romanticism around Blake, I am mindful of M. H. Abrams's admonition that it is "ultimately misleading to put Blake and Shelley, instead of Wordsworth and Coleridge, at the intellectual center of English Romanticism." See his *The Mirror and the Lamp* (New York: Norton, 1958), 313. To this, I offer Raymond Williams as a rejoinder: "Of the slower, wider, less observable changes that we call the Industrial Revolution, the landmarks are less obvious; but the lifetime of Blake, 1757–1827, is, in general, the decisive period." See his *Culture and Society, 1780–1950* (New York: Columbia University Press, 1958), 31.

6 For a more fleshed-out theoretical argument, see my "Non-Newtonian Time," *American Literature* 74 (December 2002): 911–31.

7 In his argument for "Romantic anachronism," Jerome Christensen has likewise argued that his "undertaking will involve a blurring of the distinction between Romantic and Romanticist that has been pride of the practitioners of ideology critique during the past fifteen years." See Christensen, *Romanticism at the End of History* (Baltimore: The Johns Hopkins University Press, 2000), 1.

8 A. Rupert Hall, "Newton and the Absolutes: Sources," in *The Difficulty of Difficult Things*, ed. P. M. Harmon and Alan E. Shapiro (Cambridge: Cambridge University Press, 1992), 261–85, quotation from 271.

9 Alexandre Koyre, *Newtonian Studies* (Chicago: University of Chicago Press, 1965), 10.

10 Ibid., 10–11.

11 Hall, "Newton and the Absolutes," 271.

12 Isaac Newton, *Philosophiae Naturalis Principia Mathematica* (1686), translated as *Mathematical Principles of Natural Philosophy*, trans. Andrew Motte, 2 vols. (London: Dawsons, [1729] 1966), 1:9, 12.

13 For space in Newton, see Lawrence Sklar, *Space, Time, and Spacetime* (Berkeley: University of California Press, 1977), 182–93. For an emphatic argument about the centrality in Newton of "an absolutely immobile space, distinct from body, extending from infinity to infinity," see Robert Rynasiewicz, "By their Properties, Causes, and Effects: Newton's Scholium on Time, Space, Place, and Motion," *Studies in History and Philosophy of Science* 26 (1995): 133–53; 295–321; quotation from 135.

14 Kenneth J. Knoespel, "Milton and the Hermeneutics of Time: Seventeenth-Century Chronologies and the Science of History," *Studies in the Literary Imagination* 22 (Spring 1989): 17–36; quotation from 30.

15 Albert Einstein, *Relativity: The Special and the General Theory*, trans. Robert W. Lawson (New York: Crown, 1961), 26.

16 Ibid., 30.

17 Ibid.

18 Ibid., 31.

19 For a useful account of Einstein and non-Euclidean geometry, see Rudolf Carnap, *An Introduction to the Philosophy of Science*, ed. Martin Gardner (New York: Dover, 1995), 132–76.

20 Einstein's commitment to mathematical formalization is unwavering through his life. See, for instance, Abraham Pais, *"Subtle Is the Lord": The Science and Life of Albert Einstein* (New York: Oxford University Press, 1982), 111–291.

21 I am thinking of the influential work of Benedict Anderson, which equates literature with serial publications such as the newspaper, subsuming literary time under a regime of "simultaneity," "measured by clock and calendar." See Anderson, *Imagined Community: Reflections on the Origin and Spread of Nationalism* (London: Verso, 1983), 30.

22 Unless otherwise indicated, all citations are to *The Poetry and Prose of William Blake*, ed. David V. Erdman (Garden City: Doubleday, 1970). The plate number is followed by the numbers of the lines cited.

23 Raine is speaking generally of symbols in Blake. See her *Blake and Tradition*, 2:47.

24 As Robert N. Essick and Joseph Viscomi point out, Blake seems to be suggesting, from the outset, that "his purpose in *Milton* is the same as Milton's in *Paradise Lost*, but perhaps with the implication that his attempt is necessitated by the failure of the first." See William Blake, *Milton a Poem, and the Final Illuminated Works*, ed. Robert N. Essick and Joseph Viscomi (Princeton: William Blake Trust and Princeton University Press, 1993), 111.

25 Robert Essick, *William Blake, Printmaker* (Princeton: Princeton University Press, 1980); Joseph Viscomi, *Blake and the Idea of the Book* (Princeton: Princeton University Press, 1993). For the aesthetics of Blake's calligraphic scripts, see W. J. T. Mitchell, "Visible Language," in *Romanticism and Contemporary Criticism*, ed. Morris Eaves and Michael Fischer (Ithaca: Cornell University Press, 1980), 46–86; Susan Wolfson, *Formal Charges: The Shaping of Poetry in British Romanticism* (Stanford: Stanford University Press, 1997), 31–46.

26 Newton, *Mathematical Principles*, 2:389.

27 E. P. Thompson, "Time, Work-Discipline, and Industrial Capitalism," *Past and Present* 38 (December 1967): 56–97.

28 What Blake says about Chaucer's Miller is pertinent here: "The Miller, a terrible fellow, such as exists in all times and places, for the trial of men, to astonish every neighborhood, with brutal strength and courage, to get rich and powerful to curb the pride of Man." See his "Descriptive Catalogue," in Erdman, *Poetry and Prose of William Blake*, 527.

29 For a detailed discussion of industrial capitalism and Blake's "Satanic Wheels," see Bronowski, *William Blake and the Age of Revolution*, 87–131.

30 Raine, *Blake and Tradition*, 2:56.

31 Harold Bloom, *Blake's Apocalypse: A Study in Poetic Argument* (London: Victor Gollancz, 1963), 329.

32 For a discussion of reading as a nonvolitional generator for hybridity, see my "Literature for the Planet," *PMLA* 116 (January 2001): 173–88.

33 Knoespel, "Milton and the Hermeneutics of Time," 18.

34 Northrop Frye argues that Milton's descent to earth "will do two things for him: it will enable him to see the physical world as Satanic rather than divine, and it will enable him as a result to see his 'emanation,' or totality of things he loves, as part of himself and not as a remote and objective "female will." The former is the climax of the first book of *Milton*; the latter is the climax of the second." See Frye, *Fearful Symmetry: A Study of William Blake* (Princeton: Princeton University Press, 1947), 336.

35 See Martin Heidegger, "Building Dwelling Thinking," in his *Poetry, Language, Thought*, trans. Albert Hofstadter (New York: Harper Colophon Books, 1971), 143–62. For Blake's architectural images, see Robert Essick, *William Blake and the Language of Adam* (Oxford: Clarendon Press, 1989), 11–12.

36 For Blake's weaving of the French Revolution into English political history, see David. V. Erdman, *Blake: Prophet against Empire* (Princeton: Princeton University Press, 1969). Qualifying Erdman (but still supporting my argument about Blake's interweaving of two national chronologies), W. J. T. Mitchell argues that Urizen might be seen not as an English reactionary reacting against the French Revolution but as a composite parody of the French philosophes themselves. See Mitchell, "Visible Language," 50–59.

37 Henry Crabb Robinson noted that Blake used Henry Francis Cary's translation. See *Diary, Reminiscences, and Correspondence of Henry Crabb Robinson*, ed. Thomas Sadler, 2 vols. (Boston: Fields, Osgood, 1870), 2:28. Frederick Tatham mentioned that Blake learned Italian in the course of a few weeks and was able to read the *Divine Comedy* in the original. This would have been *Dante con l'espositione di Christoforo Landino et di Alessandro Vellutello, Sopra la sua Comedia dell'Inferno, del Purgatorio, & del Paradiso* (Venice: Appresso Giovambattista, Marchio Sessa & Fratelli, 1564). See Albert S. Roe, *Blake's Illustrations to the "Divine Comedy"* (Princeton: Princeton University Press, 1953), 4 n. 5.

38 Robinson, *Reminiscences*, 2:27.

39 Drawing 101 is in Roe, *Blake's Illustrations to the "Divine Comedy."* The inscription is fairly hard to read. I quote from ibid., 31.

40 William Blake to George Cumberland, April 12, 1827, in *The Letters of William Blake*, ed. Geoffrey Keynes (Cambridge: Harvard University Press, 1968), 162.

41 William Blake to John Linnell, April 25, 1827, *Letters*, 163–64.

42 *Inferno*, 1:63, "chi per lungo silenzio parea fioco."

43 Henry Francis Cary, *The Vision of Hell, Purgatory, and Paradise, of Dante Alighieri* (London: Taylor and Hessy, 1819), 198.

44 Northrop Frye, "Poetry and Design in William Blake," *Journal of Aesthetics and Art Criticism* 10 (September 1951): 35–42; W. J. T. Mitchell, *Blake's Composite Art* (Princeton: Princeton University Press, 1978), 14–34. Mitchell largely disagrees with Jean H. Hagstrum, who sees Blake as operating within the tradition of *Ur Pictura Poesis*. See Hagstrum, "Blake and the Sister-Arts Tradition," in *Blake's Visionary Form Dramatic*, ed. David V. Erdman and John E. Grant (Princeton: Princeton University Press, 1970), 82–

87. For a discussion of the Dante illustrations, see Ralph Pite, *The Circle of Our Visi…. Dante's Presence in English Romantic Poetry* (Oxford: Clarendon Press, 1994), 58–67.

45   Cary, *Vision of Hell*, 169.

46   As John D. Sinclair points out, Nicholas III (1277–1280), Boniface VIII (1280–1303), and Clement V (1303–1314) represented "a crescendo of iniquity" for Dante: "Nicholas, reputed the first of the papal simonists and a great one, through Boniface, the protagonist in his age of the most inordinate pretensions of the Church to political predominance, a worldly, unscrupulous and powerful ecclesiastic, and incidentally the corrupter of public life in Florence and the cause of Dante's exile, to Clement, treacherous, lecherous, and servile to France, the leader of the Church into its seventy years of shameful 'exile' in Avignon." See "Note," in *Dante's Inferno: Italian Text with English Translation and Comment by John D. Sinclair* (New York: Oxford University Press, 1972), 244. Nicholas mistakenly thinks that Boniface has already arrived in hell: "*Ed el grido: 'Se' tu già costì ritto, / se' tu già costì ritto, Bonifazio? . . .*'" (19.52–53), and predicts the arrival of Clement after him: "*che dopo lui verrà di più laida opra/ di ver ponente un pastor sanza legge*" (19:82–83).

47   For Blake, reversibility is crucial to all levels of literature. As Joseph Viscomi points out, "We know that Blake changed his mind about *Milton*, adding plates and changing the plate order of copy C . . . that copy C was altered three times, that its final plate order was probably influenced by copy D rather than vice versa." See Viscomi, *Blake and the Idea of the Book*, 324.

Srinivas Aravamudan

The Colonial Logic of Late Romanticism

What are the conceptual stakes of examining and naming an Indian Romanticism? What
is the significance of such a "late" repetition,
taking place, as it does, through the late nineteenth and twentieth centuries? The colonial
and postcolonial "time lag" poses for us several
obvious questions concerning the legitimacy and
relevance of a European intellectual-diffusionist
hypothesis. When related to its European precursors, is this late Romantic strain in colonial
India an echo? a copy? a supplement? a displacement? a fantasized influence? a catachresis? If
the late eighteenth century in Europe has subsequently generated various long-lived species
of Romanticism that have subsequently bil-
lowed outward into numerous afterlives, what
are the others to this family of Romanticisms?
Dead classicisms? Liberal individualisms of various sorts? Industrial capitalism anchored in a
variety of alternative modernities? If an origi-
nary Romanticism's central theme began with
the hoped immediacy of an auto-affection philo-
sophically built up into a communitarian utopia
in the case of Rousseau, the circuit of this
itinerary gets lengthened enormously — through

The *South Atlantic Quarterly* 102:1, Winter 2003.
Copyright © 2003 by Duke University Press.

its English and German inheritors—by the time we get to the story of *Dasein* in Heidegger and postponed indefinitely in the postcommunitarian thought of Derrida. But to call all three of these philosophers Romantic is to stretch the definition of the term to the breaking point. The notion of an afterlife—in Derrida even more so than in Heidegger—would have to be predicated on the ultimate breakdown of organic coherence as a constitutive condition, even as that breakdown repeats the previous Romantic philosophical life prosthetically through a family resemblance to a past incarnation. This anachronistic continuation of Romanticism beyond the so-called Romantic Age is matched by the anatopian spread of it outside the confines of a supposed western European origin into eastern European, and also tricontinental venues.[1]

Romanticism in a late-capitalist age has also benefited from the retroactive effect of a Freudian *Nachträglichkeit* or "deferred action," appearing as the representative of many other forms of organicism, localism, and communitarianism. In this particular form of transcoding, Romanticism is the trademark name for any and all appeals to identity, community, and history. Romanticism's multiple progeny are then the result of a certain ex post facto positioning in cultural memory rather than products of a heroic narrative of documentable direct influence. Romanticism's reach as a universal lingua franca is therefore the outcome of a secret history of mergers and acquisitions—even if this is not quite the same as contemporary intellectual property ventures establishing a trademark. By way of an intercultural mimesis and a translational hybridity, various historicisms of uncertain local and foreign application resort to the modular and general theory of Romanticism as a universal solvent. There is an economic simplicity in grouping all these variants under the universalizing umbrella of Romanticism, a move that helps structure each of them as different contents, bodies of work, or subjects, competing for understanding by standing under a familiar material shape. In this regard, the resort to Romanticism as an explanation is as much a function of the vacuity and inexactness of the form as an open totality as it is evidence of the overweening intellectual or political potency of the presumed "contents."[2]

Lacking a life of its own, Indian Romanticism was a prosthesis onto the hybrid trunk of British colonialism that was obstructed by some forces even as it was enabled by others. The triumph of the Anglicists and Utilitarians such as Thomas Babington Macaulay and John Stuart Mill over starry-eyed first-generation Orientalists such as William Jones, Henry Colebrooke, Thomas Charles Wilkins, and Nathaniel Brassy Halhed was nonetheless countered by German Romantic representations of India that took over the task of representing India in a positive light that Ronald Inden has called "the loyal Opposition."[3] Johann Gottfried Herder, Friedrich Schlegel, Felix Emmanuel Schelling, Arthur Schopenhauer, and Friedrich Max Müller variously idealized what they recognized as the ancient fount of Indo-European wisdom through their encounter with translations of ancient Sanskrit texts (even if there were also early controversies generated by Hegel's downgrading of India). Abraham-Hyacinthe Anquetil-Duperron, the translator of the quirky *Oupnek'hat* (itself a translation of Dara Shukoh's partial translation of the *Upanishads* into Persian) would set the tone for many of the German idealists by claiming that "anyone who carefully examines the lines of Immanuel Kant's thought, its principles as well as its results, will recognize that it does not deviate very far from the teachings of the Brahmins, which lead man back to himself and comprise and focus him within himself."[4] Various Romantic interpretations of pantheistic monism and mysticism would also help propel the abstract philosophy of Advaita Vedanta into the position of prime representative of the construct of "Hinduism" as a new religious definition. The extended result of this operation was the prosthetic limb of the Bengal Renaissance that would twitch in response to a long-distance Romantically inspired language, generating the reformative religious vocabularies that would later be variously named "neo-Hinduism," "semitized Hinduism," "universal Hinduism," and "syndicated Hinduism."[5]

Therefore, anticolonial nationalism in India enacts a species of Romanticism that has been described by Partha Chatterjee as "a derivative discourse." Arising within a problematic of Romantic Orientalism that portrayed the native as a stereotype, a residual essence, and a negative foil to European domination, nationalist self-assertion took the form of a meticulous reversal of the Orientalist-Anglicist double hypothesis. Where the Anglicist British colonizers saw native laziness and degeneration, the Indian nationalists saw the spiritual contemplativeness and renascent subjectivity seen by earlier Orientalist forebears. The charge of native effeminacy was countered by the nationalists' embrace of androgyny and remasculinization. In addition, indigenous cultural resources were marshaled in favor of a recombinant neotraditionalism. To that extent, first-wave posi-

tive Orientalism was reclaimed and extended in a manner to refute dismissive judgments of Indian cultural competence and morality. But all this
reassertion at the level of the problematic, as Chatterjee rightly points out,
did not upset the fundamental belief in the underlying thematic of Romantic Orientalism itself that deemed the existence of cultural essences and
civilizational norms and tendencies.[6] Simple reinterpretation of specific
attributes—putting a plus sign where the colonialist had put a minus sign—
nonetheless did not unsettle the fundamental assumptions of the discourse,
that there was a difference waiting to be elaborated, and that this difference
is what testified to that central Romantic hypothesis that James Chandler
has called, after Claude Lévi-Strauss, "the historiographical-ethnographic
correlation."[7] The colonialist had to map a history onto a people and the self-
appointed representatives of the people thus named responded by arguing
about the values of the history that had been assigned unto them. One could
call this species of Romanticism reactive, reassertive, or interpellational.
A discursive shifter, initiated by the colonial language, jogs a newly created interlocutor into uttering a sentence that communicates more about
the discourse of the precedent utterance than about the subject of enunciation. That is the nature of a derivative discourse and exemplifies modular
or mimetic Romanticism in a colonial strain.

While some of the best-known lives—and afterlives—of Romanticism,
however, have incarnated in the guises of cultural nationalism, language
essentialism, and the ideal of organic intimacy among the members of
the chosen community, in this article I trace the manner in which Indian
Romanticism does not just produce the expected form. In addition to neo-
Hinduism as transcoding, Romanticism generates a supplementary religious cosmopolitanism in the outsider's language, one that would normally
be rejected as a mere add-on and indeed attacked as illegitimate by various
positions deemed Romantic and neo-Romantic. Constituting an anomaly
and therefore vulnerable to rejection, the cosmopolitan strain of Indian
Romanticism comes alive through a series of transidiomatic practices. I designate this transidiomatic lingua franca, both hyper-Romantic and insuffi-
ciently Romantic, as guru English.[8]

The colonial context of Romanticism's initial application in India was
itself highly extraneous—saturated as it was with the necessity and ideology
of English education as conceptualized by Macaulay's famous "filtration"
theory. To this idea, the Schillerian project of aesthetic education—that

promises to make good on the Kantian imperative by democratic out-reach—is simultaneously extended and compromised by the inescapable cultural bifurcation of the organic ensemble of Indianness. Unlike the folk-loric or the ethnopopular that could be appealed to by the middle class and then radicalized by popular support as in the classic model of eastern Euro-pean cultural nationalism,[9] the multiple dimensionalities and fractures of the internal ethnoreligious identity in South Asia by religion, region, language, and caste—as well as the exteriority of the prestige culture of Englishness—made Romanticism a source of middle-class aspiration with-out the prospect of unmediated popular identification. Yet, riven as this situation was by the fractured nature of the socio-intellectual field, the belief in organicity was more actualizable in practice than a theoretical under-standing would allow. While others have examined the fuller profile of Indian Romanticism as a movement, this article focuses on one of the other accretions that forms on that structure as an artificial limb that could para-doxically be said to have a more vibrant afterlife than even the organicity of the organism. Guru English is one such outcome, and one such afterlife of the colonial logic of late Romanticism. Not just perpetuating Romantic vacuity, guru English rephrases the fundamental terms of nationalist dis-course in terms of a cosmopolitan supplement in excess of functionalist interpretations about its governmentality.[10]

By taking up certain aspects of the thematic, and moving away from par-ticular toward universal essences, guru English makes visible the confusing links between "Romantic" relativism and historicism. Altering the Roman-tic thematic would mean a greater degree of freedom from the Orientalist problematic, even though guru English also frequently returns to the scene of the crime. Guru English interacts variously with imperial and national-ist vocabularies. While its Orientalist origin ensures coexistence with either dispensation, the discourse's appeal—whether cosmopolitan or national-ist—is not uniform. From the beginning, English education acquires a life of its own, generating alternate varieties of Orientalism but also this time, newer forms of subjectivity; guru English, the offspring of English edu-cation and religious rediscovery, makes for new charlatanries and contro-versies but also for a change, newer syncretisms and continuities. While there is considerable debate between the Orientalist primordialists and the subalternist constructionists regarding the manner and moment of the communalization of modern India, guru English arises precisely out of the ambivalence identified by this debate and correspondingly enjoys its multifaceted interpretive richness. Is guru English merely a translation and extension of existing religious ideas and doctrine, made available to Anglophone interlocutors? Or is it a new invention, entirely modern, and created with a view to identifying modern subjects even if it advertises itself as possessing the patina of ancient wisdom? To some extent, guru English is caught in the middle: its proponents would wish to emphasize their retailing of ancient wisdom, even as its critics are more likely to point to the neophyte status of the discourse as proof of its inauthenticity. The complex legacies of "English education" in India have occupied many scholarly lifetimes,[11] and it is not within the scope of this study to account for all that it achieved for the nation-form and all that it has wrought in terms of its very real demographic limits and reification of social inequities. Looking for a genealogy of guru English nonetheless highlights, for good measure, the perversity, excessiveness, and errancy of the newer Orientalism's productive capacities.

Bankim Chandra Chatterji's call for a renovated Indian subjectivity endorses English as the language of objectivity. This crude separation of subject and object creates a national subject who is expected to negotiate between two fatally unrelated spheres. But Bankim's innovation also recasts colonized religion within modernity. If guru English had not existed already to some degree, it is launched fully armed as an indirect consequence of Bankim's belief in nationalist modernity. Rudyard Kipling's late-guard apologia for empire, chronologically after Bankim's, has often been interpreted as uninterested in the alterity of the native, but there are peripheral recognitions of spiritual alterity and charlatanry in Kipling's work uncompromised by imperial commitments. Kipling can speak guru English and represent its metaphysics effortlessly, even if, admittedly, his sympathies tend toward voicing more familiar imperial themes.[12] Sri Aurobindo, an inheritor of Bankim's vocabulary, subjects guru English to further mystical transformations. As spiritual leader as well as literary aficionado, Aurobindo makes offbeat and futuristic contributions to guru English. Aurobindo, as pre-Independence India's premier Anglophone guru to date, heralds many of the developments in the subsequent discourse.

Even though the category of guru English allows familiar figures to be appreciated in novel ways, it might nonetheless be charged with the elitism characteristic of most Indian English literature. For instance, Tabish Khair's comprehensive reading of twentieth-century Indian English novels in *Babu Fictions*, criticizes the genre's "collapsing of all differences into a solid-state hybridity and a privileging of this hybrid subject."[13] Is guru English just a subset of this larger field of Indian English? Indeed, Indian English literature is overwhelmingly urban, cosmopolitan, Brahminized, and Anglicized; most definitely the native, rural, deprived, and marginal elements are barely visible; even more tellingly, it is true that Indian English is really a grapholect, staging and fictionalizing a written form that is never really spoken as such but hyperbolically consumed as a represented object. Despite all the overblown claims and the publishing bonanza currently under way on its behalf, Indian English is far less "real" when compared with say, American or Caribbean English.[14] Guru English, however, is a special case that overlaps not just with Indian English but with Irish, American, and New Age vocabularies. In any case, it would be odd to subject Romantic metaphysical vocabularies to the litmus test of sociological realism. Guru English, like many other cosmopolitan discourses, derives its paradoxical power precisely from its referential inadequacy. Unable to refer adequately, it can conjure excessively. Why else would William Butler Yeats and Rabindranath Tagore exchange ideas about the mystical union of Celtic and Indian spiritualism when no self-respecting philosopher of religion would venture in that direction? This willed confraternity of Irish and Indian nationalisms is none the weaker despite the flimsy intellectual grounds of their religious commonality. While the sociological imperative needs to be resolutely applied to guru English (especially to expose its bombast and bring it down to earth), it would be unfortunate if such necessary preliminaries become the reductive substitute for other forms of internal and contextual analysis. Guru English is especially potent because its language, while inflected with the past and the present, is at its most evocative when regarding metaphysical futures. This futuristic angle will especially be on display in terms of the mixture of objective science and the religion of spirit in Bankim's rhetoric, and the fusion of "overhead" poetry and spiritual anticipation in Aurobindo's predictions of a coming age of supermen. Guru English emerges equally from Bankim's cryptic representations of heroic opposition and Aurobindo's plans for mystic fellowship, which are both beholden to Jacobinical terrorist enthusiasms. Like nationalism itself, guru English is an ideology that implicates conservative, reactionary, and progressive, even as it takes into its sweep modernizers, imperialists, and revolutionaries.

Bankim's Prophecy

In an essay, "The Confession of a Young Bengal," published in *Mookherjee's Magazine* in December 1872, Bankim observes in some detail how "English-educated Bengalis are rapidly getting Anglicized." "Our conversation is nine parts broken English, and one part pure Bengali. We have exchanged the cumbrous forms of Bengali epistolary correspondence for those of Cook's Universal Letter-Writer." This change in social appearance also registers a shift in mental attitude: "Our Deism, our Theism, our Brahmoism, progressive or ultra-progressive, our Compteism [*sic*] . . . what are all these *isms* at bottom but merely so many different embodiments of a strong desire to exempt ourselves from the obligations of Hinduism."[15] Bankim's concern about the religious deracination of his middle-class contemporaries is expressed elsewhere in terms of lively satire, and indeed self-parody, of the stereotype of the Bengali *babu*. His flaying essay, entitled "Babu," describes the shallow and dissipated occupations of these representatives of the Bengali middle classes by parodic reference to the ten avatars of Vishnu.

> Like *Vishnu* they will be continually recumbent. Like *Vishnu* they too, will have ten incarnations—namely, clerk, tutor, Brahmo, commercial agent, doctor, lawyer, magistrate, zamindar, newspaper editor and idler. Like *Vishnu*, in all these incarnations they will slay powerful demons. The office-boy will be slain by the clerk, the students by the tutor, ticketless travellers by the station-master, the begging priest by the Brahmo, English traders by the agent, the sick by the doctor, the client by the lawyer, the plaintiff by the magistrate, the common man by the zamindar, the gentleman by the editor and the fish of the pond by the idler.[16]

Such self-hatred was generated by British colonial ideology that vilified the very class deliberately created by the colonizers. In keeping with Macaulay's dictum, imperial governance would be enabled by an intermediary "class who may be interpreters between [the British] and the millions whom [they] govern; a class of persons, Indian in blood and colour, but English in taste, in opinions, in morals and in intellect."[17] However, the stereotypical effeteness and effeminacy of the Bengali babu, whose languidness, according to Macaulay, came from living "in a constant vapour bath," while confirming Orientalist disparagement of native degenerescence, was also a starting point for the incipient discourses of neo-Romantic nationalism. Bankim favored a code of self-cultivation, or *anuśīlan*, that would eventually lead in the direction of cultural, religious, and national regeneration.[18] The alienation of the elites was also occasion for developing a new consciousness and rediscovering traditions that had been abandoned in hedonistic pursuit and slavish imitation of colonial masters. One result was the consolidation of a religious identity deemed "Hindu," itself created out of a welter of overlapping but also noncongruent faiths and practices present in the territorial jurisdiction of the British Indian Empire. While Bankim had set his sights mainly on a rejuvenation of Bengali culture, the earlier preparation for pan-Indian Hindu religious identity, created by European Orientalist intervention and idealization, also played into the nationalist self-perceptions of his contemporaries. Furthermore, claiming to speak for Hinduism always had the possibility of generating a wider popular basis for nationalism, even if this national community had yet to be actualized.

Bankim as babu, indeed Bankim Babu, as he was called honorifically by his associates, fulfilled the expected tasks of a competent bureaucrat in the Bengal administrative hierarchy in a number of Bengali towns, where the job entailed inspection of facilities, adjudication of disputes, and disbursing state-sanctioned relief measures toward the populace. In Khulna, he successfully tackled "the smallpox of piracy and the greater pox of Indigoism," according to Aurobindo, but ultimately fell afoul of two English superiors, who had him transferred to Jajpur in Orissa, from where he was recalled to Alipur and Hoogly.[19] Yet, as novelist and prose writer, he imaginatively defined Indian modernity, even as he dueled his way through a number of religious controversies in order to suggest a doctrinal basis for a neo-Hindu nationalism. With the exception of a failed early novel written in English, *Rajmohan's Wife* (1864), Bankim wrote fourteen other novels in Bengali in addition to a range of pamphlets and other tracts in both Bengali and English. All the same, his highly crafted middle-class social romances had been translated into all the major Indian languages (and English) by the late nineteenth century, with several works being subjected to multiple translations throughout the twentieth century. From regional novelist, Bankim rose to the status of pan-Indian author.

Bankim's later political novel, *Anandamath* (or, *Abbey of Bliss*, 1882), contributed significantly to the cultivation of nationalist sentiment after 1905. While the impact of *Anandamath* on the English-language novel has been deemed modest, this novel written in Bengali can be named as an important progenitor of the more abstract phenomenon of guru English. *Anandamath* is a peculiar political concoction, based on a willful reinterpretation of several episodes from colonial history. Known also as "Scott of Bengal" for his historical romances, Bankim clearly took something from *Old Mortality* for this implausible fantasy of martial monks engaging the government in military exchanges. *Anandamath* involves a group of renegade renunciates (self-styled *santhāns*, or Children of the Motherland) battling British tax collectors and state militia with the goal of establishing self-rule in Bengal. Bankim's rendition of these politicized warrior-monks also owes something to the late-nineteenth-century European obsession with secret societies, ranging from the Freemasons to the French Jacobins to Mazzini's nationalist carbonaries who militated for the unification of Italy. This fascination with political secrecy had influenced late-nineteenth-century social organizations in Bengal as well.[20]

As is well-known, Bankim transposed, conflated, and radically reimagined two different reactions to famine, one from 1768–69 and 1770 involving the threat posed by the "Sinassies, or wandering Fackeers,"[21] in Bengal to the Hastings government, and the other more recent trial involving Wasudeo Balwant Phadke—a militant rebel who dressed as a sannyasi and was known as Kashikar Baba—who had plotted to raise an army and loot the government treasury in Khed to relieve the populace in response to the 1876–77 famine in the West India provinces, and whose journal and autobiography were published in the *Bombay Gazette* during his highly publicized trial in 1879. And, of course, more than anything else, the novelistic revolt generated an imaginative alternative to the history of the 1857 Mutiny, and to what it could have felt like to have successfully overthrown British rule if the Mutiny had succeeded.[22] A pre-Mutiny utopian novella in English by Koylash Chunder Dutt, entitled *A Journal of Forty-Eight Hours of the Year 1945*, might have also influenced Bankim.[23]

The plot of *Anandamath* features the recruitment of a landowner, Mahendra Singha, for the nationalist cause. The Children save him, his wife, Kalyani, and their daughter, Sukumari, from robbery in the midst of famine, and secrete the family away into safety even though Mahendra is misled into believing his wife and child are dead. The Children are led by a charismatic leader, Satyananda, who disciplines his cohort by ironclad rules of personal comportment. All Children who join the cause are to renounce their family ties, abstain from sex and vice, and be willing to sacrifice their lives without notice. Satyananda's hypermasculine guerrilla ethos is nonetheless penetrated in male disguise by Shanti, the abandoned wife of one of his recruits, who demonstrates her martial prowess as a pure sublimation of her love for her husband, Jibananda, who is somewhat less successful in fighting his now-proscribed and therefore immoral passions for his wife. While Shanti, renamed Nabin, becomes one of Satyananda's most trusty lieutenants, Jibananda later loses his life in the final battle featured in the novel but is miraculously revived at the close.

While *Anandamath* identifies the British as the enemy, it also singles out the feudal Muslim rulers of Bengal as collaborators of the British and, therefore, oppressors of the populace. There has been speculation regarding Bankim's substitution of terms, edition by edition, partly to escape censorship by British colonial authorities (and there is evidence that his promotion was denied in response to one of the serialized episodes).[24] However, the fact that Muslims and British are substitutable for each other indicates the author's focalization on a militant Hindu nationalist subject. After the novel was first serialized in the monthly *Bangadarshan* in 1881–82, *rājā* in the first edition was substituted by *musalmān* in the fourth; *ingrez* (English) was replaced by *sepoy* in the second edition; and *sepoy* was replaced by *yaban* (a pejorative term for a Muslim as a foreigner) in the fourth edition. The first edition would also carry the ambivalent prefatory comment: "Revolutions are very generally processes of self-torture and rebels are suicides."[25] The novel's true nationalist impact did not occur immediately upon publication, but in 1905, when the British proposed the highly unpopular partition of Bengal. At this point, nationalists seized upon the famous song that one of the Children, Bhavananda, sings in *Anandamath*. Entitled "Bande Mataram," this composition subsequently became the most famous musical correlative of Hindu/Indian nationalism and also was adopted (and later dropped in deference to Muslim objections) as the country's national anthem.

Perhaps the most evocative scene in the novel takes place when Mahendra is taken to the hideout temple in the forest, a building architecturally reminiscent of religious periodization according to one translation: "Archaeologists could easily detect that it had first been a Buddhist *vihara*, then a Hindu temple, and then a Mohammedan mosque."[26] Within this structure, Mahendra is shown several different iconic images of India. After seeing an impressive tableau of Vishnu with his consort Lakshmi, the goddess Saraswati, and the decapitated heads of the demons Madhu and Kaitabha, Mahendra is puzzled at the marvelous form of a female figure lying on Vishnu's lap. He goes on to another room where he sees a richly ornamented image of *jagaddhātrī*, or protectress of the world, also identified as mother of the Indian nation, as she was in the past. Following this vision, Mahendra is taken to a room housing the goddess of destruction, Kali, naked and garlanded with skulls, mother of the nation as she is then portrayed to be. The mother has assumed this malefic form given the ravaged nature of the country, which currently resembles a burial ground. After this frightening vision of the present, Mahendra visits a beautiful ten-armed golden goddess (Durga), placed in the middle of a marble temple. This is what the mother will become when the country is restored to its original grandeur.[27] Bankim's vision of the nation flirts with the shadow of a primordialist version of it favored by earlier Orientalists but ultimately reveals this anterior longing as an echo effect of its wholly modern form. According to Sudipta Kaviraj, "the elaborate form of the mother, the elaborate ritual, is simply a mediation of the collective self to itself," and ultimately reflects "a certain unprincipled use of Hinduism."[28] Of course, such "unprincipled" use was also creative neo-Romantic syncretism. There are other literary successors to this evocative scene denoting a site where the nation's essence can be discerned, or inversions, as for instance in the Marabar Caves of E. M. Forster's *A Passage to India*, with their blank and atavistic echo. While refunctionalizations such as Forster's eventually displace the mythical origins of the Hindu nation into the realm of parody, guru English shares the ambivalent origins suggested by Bankim for the nation. Atavistic rediscoveries of forgotten pasts jostle with modern reinventions of ancient wisdom.

As Kaviraj's supple reading of Bankim's historical novels suggests, "the fictional narrative is exactly the opposite of what [Georg] Lukàcs found in the European historical novel." Rather, "the point of these novels is precisely to 'falsify' history. They try deliberately to probe and use counterfactuals, to extend those lines in the tree of eventuation which were not actually followed up, [to] explore the peculiar terrain of history's nonactualized possibilities."[29] Bankim's fiction of slain Englishmen is not pure fantasy, as a Captain Thomas and a Captain Edwardes[30] were killed in skirmishes of December 31, 1772, and March 1, 1773, respectively. In his hands, however, the historical novel becomes a utopian fantasy, and past and present facts of imperial subjection are gussied up into future imaginings of nationalist resurgence. High nineteenth-century European realism does not seem to have affected Indian literary sensibilities: according to Meenakshi Mukherjee, the religious allegory of John Bunyan's *The Pilgrim's Progress*, as well as the moral philosophy represented by Samuel Johnson's *Rasselas* and Oliver Goldsmith's *The Vicar of Wakefield* were far more important in determining and satisfying aesthetic taste, as were popular romance writers such as G. M. W. Reynolds and Maria Corelli, who were unheard of in Britain.[31]

Yet, what characterizes *Anandamath* is its immediate unsatisfactoriness even as wish fulfillment. At the culmination of the novel, after the Children have won the greatest battle and massacred the British-led opposition, Satyananda's dreams of political domination are shattered by the intervention of the mysterious *mahāpuruśa* (or superman). Walking amongst the wounded and dying, the *mahāpuruśa* performs the task of a physician on the battlefield. He magically resurrects the dead Jibananda. Holding Satyananda's hands, he suggests that the Children are better off conceding defeat in order to ensure that India has a still better future. Satyananda is therefore told to surrender and disband his holy army and wait for the far greater Indian future that is to follow.

The conclusion to the novel argues that the preferable outcome to seizure of the state is learning, as there is no hope for true revival if the English are not made rulers. Even if true Hinduism is based on knowledge rather than action, subjective knowledge cannot grow without first attending to objective growth. The last-minute guru intones, "The English are great in objective sciences and they are apt teachers. Therefore, the English shall be made our sovereigns. Imbued with a knowledge of objective sciences by English education our people will be able to comprehend subjective truths."[32] This concluding thought serves as a refrain for the entire Romantic genealogy of guru English that is both nationalist and cosmopolitan, both political and religious. Satyananda, who appeared to be the guru par excellence for most of the novel, is revealed to be a shortsighted chela aspiring prematurely to political subjecthood. This earlier guru-like figure is now rendered a chela to the *mahāpuruśa*, the mysterious guru of all gurus. Satyananda's disappointed objections to surrender overruled, both figures disappear, hand-in-hand: "It was as if, knowledge took the hand of Devotion, Faith of Action; Sacrifice, of active Duty." This refrain is repeated: "Sacrifice took away Active Duty."[33]

As *Anandamath* already features a subtle internal hierarchy of moral authority among the children who defer to each other based on the moral intelligibility of their views, the advice of this superhuman guru—that English education rather than armed resistance is the facilitator to self-realization—makes that chosen category the purest means of achieving nationalist ends. This final thought of a guru who believes in English education at the culmination of the original Indian nationalist novel might be seen as a blatant contradiction, a complete sell-out, or at the very best, a remarkable paradox. After all, it was not untypical for contemporary critics of it, such as Rajnarayan Basu, to have suggested that English education was "a machine for killing human beings."[34] It has been suggested that the scaling back of the military rebellion and the capitulation to English education is out of character in relation to the unfolding of the plot, which was lurching inexorably toward the seizure of the state. Pro-British voices would later argue that the novel's creed of the fearlessness of the Englishman and its finale suggesting the happy union of Britain and India, prove that Bankim could not be the nationalist icon he had been made into.[35] Other readings suggest that Bankim either lost his nerve or was worried about the colonial censor and deliberately stated the inverse of what he wished to recommend.[36]

But as Partha Chatterjee has suggested through his acute analysis of Bankim as the generational precursor of Gandhi and Nehru, such a chiastic formulation characterizes accurately the predicament of Indian nationalist discourse. Nationalism lays claim to a reversal of the Orientalist "problematic" that described Indians according to essentialized civilizational characteristics, even as it tries somewhat unsuccessfully to wrestle with the same normative "thematic" created by the Orientalist expectations and mechanisms of the colonial state. While the nationalists overthrew imperial power and reasserted colonial subjectivity (the problematic), this desire was largely framed within the moral codes, social values, parameters, and ground rules set up by colonialist epistemologies (the thematic). Hence, Bankim's proposal for a moral rejuvenation and self-discipline—through the myth of a classical Krishna—reiterates values already imposed by a colonialist mindset. Chatterjee's argument proceeds in stages, from Bankim's elite program for self-discipline (a moment of departure) through to Gandhi's popular mobilization (a moment of maneuver and ostensible rejection of Western modernity) to Nehru's deployment of the post-Independence state as the moment of nationalism's arrival, which papered over all earlier contradictions by making the state the repository of cultural specificity and scientific progress. Chatterjee argues that the moment of departure was especially prone to the combination of Eastern spiritualism and Western science, and therefore, the novel's refrain regarding an objectivist-subjectivist combination acquires special relevance.[37]

While an evolutionary (sometimes dubbed "moderate") nationalist approach to the question of social progressivism and spiritual renewal might have married Western science with Indian philosophy, or Bengal's love of Auguste Comte along with Iswarchandra Vidyasagar's intelligent traditionalism, Bankim's solution even from early in his career was to seize the offensive against Christianity. Later, Islam increasingly comes under attack, although with some qualifications. The hard-hitting essay "Mill, Darwin, and Hinduism" (1875), defends Hinduism on an entirely rational basis, even as it charges that the Christian belief in a merciful God is scientifically flawed when compared with the Hindu doctrine regarding a divine trinity. With science designated as impersonal arbiter, Hinduism, while not purely scientific, is deemed closer to science than "the Christian religion supported by the scientific European people."[38] As Tanika Sarkar has pointed out, there is a turning point in Bankim's intellectual itinerary after the publication of the liberal-rationalist *Sāmya* (Equality) in 1879. Moving from a liberal-reformist and self-ironizing spirit to the revivalist politics of nationalism, Bankim's "self-critical, radical sensibility is transformed to an authoritarian, totalitarian and intolerant voice."[39] Bankim adopted an even more aggressive approach (perhaps a precursor of the "extremist" wing in the yet-to-be-formed Indian National Congress) after the celebrated controversy over the interpretation of Hindu idolatry with William Hastie in *The Statesman* newspaper in 1882. Especially as Christian missionaries were making inroads again in the late nineteenth century after the relative stalemate of the earlier decades, advocates of a muscular Hinduism including Bankim and Vivekananda were reemphasizing what Milind Wakankar has called a "forcing-together of body-as-self and nation-as-ascesis."[40] A new ethics of individualist perfectibility obsesses this Romantic nationalist search for new theologies. Hence, we see Bankim's complete rewriting of Krishna's character in his late tract *Krishnacaritra*, undertaken again as a competitive exercise of one-upmanship against the comparative advantage the Christian religion was seen to have enjoyed because of the proven historicity of Christ's existence as compared with the legendary status of Krishna. Kaviraj summarizes very well the changes Bankim wrought on Krishna, who was transformed almost unrecognizably from "a lovable popular figure of eroticism, excess, transgression, playfulness, a subject of both admiration and admonition, to a classic figure—calm, poised, rational, perfect, irreproachable." The consequences of this neo-Krishna "ought to be seen as a Sorelian myth, an ideal condensation of energies, a focus of national-popular mobilization."[41]

The conclusion to *Anandamath* could be seen as a bizarre result of Bankim's continuing fascination with updating and modernizing Hinduism, a process that eventually "transpose[s] discipline from an external religious-pedagogic authority to the self-monitoring ethical agent."[42] This effectively meant the direct transfer of energy from a character such as the *mahāpurûsa* to the nationalist reader who continues the ethical battle as the novel closes. But this transfer is one aspect of the concern with objective sciences and English education. Beneath the superficial contradiction between indigenous culture and modern science lies a more complex synthesis that could be a veritable "meeting-ground of incongruities."[43]

In his cultural history of modern India's obsession with science entitled *Another Reason*, Gyan Prakash has analyzed in great detail the search for an archaic Hindu science that anchored nationalist attempts to fabricate a Hindu universality. Various attempts were made to bolster the truth-claims of Hinduism through rationalist revision of its doctrines. Late nineteenth-century movements from Dayananda's Arya Samaj to Blavatsky's Theosophical Society asserted that the Vedas were originally scientific texts with a materialist and experimental basis. Prakash suggests that the great emphasis on science in the nationalist movement ought not to be read "too quickly as an expression of the organicity and atavism of nationalism." Instead, a cultural translation and repositioning of the Hindu past results, even as the universality of Hinduism is put forward not as an unbroken continuity but as the return of an estranged past that had been forgotten but that miraculously renews a present in which, until recently, it had no share. Documenting the growth of local scientific societies and the inspired rediscovery of ancient Indian science and past knowledge of medicine, chemistry, and mathematics, Prakash suggests that these mechanisms, along with their encouragement by the colonial state, "materialized the imagination of India as a pre-political community" and established Indians as constituting a "fictive ethnicity."[44]

Hence, even if it were primarily thought up as a dodge to keep the novel one step ahead of the censor, the conclusion to *Anandamath* presciently reflects the neo-Romantic nationalist desire to lay claim to a resolutely Indian science and spirituality where the Orientalist problematic had juxtaposed a stark choice between a progressive Western science and a backward indigenous religion. The resulting synthesis of nationalism and modernity creates a modern India that never reaches back to the past in some simple act of retrieval and continuous tradition. Rather, there are displacements and undecidabilities that have come from the superman's precise collocation of objective sciences, English education, and subjective truths. A case in point is *Wisdom of the Rishis*, written by a brilliant young follower of Dayananda, Pandita Guru Datta Vidyarthi. The text distinguishes among "mythological, antiquarian, and contemporary methods of Vedic terminology" with a view to establishing the scientific nature of the Vedas.[45]

Understanding such troubled origins for modern Indian nationalist discourse might also lead us to realize that "English education" on Indian topics cannot be mere instruments that are discarded when the nationalist subject is made whole, even if that was the arguable intention behind the mysterious guru's comment (and even though, as is only to be expected, self-reliant wholeness never arrives at the height of crypto-nativist success). Even the infamous Macaulay Minute predicts that the intermediary class will be encouraged to "refine the vernacular dialects of the country, to enrich those dialects with terms of science borrowed from the Western nomenclature, and to render them by degrees fit vehicles for conveying knowledge to the great mass of the population."[46] Bankim's writings show that guru English has a Hindu nationalist lineage as well as a secular cosmopolitan one. In *Anandamath*, Satyananda's *kṣātratējas* (military, or kshatriya intelligence) is counterposed by the *mahāpuruśa's brahmatējas* (priestlike, or brahminical intelligence). However, such an outcome might well be a recursion as *brahmatējas* ultimately represents the sly return of the Bengali babu, whose rationale favors a solution that gives greatest advantage to his already acquired cultural capital in English. This speculative suggestion injects a greater level of playfulness and self-critique into Bankim's *Anandamath* than has ever been proposed, but after all, his literary versatility was no stranger to satire and especially self-satire of babudom. Perhaps the nationalist reception of *Anandamath* as the great political novel of modern India has hitherto precluded such a playful reading. If *Anandamath* was intended to get the nationalist subject beyond the self-perceived eunuch-like status accorded him by Macaulay's curse, its final dicta return him to where he began, as a compromised creature created for the efficient and continuing saga of colonial governmentality, but who will come to exceed that function. As Mrinalini Sinha argues, "the self-perception of effeminacy was itself an expression of the hegemonic aspirations of the Bengali elite."[47] Underneath this wide cultural agenda of nationalism—political, cultural, and moral rejuvenation—also lurk the spiritual claims that led to guru English. As nationalism attempts to turn away from Macaulay and go beyond him, the more ironically it makes a spiral return to an epiphenomenon of the initial type.

Aurobindo's Literary Cosmopolitanism

Sri Aurobindo's career as India's first modern guru[48] develops in reaction to an earlier investment in revolutionary nationalist politics. Moving in our analysis from a fictional precursor in Bankim to a historical individual, we can trace the advance of guru English discourse from a pretended fiction to a lived cosmopolitanism. Aurobindo's status is enhanced by his having been the most literarily talented modern guru who has left behind a copious archive of high Romantic argument and "overhead" poetry.

Aravinda Ghose was brought up almost entirely under European influence. He was the grandchild of Rajnarayan Bose, mentioned earlier, who had initially favored and then later opposed English education in "Then and Now" (1874). Born in 1872, and given the Western middle name "Ackroyd," in 1879 the young boy and two brothers were sent by their father to William Drewett, a clergyman in Manchester for their schooling, "with strict instructions that they should not be allowed to make the acquaintance of any Indian or undergo any Indian influence."[49] Aurobindo became very learned in English, French, Greek, and Latin literature and developed some familiarity with German and Italian as well. Continuing on to the elite St. Paul's School in 1884 and Cambridge in 1890, he passed High First Class in the first part of the Tripos but did not graduate. After passing all the written and oral requirements of the Indian Civil Service examination, he deliberately failed by not appearing for the riding test. Aurobindo lacked funds to take riding lessons and was indifferent to the prospect of becoming one of the few natives privileged to enter this exclusive imperial bureaucracy. While in Cambridge, Aurobindo was already subject to Indian nationalist influence. He was marginally active in a secret society called The Lotus and the Dagger, and he participated in meetings of the mock-parliamentary Indian Majlis. After spending nearly fourteen formative years in England, Aurobindo returned to India in 1893, employed by the Maharaja of Baroda, to take an English teaching post in the Baroda State Service, and he soon became active in the nationalist politics of the Indian Congress Party. Opposing the compromising tactics of "moderate" leaders such as Pherozeshah Mehta, who wanted incremental reforms, Aurobindo allied himself with the "extremist" wing of Lokmanya Tilak, Lajpat Rai, and Bepin Pal, who preached full independence, to be achieved through a combination of passive resistance and violent actions. Aurobindo's extensive pamphleteering and political journalism for the nationalist cause launched him into national prominence as a young militant with Jacobinical and Romantic tendencies.

When the highly unpopular partition of Bengal was proposed in 1905, Aurobindo, with his younger brother, Barindrakumar Ghose, were much influenced by Bankim's fantasy of a militant monastic brotherhood that could inspire national renewal and evict the British colonizers. Having translated *Anandamath* into English together, the two brothers collaborated on an idea to found a temple in the hills where a new order of sannyasis could be trained. Following in the footsteps of Vivekananda's epiphany about India while meditating on a rock at Kanyakumari, the southernmost tip of the subcontinent, one that is also echoed in the lama's geographical cognition at the end of Kipling's *Kim*, Aurobindo wrote a pamphlet, *Bhawani Mandir*, that delineates the mechanisms for physico-geographical rejuvenation in broad-brush strokes. Bemoaning India's want of Shakti, or strength, Aurobindo makes a bold attempt to give the Indian nation-myth a spiritual pedigree:

> For what is a nation? What is our mother-country? It is not a piece of earth, nor a figure of speech, nor a fiction of the mind. It is a mighty Shakti, composed of the Shaktis of all the millions of units that make up the nation, just as Bhawani Mahisha Mardini sprang into being from the Shakti of all the millions of gods assembled in one mass of force and welded into unity. The Shakti we call India, Bhawani Bharati, is the living unity of the Shaktis of three hundred million people; but she is inactive, imprisoned in the magic circle of Tamas, the self-indulgent inertia and ignorance of her sons.[50]

Drawing on the example of the resurgence of Japan through Westerniza-
tion and religious nationalism, Aurobindo suggests that India follow this
example. The pamphlet ends with the call for a new monastic Order of celi-
bate monks or a *deva-sangha*, who will serve the Mother Country for four
years, after which the monks would be free to continue or return to family
life. The main task of the organization would be mass instruction of all sec-
tors of society and also the education of some of the sannyasis who "will be
sent to foreign countries to study lucrative arts and manufactures," and who
will, upon their return, "establish with the aid of the Order, factories and
workshops, still living the life of Sannyasis and devoting all their profits to
the sending of more and more such students to foreign countries." Much
later, this Romantic nationalist idea will be transformed into a spiritual
utopianism. In a letter to Barindra in 1920, Aurobindo speculates that the
new association would be "a free form that can spread itself out like the sea
with its multitudinous waves—engulfing this, inundating that, absorbing
all—and as this continues, a spiritual community will be established."[51]

Aurobindo also wrote the first manifesto on nonviolent techniques, *The
Doctrine of Passive Resistance*, serialized in *Bande Mataram* in 1907, where-
upon he was tried and acquitted for seditious activities in 1907. Even though
it was for the most part theoretical, *Bhawani Mandir* became ample evidence
when Aurobindo, and his brother Barindra, were put on trial yet again by
the British authorities for the Manicktolla Bomb Factory case (otherwise
known as the Alipur Conspiracy Case) in 1908–9, during which proceeding
the manifesto was produced as prosecutorial proof of a "gigantic scheme for
establishing a central religious Society, outwardly religious, but in spirit,
energy and work political."[52] While Aurobindo was eventually acquitted for
want of evidence in both the lower court and the sessions court (in the mean-
time, one of the key witnesses was mysteriously murdered before he could
testify), Barindra was sentenced to death (later commuted to transporta-
tion) as coconspirator in an act of terrorism. Two British women had been
killed by a crude bomb that had been lobbed into their closed carriage by
an associate of Barindra's, with the intention to assassinate a British colonial official who was thought to be traveling in it. Aurobindo must have had
knowledge of the plot but was possibly a passive coconspirator, obsessed as
he was with his newly developed yogic quest that had started parallel to his
nationalist interest in 1904–5. Given these new-found spiritual interests, he
would start *Karmayogin* after his acquittal in 1909, a weekly review intended

to "unite [religion and politics] again into one mighty invincible and grandiose flood." The spiritualist turn his nationalism took, during the year he was incarcerated awaiting trial, would first be revealed publicly in his famous Uttarapara speech of May 30, 1909. Aurobindo had a mystical experience in jail, when he saw the divine forms of Vishnu—Krishna, Vāsudeva, or Nārāyana—everywhere. Early in 1908, a few months before his arrest, he had been initiated into advanced yogic practices by a Maharashtrian guru, Vishnu Bhaskar Lele. The new religious synthesis Aurobindo would put forward was, in his words, "the religion which embraces Science and faith, Theism, Christianity, Mahomedanism and Buddhism and yet is none of these, is that to which the World-spirit moves."[53]

As Aurobindo's biographer, K. R. Srinivasa Iyengar, states hyperbolically, "the idea behind *Bhawani Mandir* was something akin to 'nuclear' action. It aimed at releasing infinite energy in every Indian and fusing these three hundred million such infinities into one gigantic, one irresistible, one illimitably stupendous dynamo of Bharat Shakti. . . . India was to be the Guru of the World . . . a new religion to the world, the true religion of humanity."[54] Aurobindo states it in terms only slightly less crude in his Uttarapara speech. He sees India as "rising to shed the eternal light entrusted to her over the world. India has always existed for humanity and not for herself and it is for humanity and not for herself that she must be great."[55]

While the passage quoted earlier from *Bhawani Mandir* continues the theme identified in Bankim about the crucial necessity of English education for the objective betterment of the country, it had also silently moved from the seemingly inherent value of scientific truth to more economically viable "lucrative arts and manufactures," and from the domestic instruction of a babu elite to the foreign instruction of an avant-garde of budding gurus. But the simple instrumentalization of education never stayed within clearly defined boundaries, and Aurobindo's feelings about English education, as with those of many others, were therefore contradictory and ambivalent. He faulted British education as "disgusting[,] . . . tend[ing] to dull and impoverish and tie up the naturally quick and supple Indian intelligence, to teach it bad intellectual habits and spoil by narrow information and mechanical instruction its originality and productivity."[56] While James Cousins hewed to a Theosophical line and was a close associate of Annie Besant, his notion of "the ideal condition of true education . . . [as] a community of interest worked out in co-operation, a revival of the ancient relationship of *guru* and *chela*" matched what Aurobindo and many other gurus would later achieve through their Ashrams.[57] In his newspaper, *Bande Mataram*, Aurobindo adds that the newly proposed national education "has necessarily culminated in the production of a monstrous species whose object in acquiring knowledge cannot reach beyond the vision of mere luxurious animal life."[58] Yet it was a classic irony of colonial education that the sessions court judge presiding over Aurobindo's Alipur Conspiracy trial, C. P. Beechcroft, had stood second to Aurobindo in the Greek paper of the Indian Civil Service exam, but had done better in Bengali.[59] Aurobindo admitted to having had no facility with vernaculars in his youth except for a smattering of Hindustani. However, he immersed himself in a deep study of native languages only upon his return to India, when he mastered Sanskrit, Marathi, Gujarati, and Bengali literatures.

Aurobindo's mixture of desire and contempt for secular and economic progress is no special characteristic of Indian nationalist or religious discourse. Following Bankim's cues, Aurobindo's synthesis of nationalism with religion leads him to argue that "nationalism is an *avatār* and cannot be slain. Nationalism is a divinely appointed *śakti* of the Eternal and must do its God-given work before it returns to the bosom of the Universal Energy from which it came."[60] However, the dramatic shift made by the fiery and charismatic revolutionary after his acquittal in the Manicktolla case was a bombshell in its own right. Even as the Extremists split from the Moderates in 1907 spurred by Aurobindo's uncompromising political vision (he signed the decree mandating the split), Aurobindo himself quit nationalist politics in February 1910, on the basis of an inner spiritual command (*ādēsh*). Moving to French-controlled Chandernagore and then almost immediately to its sister colony Pondicherry partly to avoid rearrest, Aurobindo eventually established himself as a highly cosmopolitan and modern guru with a large international following. Yet the neo-Romantic whiff of Bankim's superman was still in the air, as Aurobindo's renunciation of politics was for the task of making the preparations for the evolutionary emergence of a supermind that would transform the world. Aurobindo was influenced by the Bergsonian notion of orthogenesis, grafted onto a Hindu mysticism that promulgated the belief in the necessity for human spiritual liberation by the incarnation of the divine. The ultimate and only goal for the Divine was Self-Realization through the ascent of the spirit, rising back from human to divine consciousness. In *The Human Cycle*, he would lurch toward suggesting that soul factors and psychology were present behind economic and material causes. Using Karl Lamprecht's stagist categories, he would argue that there was a historical evolution in five stages from symbolic forms such as the Vedas, to "typal" social ideas, and then to conventional conformism (all three stages having taken place in ancient India). The rise of reason and the individual constituted the fourth stage enabled by the developments in the West, but the fifth "subjective" stage of the rediscovery of the spiritual, was currently under way. Through a process of surrogation, a "gnostic individual" such as Aurobindo would accelerate the inevitable return of the subjective and pave the way for the rest of humanity's yogic salvation. Yet, even while caught up with all this, he would privately confess to his brother Barindra that he had "no confidence in guruhood of the usual type. . . . I do not want to be a guru."[61]

Ashis Nandy's provocative identification of Aurobindo as "India's first modern guru" contrasts him favorably with Kipling. According to Nandy, the latter was "culturally an Indian child who grew up to become an ideologue of the moral and political superiority of the West," whereas the former was "culturally a European child who grew up to become a votary of the spiritual leadership of India." Nandy's chiastic contrast of the two figures is meant to make the point that Aurobindo's "search for a more universal model of emancipation, however sick or bizarre that search may seem" is superior to Kipling's disowning of his Indianness.[62] Such a psychologistic reading does not help define the transnationally mobile and yet culturally fractured patterns of guru English.[63] Rather than celebrate the "confused self-definition" of Indian culture while decrying the "professional debunkers" such as Nirad Chaudhuri and V. S. Naipaul as Nandy does,[64] we need to see how Aurobindo's discourse marks a literary turn in the fortunes of a guru English that was always more free-floating than a mere pathological response to colonial humiliation by Indians with a spiritual bent. With this goal in mind, we might turn to Aurobindo's literary production for clues regarding guru English's transnational futures.

In addition to definitive metaphysical treatises such as *The Life Divine*, Aurobindo wrote vast amounts of poetry throughout his life. He is especially known for his nearly twenty-four-thousand-line poem of Dantesque and Miltonic proportions, *Savitri: A Legend and a Symbol*, indeed the longest poetic epic written in English by an Indian. Earlier, he had also written a five-thousand-line unfinished poetic treatment on the Trojan War in quantitative hexameters, entitled *Ilion*, and published a vast corpus of dramatic and narrative poetry recreating classical Greek and Hindu myth. Verse drama written includes *Rodogune* (1906), *Perseus the Deliverer* (1907), *Vikramorvasie, or, the Hero and the Nymph* (1911), *Eric* (1912–13), and *Vasavadatta* (1916). The poetic output included *Songs to Myrtilla* (1895), *Urvasie* (1896), *Ahana and Other Poems* (1915), *Love and Death* (1921), *Baji Prabhou* (1922), *The Rishi*, and *Poems in New Metres and Metrical Experiments*.[65] Deploying a vast knowledge of Greek and Sanskrit verse, Aurobindo was enough of a committed proponent of quantitative verse in English (especially the hexameter and the Sanskrit *anushtup* meter) to write a technical treatise, *On Quantitative Poetry*, justifying his prosodic innovations.[66] Always possessing considerable prosodic richness, Aurobindo's poems are often metaphysical and abstract renditions of his spiritual experiences—which make them more profound or infuriatingly impenetrable and imagistically vacuous, depending on the individual reader's receptivity to his Romantic hierophany. While he later theorized his investment in the genre of "overhead" poetry, its effects can perhaps be best understood by considering a passage on the stilling of thought by meditation from an early poem, *Thought the Paraclete*:

> Hungering, large-souled, to surprise the unconned
> Secrets white-fire-veiled of the last Beyond,
> Crossing power-swept silences rapture-stunned
> Climbing high far ethers eternal-sunned,
> Thought the great-winged wanderer paraclete
> Disappeared slow-singing a flame-word rune.
> Self was left, lone, limitless, nude, immune.[67]

When it came to the magnum opus, *Savitri*, Aurobindo was anxious to remind his readers that it is not "a poem to be written and finished" but "a field of experimentation to see how far poetry could be written from one's yogic consciousness." He characterized his lifelong devotion to the production of this epic (barely finished when he died) as "an attempt to catch something of the Upanishadic and Kalidasian movement."[68] The end-stopped line gives the poem a subtle intensity despite its inordinate length. Giving up the weighty hexameter he loved earlier, and for the most part also eschewing the run-on line, he composed *Savitri* as a blank-verse structure that displays many different aspects of "overhead" poetry. Mostly obsessed with psychic liberation, spiritual consciousness, and meditative epiphany, the poem provides a record of the poet's spiritual autobiography and with it, a theodicy and a cosmology. Based on the well-known episode from the Mahabharata involving a devoted wife, Savitri, who cajoles the god of death, Yama, into returning her husband, Satyavan, from suffering his foretold untimely demise, the poet introduces the allegorical method of the poem through this short note that is worth quoting in full:

> The tale of Satyavan and Savitri is recited in the Mahabharata as a story of conjugal love conquering death. But this legend is, as shown by many features of the tale, one of the many symbolic myths of the Vedic cycle. Satyavan is the soul carrying the divine truth of being within itself but descended into the grip of death and ignorance; Savitri is the Divine Word, daughter of the Sun, goddess of the supreme Truth who comes down and is born to save; Aswapati, the Lord of the Horse, her human father, is the Lord of Tapasya, the concentrated energy of spiritual endeavour that helps us to rise from the mortal to the immortal planes; Dyumatsena, Lord of the Shining Hosts, father of Satyavan, is the Divine Mind here fallen blind, losing its celestial kingdom of vision, and through that loss its kingdom of glory. Still this is not a mere allegory, the characters are not personified qualities, but incarnations or emanations of living and conscious Forces with whom we can enter into concrete touch and they take human bodies in order to help man and show him the way from his mortal state to a divine consciousness and immortal life.[69]

Aurobindo's final claim is of course the most arguable one, since the position of belief and individual spiritual experience would radically alter the meaning of the poem from an aesthetic appreciation to spiritual revelation, as many interpretations of religious poetry also suggest.

Originally planned in two parts — dividing Savitri's birth, quest, and marriage from her epic struggle with Death, the poem mushroomed into serial descriptions of a number of preparatory yogas and various steps on the ladder of spiritual evolution. To characterize it in its own words, the theme of the poem is perhaps about "the secret crawl of consciousness to light."[70] The epic grandeur is still maintained by the imposition of unities and double time (the entire action takes less than a single day). Dawn is the most potent symbol of the poem, symbolizing the incipient defeat of death, the advent of the supermind, and the moment of cosmological creation:

It was the hour before the Gods awake.
Across the path of the divine Event
The huge foreboding mind of Night, alone
In her unlit temple of eternity,
Lay stretched immobile upon Silence' marge.
Almost one felt, opaque, impenetrable,
In the sombre symbol of her eyeless muse
The abysm of the unbodied Infinite;
A fathomless zero occupied the world.[71]

After all the epic tribulations, including Aswapathy's astral time-travels on the world-stair, which takes up fifteen cantos in book 2, the prediction of the appearance of the Divine Mother in book 3, yogic quests from book 4 to book 8, and Savitri's preparation and confrontation with death in book 9, the poem ends in book 12 just before the break of the "greater dawn," even as the triumphant couple returns to Earth unharmed by Death to fulfill a salvational mission.[72]

While the myth provides the poet with an objective correlative for his spiritual experiences,[73] the allegorical, or indeed anagogic overlay, however, is complicated in Aurobindo's case. The involved yogic quests by Aswapathy are thinly veiled spiritual autobiography, combined with intimations of divine incarnation: "His was a spirit that stooped from larger spheres / Into our province of ephemeral sight, / A colonist from immortality."[74] Aurobindo's organization and personal life was run by a Frenchwoman, Mirra Richard, whom he anointed as the spiritual coleader even while the Ashram was in its infancy, in 1922 (the Ashram was not formally established till 1926). She first visited Aurobindo in 1914 with her husband and returned permanently in 1920. Mirra was accepted by Aurobindo and his disciples as the living incarnation of Savitri, "the Divine Mother." Influences from Christian mariolatry, Bengali Shakti worship, Bankim's nationalist motherland worship, English Romantic epic, as well as the more generalized Hindu notion of incarnation are indicated in Aurobindo's theology and personal practice, just as much as the specific contours of the ancient Savitri myth. The worship of the feminine principle in Aurobindo's case also has the contingent flavor of his earlier admiration of French (as opposed to English) values in his earlier political writings, and his operation out of a French colony adjacent to British Indian territory for most of his life, dying as he did, in 1950, shortly after Independence.[75] Yet, while the acceptance and promotion of a mystically chosen Frenchwoman into the top slot of the hierarchy contributed greatly to the organization's international appeal, it is worth speculating whether this factor correspondingly diminished Aurobindo's appeal to many more conventionally minded Indians. Entry into the organization was difficult, and hundreds of prospective disciples were turned away from Pondicherry. Access to Aurobindo was next to impossible after the mid-1920s except to a closed circle of initiates, and the Master, closely guarded by an inner coterie, appeared in public only three times (later four times) a year. A remarkable spiritual experience on November 24, 1926, led Aurobindo to the conclusion that Lord Krishna, "the consciousness of the Overmind," had descended upon his body, and that this was eventually to make way for the descent of "the Supermind," which would culminate in the accelerated spiritual evolution of humanity. He was quick to remind the residents of the Ashram that their aim was not personal salvation as much as it was "the perfection of life" that would have a collective and cosmic impact. Given this aim, Aurobindo's renunciation of politics was never entire, as he claimed to follow world events and intervene on a spiritualist plane. Unlike many Indian nationalist leaders who were at best indifferent to Britain's war effort and who sometimes actively courted Britain's enemies (witness Subhas Chandra Bose's famous alliance of the outlawed Indian National Army with Japan), Aurobindo was convinced that Hitler and his followers represented "Asuric" (demonic) forces. Aurobindo and the Mother issued a joint declaration in favor of the Allies in September 1940. An especially intriguing claim he put out was that he foresaw the Allied victory and "inwardly, he put his spiritual force behind the Allies from the moment of Dunkirk." As such, this psychic intervention was acknowledged as hit-and-miss in its effectivity, because it was not from the highest and transcendental fifth-level "supramental" force but from its materially constrained inferior, the fourth-level "Overmind force." Aurobindo's claimed psychic intervention in the fortunes of world history also paralleled what he saw as "India's spirituality . . . entering Europe and America in an ever increasing measure."[76]

Despite Aurobindo's partiality for the Allies, there was of course no assurance that, putting aside the obvious Aryan genealogy of the swastika, guru English could not collaborate with Nazism as well. The strange and fascinating case of a French-Greek woman devotee of Hitler, Savitri Devi Mukherjee (née Maximiani Portas) has been highlighted in a recent biography. An inveterate Hitler follower, Savitri Devi argued that Hitler was a reincarnation of Vishnu as the tenth avatar, Kalki. Hitler represented for her a true Aryan paganism, as opposed to the Judeo-Christian weakness that had vitiated Western society with the cancer of humanism for two thousand years. Savitri Devi's bizarre genealogy included the Egyptian pharaoh Akhnaton and Genghis Khan as predecessors of Hitler, who were also, like him, Men Against Time. Several of Savitri Devi's tracts, especially *The Lightning and the Sun*, are very popular with those underground neo-Nazi movements that are synthesizing their pernicious philosophies with those of the New Age religions.[77]

Aurobindo's phenomenal productivity of political prose, narrative poetry, philosophical tracts, and especially literary criticism more than confirms the close coordination of his spiritual with his literary quest, and the precision of his guru English in its attempted act of the spiritual reverse penetration of the Western colonizers. Writing about Aurobindo's extensive poetic output (well before the composition of *Savitri*) as "a meeting-place of Asiatic universalism and European classicism," the Irish Theosophist James Cousins predicts a new wave of spiritual poetry that includes neo-Romantic prophetic voices such as Walt Whitman, Æ, and Tagore in a kind of transcendental fellowship. As readers of the following movement of the "new writers of the West we catch the large accent, the forward vision of the self-realized and ecstatic soul."[78] Inspired by Cousins's essay, Aurobindo wrote a long justification of the spiritual and literary aims of his poetic endeavors, entitled *The Future Poetry*. The powers of English poetry and ancient Vedic incantation can be combined by "the discovery of a closer approximation to what we might call the mantra in poetry, that rhythmic speech which, as the Veda puts it, rises at once from the heart of the seer and from the distant home of the Truth."[79] In rhythmic movement, verbal form, and visionary insight, English poetry can match the mantric achievements of Vedic seers. Furthermore, "the Indian spirit could seize powerfully the spiritual motive in an age which lived a strenuous objective life and was strongly objective in its normal outward mentality."[80]

Aurobindo had celebrated Bankim's "Bande Mataram" as a powerful nationalist mantra, but as one that had eventually lost its effectivity. The greater mantra now had to come from a more rarefied transcendental plane.[81] We are one step beyond Bankim's dictum regarding the objective instrumentality of English here, as the spiritual initiative will be seized in the language of the objective, English, which will itself be subjectively deep-

ened. It is perhaps unsurprising that Aurobindo strongly favored visionary Romanticism. His own poetry could be classified as extending a strain
of Indian Romanticism, strongly influenced by Orientalist and Victorianist
classicism. Shelley's *The Revolt of Islam* was Aurobindo's favorite poem as a
youth.[82] Shelley is clearly Aurobindo's favorite among the Romantics, and
his comparative assessment of Shelley's superiority to his Romantic contemporaries is worth appreciating in full. The following passage gives us an
economical sense of how guru English can be a subject-position for metaphysical literary criticism, one that is, to date, strongly echoed in a section of
South Asian literary criticism of English literature. Shelley, says Aurobindo
the literary critic,

> is a seer of spiritual realities, much more radiantly near to them than
> Wordsworth, has, what Coleridge had not, a poetic grasp of metaphysi-
> cal truths, can see the forms and hear the voices of higher elemental
> spirits and natural godheads than those seen and heard by Blake, while
> he has a knowledge too of some fields of the same middle realm, is
> the singer of a greater and deeper liberty and a purer and nobler revolt
> than Byron, has the constant feeling of a high spiritual and intellectual
> beauty, not sensuous in the manner of Keats, but with a hold on the
> subtler beauty of sensible things which gives us not their glow of vital
> warmth and close material texture, but their light and life and the rarer
> atmosphere that environs there on some meeting line between spirit
> and body. He is at once seer, poet, thinker, prophet, artist.[83]

Following Cousins, Aurobindo will deem vatic poets such as Whitman to
be the true successors to Shelley, because of a foresight and an enthusi-
asm that can include the cosmic, the universal, and the democratic within
its vision. The future poetry, Aurobindo claims, will focus on Truth, Life,
Beauty, Delight, and Spirit, in equal measure.

   The new poetry of the future will be ushered in as a concrete reality,
even as it will be more intuitive, less recondite, and better connected to
the material life of man. While Aurobindo shies away from direct self-
identification within this lineage, self-reference hovers in the background:
"The idea of the poet who is also the Rishi has made again its appearance."[84]
Guru English does not mean only literature about the spirit; it means also
the bonus, that of English poetry written by gurus, foremost exponent being
Aurobindo himself. Why would this not be true, especially when "the voice

of poetry" is deemed to appear "from a region above us, [from] a supermind which sees things in their innermost and largest truth"? The "adequate" and "dynamic" degrees of poetic speech will correspondingly be raised to "intuitive and illuminative" powers, and this revitalized guru English will be the distinctive feature of "nations of the coming dawn."[85] The guru, armed with the mantra of overhead poetry, will sing of the imminent arrival of the spiritual superman. Bankim's stirring song, "Bande Mataram," had been deemed by Aurobindo to function as potently as any mantra, and we might wonder whether, at this higher plane of overhead poetry, the verities of universalism, cosmopolitanism, and nationalism—and the desires for science, statehood, and spirituality—merge into one. From Bankim's physician to Aurobindo's poet can be seen a transition to the higher Romantic universalist synthesis of object and subject that had been kept apart. By either wonderful coincidence, or overhead poetic justice, an independent India would come into being on August 15, 1947, Aurobindo's seventy-fifth birthday.

So what have we learned about the colonial logic of late Romanticism through the examples of Bankim and Aurobindo? These figures expose an unsurprising paradox, revelatory of universalizing Romanticism and its mergers-and-acquisitions process more generally. What seems most natural, organic, and authentic about Indian culture—whether in its national or its cosmopolitan version—is shown to be invented, prosthetic, and supplementary. This is perhaps no great discovery, even while Indian Romanticism can be allowed to take its rightful place alongside all the other products of modernity that ceaselessly invented a nominalized cultural tradition in the place of the multiple practices they erased. Despite their chronological priority, German and English Romanticism did no better, and perhaps no worse. The history of the colonial detour of Romanticism is necessary not just in order to fill out the picture but to account for other transitions that have since occurred: nostalgia for the present, the logic of the simulacrum, and phenomena such as guru English, all of which were incipient in early Romanticism. If early Romanticism indulged in premodern nostalgia and a lament for lost community, late Romanticism put forward revolutionary agendas while inventing both past and future. Scapegoated as they can be for their recognizable inauthenticity and less credible cultural vocabulary, such time-lagged Romanticisms are not housed easily in narratives of identity, whether high or low. Post-Romantic archivists might want to reject characters such as Bankim and Aurobindo as pale shadows for their hybrid awkwardness. While imitation is the sincerest form of flattery, it becomes diffi-cult for Indian Romantics to confess to it especially when official Romantic values continue to foreground originality, creativity, and individuality in great measure even if derivation, forgery, and prosthesis, subtended by the anxiety of influence, are more accurate attributes of early Romantic energy. In guru English is expressed the efficiencies of a cosmopolitanism, cease-lessly mopping up the various remaindered fractions that earlier Romantic particularisms and universalisms could not reach. Romanticism's afterlife is ensured in the flourishing of prosthetic devices, or derivative discourses, such as guru English.

Notes

1   For an extended discussion of anachronism and anatopism in relation to the "preroman-tic" thought of Giambattista Vico, see Srinivas Aravamudan, "The Return of Anachro-nism," in *Periodization: Cutting Up the Past*, a special issue of *Modern Language Quarterly* 62.4 (December 2001): 331–53. For further discussion of anachronism and anatopism, see also James Chandler, *England in 1819: The Politics of Literary Culture and the Case of Roman-tic Historicism* (Chicago: University of Chicago Press, 1998), 107–9. For an exposition of Anouar Abdel-Malek's notion of tricontinentalism, see Robert J. C. Young, *Postcolo-nialism: An Historical Introduction* (Oxford: Blackwell, 2001), 4–5, 170–74. For a decon-structive meditation on prosthesis and the (crypto-Romantic) myth of origins, see Jacques Derrida, *Monolingualism of the Other; or, The Prosthesis of Origins*, trans. Patrick Mensah (Stanford: Stanford University Press, 1998).

2   For a fuller definition of Freudian *Nachträglichkeit*, see J. Laplanche and J. B. Pontalis, *The Language of Psycho-Analysis*, trans. Donald Nicholson (New York: Norton, 1973), 111–14. For an analogical application that interprets the backward creation of the "Enlight-enment" by the French Revolution, see Roger Chartier, *Les Origines culturelles de la Révolution française* (Paris: Seuil, 1990). For a postcolonial reading of eighteenth-century colonialist literature on similar lines, see Srinivas Aravamudan, *Tropicopolitans: Colonial-ism and Agency, 1688–1804* (Durham: Duke University Press, 1999).

3   Ronald Inden, "Orientalist Constructions of India," *Modern Asian Studies* (1986): 401–46; *Imagining India* (Oxford: Blackwell, 1990).

4   Wilhelm Halbfass, *India and Europe: An Essay in Understanding* (Albany: State University of New York Press, 1988), 67.

5   Romila Thapar, *Interpreting Early India* (Delhi: Oxford University Press, 1992), 60–88; Veena Das, *Critical Events: An Anthropological Perspective on Contemporary India* (Oxford: Oxford University Press, 1995); Chetan Bhatt, *Liberation and Purity: Race, New Religious Movements, and the Ethics of Postmodernity* (London: University College London Press, 1997); and Richard King, *Orientalism and Religion: Postcolonial Theory, India, and "The Mystic East"* (London and New York: Routledge, 1999).

6   Partha Chatterjee, *Nationalist Thought and the Colonial World: A Derivative Discourse* (Min-

neapolis: University of Minnesota Press, 1986), especially chapter 2, "The Thematic and the Problematic," 36–53.

7   Chandler, *England in 1819*, xvi.

8   For a fuller elaboration of the idea, see Srinivas Aravamudan, "Guru English," *Social Text* 66 (Spring 2001): 19–44.

9   See E. J. Hobsbawm, *Nations and Nationalism since 1780: Programme, Myth, Reality* (Cambridge: Cambridge University Press, 1990).

10 In this respect, I am somewhat skeptical of the governmentality thesis in relation to the Bengal Renaissance as elaborated in Henry Schwarz, "Aesthetic Imperialism: Literature and the Conquest of India," *Modern Language Quarterly* 61.4 (December 2000): 563–86.

11 Take, for instance, the two brilliant books by Gauri Viswanathan, *Masks of Conquest: Literary Study and British Rule in India* (New York: Columbia University Press, 1989) and *Outside the Fold: Conversion, Modernity, and Belief* (Princeton: Princeton University Press, 1998).

12 In a longer version of this argument, I take into account *Kim* and also some of Kipling's short stories with Indian religious themes; see my *Guru English: South Asian Religion in Cosmopolitan Contexts* (Princeton: Princeton University Press, forthcoming).

13 Tabish Khair, *Babu Fictions: Alienation in Contemporary Indian English Novels* (Delhi: Oxford University Press, 2001), 86.

14 Ibid., ix, 123. Furthermore, when conflicts erupt within the field, they are between Brahminized, colonial, and cosmopolitan babus; these positions represented by Raja Rao, V. S. Naipaul, and Salman Rushdie, respectively (xiv).

15 Bankimchandra Chattopadhyay, "The Confession of a Young Bengal," in *Bankim Rachanavali*, ed. Jogesh Chandra Bagal (Calcutta: Sahitya Samsad, 1969), 137, 138, 140.

16 "Lokrahasya," in Bankimchandra Chatterjee, *Sociological Essays: Utilitarianism and Positivism in Bengal*, trans. and ed. S. N. Mukherjee and Marian Maddern (Calcutta: Rddhi, 1986), 28. For a discussion, see Partha Chatterjee, *The Nation and Its Fragments: Colonial and Postcolonial Histories* (Princeton: Princeton University Press, 1993), 68–71.

17 George Malcolm Young, ed., *Speeches by Lord Macaulay with His Minute on Indian Education*, intro. G. M. Young (London: Humphrey Milford for Oxford University Press, 1935), 359.

18 Thomas Babington Macaulay, "Warren Hastings," in *Critical and Historical Essays* (London: Longman, Brown, Green, and Longmans, 1843), 3:345; John Rosselli, "The Self-Image of Effeteness: Physical Education and Nationalism in Nineteenth-Century Bengal," *Past and Present* 86 (February 1980): 121–48; Milind Wakankar, "Body, Crowd, Identity: Genealogy of a Hindu Nationalist Ascetics," *Social Text* 45 (1995): 45–73; Mrinalini Sinha, *Colonial Masculinity: The "Manly Englishman" and the "Effeminate Bengali" in the Late Nineteenth Century* (Manchester: Manchester University Press, 1995).

19 Sri Aurobindo, *Bankim Chandra Chatterjee* in *The Harmony of Virtue: Early Cultural Writings*, Birth Centenary Library, vol. 3 (Pondicherry: Sri Aurobindo Ashram Trust, 1972), 83.

20 Sisir Kumar Das, *The Artist in Chains: The Life of Bankimchandra Chatterji* (New Delhi: New Statesman, 1984), 140.

21 George Robert Gleig, *Memoirs of the Life of the Rt. Hon. Warren Hastings*, 3d ed. (London: R. Bentley, 1841), 1:282.

22 Bimanbehari Majumdar, "The Ananda Math and Phadke," *Journal of Indian History* 44, pt. 1, no. 130 (April 1966): 93–108; William Wilson Hunter, *Annals of Rural Bengal* (London: Smith, Elder, and Co., 1897), 13–55. Bankim added an introduction to the second edition (1884) that quoted from Gleig (*Memoirs*) and Hunter (*Annals*), even while he still was uncomfortable about owning up to the novel as a political allegory or historical fiction regarding the current national situation. See also William R. Pinch, *Peasants and Monks in British India* (Berkeley: University of California Press, 1996). See also Koylash Chunder Dutt, *A Journal of Forty-Eight Hours of the Year 1945* (Calcutta: [n.p.], 1835).

23 Cited in Apurba Kumar Ray, "History and the Romantic Imagination," in *Bankimchandra Chatterjee: Essays in Perspective*, ed. Bhabatosh Chatterjee (New Delhi: Sahitya Akademi, 1994), 513. Dutt might have been himself influenced by Sebastien Merçier's Rousseauistic utopian novels such as *The Year 2440*.

24 Tapan Raychaudhuri, *Europe Reconsidered: Perceptions of the West in Nineteenth-Century Bengal* (New Delhi: Oxford University Press, 1988), 117–19.

25 Bankimchandra Chatterjee, *Abbey of Bliss*, 5th ed., trans. Nares Chandra Sen-Gupta (Calcutta: Cherry Press, 1905), xi. I refer to this translation unless otherwise indicated. Unfortunately, the only currently available English translation of *Anandamath*, trans. Basanta Coomar Roy (New Delhi: Vision Books, 1992), is clearly the least faithful, as it omits some key passages, including the encounter with the *mahāpuruśa*. See also Das, *Artist in Chains*, 142.

26 This is an interesting twist quoted from the otherwise corrupt Basanta Coomar Roy translation.

27 For Aurobindo's evocative translations of the *Bande Mataram* song and of the scene in the temple, see *Translations from Sanskrit and Other Languages*, Birth Centenary Library vol. 8 (Pondicherry: Sri Aurobindo Ashram Trust, 1972), 307–14, 343–46. For a discussion of the gendered aspects of *Anandamath*, see Sangeeta Ray, *En-Gendering India: Woman and Nation in Colonial and Postcolonial Narratives* (Durham: Duke University Press, 2000), 39–48.

28 Sudipta Kaviraj, *The Unhappy Consciousness: Bankimchandra Chattopadhyay and the Formation of Nationalist Discourse in India* (Delhi: Oxford University Press, 1995), 140, 141.

29 Ibid., 133.

30 In the prefatory note to the third edition, Bankim adds "the name of Major Wood has been used in the place of Captain Edward[e]s" (*Abbey of Bliss*, xi).

31 Meenakshi Mukherjee, *Realism and Reality: The Novel and Society in India* (Delhi: Oxford University Press, 1985), 10. See especially Priya Joshi, *In Another Country: Colonialism, Culture, and the English Novel in India* (New York: Columbia University Press, 2002), 74–87.

32 Chatterjee, *Abbey of Bliss*, 199. Aurobindo's brother Barindrakumar Ghose renders the key phrase as follows: "The English are past masters in the knowledge pertaining to the material world. They are adepts in the art of teaching. So we shall make the British our rulers. Through English education our people attaining knowledge of the material world will also be made capable of understanding inner knowledge." See Bankim Chandra Chatterjee, *Anandamath*, trans. Aurobindo Ghose and Barindra Kumar Ghosh (Calcutta: Basumati Sahitya Mandir, 1909), 192.

33 Chatterjee, *Abbey of Bliss*, 200–1.

34 Rajnarayan Basu, "Then and Now" (1874), quoted in Roselli, "Self-Image of Effeteness," 124; Chatterjee, *Nationalist Thought*, 65.

35 J. N. Samaddar, *The Creed of Bankim Chandra* (Calcutta: Kuntaline Press, 1922).

36 For instance, Nirad Chaudhuri suggests that the contradiction arises from Bankim's confusion regarding the role of the British. Priya Joshi has ingeniously argued that Chaudhuri's reading is itself a subterfuge as it is on page 420 of his text (420 being the section number of the Indian Penal Code drafted under the aegis of Lord Macaulay to deal with fraud). See Nirad C. Chaudhuri, *Autobiography of an Unknown Indian* (New York: Addison Wesley, 1989), 420; Joshi, *In Another Country*, 288n. 41.

37 Chatterjee, *Nationalist Thought and the Colonial World*, 36–53; and also *The Nation and Its Fragments: Colonial and Postcolonial Histories* (Princeton: Princeton University Press, 1993).

38 See Bankim Chandra Chatterji, *Sociological Essays: Utilitarianism and Positivism in Bengal* (Calcutta: Rddhi, 1986), 60–70; quotation from 70.

39 Tanika Sarkar, "Bankimchandra and the Impossibility of a Political Agenda," in *On India: Writing, History, Culture, Post-Coloniality*, ed. Suvir Kaul and Ania Loomba, special issue of *Oxford Literary Review* 16.1–2 (1994): 195.

40 Wakankar, "Body, Crowd, Identity," 46.

41 Kaviraj, *Unhappy Consciousness*, 91, 106.

42 Sarkar, "Bankimchandra and the Impossibility of a Political Agenda," 195. Priya Joshi has recently suggested that in genre terms, the use of the swami or mahatma figure in Bankim's later novels helps transform the indigenous novel form into "an encyclopedic compendium of narrative modes with epic, history, and fiction coexisting in powerful synergy." See Joshi, *In Another Country*, 168.

43 To quote one critic about the terrain covered by Bankim's neo-Hindu doctrinal synthesis: "In this meeting-ground of incongruities, here held up in perspective, one recognizes Pantheism and Agnosticism, Positivism and Asceticism, Renunciation and Ritualism, Gnosticism and Justification by Faith, the Gospels of Work and Prayer, Church Authority and Individual Judgment, Free Will and Fate, Progress and Order, Spiritual Worship and *Avatārism*, Historic Religion and Evolution, Hindu Nationalism and cosmic Propagandism, the Material Civilization of the West and the Spiritual Renunciation of the East." See Brajendranath Seal, "Neo-Hinduism," in *Bankimchandra Chatterjee: Essays in Perspective* (New Delhi: Sahitya Akademi, 1994), 86.

44 Gyan Prakash, *Another Reason: Science and the Imagination of Modern India* (Princeton: Princeton University Press, 1999), 89, 202.

45 Pandita Guru Datta Vidyarthi, *Wisdom of the Rishis* (Lahore: Arya Pusthakalaya, 1930), 6. The brilliant Vidyarthi died of consumption at the age of twenty-six in 1890.

46 Young, *Speeches by Lord Macaulay*, 359.

47 Sinha, *Colonial Masculinity*, 7.

48 Ashis Nandy, *The Intimate Enemy: Loss and Recovery of Self under Colonialism* (Delhi: Oxford University Press, 1983), 97.

49 Sri Aurobindo, *On Himself Compiled from Notes and Letters*, Birth Centenary Library vol. 26 (Pondicherry: Sri Aurobindo Ashram Trust, 1972), 1. All quotations and refer-

ences to Aurobindo's writings are from this 30-volume Birth Centenary Library edition by volume number unless cited otherwise.

50 Aurobindo, *"Bande Mataram": Early Political Writings*, 1:65.

51 Ibid., 1:73, 74; letter to Barindra cited in Peter Heehs, *Sri Aurobindo: A Brief Biography* (Delhi: Oxford University Press, 1989), 132.

52 K. R. Srinivasa Iyengar, *Sri Aurobindo: A Biography and a History*, 2 vols. (Pondicherry: Aurobindo Ashram Trust, 1972), 1:26.

53 Aurobindo, *Karmayogin: Early Political Writings*, 2:11, 19.

54 Iyengar, *Aurobindo*, 1:328.

55 Aurobindo, "Uttarpara Speech," *Karmayogin: Early Political Writings*, 2:4.

56 Aurobindo, *On Himself*, 26:57.

57 James H. Cousins, *The Kingdom of Youth: Essays Towards National Education* (Madras: Ganesh and Co., 1917), 45.

58 Cited in Iyengar, *Aurobindo*, 1:424.

59 Heehs, *Sri Aurobindo*, 48.

60 Aurobindo, "The Life of Nationalism," in *On Nationalism, First Series* (Pondicherry: Sri Aurobindo Ashram, 1965), 39.

61 Sri Aurobindo, *The Human Cycle in Social and Political Thought*, vol. 15; for the letter to Barindra, see Heehs, *Sri Aurobindo*, 134.

62 Nandy, *Intimate Enemy*, 97, 85.

63 Nandy's book is itself caught up in the dubious project of justifying an alternative cultural universality with an Indian origin that somehow goes beyond the psychic damage created by colonialism. Even though Nandy attempts to separate his notion of culture from religious essentialism, this universality in his treatment is ultimately one that updates Gandhi's synthesis of Hindu Brahmanical tendencies with a Christian ethics of martyrdom and self-sacrifice.

64 Nandy, *Intimate Enemy*, 83. Similarly, Nandy is not entirely persuasive when he suggests that Kipling saw India only in terms of Kshatriyahood. While martial values are clearly of great importance within Kipling's imperialist ethics, it would be more accurate to suggest that Kipling perceives Indian religions (with Brahminism being one strain within this vast spectrum) as esoteric oddities that he occasionally incorporates but cannot quite fully define. The residual Orientalism in Kipling makes him overvalue the highly elaborated religious character of India and at the same time dismiss what he sees as its irrational effects.

65 See Aurobindo, *Collected Poems: The Complete Poetical Works*, and *Collected Plays and Short Stories: Parts One and Two*, vols. 5, 6, 7.

66 Aurobindo, *On Quantitative Metre*, 5:339–87.

67 Aurobindo, *Poems in New Metres and Metrical Experiments*, 5:582.

68 Aurobindo, *On Himself*, 26:229; Aurobindo, *Savitri: A Legend and a Symbol*, vols. 27 and 28.

69 Ibid., preface.

70 Aurobindo, *Savitri*, 28:138.

71 Ibid., 1.

72 Ibid., 29:724. For full-length expositions of *Savitri*, see Aurobindo's *Letters on Savitri*,

29:725–816; Iyengar, *Aurobindo*; A. B. Purani, *Sri Aurobindo's "Savitri": An Approach and A Study* (Pondicherry: Sri Aurobindo Ashram Trust, 1956); Prema Nandakumar, *A Study of "Savitri"* (Pondicherry: Sri Aurobindo Ashram, 1962); Prema Nandakumar, *Dante and Sri Aurobindo: A Comparative Study* (Madras: Affiliated East-West Press, 1981); K. D. Sethna, *The Poetic Genius of Aurobindo* (Pondicherry: Sri Aurobindo Ashram Trust, 1974); V. Madhusudan Reddy, *"Savitri": Epic of the Eternal* (Hyderabad: Aurodarshan Trust, 1984); R. K. Singh, *"Savitri": A Spiritual Epic* (Bareilly: Prakash Book Depot, 1984); and D. S. Mishra, *Poetry and Philosophy in Sri Aurobindo's "Savitri"* (New Delhi: Harman Publishing House, 1989).

73 See Stephen H. Phillips, *"Savitri* and Aurobindo's Criterion of 'Spiritual Objectivity,'" *Journal of South Asian Literature* 24.1 (Winter–Spring 1989): 37–49.

74 Aurobindo, *Savitri*, 28:22.

75 "We in India, or at any rate those races among us which are in the vanguard of every forward movement, are far more nearly allied to the French and Athenian than to the Anglo-Saxon, but owing to the accident of British domination, our intellects have been carefully nurtured on a purely English diet." See Aurobindo, "New Lamps for Old-5," (*Indu Prakash*, October 30, 1893), in *Bande Mataram: Early Political Writings* 1:32.

76 Aurobindo, *On Himself*, 26:69, 245, 393, 403. The five levels are inanimate matter, life, consciousness, overmind, and supermind.

77 See Nicholas Goodrick-Clarke, *Hitler's Priestess: Savitri Devi, the Hindu-Aryan Myth, and Neo-Nazism* (New York: New York University Press, 1998); and Savitri Devi Mukherjee, *The Lightning and the Sun* (Calcutta: Savitri Devi Mukherjee, 1958).

78 James H. Cousins, *New Ways in English Literature* (Madras: Ganesh and Co., 1917[?]), 27, 15.

79 Sri Aurobindo, *The Future Poetry and Letters on Poetry, Literature and Art*, 9:8. See also, Dilip Kumar Chatterjee, "Cousins and Sri Aurobindo: A Study in Literary Influence," *Journal of South Asian Literature* 24.1 (Winter–Spring 1989): 114–23.

80 Aurobindo, *Future Poetry*, 9:42.

81 Aurobindo, "The New Mantra" (August 22, 1920), in *Karmayogin: Early Political Writings* 2:431.

82 See K. D. Verma, "Observations," in *Sri Aurobindo*, a special issue of *Journal of South Asian Literature* 24.1 (Winter–Spring 1989): 1–9.

83 Aurobindo, *The Future Poetry*, 9:126.

84 Ibid., 203.

85 Ibid., 279, 281, 288.

Frances Ferguson

The Afterlife of the Romantic Child: Rousseau and Kant Meet Deleuze and Guattari

It has so long been recognized that children had a special status in the Romantic period that to say so is perhaps merely to rehearse a cliché. A host of examples could be cited to illustrate this uncontroversial claim: Wordsworth's use of children as speakers in his poems from *Lyrical Ballads*; Anna Laetitia Barbauld's efforts to develop age-coordinated readers for children; and Thomas Day's sense that children justified Christianity, which had early found a use for them.[1] The Romantics, we have come to see, created a new economy of respect by seeing children as different from adults. No longer were they deficient adults. Now they were, finally, completely adequate children. Yet if Wordsworth, Barbauld, and Day maintained that children had their own capacities and ways of thinking, their respect for children as children also confronted an obvious problem—that one could value the traits of children only by establishing a way of singling them out and separating them off from other, older people.

Rousseau had preceded Wordsworth, Barbauld, Day, and a host of others in this double move. On the one hand, he had sequestered his

The *South Atlantic Quarterly* 102:1, Winter 2003.
Copyright © 2003 by Duke University Press.

imaginary pupil Emile to cut him off from a world of adult influence, the better to identify and show off his capacities. On the other hand, this act of acknowledging the child's age-specific capacities was part of an educational project that rested on constant age-segregation of children. If Emile's tutor was both solicitous and admiring (albeit in his Spartan fashion), he was also leading the child along a very distinctly identified track. Rousseau's attempts to see children and to see them clearly also involved segmenting the time of their lives into a series of stages and treating those stages as if they could be coherently described and predicted. The time of childhood, that is, became a space, and children came to have their own institutions and live in a world apart from adults.[2]

To put this point another way, Rousseau's acknowledgment of childhood in itself was no simple act of perception; it also involved the practical development of a pedagogy that would usher children through a series of developmental stages and the practical sequestration of children from most adults. For if Rousseau argued against sending children to wet nurses and thus separating them from their mothers, it was inevitable, once one escaped the confines of the world of the *Emile* itself, that children would, on any extension of his scheme, spend ever-increasing amounts of time with one another. A version of the Malthusian problem of population emerged as soon as one confronted education on the Rousseauvian plan. While there might be enough of the necessaries of life to support a substantial number of people, education as Rousseau conceived it introduced even the most Spartan education as a new kind of need. Each child needed, in order to fulfill the distinctive capacity that might lie unacknowledged and thus undeveloped, the undivided attention of an adult—a tutor to direct him or her to the age of independence and marriage. Any couple having more than two children would necessarily have to rely on other adults to remain childless and lavish their attentions on other people's children. Were the adult labor pool to be inadequate to the educational task, children would necessarily be recruited to become both consumers and producers of attention.

The controversial aspect of Rousseau's scheme, as William Blake was quick to see, was that it went well past the traditional bounds of the empiricist project of expecting children to come to agreement with adults about how objects existed in the world. Rather, Rousseau's educational plan proposed to jettison the notion that education might involve agreement on names and the concepts that they betokened, and to proceed directly to an organization of the conditions of perception. Time and space might be impalpable in themselves, but Rousseau aimed to treat education as a venue in which they might be given distinct form. The Rousseauvian stages that Blake so derisively called "ratios" accorded a child reason by segmenting the child's reason out of a more nearly universal reason.[3] Rousseau presented thought as graduated and argued that reason came in all sizes — that it was not able, and did not need, to speak the language of a common reason.

This aspect of the Rousseauvian project remains controversial today. For even if we no longer echo Blake in linking Rousseau with Newton and attacking their reification of time and space into "mind-forged manacles," many of the debates about culture following on from Gilles Deleuze and Félix Guattari address questions of the organization of thought rather than specific beliefs and opinions. In other words, Rousseau and Kant might have authored modern liberalism by arguing for the accommodation of many different beliefs, but modern liberal toleration creates a new ground for politics: in representation itself. If Rousseau and Kant relocate the questions of philosophy to replace perceptions and statements with the conditions of the possibility of perceptions and statements, they quickly replace the abstractness of those conditions with techniques for coordinating the practice of reason. In this process, children are not merely the beneficiaries of greater attention and respect. They also become the focus for intense debates about whether reason can be made social reason, whether it can be coordinated among persons and given practical purchase. They become the occasion for debating the meaning of the old notion of an age of reason or consent, because the very distinction between childish unreason and adult reason comes to look like the paradigmatic instance of apportioning the world and segregating some persons from others.

The most recent version of this debate has focused on sexuality and its division into separate spheres for children and adults — and penalties for adults who fail to recognize that the segregations of the school extend past the schoolyard. The discussion that follows is not an attempt to identify prescriptive rules of conduct or to develop legislation and recommendations for its enforcement. It is, rather, an effort to see how a debate that appears to be rooted in an immediate politics is a skirmish in a longer-running political and intellectual war about what constitutes majority and minority for persons.

≣

In a program called "Dialogues" broadcast by France-Culture on April 4, 1978, Michel Foucault, Guy Hocquenghem, and Jean Danet assessed the state of then-current French law on sexuality. They attacked, in particular, the Mirguet amendment (promulgated July 18, 1960, as an amendment to article 38 of the 1958 French constitution, Cot. 4, 1958), which declared the necessity of fighting "against all threats to public hygiene" and specifically named tuberculosis, cancer, alcoholism, prostitution, and homosexuality as objects of attack.[4] But if the Mirguet amendment had used a scattershot approach to hint—loudly—that prostitution and homosexuality were diseases just as tuberculosis, cancer, and alcoholism were, Foucault, Hocquenghem, and Danet did not respond simply by saying that the Mirguet amendment represented an episode of sexual panic, of the kind that Gayle Rubin has pointed to and denounced in her work.[5] They sounded a note of alarm at the panic and then immediately proceeded to do something that might best be described as throwing fuel on the fire. They had, they said, "launched a petition demanding the abrogation of a number of articles in the law, in particular those concerning relations between adults and minors, those forbidding the incitement of minors to 'debauchery' and the decriminalization of relations between minors and adults below the age of fifteen" (*Foucault*, 272–73).

They were, that is, taking issue with laws that revolved around the notion of sexual minority. Danet asserted that psychiatrists who "consider that sexual relations between children and adults are always traumatizing" manipulate "the children's words in court" (274). Foucault elaborated, ventriloquizing the manipulative psychiatrists as saying:

> It could be that the child, with his own sexuality, may have desired that adult, he may even have consented, he may even have made the first moves. We may even agree that it was he who seduced the adult; but we specialists with our psychological knowledge know perfectly well that even the seducing child runs a risk, in every case, of being damaged and traumatized by the fact that he or she has had sexual dealings with an adult. Consequently, the child must be protected from his own desires, even when his desires orientate him towards an adult. (277)

For Hocquenghem, the particular danger was that the process of finding a victim for victimless crime also made it particularly easy to dispense with evidence. Referring to a case in which "the police" had been "unable to find anything" that might support "the notion of violence," Hocquenghem pointed out that the lack of evidence itself had been used to argue that the very existence of persons with certain sexual preferences was itself an affront: "The criminal is simply a criminal because he is a criminal, because he has those tastes. It is what used to be called a crime of opinion" (278).

A series of excellent arguments converge in these statements: first, that an institutionalization of psychiatry has substituted its predictions for descriptions of actual experience; second, that the refusal to credit a child's sexual interest in an adult constitutes a paternalistic gesture of protecting the child from his own desires; and third, that the choice of a sexual object is a matter of taste or opinion and ought not to be regulated any more than religious belief or aesthetic preferences are. I do not mean to dismiss these arguments out of hand. But I do mean to point to a peculiarity of the discussion—a peculiarity that repeatedly registers itself in Foucault's discussions of sexuality in the form of a nostalgia for the days in which there were far fewer constraints on sexual relations between adults and children. (Think, for example, of the adult of limited mental powers whose game of "curdled milk" with village children is so compellingly described in *The History of Sexuality*.)[6]

Foucault, Danet, and Hocquenghem bring out the importance of the fact that it is easy to imagine that the prohibition on sex between adults and children is not nearly as timeless and universal as it might sound in a Freudian account. They make it easy to see the contingency of the representational schema, and make it possible to ask not simply, What if Freud had never lived? but also, What if psychoanalysis had never invented the Oedipus complex and its generationalizing account of sex? Yet, we might ask, is the use of the past to produce skepticism about the present not itself a rather peculiar move? What I want to point out here is the strangeness of the fact that Foucault, Danet, and Hocquenghem sound very much as though they believed—or, at least, wished—that one could choose when and where to have historical development stop. On this view, one might decide that the history of moral philosophy developed until it produced Kant and the world that he could recognize, that the history of sexuality developed until it produced Sade and his contemporaries, and so forth. It is worth observing that it is a very strange view for someone who is working as a historian and an even stranger view for someone who is living a century or two after the ideal relationship between children and adults had been arrived at and lost sight of.

Yet even as I have my doubts about the temporal pastoralism of the view that sexual relations between children and adults were once right because unregulated, I also think that it is worthwhile to notice the extent of the change that has taken place. What altered the world to cause regulation—both internal and external—to develop? Why did it cease to be an acceptable part of rather widespread child-rearing practices to masturbate an infant to soothe it to sleep? After all, already in 1799 Byron's mother would dismiss Byron's nurse as soon as she learned that the nurse had made sexual advances to the eleven-year-old boy.[7] Prohibitions on sexual relations between adults and children were firmly enough in place for their violation to seem to afford plausible grounds for sacking the adult. So it does not come as a surprise when Anthony Giddens's *The Transformation of Intimacy* provides a capsule summary of the current practical impact of the incest taboo in the late twentieth century:

> Incest has come to be understood not just as a secret wish, but as a reality in very many families, stretching across all social classes. Even when defined quite narrowly, to exclude visual and verbal sexual harassment, and include only the direct stimulation of the erogenous zones of the body, incest is vastly more common than once was generally thought by welfare professionals and specialists in the study of the family. Research suggests that some 5 per cent of all children under the age of eighteen have at some point been sexually molested by one or another parent (including step-parents).[8]

It is clear that what looks to Danet (and Foucault and Hocquenghem) like a simple matter of sexual object-choice looks to Giddens like a pathological situation. It is equally clear that Giddens's view and Danet's are not just trivially different views but absolutely opposed—that anyone who sees the sexual world as Giddens does is going to see what Danet treats as an opinion as a crime or a pathology.

This competition between opinions is not, I think, a competition between equally persuasive views. If Gayle Rubin's work enables us to understand the force of the claim that members of the North American Man-Boy Love Association might be thought of as sexual dissidents, it is a claim that I think is basically mistaken.[9] It is mistaken, moreover, because it tries to identify a representational schema for power that applies equally to all views that can be said to have any kind of minority status. As same-sex relations between adults and as sadomasochistic relations between gay and heterosexual adults win increasing acceptance, it is worth asking why adult-child sex is increasingly disapproved. It is clear that this is not a straightforward question of power *within* sexual relations. If it were, then the inability of sexual experience to act itself out in terms of absolute equality would be as problematic as Leo Bersani and the child's-eye view of the Wolf Man suggest: all sex acts, in requiring the physical enactment or impression of domination and subordination, could be shown to be unacceptable. People might thus feel the need of sex without being able to like it, as Bersani suggests in "Is the Rectum a Grave?"[10] It is also clear that it is not exactly a straightforward matter of the dialogue of different kinds of minority identity groups with majority culture. If it were, then our culture's incredible genius at converting private acts into class consciousness and collecting the small-scale transactions of sexual relations into significant masses would make more headway. It is clear that it is not a straightforward matter of our society's subscribing to a fundamental doctrine about the proper nature for human relations, or else Hoquenghem and Foucault would sound infinitely more convincing than they do when they point out that "consent is a contractual notion" that is "nonsense" applied to sex, since "no one signs a contract before making love" (285).

I am arguing that not all kinds of sexual dissidence (to use Gayle Rubin's term again) are equally dissident, and I am predicting that adult-child sex is unlikely to win greater acceptance no matter how many times people run the argument that all pedagogy is essentially seduction, no matter how many times they affirm that Freud acknowledged the sexuality of children only to take it away by insisting that it must be straitjacketed by being processed through the Oedipus complex. In making that claim, I mean to point to the fact that sex has been strongly generationalized over the past several centuries. I also want to argue that that historical development has strong support in formulations that reach deep into the ways in which democracies of a basically liberal cast enable their citizens to express beliefs and, at least as important, to enjoy freedom from the necessity to provide beliefs and doctrines for their actions. My reasons for thinking that there is a real intractability on this issue are not universalist, in that they do not involve me in saying that the generationalizing of sex was always equally pronounced in our society, much less other ones. Nor are they formulations of the basic doctrines of our society, and in that sense practical assessments of the political field. Instead I am claiming that the ability to treat children as different from adults is almost as fundamental to modern political thinking—of a more or less liberal cast—as any distinction we make politically. I also want to claim that it is a distinction that is all the more fundamental for being extraordinarily difficult to correlate with actual empirical descriptions and a specification of one's criteria.

This is to say that a difficulty enters here, in the form of a question about whether the repudiation and the defense of sexual relations between adults and children revolve around actual cases. Giddens's assessment of the current understanding of parent-child incest raises that very point: while "welfare professionals and specialists in the study of the family" once thought that incest was merely notional, a representation with no empirical correlate, "research [now] suggests" that it is more common than that older understanding would have allowed (107). What Giddens's statement suggests is that we are dealing with an issue that is at least as much a matter of the representation as of the reality. Indeed, the prominence of views of representation here is extreme. It is extreme, first, because of the notorious unreliability of the reports that people make to sex researchers who are interviewing them about their experience. Sex researchers regularly assert that men significantly overreport their sexual experiences and that women tend to underreport theirs, and this social-scientific perspective merely echoes the psychoanalysts and the welfare professionals that Giddens invokes. Moreover, this problem about reporting—the time-honored suggestion that the analyst or the welfare professional cannot trust the reports of the persons who have or have not had the experience—is not simply a matter of experiences that take place *avant la lettre*, so much in advance of the currency of their terms that designate them that it becomes impossible to apply them. The problem is also, and more fundamentally, that our understanding of the relationship between children and adults is a representational one that does not rest with any security on empirical bases.

The crucial point is that the difference between children and adults is a difference that cannot establish itself in terms of any appeal to differences in genetic material or environment. (The simple process of continuing as a child to replace one's cells causes one to cease to be a child.) Moreover, it is significant that this is a distinction that individuals in our society make almost completely without the aid of explicit initiation rituals that mark the passage to adulthood publicly and to an entire community. Sexual difference and differences in sexual orientation may be in the culture or in the genes; generational difference as we deploy it is neither. It is instead our society's most basic representational device for setting a limit to the level of agreement we demand from persons.

The claim that I am advancing is that the explosion of an interest in the education of children in the work of Locke, Rousseau, and Kant is essential to the liberal tradition that they initiate, in that children become the representatives of the inevitable limitation of the reach of doctrine, of belief, of being able to say what you mean and mean what you say in every moment. In liberalism's treatment of the child, in other words, it becomes clear that there is no issue of interpreting when consent to sex or anything else really, really, really is consent. Rather, the introduction of a divide between adults and children insists that the two groups may speak the same language and, indeed, use the same words but that the child will not mean what the adult does by them. As Rousseau says of the inevitability that a young child's liberality with gifts will be merely apparent, the child will never actually be able to give a gift, since there is no idea of property, no idea of a gift at what Rousseau regularly calls, with calibrated vagueness, "that age."

What I am arguing, then, is that liberalism crucially replaces the question of meaning with the question of representation. Now in Foucault's view, this kind of distinction is mistaken because it operates imprecisely. Thus, he objects to the laws governing sexual relations between adults and minors, on the grounds of their vagueness. He points to what looks like a lack of specificity in sex law generally, the kind of thing that has made the U.S. Supreme Court justice Potter Stewart's remark that he did not know what pornography was but that he knew it when he saw it the most frequently quoted remark in the discussions of pornography. Moreover, there is a difficulty in knowing, if you happen to be an adult, if the person you are meeting is in fact a minor or not. Since we do not ask for identification cards from people on meeting them, there will be many times when we will make mistakes about someone's age. What that means for Foucault is that the distinction ought not to be made at all, that the inevitability of mistakes completely vitiates the distinction. And he thus endorses taking children at their words. We should, he says, believe the children. We value them by taking their statements as valuable, by according them "their sexuality" and their decisions on it.

This commitment to a rigorously superficial account of consent and intention is, of course, a sophisticated version of simplicity. It aligns itself with the rejection of the psychoanalytic Oedipal narrative—mother, father, and me—that Deleuze and Guattari so brilliantly lay out in *Anti-Oedipus*.[11] There, they argue against the very notion of the analytic divisions that operate in economies (the relatively autonomous spheres of production, distribution, and consumption) and against the very notion of the conceptual devices of psychoanalysis (the unconscious, the ego, the drives, the Oedipus complex, neuroses, psychoses). All such categorizations are fundamentally mistaken, they argue "for the real truth of the matter—the glaring, sober truth that resides in delirium—is that there is no such thing as relatively independent spheres or circuits: production is immediately consumption and a recording process without any sort of mediation, and the recording process and consumption directly determine production. . . . Hence everything is production. . . . Everything is production, since the recording processes are immediately consumed" (4).

What Deleuze and Guattari insist upon here is an assault on representation-based analysis as such. And what they are arguing for is, despite the language of delirium, a repudiation of the fact-value distinction. Facts are facts, they say, not by having their values represented but by carrying those values within themselves. A child consents if a child consents. Yet the curious thing about this move to treat facts and values as identical, inseparable, and uninterpretable is that it must treat all facts as equally timeless. Treating facts as revisable, imagining anyone's wants as changeable comes to look like a denial of their facticity, since their facticity is identical to their value. Thus, the assumption that what it means to be a child is constantly to alter the value of one's ideas and experiences does not look like an indulgence of children but like dismissiveness.

What seems to me fundamentally mistaken about this position and its application is that it deploys the language of the most tightly organized social instruments ever devised as if that operation simply occurred without any preliminary organization. The locus classicus for the practical and effectual elimination of the fact-value distinction is the monitorial classroom of Andrew Bell and Joseph Lancaster and Jeremy Bentham, with its insistence on making itself into a constant read-out of the value of facts. Those systems taught reading and math and so forth by making oral examination into what Bentham called an arrangement for "place-capturing." An incorrect answer would immediately consign an individual student to a lower-ranked seat; a correct answer would enable him to continue in the running for the higher-ranked places. In this system, incentives that existed outside the classroom were unnecessary, because the system had found a way of making its own recognition the crucial reward and of producing no facts without that basic assessment of its relative value. When Dick's spelling of a word put him into the fourth seat and Jane's competence at doing arithmetic gave her the first seat, the value of what they did was completely apparent. It was visible to others, and visible to them. It needed no further analysis. But it needed no further analysis because it did not stop by simply affirming the value of what a child says but rather by running a common task down the line in spelling-bee fashion until each individual was distinguishable from every other. There were no ties and, thus, no separable groups to be acknowledged or affirmed as groups.[12]

Facts could not be distinguished from their values in utilitarian social structures like these, but that indistinguishability between facts and values went hand in hand with constant discriminations between the value of one student and the value of every other. In that sense, the monitorial schools were producers of inequality. But if they obviously did not revolve around having students debate with one another about their doctrines or express their ideas, the monitorial schools were enthusiastically liberal institutions both because they provided credentials for the previously unlettered and, perhaps even more important, because they introduced generationalism and rigorous age-segregation into modern society. For the development of these schools, with their classes divided by grade and age, substantiates Philippe Aries's claim that "the age groups in our societies are organized around institutions; thus adolescence, never clearly defined under the ancien regime, was distinguished in the nineteenth century and indeed already in the late eighteenth century by conscription and military service."[13]

Aries was interested in documenting the fact of age segregation itself, of the development of an extended period of childhood that endured past the time when a child "still walked on a 'leading-string' or spoke his 'jargon'" and of the development of an intermediate stage, adolescence, between the period of childhood and that of the recognized adult (329). What I would like to add to that account is the force of institutional logic in expressing and promoting certain basically liberal approaches without benefit of explicit liberal doctrine. Age-segregation, that is, is not a neutral institutional fact or simply a biased institutional fact but rather an effective if unarticulated claim of utilitarian liberalism—that a basic duty of society is to organize the competition between persons so that individuals are always being compared with persons who are, at least in terms of age, their equals. Age-segregation gestured toward the similarity and virtual equality of the members of the class. Indeed, the very inequalities that the monitorial classroom was designed to display in its insistent differentiation of one student from another relied upon the basic assertion of the virtual equality of the members of the class. Those inequalities of value—the fact that individuals get diagnostically produced in terms of exactly how good they are in comparison with the others of the class—are said to be tolerable only within a certain restricted range. The monitorial school continually guarantees that restriction: it says that the first-grade poetry prize does not need to admit Homer to the competition, and that we do not have to measure the quality of our little local basketball game by Michael Jordan.

In this view, the narcissism of small differences is not contemptible. Rather, if what it means for anything to have value is for it to be unequal and thus perspicuous by contrast with other things, the liberal utilitarian claim is that the conspicuousness of values disappears with the progressive expansion and disorganization of the group of people being compared.

When Catharine MacKinnon talks in *Only Words* about how hate speech is intolerable in schools and workplaces because schools and workplaces are venues where equality is guaranteed in our society, I think that she is wrong to use the word *equality* as a starkly single term.[14] Inequality within a limited range would come closer to the truth. The basic idea of her position, however, has considerable force. That idea, I take it, is that modern society can point to a tradition of restricting the demands it places on us to identify the value of our statements as facts to all the world. Whether physically (as with the utilitarian social organizations) or representationally (as with the distinctions of Locke, Rousseau, and Kant), the effort is not to say what adult-child relations (pedagogical, social, or sexual) mean. It is to acknowledge the limits on our abilities to resolve our statements into beliefs that we can live with.

Let me recapitulate the basic contours of the problem I am trying to lay out. Foucault, Hocquenghem, and Danet describe adult-child sexual relations as part of a belief system, an opinion that ought to be tolerated by any society in the modern liberal tradition—or, rather, by any society that is suspicious of its categories of representation. If I were Stanley Fish, I would make the Foucault, Hocquenghem, and Danet point by saying that beliefs and opinions are all that we have, and that what we do not have available to us *ever* is a principled position independent of our beliefs from which we can evaluate them. Since we are our beliefs, we must desperately seek to promulgate and prosecute them in the same way that we strive to sustain our own organic existences.[15] In the panel discussion that I have cited, Foucault, Hocquenghem, and Danet adopt this view insofar as they argue for an almost biological identity between persons and their beliefs and for the essential simplicity of this process. (The possibility that they might redescribe matters to say that sexuality is unreason would not materially change matters.) For Foucault, Hocquenghem, and Danet—as for Sade, the basic point is that we cannot choose not to be who we are and that part of what that means is that we cannot choose our beliefs and our actions. We can only say what they are.

At this juncture we can see the affinity between the position that Foucault and the others take here and the Foucauldian notion of disciplinarity. The language of belief and opinion that gets invoked as a description of an adult's desire to have sex with children may seem strange in conjunction with the sense that disciplinarity enables individuals to do things without needing to summon up a sense of their own personal beliefs, but they converge in the insistence on what Deleuze and Guattari characterize as "desiring-production." Disciplines in Foucault's terms and "desiring-production" in Deleuze and Guattari's are terms that designate the limitations on appeals to beliefs, and specifically, to an genealogical perspective. The disciplines make it possible to say that one did something because that is the way things like that are done, that one spelled the word *cat* or *Oedipus* because that was the word one was asked to spell, and that one need seek no further for motivation than that. "Desiring-production" seeks to capture how "desiring-machines" involve "no distinction between man and nature," so that "industry is then no longer considered from the extrinsic point of view of utility but rather from its fundamental identity with nature as production of man and by man" (*Anti-Oedipus*, 4). In both cases, the technique and the mechanical bring an end to the search for motivation, or what Bentham called "the springs of action." One need not ask a machine why it runs, or why it wants to do what it does.

Were the end to the search for motivation (for belief and the cause of belief) the whole story, however, this perspective would not be particularly distinct from the shift that David Hume and Bentham introduced into their versions of utilitarianism in emphasizing not what things are but how they are used. It would simply recapitulate that gesture while simultaneously disallowing the utilitarian commitment to comparing and evaluating various kinds of "use." The Deleuze-Guattari position in *Anti-Oedipus*, however, reaches farther. And it does so by proposing schizoanalysis as a replacement to psychoanalysis, insofar as schizoanalysis attempts to discover the "deterritorialized" flows of desire and thus to attack the cure that psychoanalysis claims to effect with its Oedipal codes and neuroticized territorialities. In that sense, what *Anti-Oedipus* attacks is psychoanalysis specifically but also interpretation more generally. It substitutes, instead, what Fredric Jameson describes as "a kind of articulated thinking that fails to reach its ultimate translation in propositions or concepts."[16] While Bentham or even Wittgenstein would rest content with the idea that one might explain the meaning of something by explaining its use, for Deleuze and Guattari even use-as-meaning is irrelevant. Thus they write that "desire makes its entry with the general collapse of the question 'What does it mean?' No one has been able to pose the problem of language except to the extent that linguistics and logicians have first eliminated meaning; and the greatest force of language was only discovered once a *work* was viewed as a machine, producing certain effects, amenable to a certain use" (109).

But if it might sound as though Deleuze and Guattari are endorsing the method of the social sciences that enabled the modern study of language to make its breakthroughs and become linguistic science, that conjecture would be deeply mistaken. For Oedipalization is nothing other than the process of accepting one's individual story from such a systemic analysis, of imagining that one can discover one's own experience so radically outside oneself that one must continually read the mythic cycles of one's culture as if they ought to be one's autobiography. Oedipalization involves replacing the schizophrenic body without organs with a collection of organs and organ systems, and developing an "egoic" perspective that is heroic to exactly the degree that it is fascistic. "There is," they write, "no more an individual Oedipus than there is an individual fantasy. Oedipus is a means of integration into the group, in both the adaptive form of its own reproduction that makes it pass from one generation to the next, and in its unadapted neurotic states that block desire at prearranged impasses" (103). The social scientific perspective from nowhere that enables Claude Lévi-Strauss to treat all versions of the Oedipus story as parts of the story itself so that the collective account is the only available one is what has made "interpretation . . . our modern way of believing and being pious" (171), because it takes the nonintuitive approach of social scientific aggregation as a model for individual experience, making it seem as though we should actually be trying to have 1.7 children per family or 2.3 cars in every driveway.

Schizoanalysis eliminates the ego and the individual. Thus, Deleuze and Guattari write:

> The schizoanalytic argument is simple: desire is a machine, a synthesis of machines, a machinic arrangement—desiring-machines. The order of desire is the order of production; and production is at once desiring-production and social production. We therefore reproach psychoanalysis for having stifled this order of production, for having shunted it into *representation*. . . . In reality, social production becomes alienated in allegedly autonomous beliefs at the same time that desiring-production becomes enticed into allegedly unconscious representations" (296)

And, they propose, "Schizoanalysis must devote itself with all its strength to the necessary destructions. Destroying beliefs and representations, theatrical scenes" (314). Such destruction is necessary because "beliefs and representations, theatrical scenes" are, in their view, never inert translations: they produce the games of guilt as Freud scripted them. Freud, "the Luther and the Adam Smith of psychiatry," echoes Luther's recognition of the essence of religion as "interior religiosity" and Adam Smith's recognition of the essence of wealth as the "subjective essence of the activity of production in general" (270) by making guilt an interior essence of both the family and the individual.

Now for Deleuze and Guattari the project of discovering "beneath the familial reduction the nature of the social investments of the unconscious" and "beneath the individual fantasy the nature of group fantasies" involves in particular liberating persons from "Reason-the-father and madness-the-child or minor, the parents who are ill only from their own childhood" (271). And Freud's abandonment of his theme of the seduction of the child by the adult in favor of an account of individual fantasy in no way alters Deleuze and Guattari's basic line of attack. For when Freud posits what they call "an autonomous repression independent of social repression," he "exonerates the real exterior family of any wrongs, the better to internalize the family and the wrongs in the person of the family's smallest member, the child" (270). But if it begins to seem that Deleuze and Guattari are simply affirming their sympathy for the powerlessness of the child, their account also brings out a crucial ambivalence in Freud's work. The family is guilty but "confounded with the child's own guilt," and the family is "a tribunal before which one stands as a guilty child, and in relation to which one becomes a responsible adult" (271).

With Deleuze and Guattari's emphasis on the necessity that the family "appear in two forms," the victim and the judge, we begin to see a crucial feature of their analysis—in the form of a direct challenge to the kind of representational reduction that Freud frequently offers up. If, for Freud, there is one sexual organ (the penis), there is also one emotion (guilt). And while Deleuze and Guattari imagine that this creates a situation in which everyone seeks to apply a universal schema to themselves, what it in fact introduces into the scheme is a scarcity of available actions. The phallus precedes the penis just as guilt precedes crime. And this is true less because sexuality and wrongdoing have been internalized than because the reduction brings out a basic claim of modern utilitarian societies—that all actions are, essentially, assisted actions. From Mrs. Gradgrind's conviction when she has a toothache that there is a pain somewhere in this room but that she does not know where, to the organized spaces of the monitorial classroom, the reason actions and uses have replaced beliefs and doctrines as the central focus of discussion is not that actions and uses are ultimately more material and more reliable than beliefs and doctrines. Nor is it that actions and uses are more readily disseminated than beliefs and doctrines so that anyone and everyone can with practice come to do almost anything and everything. Rather, the reduction of rewards and punishments into punishments, like the reduction of clitoris and penis to penis, brings out the extent to which the production of an action is a collective action.

What I mean to call attention to in Deleuze and Guattari's account is that the regular appeal to things like collective fantasy and a deterritorialization of desire actually is a more individualistic account than those that they critique. For in imagining that everyone could tap into collective desire in such a way as to increase their gratification, they may attempt to defeat the internal monitor that keeps asking us whether we are doing our best, being all we can be, and emulating our culture in cultivating ourselves. But they also are, oddly, not merely attacking representation but insisting that all representation should be direct representation, in which every agent speaks for itself and in which the self is schizophrenized so that the halves speak for themselves. Schizophrenia, that is, constitutes a refusal of self-reflexiveness along with a refusal of the reflexiveness of the group. Indeed, the strong claim to be made on behalf of the account of schizophrenia that Deleuze and Guattari give is that they at least recognize the efficacy of utilitarian social structures such as the monitorial classroom — and the efficiency with which they convert the reflective process into an instantaneous statement of what the value of one's activity amounts to.

There is, nonetheless, something very peculiar about this theoretical commitment to the heroism of the schizophrenic out for a walk, since the main thing one can say about the schizophrenic is that he escapes the utilitarian evaluative structures largely by being foregoing representations of himself. In a book published three years in advance of *Anti-Oedipus* Deleuze had found another hero of unreflexiveness. The book was *The Logic of Sense*, and the hero was the child, particularly the child of Lewis Carroll's Alice books with their commitment to replacing the effort to root underground for "the secret of events" with a recognition of the interest of "card *figures* which have no thickness," no interiority or internal depth.[17] For Deleuze the basic subject is the Stoic discovery of a logic that does not rest in the present and concern itself with bodies and states of affair. Such logic instead treats "'incorporeal' entities or events. For him, the Stoic discovery of sense replaces appeals to sensation with sense as "the expressed of a proposition," which is "incorporeal" and an "irreducible entity, at the surface of things, a pure event that inheres or subsists in the proposition" (19). As with Alexius Meinong's square circles, the Stoic proposition has sense — even if it is an absurd or self-contradictory sense — that is part of its being significant even if it is not actualizable. It has sense even though it does not have reference now and will not have reference in the future.

For our purposes, the particular interest of Deleuze's concern with the sense of expressed by nonactualizable propositions lies in his preoccupation with these issues as entirely bound up with the figure of the child. For it is not at all that Deleuze is imagining that the logical games of the mathematician Charles Dodson simply happen to be the resources that he, as Lewis Carroll, has available to him for amusing little girls. Rather, Deleuze essentially treats Carroll's logical games of absurd sense as if they were the only language appropriate to children's books.

This is as much as to say that Deleuze, in *The Logic of Sense*, discovers Lewis Carroll as the archetypal progenitor for minority literature, a literature that revolves around the child's minority as simultaneously indicating her own lack of reflection and what Deleuze calls the "being infinite" of the nonactualized. While the economic account of children might treat them as the produce of society in general or their parents' intercourse in particular, for Deleuze children are, strictly speaking, not measurable.

The question worth ending with is how Deleuze's position relates, finally, to the liberal tradition that I have associated with Rousseau and Kant. Although Locke and Rousseau may regularly enjoin their readers to pay attention to their particular pupils, they also have a great deal to say about the impracticability of their practical wisdom. For Locke and Rousseau, as for Deleuze, the child is unrepresentable—though Locke and Rousseau do not describe the unrepresentable as unreason. Although Deleuze might have been appalled to hear it, his treatment of the child in its minority echoes Rousseau and Kant in their regular appeals to an unactualized but perfectly sensible standard—the child's-eye view. As they invert a notion of citizenship that can and does imagine the child's judgment of the choices that people make, they are talking about neither rights nor duties but, instead, a sensible if unactualized standard. The classic liberal perspective, in other words, is not nearly as abstract or as principled as it is frequently thought to be. Rather, it also commits itself to the logic of sense as Deleuze describes it. Far from resolving itself into a simple idealization of childhood innocence or a commitment to potentiality, this account treats the sense of childhood as a statement of the fundamental unactualizability of a knowledge of our own positions. Further, it affirms that just this sense of the unactualizability of a knowledge of our own positions makes it possible for people to imagine that modern democratic societies are not just being disingenuous when they talk about the distance of people's judgments about fairness from their own self-interest. If John Rawls's notion of a veil of ignorance captures the basic Stoicism of the classic liberal view that we cannot know our positions without also knowing how much they are subject to complete reversal and alteration, the child comes to be something like the embodiment of the veil of ignorance, a figure who represents a principle of the nonactualized that keeps our relations with other people from involving a simple expression of our own needs, desires, opinions, and interests. It is no accident that, as J. L. Austin points out, Kant was the modern philosopher who systematically described the importance of nonsense.[18] For it is nonsense of the kind that increasingly comes to be associated with the figure of the child that indicates the distance between representations and prescriptions, acknowledgment and coercion.

Notes

1   William Wordsworth, *Lyrical Ballads*, ed. R. L. Brett and A. R. Jones (London: Methuen and Company, 1963). See especially "We Are Seven." Anna Laetitia Barbauld, *Lessons for Children, from Two to Four Years Old* (Philadelphia: B. F. Bache, 1788); *Lessons for Children from Four to Five Years Old* (Philadelphia: B. J. Bache, 1788); Day had his Harry Sandford characterize the "simple, hardy lives of Christ and his apostles" as if they had been Rousseauvians *avant la lettre*, and a reviewer immediately noted that the "motto" of the author of *Sandford and Merton* "is, *Suffer little children to come unto me and forbid them not.*" See George Warren Gignilliat Jr., *The Author of "Sandford and Merton": A Life of Thomas Day, Esq.* (New York: Columbia University Press, 1932), 265, 298.

2   Jean Jacques Rousseau, *Emile; or, On Education*, trans. Allan Bloom (New York: Basic Books, 1979).

3   William Blake, *The Poetry and Prose of William Blake*, ed. David V. Erdman (Garden City, NY: Doubleday, 1965). See especially *Europe: A Prophecy, Milton, a Poem in Two Books*, and *The Four Zoas*.

4   Michel Foucault, Guy Hocquenghem, and Jean Danet, "Dialogues," *France-Culture*, April 4, 1978. For an English version of the exchange, see Lawrence D. Kritzman, ed., *Michel Foucault: Politics, Philosophy, Culture: Interviews and Other Writings, 1977–1984* (New York: Routledge, 1988), 271–85.

5   Gayle Rubin, "Thinking Sex," in *Pleasure and Danger*, ed. Carol Vance (Boston: Routledge and Kegan Paul, 1984), 267–319. See also Dierdre English, Amber Hollibaugh, and Gayle Rubin, "Talking Sex: A Conversation on Sexuality and Feminism," in *Sexuality: A Reader*, ed. Feminist Review (London: Virago Press, 1987), 63–81.

6   Michel Foucault, *An Introduction*, vol. 1 of *The History of Sexuality*, trans. Robert Hurley (New York: Random House, 1980), 31.

7   The headnote on Byron in a prominent anthology rehearses the story in the following manner: "During this time [at Newstead Abbey] (around 1799), when he was eleven, he was the subject of sexual advances from his nurse, May Gray, who was dismissed when her misdemeanors were discovered." See *Romanticism: An Anthology*, ed. Duncan Wu (Oxford: Blackwell, 1998), 661.

8   Anthony Giddens, *The Transformation of Intimacy: Sexuality, Love, and Eroticism in Modern Societies* (Stanford: Stanford University Press, 1992), 107.

9   Rubin, "Thinking Sex." See also English, Hollibaugh, and Rubin, "Talking Sex."

10 Leo Bersani, "Is the Rectum a Grave?" 43 (October 1987): 197–222.

11 Gilles Deleuze and Félix Guattari, *Anti-Oedipus: Capitalism and Schizophrenia* (Minneapolis: University of Minnesota Press, 1983).

12 Andrew Bell, *An Experiment Made at the Male Asylum of Madras, Suggesting a System by which a School or Family may teach itself under the Superintendance of the Master or Parent* (1797); Joseph Lancaster, *Improvements in Education, as it respects the Industrious Classes of the Community* (Clifton, NJ: Augustus M. Kelley, Publishers, [1805] 1973); Jeremy Bentham, *Panopticon Writings*, ed. Miran Bozovic (London: Verso, [1816] 1995).

13 Philippe Aries, *Centuries of Childhood: A Social History of Family Life*, trans. Robert Baldick (New York: Vintage, 1962), 329.

14 Catharine MacKinnon, *Only Words* (Cambridge: Harvard University Press, 1993), 54.

15 For a recent statement of this position, see Stanley Fish, "Mission Impossible," in *The Trouble with Principle* (Cambridge: Harvard University Press, 1999), 186.

16 Fredric Jameson, *The Cultural Turn: Selected Writings on the Postmodern, 1983–1998* (London: Verso, 1998), 64.

17 Gilles Deleuze, *The Logic of Sense*, trans. Mark Lester with Charles Stivale, ed. Constantin V. Boundas (New York: Columbia University Press, 1990), 9. Deleuze's announcement of his themes in 1–11 is particularly powerful. Note that although *The Logic of Sense* appeared in French three years before *Anti-Oedipus*, the English translation of *Anti-Oedipus* appeared before the translation of *The Logic of Sense*.

18 J. L. Austin, *How to Do Things with Words*, ed. J. O. Urmson and Marina Sbisa (Cambridge: Harvard University Press, 1962).

James Chandler

About Loss: W. G. Sebald's Romantic Art of Memory

All the new thinking is about loss." So wrote Robert Hass to open his now widely anthologized poem of 1979, "Meditation at Lagunitas." But neither the poem that followed nor the thinking that it engaged proved to be so new. Many commentators have noted this poem's reliance on Romantic models. And when Hass completes his opening idea, "In this it resembles all the old thinking," we are surely invited to recall the extensive poetry of loss that was British Romanticism.[1] If the topic of this issue were afterlives of Romanticism in the 1970s, one might well have centered a discussion on this graceful lyric, written as it was less than two decades after Frederick Pottle's announcement of the death the Romantic sensibility in a famous essay of 1952.[2] It is a poem, like A. R. Ammons "Corson's Inlet" (1965), that seems to mimic the mode, tone, and structure of the sort of verse meditation in a landscape that had come in those days to be called "the Greater Romantic lyric," the poem that conversationally describes a landscape, offers a personal meditation, and then represents the scene in a new light.[3]

Hass leaves the initial part of the out-in-out

The *South Atlantic Quarterly* 102:1, Winter 2003.
Copyright © 2003 by Duke University Press.

structure largely implicit. He begins with a reflection that is prompted by the California landscape suggested in the poem's title. And as often happened with the landscape reflections of Coleridge, Wordsworth, and Shelley, Hass's reflection is cast in terms of contemporary philosophy, especially skeptical philosophy.

> The idea, for example, that each particular erases
> the luminous clarity of a general idea. That the clown-
> faced woodpecker probing the dead sculpted trunk
> of that black birch, is by his presence,
> some tragic falling off from a first world of
> undivided light. Or the other notion that,
> because there is in this world no one thing
> to which the bramble of *blackberry* corresponds,
> a word is elegy to what it signifies.

Working through his reflection on the idea of words as afterlives, and especially recalling the vividness of certain memories associated with the woman he loves, the speaker of Hass's meditation finds a vivid persistence that is not to be gainsaid by theoretical doubts.

> But I remember so much, the way her hands dismantled bread,
> the thing her father said that hurt her, what
> she dreamed. There are moments when the body is as numinous
> as words, days that are the good flesh continuing.
> Such tenderness, those afternoons and evenings
> saying *blackberry, blackberry, blackberry.*

I heard Hass read this poem in the late 1970s, and I found it mysterious and moving. I was at that time unable to see its embeddedness in Vietnam War–period Romanticism. Nor could I register its distinctive brand of poetic diction, self-consciously marked: "After a while I understood that, / Talking this way, everything dissolves: justice, / pine, hair, woman, you and I." And I certainly did not grasp how its representation of the bodily might figure as a sign of things to come. Not that this representation is so clear: What do we make, in the end, of that apposition between the moments when the body is as numinous as words and the days that are the good flesh continuing? Just what kind of loss is being compensated here, and how?

Hass's first book of poetry was called *Field Guide*. One of Seamus Heaney's important early volumes, also of the 1970s, was called *Field Work*, and the respective titles mark a difference between these two roughly contemporary poets in the Wordsworthian line. Hass's poetry—"At Stinson Beach" and "Songs to Survive the Summer" would be other examples—is identified with the field of leisure, Heaney's with the field of labor, and especially labor metaphorized as "opening ground" (to draw on the title of his recently issued collected poems). Heaney's poetic transformation of the characteristically Irish labor of digging was made explicit in a celebrated early lyric about the difference between his own work and his father's. It often amounts to digging into the meaning of moments or events called up in memory or imagination, and sometimes the particular mix of memory and imagination assumes a distinctively Romantic cast.

In "Casualty," a poem from *Field Work* about the events of Bloody Sunday (1972) and its aftermath, Heaney records the terrible massacre with all the economy of a knowing graffiti stylist: "PARAS THIRTEEN, the walls said, / BOGSIDE NIL."[4] But he frames the events of Sunday and the subsequent funeral of the victims in terms of his more everyday encounter with a local fisherman—a heavy drinker, on the dole—and that man's less-heralded funeral of that same week, after he ignored IRA warnings and died in a retaliatory bombing of a local Protestant pub. It is a distinctively Wordsworthian displacement of the politics of great events onto the encounter with the outcast—blind beggar, discharged soldier, leech-gather, vagrant dwellers in the houseless woods. And as with Wordsworth, Heaney's conjuring of this figure lends to him a status between memory and imagination. This status allows his haunting presence, however disturbing, to compensate for his loss. Thus, recalling the man's earlier efforts to ask Heaney about his poetry, efforts Heaney had deflected, Heaney closes his visionary account of the man's funeral, and, in the same stroke, ends the poem, with this invocation: "Dawn sniffing revenant, / Plodder through midnight rain, / Question me again." But the revenant haunts the poem from the start, and his questions set its agenda, especially the question Heaney poses on his behalf.

> How culpable was he
> That last night when he broke
> Our tribe's complicity?
> "Now you're supposed to be
> An educated man,"
> I hear him say. "Puzzle me
> The right answer to that one."

That Wordsworthian slide into the visionary present tense ("I hear . . .") insists on the surviving connection with what seemed to have been lost even as it hearkens back to moments in Wordsworth's poetry of encounter in which the imaginative recuperation is similarly represented.

I would not want to overgeneralize from a pair of examples of the Romantic afterlife in 1970s poetry in English. Suffice it to say that both of these poems hew closely to Romantic predecessors in their styles and forms: Hass's meditation in the tradition of the "conversation poem" is haunted in places by the blank-verse line (e.g., "some tragic falling off from a first world") and Heaney's exercise in the tradition of the *Lyrical Ballads* is in fact loosely structured by ballad-quatrain patterns underlying the long verse paragraphs:

> Sure-footed but too sly,
> His deadpan, sidling tact,
> His fisherman's quick eye
> And turned, observant back.

While not quite the sort of Wordsworthian pastiche that one finds in the poetry of Geoffrey Hill from the same period (often of course with more pointed allusions), this is neo-Romantic meditation on loss in a neo-Romantic verse modality. And though one can find echoes of Wordsworth in poets of the previous generation (Elizabeth Bishop, Denise Levertov, Wallace Stevens among U.S. poets), Hass and Heaney seem programmatically invested, in both topic and treatment, in a way that few recent poets had been before or have been since. It is not easy to tell whether this had something to do with the general academic revival of Romanticism after the 1950s when Pottle's own student, Harold Bloom, did his part to give the lie to his teacher's passing of Romanticism's death sentence. The cultural revolutions of the 1960s were obviously far broader and deeper in their sources and currents. I can say that, looking back from a quarter century later, it seems harder to identify major voices attuned to Romanticism in the way Hass and Heaney were in the 1970s. Insofar as one can, it seems to be easier to do so in the realm of contemporary fiction.

One might consider, for example, the range of contemporary novels that make explicit or strongly implicit use of Wordsworth, especially fiction from the periphery of the former British Empire. Jamaica Kincaid's second novel, *Lucy* (1991), for example, not only involves a protagonist with a name borrowed from Wordsworth's famous lyric sequence. It also crucially highlights how the young West Indian woman, having gained employment as an au pair with a white upper-middle-class family in a North American metropolis, marks her difference from Mariah, the woman she works for, by way of Wordsworth's most famous poem.

> She said, "Have you ever seen daffodils pushing their way up out of the ground? And when they're in bloom and all massed together, a breeze comes along and makes them do a curtsy to the lawn stretching out in front of them. . . . When I see that, I feel so glad to be alive." And I thought, So Mariah is made to feel alive by some flowers bending in the breeze. How does a person get to be that way?
>
> I remembered an old poem I had been made to memorize when I was ten years old and a pupil at Queen Victoria Girls' School. I had been made to memorize it, verse after verse, and then had recited the whole poem to an auditorium full of parents, teachers, and my fellow pupils. After it was done, everybody stood up and applauded. . . . And so I made pleasant little noises that showed both modesty and appreciation, but inside I was making a vow to erase from my mind, line by line, every word of that poem.[5]

This is the first articulation of Lucy's sense of her difference from a woman who is consistently identified with the color of daffodils throughout the book—a heart of gold in a book structured as an inverted *Heart of Darkness*.

Also published in 1991, Margaret Atwood's *Wilderness Tips* features a story, "Death by Landscape," about the disappearance of a young girl at a Canadian summer camp. Mark Bruhn sees in Atwood's tale a reworking of Wordsworth's Lucy poems in what he calls a postmodern "memorial poetics of the altered self," a way of seeing the story as neo-Romantic in its postmodernism.[6] More recently, another novel from the imperial periphery has invoked the Romantic poets in general, and the Lucy poems in particular, in framing its narrative about race and the transformations of modern life. J. M. Coetzee's *Disgrace* features an academic protagonist, David Lurie, author of a book on Wordsworth and history, whom we early on see lecturing on *The Prelude* to his students at Cape Technical University. His daughter, about whom much of the story turns, is called Lucy. Lurie also has an interest in Byron and will eventually find himself writing a musical play about Byron's relation to Teresa Guiccioli. Lurie is not Romantic in any ordinary sense. That much will be clear from the book's arresting first sentence: "For a man of his age, fifty-two, divorced, he has, to his mind, solved the problem of sex rather well." Both Wordsworth and Byron, like the professor, have scandalous sexual affairs (his is with a student). Both, like him, see their private scandals getting caught up in the great social movements and transformations of the times. Whether the Wordsworth frame is superceded by an alternate but still Romantic framing by way of Byron is a matter of some interpretative consequence in the book.[7]

In *Lucy* and *Disgrace*, however, as in Atwood's "Death by Landscape," we have texts that mark their relations to Romanticism with fairly clear allusive gestures. Yet at the same time, these works are not, in respect to such Romantic invocations, especially typical of their respective authors. Nor, in the Kincaid and Coetzee novels, is there a sense that these works are structured by Romantic methods and principles. The allusions mark off an object to be reckoned with but not, for the books themselves, a means of reckoning. In lieu of pursuing these examples, then, I propose to look in more detail at an author whose work, though less obviously so, may prove more typically and characteristically apposite for a discussion of Romantic afterlives in contemporary literary culture: W. G. Sebald.

At a relatively advanced point in his career as a scholar of German and English literature the German-born expatriate W. G. Sebald began the series of four remarkable books — *Vertigo, The Emigrants, The Rings of Saturn*, and *Austerlitz* — that have earned him much acclaim from a widening chorus of serious readers. It is said that he may have been headed for a Nobel Prize had he lived and written on. These books show an adroitness with narrative complexity, a boldly innovative approach to genre categories, and an impressive stylistic flair. The stylistic virtuosity comes across very powerfully in the English texts on account of Sebald's personal attention to the translations and his professional commitment to translation studies. True, though Sebald is supposed to have preferred English readers,[8] there is a recurring sense that an implied German reader looms large among the various audiences for these books. Thus, in *The Rings of Saturn*, which records a meditative pilgrimage along the Suffolk coast from late summer 1992, Sebald concludes with a long discussion of the silk industry in East Anglia since the Middle Ages that evolves into an analysis of the silk industry in

Germany, and indeed an analysis of the didactic uses to which the Germans put the practice of *breeding* silk worms both before and during the Nazi period. At such moments the English-speaking reader of the book is reminded that one is actually reading a translation of *Die Ringe des Saturn*, for the associations seem unmotivated in the absence of such a connection. One is not otherwise, however, distinctly aware of this fact—certainly not from the quality of the translated prose. The translations, one wants to say, are impressive works in their own right, much as Samuel Beckett's English translations are.[9]

These are books with a markedly European purview, and they range widely over the continent, with just a single excursus to the United States late in the fourth and final narrative in *The Emigrants*. Yet their reception on both sides of the Atlantic has been warmly enthusiastic from the toughest of audiences. It is noteworthy, too, that the list of British and American writers who have touted Sebald's narratives—A. S. Byatt, Michael Ondatje, Michael Hamburger, Susan Sontag, W. S. Merwin, Paul Auster, Cynthia Ozick, W. S. Di Piero, Anthony Lane, and Richard Eder—includes not only critics and novelists but also poets. Sebald has become something of a literary phenomenon for the turn of the twenty-first century.

Many of his readers, I suspect, might well concede that his quartet of prose narrative works deserves and rewards closer critical scrutiny than it has received. Those who have tried to gain critical purchase on these slippery and generically hybrid works, however, have not inclined to see in them intimations of the afterlives of Romanticism.[10] There are, moreover, good reasons for looking elsewhere. Sebald is an aggressively allusive writer, and his reviewers have in many instances been tempted to identify a literary master or master corpus among the many texts echoed and cited in these narratives. The names that come up, however, are for the most part not in the first instance Romantic ones: Proust, James, Borges, Calvino, Nabokov, Kafka, Primo Levi, Thomas Bernhard.

Moreover, the most recurring and explicit frame of reference for these fictionalized memoirs-cum-histories is the German experience of World War II. It is not just that the novels reveal a sense of attention to their original German-speaking readership. It is also a matter of a particular preoccupation with the events of World War II. Sebald's is a mnemonic imagination obsessed with the German failure to deal with the terrible events of the era into which Sebald was born—in 1944, in the Bavarian village of Wertach im Allgäu (usually "W." in these narratives). Sebald has explained, in rare interviews and published comments, that he first met his father, when he returned from a French POW camp in 1948. The telling point about this event is that neither his father nor anyone else in the family ever discussed the events that so massively overhung their lives for years to come.

So in *The Rings of Saturn*, clearly, what brings Germany into the discussion of the silk worm industry has to do very specifically with the thematics of "breeding" in relation to Nazi policies of mass destruction. Moreover, the entire book, though ostensibly framed as a pilgrimage along the East Anglian coast, meditates on the English shoreline as a site of war, death, and catastrophe. It takes its title, after all, from the phenomenon explained in one of its epigraphs—an encyclopedia entry, characteristically—in which we learn that the "rings of Saturn consist of [orbiting] ice crystals and probably meteorite particles . . . fragments of a former moon that was too close to the planet and was destroyed by its tidal effect."[11] The idea of patterns formed in destruction, particularly in mass destruction, is this book's central theme—whether it is the degeneration of bodies in death, the huge slaughters of the North Sea herring fishery, the 1672 Battle of Sole Bay between the Dutch and English fleets, or the great hurricane of 1987 that felled whole stands of trees in its battering of the East Anglian coast. In each of these events, after the manner of the book's East Anglian presiding genius Thomas Browne before him, Sebald finds illumination in the catastrophe, light in the destroyed particles, a kind of beauty in death. The way in which this great orrery of a book makes World War II and the Holocaust central to its story and its sentiment is a tribute to Sebald's deft handling of narration. The East Anglian coast fronts, of course, on what Sebald throughout calls "the German sea," and the shoreline retains marks from centuries of conflict between English and German (and Dutch) powers. So as "Sebald" proceeds down the coast from Somerleyton, he moves inexorably, it comes to seem in retrospect, toward the other-worldly 1940s military installations on the island of Orfordness where the eerie, somber crossing to the ruins of the defense system is described in terms that echo a journey to Hades: "Once we were on the other side, I took leave of my ferryman. . . . With each step I took, the emptiness within and the emptiness without grew ever greater and the silence more profound" (234). The sense of entering "a mysterious isle of the dead" is initially heightened by military structures (illustrated by photographs, of course) that "Sebald" inclines to see as temples, though in the end he comes to imagine himself among the ruins of contemporary civilization as seen from the point of view of a future stranger.

The Rings of Saturn thus seems to exemplify Kristin Ross's point, in a book about the "afterlives" of May 1968 in Paris, that World War II and the Holocaust have determined much of what historians count as questions of memory and mass history in our time, especially history in the mode of mass destruction.[12] Understood in these terms, certainly, Sebald does not seem on first blush to owe particular debts to Romantic writers. Even less does his recurring historical subject matter and central preoccupation. For all this, however, I want to suggest that Sebald's new *memoria technica*— though punctuated by the technological effects of modernity—may actually follow some Romantic principles of construction. Understood in such a frame of reference, some of Sebald's most puzzling tactics and topics achieve a kind of intelligibility, and his preoccupation with photographs, say, comes into focus as part of a longer history of Romanticism and what Wordsworth called the ever-reviving "picture of the mind."

I was prompted to this inquiry in part by the way reviewers of Sebald's book return again and again to terms such as *eerie, sublime, ghostly, spectral,* and above all *haunting* (perhaps the most frequently recurring adjective used for his narratives). I was prompted to it in part, too, by the peculiar sense of narrative involution and self-incommensurate temporality in Sebald ("time out of joint") that, for present purposes, we are taking as a possible marker of a Romantic afterlife. But these intuitions required some looking into, and the results demand some careful spelling out.

Let us then begin again at the beginning. Sebald's first novel, *Vertigo,* opens with a straightforward past-tense declarative sentence about a long-dead Romantic hero in a remote Romantic setting: "In mid-May of the year 1800 Napoleon and a force of 36,000 men crossed the Great St. Bernard pass, an undertaking that had been regarded until that time as next to impossible."[13] The statement seems to be delivered in a kind of vacuum, writing degree zero. By the opening of the second paragraph, however, the narrative has located a personal witness to—and indeed participant in— that momentous event: "Among those who took part in that legendary transalpine march, and who were not lost in nameless oblivion, was one Marie Henri Beyle." By the end of that paragraph, the narrative has made explicit that the source for Beyle's account of that crossing is a series of notes that Beyle wrote out thirty-six years later, after launching his career as the novelist Stendhal. This is the celebrated *Vie de Henry Brulard*, one of the most raw and compelling autobiographies of a century of autobiography. It is, for Sebald, an attempt at "afterlife" and an exercise in frustration: "The notes in which the 53-year-old Beyle . . . attempted to relive the tribulations of those days afford eloquent proof of the various difficulties entailed in the act of recollection" (*Vertigo*, 5).

In *Vertigo*, such difficulties in turn become part of the explicit subject of Beyle's sketchy accounts, as those accounts begin to be ventriloquized by the narrator, a figure closely identified with (but not identical to) W. G. Sebald, expatriate German literature professor born in wartime Bavaria but resident in England since the 1970s. Beyle is said to have been "so affected" by the carnage of the campaign "that he now has no clear idea whatsoever of the things he found so horrifying then" (5–6). Thus, when the narrator goes on to the next stage of Beyle's account, in which Beyle characteristically produces a sketch to aid his memory of the battle that followed upon the transalpine march, he comments on the internal inconsistency of the drawing. The sketch, which Sebald (also characteristically) includes as a "figure" in his text, is supposed to show how his column came under fire near a fortress, notating various positions with different letters and locating his own position in the scheme with an "H." But the narrator points out that the scene could not have been viewed in just this way from a position that the sketch itself includes in its representation. If strong emotion can erase the very impression it generates, the images by which we try to revive those impressions can be all the more treacherous for their air of reliability.

Likewise, Sebald's Beyle records that the descent from the heights of St. Bernard's pass made "an indelible impression on him." Beyle writes that he "gazed and gazed" upon the scene and reports in this memoir that for years he "lived in the conviction that he could remember every detail of that ride, especially the panoramic view of the town of Ivrea" (7). It was therefore, we learn, a matter of "severe disappointment . . . when some years ago, looking through old papers he came across an engraving entitled *Prospetto d'ivrea* and was obliged to concede that his recollected picture of the town in the evening sun was nothing but a copy of that very engraving" (8). The moral of the story for Beyle is that one should not "purchase engravings and fine views and prospects seen in one's travels, since before long they will displace our memories completely, indeed one might say they destroy them" (ibid.).

The moral of the story for Sebald is far less clear. His four books all address vexed questions about how to understand one's relation to the past in the light of the treacherous work of memory and forgetting, image and impression. No simple rule (such as not to purchase pictures of the places one visits) can be said to govern the complex evolution of cases throughout these books. Sometimes images displace memories, but such displacement is often a form of conservation—a trace that enables someone to track back to something crucial. It is seldom an easy matter in a Sebald narrative to tell whether one is moving in the direction of remembering or of forgetting; one is often doing both, and neither, all at once.

The handling of Beyle's account of the battle of Marengo is a case in point. Beyle had not fought in this battle, but in the 1836 memoir he did record his 1801 visit to the scene of the battle fifteen months after it took place. On arriving at the battlefield he was already familiar with the famous events that had taken place there from "many and various tellings, and he had himself pictured it in numerous forms and hues" (17). At the scene itself, Beyle recalls, in confronting "the few stark trees, and . . . the bones of perhaps 16,000 men and 4,000 horses that had lost their lives there, already bleached and shining in the dew," he was thrown into "a vertiginous state of confusion such as he had never previously experienced" (17). When Ezekiel witnessed the miracle of a skeleton brought to life, he famously put the question—"Can these dry bones live?" The bones at Marengo are moist— still moist, as it were—and yet this is not in any straightforward sense an act of revivification. The effect of the shining bleached-white bones on Beyle is less to bring the battle back to life than to erase a surviving image of the battle, the one he had been carrying around in his head in its "numerous forms and hues." The extinction of this surviving picture seems to be the immediate occasion of the fit of vertigo, the first one mentioned in the book. The loss of the image (of such loss) leaves Beyle without temporal and historical bearings.

The sense of vertigo here is also a function of the narrative rhetoric, as this passage seems to orbit among several tenses or times: the time of the battle, the times of his hearing of the battle, the time of Beyle's seeing the battlefield, and the time of Beyle's recollection of the visit. Moreover, Sebald goes on to cite a reflection in which Beyle finds a tense structure to address even the years between 1801 and 1836, to the following effect: "Later, think-ing back to that September day on the field of Merengo, it often seemed to Beyle as if he had foreseen the years which lay ahead, all the campaigns and disasters, even the fall and exile of Napoleon, and as if he had realised then that he would not find his fortune in the army. At all events, it was in the autumn that he resolved to become the greatest writer of all time" (18). In the space of a few pages Sebald has almost impossibly complicated the configuration of time and tense underlying that initial simple declara-tion about Napoleon's "historic" 1801 crossing of the Great St. Bernard pass. And as with the account of the visit to the Marengo battlefield, the effect of this complication is as much a matter of making the moment live as it is of rendering it ghostly.

What Sebald accomplishes in these opening pages of his first novel is cer-tainly already a feat of narrative virtuosity. But in fact further temporal and mnemonic complications still lie ahead as we learn that what this book is really about is the vertigo not of Stendhal but of the narrator, a character named "W. G. Sebald," who is traveling around northern Italy researching Stendhal's (and Kafka's) periods of residence there. This "Sebald" is a char-acter who, like the author of the book, is a German-born literature scholar who left Germany years before to live and work in East Anglia, and who has not revisited his homeland since 1970. At one point we actually see an illus-tration showing "Sebald's" (and presumably Sebald's) 1987-issued German passport. It is "Sebald"—the *author* of the account of Beyle's account of his Napoleonic past—whose travels we follow in Venice, Verona, and Riva. It is "Sebald" whose fits of vertigo in these places are made the driving force of the narrative, "Sebald" who revisits all these places to understand what plagued him in them, and "Sebald" whose travels we eventually follow to the Bavarian village where he was born, as he looks for answers among the scenes, objects, and people of his German childhood.

It is in this sense that *Vertigo* sets a pattern for Sebald's quartet of novels. Different as they are, they nonetheless hang together with a programma-tic sense of mission. Each involves a narrator rather like himself. And of course each produces extraordinary feats of narrative virtuosity in weav-ing problems of memory and history. Each finds its way to Germany, the place where, for Sebald, memory and history were put to the hardest tests in the previous half-century or so. The convoluted narrative of *Austerlitz*, as we see below, spirals steadily back to a Jewish detention center in Prague at the start of the war. In "Max Ferber," the longest and richest tale in *The Emigrants*, curiosity about a Manchester painter (a composite of two actual personages) eventually leads "Sebald" to, and into, the memoirs written by Ferber's mother, Luisa Landsberg, at Bad Kissingen in the two years before her execution in 1941, a document from which the narrator "quotes" extensively before reporting on his trip to her gravesite. (As usual with Sebald we do not know whether the quoted document or reproduced illustration is factual, merely rooted in fact, or basically fabricated.) The narrator tells us that he stays there, writing up the account, until he realizes that "the lack of memory that marked the Germans, and the efficiency with which they cleaned everything up, were beginning to affect my head and my nerves."[14]

This kind of drive toward the German scene thus exerts its power throughout these books. By the same token, however, the use of Stendhal as the starting point for the entire project should not be taken to be a matter of serendipity—not in view of Sebald's evident emulation of the hybrid fiction-memoir, not in view of Sebald's marked imitation of Stendhal's practice of sprinkling his text liberally with figures and illustrations, and especially not in view of the kind of epistemological conundrums that Sebald highlights in his "reading" of Stendhal's text. Such conundrums occur all over the *Vie de Henry Brulard*. Sometimes Stendhal emphasizes the surety of the images at the expense of undermining the explanations he attaches to them: *"Le lecteur, s'il s'en trouve jamais pour ces fariboles, verra sans peine que tous mes pourquois toutes mes explications peruvent être très fautives. Je n'ai que des images fort nettes; toutes mes explications me viennent en écrivant ceci, quarante-cinq ans après les événements."* Sometimes he emphasizes the uncertainty of the image itself: *"Je me figure l'événement, mais probablement ce n'est pas un souvenir direct, ce n'est que le souvenir de l'image que je me formi de la chose fort anciennement et à l'époque des premiers recita qu'on m'en fit."*[15] These observations, it seems to me, could as easily apply to Sebald's blend of memoir and fiction and history as to what we find in the *Vie de Henry Brulard*. If Sebald is preoccupied with the recent German past, the question I want to pose is whether his circuitous path to it is being mapped with Romantic resources.

=====

To appreciate the deep propriety of Sebald's framing of the first of his series of books by way of Stendhal's memoir, it helps to grasp the importance of a particular set of concepts informing Sebald's practice: impression, image, trace, layer, association, digression, and order or design. These concepts are everywhere important in what Sebald sets out to accomplish, and together they help to furnish the peculiar brand of "narrative" in his books. The epistemology that underlies this vocabulary and this sort of narrative, I want to suggest, is one that underlies British Romanticism. It belongs, ultimately, to the so-called theory of ideas as that was developed over the course of the eighteenth century by the likes of Frances Hutcheson and David Hume.[16] The theory of ideas is summarized fairly clearly in the exposition with which Hume begins *The Treatise of Human Nature*. And as Annette Baier has suggested, this theory provides the basis for the understanding of a *sentiment* in its early and technical sense.[17]

To state the crux of the matter briefly, an impression on this account is something that we feel, and an idea is an afterimage of the impression. It is what survives the initial impression and resembles it in all ways except in the degree of vivacity. The image that is the idea might therefore not inaptly be termed the specter or afterlife of the impression. What becomes crucial in the theory of sentiments that grows out of the theory of ideas, however, is that our minds work in such a way that the idea or image-of-the-impression has the capacity to return to us in a reflective modality. Such a return of the idea, itself cognitive in character, occasions a new affective event in our experience. Hume's name for this new reflective event is an "impression of reflection." This (as it were) second-order impression likewise leaves behind its trace image, its idea. That idea can in its turn recur to the mind, and so on.

There are two ways in which ideas can recur to the mind to create new impressions and thus new ideas. These are memory and imagination. And the difference is simply that the ideas of memory arrange themselves just as they did in our experience, whereas the ideas of imagination do not. Needless to say, the distinction between memory and imagination here is not a clear and bright one, and neither, therefore, is the distinction between the image and its source impression. Nonetheless, this basic scheme, it seems to me, became the framework of the so-called Romantic revolutions in poetry, especially the one led by Wordsworth and Coleridge in the *Lyrical Ballads* collaboration of 1798–1800. The preface that Wordsworth wrote for the volume in 1800, the very year young Henri Beyle marched with Napoleon into Italy, announced its epistemological premises in terms that deviated from the Humean exposition only trivially. Describing the act of meditation that he felt entitled him to the authority of the poet, Wordsworth explained its operations in terms of his disciplined attention to "thoughts" (what Hume calls "ideas") that are the "representatives of past feelings" (what Hume calls impressions).[18] And in a versified passage written at about this same time for *The Prelude*, Wordsworth reproduced the schema in much the same form when he spoke of how "objects and appearances" were "impressed" on the mind: "And if the vulgar joy [or fear] by its own weight / Wearied itself out of the memory, / The scenes which were a witness of that joy / Remained, in their substantial lineaments / Depicted on the brain, and to the eye / Were visible, a daily sight." This practice, grounded in what he punningly calls an "impressive discipline," was itself the basis of his great art of memory.[19]

Behind the *Lyrical Ballads* project, of course, were the tumultuous years of the 1790s whose developments Wordsworth specifically pointed to when he argued the need for his new form of meditative poetic discipline: "A multitude of causes, unknown to former times, are now acting with a combined force to blunt the discriminating powers of the mind" (*Prose Works*, 1:128). Wordsworth develops his new mental discipline to address an age that has reduced the mind to "a state of almost savage torpor" (ibid.). But the very discipline he forges, his new *memoria technica*, has as one of its consequences that he cannot tell—can neither see nor say—just what it is for sure that lies behind his images. This is why, in that passage from book 1 of *The Prelude*, he is able to understand something about why beginning the poem had been such a vexing task for him.

> I began
> My story early, feeling, as I fear,
> The weakness of a human love for days
> Disowned by memory—ere the birth of spring
> Planting my snowdrops among winter snows.
> (*Prelude*, 640–44)

Wordsworth begins his story "early" in the sense that any story he tells must construct a content for the emotion he feels in confronting a thought-image that is a representation of a feeling no longer available. Any story he tells must offer an etiological speculation for the thought-images he carries with him (or those he finds in the world around him). He must begin his memoir in a place and time where memory itself cannot help him.

This kind of conundrum is a version of what Richard Terdiman, writing about Alfred de Musset in France, calls the problem of Romantic mnemonics, the problem of the past pitted against the present for determinative priority.[20] It is the kind of conundrum that informs the autobiographical speculations of Musset's great contemporary Stendhal. It is the kind of conundrum that shaped the greater Romantic lyric that Wordsworth and Coleridge (before his Kantian conversion) together elaborated from 1797 to 1800, and that Hass and Heaney were working from in their own variations on the Romantic afterlife in the 1970s. And it is the kind of conundrum that one can discern in a more recent poem with the archly Romantic title, "Dark Night Sallies Forth," that opens like this:

> If I see before me
> the nervature of past life
> in one image, I always think
> that this has something to do
> with truth. Our brains, after all,
> are always at work on some quivers
> of self-organization, however faint,
> and it is from this that an order
> arises, in places beautiful
> and comforting, though more cruel, too,
> than the previous state of ignorance.
> How far, in any case, must one go back
> to find the beginning? Perhaps
> to that morning of January 9, 1905,
> on which Grandfather and Grandmother
> in ringing cold drove in an open
> landau from Kloster to Lechfield
> to Obermeitingen, to be married.[21]

By the end of this passage it probably becomes clear that this is a poem by W. G. Sebald. It was translated by Michael Hamburger and published posthumously in *The New Yorker* magazine in 2002. Is it not fair enough to call it a poem of the Wordsworthian afterlife? True, Sebald's beginning before the beginning characteristically extends to a time before his own birth and a place beyond his own "sweet birthplace." He seems more willing than Wordsworth to think of the field of history as a kind of "extended memory," though such extension also ultimately becomes part of Wordsworth's own argument in *The Prelude*.[22]

═══

But what of the prose work? What more can be said for placing Sebald's fiction in the Romantic line, as *Vertigo* seems to invite. Let me turn now to *Austerlitz*, the last of the four novels and arguably the most accomplished. It is the most "novelistic" of Sebald's four books, and in that sense the least generically mixed, but to say that much is to risk underestimating its singularity and complexity. It records two series of encounters (one beginning in 1967, the other in 1996) between the unnamed narrator and a character called Jacques Austerlitz. Austerlitz is supposed to be in his early thirties when he and the narrator first meet—stranger to stranger—in the Belgian train station where they begin their long conversation. They meet again by accident, then later by design. The novel is given over to their conversation, somewhat in the manner of Louis Malle's *My Dinner with André*, with most of the words in the novel being put in the mouth of Austerlitz. He holds forth on a variety of historical subjects, especially architecture, and increasingly on the events of his own life, about which he discovers—and recalls—more and more detail over the three decades spanned by the narration. Whereas early on in the narrative his autobiographical comments address the period of his early schooling in Wales, where he was raised by foster parents, they eventually zero in on his first four years as a Jewish child in Prague and his being sent away in 1939 by parents anxious for his safety who themselves did not survive the Holocaust.

Like its three predecessors, *Austerlitz* is narrated by a character recognizably like W. G. Sebald—we know that he is professorial, was born in Germany, and has long lived in England. Like the others, it is drawn inexorably toward the war years with a deep and powerful homing instinct. Like the others, too, most conspicuously, it is liberally illustrated with photographs, drawings, and other visual materials. But it also departs from the other books in key respects. First, it presses hard with a tendency present in the other works to conflate narrative voices by leaving interpolated stories unpunctuated. In encountering pronouns, we are often at least momentarily confused—deliberately so, it would seem—about who is talking and when. Second, a closely related point, the Sebaldian narrator cedes his centrally authoritative position and many of its functions to Jacques Austerlitz.

Thus, where in *Vertigo* "Sebald" himself is the one who returns to the place of his childhood for the first time in many years, in *Austerlitz* it is the titular character who makes this pilgrimage—revisiting his surrogate mother and exploring the painful objects collected at Terezìn, the Prague site where the Germans imprisoned Czech Jews under the flimsy pretext of creating an art center.

Austerlitz not only occupies center stage in the narrative, he also holds a kind of psychological sway over the narrator by virtue of his elaborated views of how to understand the encounter with the past—his own version of *memoria technica*. In the initial chance encounter at the Antwerp Centraal Station, Austerlitz, who stands out among the other waiting passengers because of his conspicuously attentive habits of observation and his diligence in note taking, offers a discourse on the history of train stations in general and the Antwerp Centraal Station in particular. After reproducing Austerlitz's virtuoso commentary on the placement, construction, and ornamentation of the great clock in the Antwerp station—a commentary that evolves into a meditation on railways, time, and modernity—the narrator recollects his own early admiration for the *method* he found in Austerlitz discourse, its a mix of memory and history: "From the first I was astonished by the way Austerlitz put his ideas together as he talked, forming perfectly balanced sentences out of whatever occurred to him, so to speak, and the way in which, in his mind, the passing on of his knowledge seemed to become a gradual approach to a kind of historical metaphysic, bringing remembered events back to life" (*Austerlitz*, 13). The narrator finds in Austerlitz a scholar of the secular afterlife, and this fact binds them in their asymmetrical intercourse of *longue durée*.

Thus, in one of the rare self-characterizing remarks by this narrator, we find him elaborating his respect for Austerlitz's form of pedagogy as an explanation for his repeated visits to Austerlitz in his Bloomsbury flat during the early 1970s.

> When I began my own studies in Germany I had learnt almost nothing from the scholars then lecturing in the humanities there, most of them academics who had begun their careers in the 1930s and 1940s, and still nurtured delusions of power, and I found in Austerlitz the first teacher I could listen to since my time in primary school. I remember to this day how easily I could grasp what he called his tentative ideas when he talked about the architectural style of the capitalist era,

a subject which he said had fascinated him since his own student days, speaking in particular of the compulsive sense of order and the tendency towards monumentalism evident in law courts and penal institutions, railway stations and stock exchanges, opera houses and lunatic asylums, and the dwellings built to rectangular grid patterns for the labor force. (33)

With his trademark rucksack, and his penchant for resituating history and memory over an analysis of built space, Austerlitz appears early on in the book as a kind of vagabond Walter Benjamin—vaguely suicidal, laboring away at an unfinishable project, driven by passions created in historical conditions with which he eventually and obliquely manages to come to terms. Indeed, looking back on this period of his architectural project from the point of view of his later discoveries about his own past, Austerlitz will acknowledge that "the whole history of the architecture and civilization of the bourgeois age, the subject of my research, pointed in the direction of the catastrophic events already casting their shadow before them at the time" (240). Here, as in the complex sentence Sebald ascribes to Stendhal in the opening section of *Vertigo*, we find that multiplicity of times and tenses that is crucial to Sebald's vertiginous narrative sublimity.

Sebald's Jacques Austerlitz, then, is a teacher of time, history, and memory who is repressing his own relation to his past. The engagement with it will be the story of the post-1996 conversations, by far the bulk of the book, where Austerlitz explains how, in effect, his sense of himself came to be developed in a kind of a double contingency—moral luck working both on the level of how accident and circumstance made possible chance discoveries about one's past life and on the level of how historical and biographical conditions shaped that past life in the first place. In retrospect it makes sense that our introduction to Austerlitz, and the narrator's, occurs in a place called "the lost steps": "One of the people waiting in the *Salle des pas perdus* was Austerlitz, a man who then, in 1967, appeared almost youthful" (7). How does Austerlitz find his way? The Ariadne's thread that leads him back is in fact the first thing we learn about him, his own name. But the thread proves to be a fraying multi-stranded braid, and it does not lead by a continuous route to a fixed center.

Though we learn Austerlitz's name from the outset, Austerlitz himself had spent much of his life in Wales as Dafydd Elias. It is not until 1949, at the age of fourteen, his foster parents out of the picture, that he was summoned by the headmaster of his school and informed that he must sign the name Jacques Austerlitz on his exam papers for them to be official. The headmaster knows that this is his true name, but little else about him. For the boy, the name draws a blank: "At first, what disconcerted me most was that I could connect no ideas at all with the word *Austerlitz*" (68). When the boy asks the headmaster what the name means, the headmaster replies: "I think you will find it is a small place in Moravia, site of a famous battle, you know" (ibid.). Of course, readers of this novel are aware that by its conclusion the name Austerlitz figures crucially in the denouement in a number of ways. Once he begins to discover his painful origins in Prague, and to learn of the sacrifice his parents made while saving him, the titular character embarks on a journey in quest of some image of them or knowledge of their exact fate. This quest leads him to Paris, to the new Bibliothèque Nationale, and there Austerlitz visits yet another of the many railway stations of this novel, the one named, precisely, for that Napoleonic victory in Moravia. Indeed, much of the action at the end of the novel takes place in or around a zone that Austerlitz describes as "the half-deserted area between the tracks of the gare d'Austerlitz and the quai d'Austerlitz on the left bank of the Seine, . . . among abandoned dockyards, boarded up warehouses, goods depots, customs halls, and a few garages and a car repair shops" (272).

This is a zone of vision, dreams, and encounters with afterlives—including a trance induced by the conjuring music of some circus performers under a tent in an open space. It is also a territory charged with historical freight that becomes as unbearable for Austerlitz as (we learn) it did for officials responsible for reshaping it. The most recent project, the Mitterand Library, satirically treated throughout, is pointedly described as "the official manifestation of the increasingly importunate urge to break with everything which still has some living connection to the past" (286). It is an edifice dedicated to learning about the past but that—in its structure, style, and location—obliterates it. Nowhere is this point more evident than in Austerlitz's account of yet another of the novel's eponymous sites: the terrible German storage depot of the early 1940s that was once mordantly called "Les Galleries d'Austerlitz" by the prisoners forced to work there: "On the waste land between the marshalling yard of the gare d'Austerlitz and the pont de Tolbiac where this Babylonian library now rises, there stood until the end of the war an extensive warehousing complex to which the Germans brought all the loot they had taken from the homes of the Jews of

Paris" (288). In a grotesque inversion of the kind of attention to past objects that characterizes Austerlitz's own disciplined observations, the place functioned as a massive infernal vetting and recycling center. "Over five hundred art historians antique dealers, [and] restorers . . . were employed day after day in fourteen-hour shifts, to put the goods coming into the depot in proper order and sort them by value and kind" and what was not picked over by party grandees and SS officers would be shipped out to the "ruined cities of the Reich" in over seven hundred train loads (289).

The account of the eponymous storage depot seems to take us to a sort of ground zero in the novel, a stratigraphic layer that carries particular force as part of a massive perversion of culture and civilization, an "affair buried in the most literal sense beneath the foundations of [the] Grande Bibliothèque" (ibid.). Another kind of eponymous ground zero is reached with the Gare d'Austerlitz itself. For there Austerlitz has a premonition that brings him as close as he will come in his quest for his father (the closest he comes in his quest for his mother is a fond hope in an archive, a "photograph of an anonymous actress who seemed to resemble my dim memory of [her]"): "An idea came to him of his father's leaving Paris from this station, . . . soon after the Germans entered the city. I imagined, said Austerlitz, that I saw him leaning out of the window of his compartment as the train left, and I saw the white clouds of smoke rising from the locomotive as it began to move ponderously away" (291). The Gare d'Austerlitz supplies beginnings, middles, and ends for this novel. It is the place where the quest for his father effectively terminates, in spite of his unrelenting pursuit. Since his parental name proves to be Aychenwald, and since he himself passed through this station en route to Wales in 1939, we are invited to think of this place as the source of his name. And finally, it becomes clear, as his memories of it develop, that it is in this place, or its repression, that Austerlitz's Benjaminian preoccupation with the history of railway stations begins. In the final pages of the novel, Austerlitz begins to see this: "That station, said Austerlitz, has always seemed to me the most mysterious of all the railway terminals of Paris" (292). Austerlitz had *not* included the Gare d'Austerlitz in his earlier account, when he said that in Paris at the beginning of his studies "he used to visit one of the main railway stations almost daily, usually the Gare du Nord or the Gare de l'Est" (33).

But with Sebald, we must be wary of assuming that we have actually reached a ground floor, a point of origin, a master scheme or structure for the past. If Jacques Austerlitz is named for the famous Paris station, the Paris station is named for that place in Moravia, as Austerlitz's headmaster says, where Napoleon fought a famous battle. Just as in *Vertigo*, where a storyteller's sense of being stymied by the recent German past is framed within a context of Napoleonic struggle and Romantic epistemology, so here in *Austerlitz* Sebald takes some pains to contextualize Austerlitz's own historical preoccupations. When the young Austerlitz, now so called for the first time, passes his exams with flying colors, he qualifies for a scholarship to study history. In the ensuing years, his most important teacher—that is, the teacher of this boy whose own teaching will later be revered by the Sebaldian narrator—is a man named Hilary, whose course in European history was "confined to the period from 1789 to 1814" (69). He is said to have known "every detail" of this era, including the life of Napoleon and its string of celebrated military exploits: "the crossing of the Great St. Bernard, the battles of Marengo, Jena and Auerstedt, of Eylau and Friedland, of Wagram, Leipzig, and Waterloo—Hilary brought it all vividly to life for us, partly by recounting the course of these events, often passing from plain narrative to dramatic descriptions and then on to a kind of impromptu performance distributed among several different roles, . . . and partly by studying the gambits of Napoleon and his opponents with the cold intelligence of a non-partisan strategist, surveying the entire landscape of those years from above with an eagle eye" (70). When Austerlitz reports that Hilary sometimes gave these lectures on his back on the floor, because of his slipped disks, and that these lectures were more rather than less compelling on that account, the detail does not seem meant to detract from Hilary's authority. Austerlitz himself says that the students themselves did not find this "at all comic" since at these times "Hilary spoke with particular clarity and authority" (ibid.).

Of all Hilary's acts of historical revivification, however, one stood out for its brilliance: "His undoubted *pièce de resistance* was the battle of Austerlitz" (ibid.). Nearly two pages of the novel is given over to Austerlitz's recollection of how Hilary represented the events of December 2, 1805, in that "small place in Moravia," pedagogical performance that waxes Tolstoyan in its eloquence and dramatic intensity. (Hilary's first name, like Tolstoy's protagonist, is André—though the world-historical account of Austerlitz in *War and Peace* is not directly referenced in the text.) More important, the Battle of Austerlitz occasions some extended commentary on Hilary's part about inevitable limits of the historiographical operation. Though he would "talk for hours" about this battle, Hilary nonetheless felt that he was giving the event short shrift, because "as he several times told us, it would take an endless length of time to describe the events of such a day properly, in some inconceivably complex form recording who had perished, who survived, and exactly where and how, or simply saying what the battlefield was like at nightfall with the screams and groans of the wounded and dying" (71). The impossibility of this fantasy of total representation, in turn, occasions some reflections on the relation of historiography to questions of rhetoric and human psychology, and in enunciating them Hilary sounds themes very close to the heart of the book in which he appears.

> In the end all anyone could ever do was sum up the unknown factors in the ridiculous phrase, "The fortunes of battle swayed this way and that," or some similarly feeble and useless cliche. All of us, even when we think we have noted every tiny detail, resort to set pieces which have already been staged often enough by others. We try to reproduce the reality, but the harder we try, the more we find the pictures that make up the stock-in-trade of the spectacle of history forcing themselves upon us: the fallen drummer boy, the infantryman shown in the act of stabbing another, the horse's eye starting from its socket, the invulnerable Emperor surrounded by his generals, a moment frozen still amidst the torment of battle. Our concern with history, so Hilary's thesis ran, is a concern with preformed images already imprinted on our brains, images at which we keep staring while the truth lies elsewhere, away from it all, somewhere as yet undiscovered. (71–72)

In this crucial passage from what would prove to be his last novel, Sebald returns to topics with which he opened his first one, a discussion of historical epistemology framed in the concepts of impression, idea (image), and impression of reflection, all from the eighteenth-century theory of ideas. As in *Vertigo*, the basic principles of this theory, pre-Romantic in itself, are given a Stendhalian (and Wordsworthian) inflection with the emphasis on the dialectics of misdirection in the reflective process. The images that survive for our contemplation, either in personal memory or in historical memory, as photographs or sketches or ideas, have meanings that must be themselves imagined, rather than remembered, and *that* means that they can mislead, will mislead.

If I am right in sensing that Tolstoy's famous descriptions of Austerlitz lie behind this passage, then they themselves might count among the already-staged set pieces of which Hilary professes wariness. But more to the larger point, if I am right about Sebald's emphasis on Hilary's teaching the great Romantic scenes of Austerlitz in relation to the great Romantic theories of that age, then there are implications for how we understand the "modernity" of a book that so conspicuously features post-Romantic technologies. To the extent that he is using Hilary's early-nineteenth-century Austerlitz problematic as a paradigm for (as it were) the *twentieth*-century Austerlitz problematic, Sebald seems to suggest that photography, say, and the façades of the great train stations are rather incidental than otherwise to his art of memory and the treachery of its supplements.[23]

On Hilary's account of the historiographical operation, the historian is caught between the Scylla of "inconceivable form" (the fantasy of total representation) and the Charybdis of cliché form (the false synecdoche of the time-worn set piece). The solution, insofar as the book suggests one, seems to lie in the use of multiple conceivable forms. Hilary's own practice alternates between two forms, the form of dramatic immersion in which the historian assumes the point of view of various agents by turn, and the panoramic form, in which the historian presumes to hover above the event assuming "the view from nowhere." Sebald's *Austerlitz* itself is a book in which an array of historical forms is marshaled, including most prominently the panorama (which is invoked in half a dozen instances in the book, often accompanied with illustrations) and the immersive dialogue, along with the collection, the historical painting, the photographic essay, the archaeologists strata, the messianic epiphany, and the found document. It would not be hard to argue that the generic hybridity of Sebald's four books taken as a whole, a feature noted by every serious reviewer they have had, is meant as a similar kind of response to Hilary's problem: if history is necessary to the purposes of human memory, and history needs a form, and if its forms have degenerated into cliché, then the forms of historiography as we know it must be revitalized by rhetorical genre crossing.

Here I think we come to the other great Romantic contribution to Sebald's art, and another respect in which it can be seen as a Romantic afterlife. I have all along been stressing one kind of Romantic approach to history and memory: through elegiac meditation. This is the Romantic line that leads from Coleridge's conversation poems to the neo-Romantic instances of Hass and Heaney with which I began. But the other great innovation of the Romantic period—far greater in its world-historical impact—was the historical novel form usually dated from the publication of Sir Walter Scott's *Waverley* in 1814 and, if we can believe Georg Lukàcs, a historical epitome of the period 1789–1814, the very period on which Austerlitz's Hilary focused his teaching.[24] I will refrain from repeating here arguments I have made elsewhere, or rehearsing familiar points about Scott's contribution to European historiography. But it is perhaps important to recall that for many historians from Lord Macaulay to Carlo Ginzburg, the early-nineteenth-century form that Scott invented (with much help, to be sure, from, among others, Maria Edgeworth and the philosophical historians of the Scottish Enlightenment) managed just the sort of genre-crossing feat that Sebald's Hilary seems to call for and that Sebald himself delivers in this remarkable series of books. Thinking back to Sebald's use of Stendhal on the field at Marengo, we should not fail to recall here that, in introducing *Ivanhoe*, Scott famously reflected on his own "magic" in bringing life to the past by way of an allusions to Lucan's witch Erictho conjuring over the bodies of the battlefield and to the biblical bones of the Valley of Jehosephat.[25]

Like Hilary on his hobbyhorse about the Battle of Austerlitz, I feel that one could go on forever about this subject and never properly qualify one's account. I do not mean to claim that the Napoleonic period—rather than the German 1940s—is the "real" or the "true" center or foundation of Sebald's interests, though neither do I see Romanticism as just another displacement of attention from such suppressed sites as the horrendous Galleries d'Austerlitz under the Mitterand Bibliothéque Nationale. I do claim that Romanticism haunts these books in a way that argues a more than casual involvement, that it deeply "informs" them. It is not an alternative site of origin for memory and history but rather a dialectic principle of mapping them. And one could particularize in a number of ways. With world enough and time, for example, one would want to look in detail at those various forms that Sebald puts into play—analyze virtuoso passages describing Austerlitz's visit to the museum at Greenwich or his apocalyptic vision in London's Liverpool Street Station. One would want to return to the books between *Vertigo* and *Austerlitz*, especially to faces and façades of *The Emigrants*, where Max Ferber's mode of painting—his way of erasing "excavat-

ing the features of his model" (*Emigrants*, 162) through the twinned practices of painting and scraping—clearly supplies another internal paradigm
for Sebald's own practice.

One would certainly want to discriminate, too, between Sebald's deep
literary melancholy and the characteristic moods and modes of consolation that link Romantic writers as distinct as Wordsworth and Scott in their
response to loss, and link them both with the likes of Hass and Heaney in
the 1970s. I find little or nothing of the impulse to compensate or comfort
in any of Sebald's four remarkable books of the 1990s. The circular light
born of the destruction of Saturn's satellites may be beautiful, but it is a
cold, distant, and disconsolate kind of beauty, and *The Rings of Saturn* is as
saturnine as a book can be. The extraordinary reception that Sebald's books
have had in the past decade raises the question whether there is something
to be said about a changing spirit of the age from the 1970s to the 1990s.
Should we conclude that the 1990s was a gloomier time? Is there a way of
linking Sebald with the revival of Romantic modes in *cultural* criticism, or
indeed the intense recent interest in the topic of cultural afterlife?[26] Hard to
say. The spirit of the age is seldom so easily captured. Within Romanticism
itself, after all, the inconsolable figure of Byron generated his influential
alternative for "thinking . . . about loss." In any case, we may have to leave
behind the period 1989–2001 before we can begin to speculate about such
things in earnest.

Notes

I would like to thank Ian Baucom and Bill Brown for helpful suggestions with this essay, and
John Maki for his research assistance.

1   Robert Hass, *Praise* (New York: Ecco Press, 1979), 4–5.
2   Frederick A. Pottle, "The Case of Shelley," *PMLA* 67 (September 1952): 589–608.
3   Ammons was poet-in-residence at Cornell University at the time, which is where M. H.
    Abrams developed his influential scheme, published in fact in the same year as "Corson's
    Inlet," in "Structure and Style in the Greater Romantic Lyric," part of a volume dedicated
    to Pottle: *From Sensibility to Romanticism*, ed. Frederick W. Hilles and Harold Bloom (New
    York: Oxford University Press, 1965), 527–60.
4   Seamus Heaney, *Field Work* (New York: Farrar, Strauss, & Giroux, 1979), 21–24.
5   Jamaica Kincaid, *Lucy* (New York: Penguin, 1991), 17–18.
6   Mark Bruhn, "Margaret Atwood's Lucy Poem" (paper presented at the conference
    "Wordsworth's Second Selves: The Poetic Afterlife," Lancaster University, July 23–26,
    2002).
7   Jerome McGann sees the book as tilting toward Byron in a chapter entitled "Is Roman-

ticism Finished?" for *The Cambridge History of English Romantic Literature*, ed. James Chandler (Cambridge: Cambridge University Press, projected for 2004).

8 Obituary in *The Guardian*, December 17, 2001.

9 Sebald does make use of a translator for all four books. But it is well-known that Sebald's English was impeccable and his dedication to translation studies is evidenced by his directorship of Britain's most important center for that subject.

10 The one partial exception I have found is the oblique comment by Michael Scorra to the effect that Sebald's is "a melancholy at once exhilarating and too deep for tears." See review of *Austerlitz*, *Atlantic Monthly*, November 2001, 146; but see note 21 below.

11 W. G. Sebald, *The Rings of Saturn*, trans. Michael Hulse (London: New Directions, 1998), epigraph. Subsequent references cited by page number in the text.

12 Kristin Ross, *May '68 and Its Afterlives* (Chicago: University of Chicago Press, 2002), 2. This is one of several recent studies relying on the notion of an afterlife, about which more below.

13 W. G. Sebald, *Vertigo*, trans. Michael Hulse (New York: New Directions, 2000), 3. Subsequent references cited by page number in the text.

14 W. G. Sebald, *The Emigrants*, trans. Michael Hulse (New York: New Directions, 1996), 225.

15 Stendhal, *Vie de Henry Brulard* (Grenoble: Edition Glénat, 1988), 54 and 57.

16 For a good account of the "theory of ideas" as Hume inherited and developed it, see Barry Stroud, *Hume* (London: Routledge and Kegan Paul, 1977), 17–41. Strould is critical of this theory and sees Hume's best impulses as working against its requirements.

17 Annette Baier, *A Progress of Sentiments: Reflections on Hume's Treatise* (Cambridge: Harvard University Press, 1991), 180–81.

18 William Wordsworth, *Prose Works*, ed. W. J. B. Owen and Jane Worthington Smyser, 3 vols. (Oxford: Oxford University Press, 1974–76), 1:126. Hereafter cited by page number in the text.

19 William Wordsworth, *The Prelude*, ed. Jonathan Wordsworth, M. H. Abrams, and Stephen Gill (New York: Norton, 1979), 1:590–631. Hereafter cited by line number in the text.

20 Richard Terdiman, *Present Past: Modernity and the Memory Crisis* (Ithaca: Cornell University Press, 1993), 84–85.

21 After this essay went into page proofs, the full English version of "Dark Night Sallies Forth" appeared as *After Nature*, trans. Michael Hamberger (New York: Random House, 2002). The full text confirms my sense of its debt to English Romanticism. Indeed, commenting on this verse narrative in *The New York Review of Books*, J. M. Coetzee says it is "written with a nod in the direction of *The Prelude*," October 24, 2002, 26. I have tried here, in effect, to give an account of the contexts and implications of that "nod."

22 See my discussion of Wordsworth's linkages of memory and history in *Wordsworth's Second Nature* (Chicago: University of Chicago Press, 1984), 184–215.

23 This may be the place to mention Sigfried Kracauer, whose analysis of the opposition between the "realistic" and the "formative" tendencies in historiography bear some resemblance to Terdiman's notion of the struggle for determination between the past and the present. Kracauer seems to have a certain relevance to Sebald's Austerlitz because of his interest in architecture and, especially, photography. Indeed, Kracauer's account of "the historical approach" is based in what he calls "a fundamental analogy between his-

toriography and the photographic media," and in a "parallel" between "camera-reality" and "historical reality." *History: The Last Things before the Last* (New York: Oxford University Press, 1969), 56, 58. My account of Sebald will not seem inconsistent with such arguments so long as we take the long view of the history of the photographical media, understanding that such media were important to, for instance, the eighteenth-century epistemology I have sketched out. And one historian of technology who has attempted a longer history of this sort has concluded that the decisive turn in it occurs around 1820, well before the invention of the modern camera as we know it. See Jonathan Crary, *Techniques of the Observer: On Vision and Modernity in the Nineteenth Century* (Cambridge: MIT Press, 1990).

24   Georg Lukàcs, *The Historical Novel*, trans. Hannah Mitchell and Stanley Mitchell (Lincoln: University of Nebraska Press, 1983), 19–34. Of course, Lukàcs sees Scott as an anti-Romantic writer, rather than another kind of Romantic writer, but his is a far more restrictive sense of the term that I employ here.

25   I discuss this passage in Scott's "Dedicatory Epistle" for *Ivanhoe*, and its implication for the form he helped to elaborate, in *England in 1819: The Politics of Literary Culture and the Case of Romantic Historicism* (Chicago: University of Chicago Press, 1998), 166–70.

26   The afterlife is everywhere in contemporary criticism. Recent and relevant publications in Romantic studies would include Andrew Bennett, *Romantic Poets and the Culture of Posterity* (Cambridge: Cambridge University Press, 1999), a book about the "textual afterlife" as an increasingly important impulse for poetry in the eighteenth and early nineteenth centuries, and Ted Underwood, "Romantic Historicism and the Afterlife," *PMLA* (March 2002): 237–51, which actually does try to make the link between the notion of a Romantic revival in criticism and the notion of the afterlife in Romanticism as what might be revived.

Alan Liu

Remembering the Spruce Goose: Historicism, Postmodernism, Romanticism

We enter the great, white dome and gather in the recep-
tion theater. Computer-coordinated slide projectors whir to
life to tell us in a rapid montage of images and voices
the Story. "A success story, a driving power, a dynamic
tycoon, the envy of Wall Street, a world-record-breaking
pilot, the toast of the nation: a man who could make
things happen," the voices recite. "Who was this man?
Howard Hughes. His mission: to build the world's largest
airplane. . . ."

The story draws to a close; the screen rises slowly; we
walk through *the space of the screen to see—alone in its*
black, reflecting pool—the Plane.

Commonplaces

Whether we read Baudrillard on Disneyland,
Jameson on the Hotel Bonaventure, Lyotard
on the "Pacific Wall," or Virilio on Howard
Hughes, we know that Southern California—
more broadly, the North American Pacific Rim—
has become the commonplace of the postmodern world.[1] Installed all along the arc that runs
up from La Jolla through Anaheim, Hollywood,
Silicon Valley, Bill Gates's or David Lynch's
Washington, to William Gibson's Vancouver are

The *South Atlantic Quarterly* 102:1, Winter 2003.
Copyright © 2003 by Duke University Press.

the *topoi*—small as a microchip or large as the LA sprawl—of the postmodern dystopia. This dystopia appears variously on phenomenal, psychosexual, socioeconomic, and other planes as the society of "simulation," "hyperreality," "hyperspace," "depthless surface," "cyborg couplings," "flexible accumulation," "schizophrenia," "speed," and so on. Perhaps most fabulously, it appears on the historical plane as "the end of history"—as the fabled new world order, that is, where the completion of history's work rewards us with a leisure of pure *representations* of history modeling the past (in Jameson's words) "as fashion-plate images that entertain no determinable ideological relationship to other moments of time."[2] Postmodern buildings thus wear façades of history, postmodern cities fill with gentrified Old Townes or Retro-Malls, postmodern TV goes Nick-at-Nite, and everywhere on the LA dial we hear Oldies Rock. As Baudrillard says in his 1985 essay "The Year 2000 Has Already Happened," "History itself is or was only an immense model of simulation."[3]

I wish here to install in the postmodern canon yet another Pacific Rim commonplace. But I do so to challenge the very theory of the commonplace that underlies postmodern thought. The theory is that at the center of popular culture there is a commonplace that once functioned as an agora but that is now dysfunctional—that no longer grounds the truth-difference between agora and allegory, reality and hyperreality; that fractures the universality of ethical standards; that similarly scandalizes the generality of aesthetic criteria; and that at last revokes the very language-pragmatics designed to negotiate agreement upon (and between) truth-, morality-, and art-claims. The village square of the global village, in short, has been emptied of the kind of founded, integral cognition—total cognition, we may say—that once made the *sensus communis* a closed circuit of the true, good, and beautiful. And so in the agora where people once spoke the mutuality of their cognition and hence *re*cognized each other there remains only something other than total cognition.

Or more precisely (and this is the particular trauma of postmodern theory), there remains an agonic contest between two forms of other-than-total-cognition. One, the antagonist, is the Weberian regime that Lyotard names "performativity" and Habermas the "colonization of the lifeworld": the modernizing regime, in other words, that in the abeyance of total cognition reifies just one faculty of cognition, the truth-function, into an "instrumental rationality" capable of absorbing all other faculties into a bureaucratized, "expert"-culture of specialized subsystems.[4] To vary upon Max Weber's "iron cage" image: society becomes something like a computer motherboard on which dedicated ethics and aesthetics chips now serve the truth-processor at the top of the instrumental hierarchy. The second form of "other-than-total-cognition" is then the tragic or sublime agonist of postmodern theory. This hero, as often mourned as celebrated, is the stubbornly noncognitive *and* noninstrumental aesthetics—a sort of survivor's or guerrilla aesthetics—that Walter Benjamin in his "Work of Art in the Age of Mechanical Reproduction" early on dubbed "reception in a state of distraction" and that postmodern theory has updated into a whole aesthetics of everyday distraction.[5] I refer to the microstylistics of sensation that so fascinates postmodern theory: Lyotard's "feeling" for the "unpresentable"; Deleuze and Guattari's "pure intensities"; Baudrillard's "ecstasy"; Haraway's "pleasure in the confusion of boundaries"; de Certeau's "almost invisible pleasures, little extras"; Jameson's "*boredom* as an aesthetic response," "'hysterical' sublime," video "panic"; and so on.[6]

The best we have to hope for, it seems, is to live in a gigantic, mindless commonplace—named "America" or "California"—that distracts us eternally from total cognition and its head administrator, performativity, through an aesthetics so mind-numbing (borrowing here from Susan Buck-Morss's essay on Benjamin) that it is precisely "*an*esthetic."[7] "Eternally," I add, because the ultimate postmodern anesthetics is the rigorously mindless assertion—a sort of parody of Hegel's teleology of Absolute Knowledge—that history has ended and the feeling of distraction is for all time. Distraction, the simulation of historical contingency, is how we pass the time.

My suggestion in this essay is that we have been too quick to believe that total cognition has vanished totally, and thus also too quick to make a triage choice between the two, consequent postures of postmodern theory: the one that looks to aesthetic distraction for resistance to the reification of instrumental rationality (the Lyotardian heresy), and the other that looks past aesthetics to a revenant *return* of total cognition (the Jamesonian and Habermasian piety). We have been too quick because the preoccupation of postmodern theory with the family quarrel between postmodernity and modernity has made it easy to forget a crucial fact about the "totality" in such concepts as "total cognition." The only totality there has ever been is history, where history (in the view I have espoused elsewhere) is understood as that which teaches by contingency that there has never been any such thing as *a* totality—universal, unified, stable—with enough bounded presence to be judged either totally "here" or "not here."[8]

Imagine, then, that the postmodern commonplace is cannier, just plain smarter than we give it credit for because total cognition has never totally vanished but is still resident in a retrievable *history* of cognition. Imagine that within the state of distraction—the state of an "everyday" consciousness suspended between the horizons of the collective and individual, the necessary and contingent, the mind and body—there exists a whole archive of negotiations between rational, ethical, and aesthetic thought. Imagine in particular that the aesthetics of distraction is thus always also cognitive *traction*: an engagement of aesthetics *with* cognition capable on various occasions of drawing upon all the permutations in the dialectical relationship between sensation and thought that Terry Eagleton reminds us is the *history* of aesthetics.[9]

Imagine, if you will, the visit of a Wordsworth critic to the Disney-managed Spruce Goose installation in Long Beach, California, as it stood in spring and summer 1992 soon before it became history.[10]

> *On our way to the plane, we are distracted by the exhibits scattered across the dome floor. Here is the original mock-up of the Spruce Goose cockpit, in which the sign tells us Hughes "spent more time . . . than in the actual . . . cockpit." Next is an "authentic Sherman tank" rolling out of a dummy version of the plane's front bay doors.*
>
> *Let's sit and rest for a moment at the Hughes the Filmmaker exhibit, where the video shows clips from* Hells Angel *featuring Hughes's fleet of original WWI airplanes. And there's Jane Russell in a clip from* The Outlaw *showing off the breasts for which Hughes designed extra lift. (A woman near us laughs and walks away.)*
>
> *Finally, we are climbing the staircase that takes us over the reflecting pool to the Spruce Goose. They've cut a hole in the fuselage to let us in. Only, what we see when we enter is not the full length of the interior, which extends back from where we stand a hundred feet or so to the tail, but instead a false-perspective mock-up of the interior going back only some 50 feet. There's even a miniature dummy of a crew member.*

Exit Nature

We can best describe the postmodern agora installed at the Spruce Goose by adopting a socioeconomic analytic—one that, up to a point, will be predictable. Where Benjamin had his Arcades, we can say, LA had its Spruce Goose. The Spruce Goose, that is, structured the contemporary agora as an exemplary spectacle-market of commodity logic. Or rather, it structured a distracting transition between two such commodity logics, one the heartland of Benjaminian modernity and the other that of postmodern simulation.

Modernity, first of all. In Benjamin's terms, the Spruce Goose installation was a paradigm of the fetishism with which the age of mechanical reproduction transfigures auratic "originals" and "uniques" into equipment-assisted facsimiles. From the moment we walked *through* the space of the slide-screen to see the original plane—the one and only Spruce Goose flown one time by the one and only Howard Hughes—all the dome's phantasmagoria of reproduction was foreseen: all its transference of aura from originals into images, mockups, models, and dummies; all its origami-ontology folding "authentic" Sherman tanks into trompe-l'oeil bay doors; even the inexplicable insertion of a stage-set-like replication within the body of the original. And just in case we missed the "modern" in all this, the entirety of the phantasmagoria, of course, was mounted in a Disney-perfect ambience of modernity finished in excruciating detail with music, photos, mementos, planes, cars, and other bric-a-brac from the period of that great, Fordist entrepreneur of speed and mass entertainment: Howard Hughes. In this context, indeed, Hughes's twin manias for airspeed and film production are equivalent registers of the need for reproduction. World-record speed was what allowed Hughes to reproduce himself as if instantly before cameras in New York and Paris; and film was what allowed him to change one instrument of reproduction, the airplane, for an even faster one, the camera itself.

Modernism (as opposed to modernity) was then the critical or utopian myth that arose to represent reproduction: "dreamwork," Benjamin calls the myth in his Arcades Project; a "dream" of progress, the Spruce Goose exhibits said instead. We note, however, that modernist myths of reproduction rest upon a prior, foundational myth secreted within the notion of the original itself. The myth is "nature." Consider these two statements together:

> *From Benjamin's Artwork essay*: The concept of aura ... may usefully be illustrated with reference to the aura of natural [objects]. ... If, while

resting on a summer afternoon, you follow with your eyes a mountain range on the horizon or a branch which casts its shadow over you, you experience the aura of those mountains, of that branch.[11]

Voiceover in the video at the Hughes as Filmmaker exhibit: Howard Hughes was a man of great natural talent, ability, and intelligence. . . . It was only natural that . . . Hughes would make a name for himself [in Hollywood].

Whether reproduction is seen as the Fall or, instead, *felix culpa* of originality, in other words, there *was* a primordial originality as real as nature. Or at least, such originality could be fabricated.[12] For what is curious about such eminently modern artifacts as the Spruce Goose, we recognize, is that their authenticity depends on conflating the categories of the "natural-original" (as it may be called) and the "manufactured-original." The result is that highly interesting, synthetic category (mock-heroicized by Duchamp's Readymades) of the "found-original." Hughes, after all, had meant to build three prototypes of the Spruce Goose and eventually a working fleet. If the plane turned out to be uniquely original, therefore, such singularity has at best a "found" status akin to that of a *hapax*: authenticity derives only from the extinction or suppression of reproductions *contemporary* with originality.

But now we come to postmodern commodity logic. The crucial fact here, of course, is that the Spruce Goose installation was unable to let the modernist conflation of natural- and artificial-originals alone. Rather, it worried at that seam of foundation so obsessively that it at last disclosed the fissure of postmodern "hyperreality." Item: we notice that curious, *other* "found-original" sharing the pool with the Spruce Goose: the one-of-a-kind 1939 Cadillac. Item: Hughes's originality was dogged throughout the exhibits by the specter of another, prior original: Charles Lindbergh. "In 1927," the sign at the Hughes and Aircraft exhibit proclaimed, "Charles Lindbergh completed a historic flight . . . launching the golden age of aviation. Hughes became caught up in the excitement of the age." Again, in the exhibit's video: "President Roosevelt himself presented the Harmon Trophy to Hughes, whose fame was now equal to Charles Lindbergh's." And item: the entirety of the Spruce Goose installation competed with an even more massive singularity tied up at the same Long Beach dock—the Disney-run Queen Mary with its homage to the identical era of modernity (complete with historical photos, mementos, restored staterooms, etc.). At the Spruce Goose, in sum, the modern market of exchange between auratic originals and mechanical reproductions was overlaid by a gigantic double image: the ghost image of a whole, other market of exchange between *competing* originals each of which hollows out the authenticity of other originals.[13]

Thus it is that we discover ourselves in the postmodern agora. This agora is not the scene of modernist alienation or (put spatially) "spacing" between originals and reproductions. Nor is it in any fully stabilized way the postmodern spacing *within* originality that alienates us from modernist myths of alienation themselves. Rather, the postmodern agora is what Jameson calls a cognitive hyperspace yawning open in strange, disorienting torsion *between* those two, primary spaces of alienation—a meta- or hyperspace in which, as Margaret Morse says in her study of the "ontology of everyday distraction" on freeways, malls, and TV, we are profoundly "spaced out."[14] If modernity had witnessed the diaspora of reproductions away from their originals, after all, at least it had a compass bearing on those originals by which to measure its own exile. As in the bold diagonals of modernist graphic design (e.g., El Lissitzky or Jan Tschichold), modernism cut athwart all the old symmetries at a critical slant, yet implied in that very slant its own grid of right-angled certitudes (the "grid" principle of layout within which diagonals worked their precise transgressions).[15] But now we have neither the old symmetries nor any clear diagonals designed to snap everything back into an alternative, critical focus. As in Jameson's paradigm of the Hotel Bonaventure, the Benjaminian *flaneur* gives way to the postmodern consumer-tourist wandering in malls and Spruce Goose installations through a cognitively unmappable zone of hyperalienation where the only foundation to be grasped is somatic: the purely local universe of the body in which we "feel" our estrangement from total cognition.

> *We visit the Spruce Goose once more in late summer soon before it is to be disassembled. Jazz Age music plays to no one at the snack bar; just a few people sit at the video exhibits, faces lit by flickering screens; one child stands before the Cutaway Engine display, watching a mock-up of the plane's gigantic engines ceaselessly propelling itself nowhere.*
>
> *Looking around, we notice that the trees in pots are gone—all except one left out in the refuse for Art to pick up.*[16]

Toward a History of Distraction

My sketch of the postmodern agora, as indicated, is so far predictable. What is *un*predictable because unthought by postmodern theory?

It is time to remember the laugh of that woman at Jane Russell's breasts (exhibited without irony as yet another Hughes engineering project along-side the world's largest airplane).[17] The laugh itself, perhaps, is theoreti-cally accountable. The woman utters a great, Foucauldian laugh, we deduce, because she sees in the Russell icon the exposure not just of the modern gap between the natural or original woman and her inflated screen-image but also the postmodern scission or cleavage we previously remarked within the status of the natural/original itself.[18] According to the exhibit, after all, Russell was in effect man-made: it was the man Hughes who originated the image of the natural woman. (And extending the analysis further, we notice that not even the "man Hughes" is fundamental but is instead a con-struction constantly effeminized in the exhibit by allusions to his shy and retreating boyhood spent under the wings of his mother.)

What is theoretically unpredictable, however, is simply that the woman walked away—an act that may stand here for the larger fact that so many people walked away from the Spruce Goose that Disney at last had to shut it down. To my knowledge, nothing in current postmodern theory ade-quately explains such a discrimination *within* the realm of the common-place. While theory deploys sophisticated analytics to describe the distrac-tions of hyperreality, it has assumed that such a postmodern condition is essentially homogeneous (homogeneous in its heterogeneity, it might be said) and so, too, that our distracted navigation through this condition also is indiscriminate. But what we learn from such commonplaces as the Spruce Goose is that some distractions are more attractive than others—Disney-land itself, for example, as opposed to Hughes-land. And while the dis-crimination involved in choosing distractions is in part aesthetic (one could, I suppose, build a case for Disneyland as an extra-hyperreality furnish-ing *more* feeling, more pleasure, more boredom, more panic, etc.), surely in everyday practice aesthetic and rational discriminations mix. Rationally considered, for instance, the Spruce Goose was simply harder to get to and offered relatively little bang for the buck compared with other acmes of hyperreality. So, too, it is at least conceivable that ethical discriminations may have come into play: shadowed by the eccentricities of his late life, Howard simply could not be Walt on the family circuit.

Of course, my particular speculations here are disputable. But more interesting than any such dispute is what the very possibility of making speculations of this sort points to: the great, blind zone of cognition *in* the commonplace that theory elides because it characteristically stops just at the point of discovering the sublime, panicked, ecstatic, bored, and other aesthetics of distraction prior to looking closely *into* those aesthetics to descry their internal dynamics and external affiliations. This blind zone where aesthetics links up with other cognitive domains has been the absolute limit of inquiry that Baudrillard personifies as the "silent majorities": "What are they; what do they do; what do they become?," he asks about the silent masses and immediately answers in his usual spirit of burlesque-sublimity, "They turn themselves into an impenetrable and meaningless surface."[19] So, too, for Lyotard the blind zone where aesthetics links up with other cognitive "phrase regimes" marks the absolute limit of knowledge he calls— with a much more serious invocation of the sublime—the "differend." But pause to look closely *into* the "meaninglessness" of distracted "feeling," I am saying, and discover that the horizon of postmodern aesthetics merely opens up rather than closes off a whole, further horizon of questions—questions about the commonplace imbrications of reason, ethics, *and* aesthetics that allow some people on some occasions to be critical in their distraction.

I come now to the core suggestion of this essay: How do we look into the blind zone of commonplace intelligence? What is required, I believe, is a hermeneutic of the commonplace designed to be sensitive to the peculiar combination of meaninglessness *and* cognition constitutive of the blur of everyday consciousness—the blur of *collective* practical thought, in other words, that other hermeneutics still busy affirming or negating the notion of individual cogito pass over. And the best hermeneutic in this regard is historical understanding.[20] While the sometimes bizarre linkages of reason, ethics, and aesthetics created in commonplace thought have no transcendental foundation (they are in this sense "meaningless"), they *are* founded in the contingency of the *history* of thought. There are historically different kinds of "meaningless" engagements or "differends" between reason, ethics, and aesthetics, in other words; and at least some past kinds (historiography has a wealth of collectivist names for these kinds: custom, habitus, episteme, mentality, ideology, and so on) enter into conjunction with postmodernity as a repertory of habitual ways of thinking *about* and *through* feeling. To understand how it is possible to think in the postmodern agora, therefore, we need to look into the archive of prepared forms of cognition to see just what past commonplaces (and in what configurations) are available to the present commonplace.

I cannot here provide the history of distraction I am calling for except (as I have also done in essays during the 1990s) to suggest the usefulness of exploring a particular episode in such history: what might be called the "Romanticism of postmodernism."[21] After all, consider that tree, of many one, left standing outside the Spruce Goose dome.[22] Whatever one thinks of the ultimate conclusions of Habermas's work, I believe, the historicizing impulse he demonstrates in such writings as the chapter on Nietzsche and Romantic aesthetics in his *Philosophical Discourse of Modernity* is worthy of emulation.[23] Romanticism—which originally worried the relation between cognition and the commonplace, which inflected that cognition in the direction of feeling, which named the resulting distraction "memory" or "imagination," and which finally subjectified the whole problem in a tense relation between nature and originality—such Romanticism is not the same as postmodernism. But without the historical lens provided by such topics as Romanticism *and* postmodernism, neither term in the comparison can now be illuminated.

Methodological Afterword

A defining feature of the debate on postmodernism has been what may be termed the "historicism paradox." On the one hand, postmodern experience has been described as the aestheticization of historical reality. Where once things mattered, historical matter (economic, social, political, cultural) now appears indistinguishable from the phantasmic. Nothing matters except the imagery, spectacle, or simulacra of reality; and the essence of such simulation is that—as when we surf effortlessly across channels on cable or sites on the Web—it seems to have none of the stubborn, gritty determinacy or resistance of historical matter. Even late- rather than postmarxists such as Fredric Jameson, David Harvey, and Edward W. Soja have effectively abandoned the materialist premise to cleave to a hollower notion of geo-social "space."[24] Postmodern space is all configurations, relations, distances, and timings: it is a circuit etched on a world-size silicon chip whose material substrate (the equivalent of silicon) is functionally neutral, history-less. As Baudrillard sums up in his essay on the end of history ("The Year 2000 Has

Already Happened"): "History itself is or was only an immense model of simulation." History becomes an image-generating circuit that "models," rather than constitutes, reality.

But on the other hand, formulations of postmodernism have been simultaneously haunted by the need to account *historically* for postmodernism as the end of history. Characteristically, therefore, postmodernism is inflected as a "postmodernity" or "postmodern condition" whose origin is sought above all in its relation to modernity. And the fierce debate over whether this period-relation is discontinuous or continuous proceeds precisely on the grounds of economic, social, political, and cultural matter—that is, on the presumption of a substrate able to determine the rise of the new world order of indeterminacy. Jameson puts the paradox nicely when he says about his "late-capitalism" thesis: "What follows is not to be read as stylistic description. . . . I have rather meant to offer a periodizing hypothesis, and that at a moment in which the very conception of historical periodization has come to seem most problematical indeed."[25] In a manner similarly problematical, postmodernism has been determined as post-Fordism, post-use-value, post-"performativity," postrepresentation, posthumanism, and so on.

Interpreters crave a history of postmodernism, in sum, but have no ground to stand on. For, if postmodernity is the period that conditions us to experience sim-history rather than history, then to what period or condition do interpreters themselves belong when they seek to explain the end of history historically?

The methodological premise of this essay is that the hermeneutic groundlessness fostered by the historicism paradox is in great part a function of the narrowness of the "modern versus postmodern" debate. When attempts to explain the historical emergence of postmodernism restrict their baseline to twentieth-century "modernity," then the conceptual ground of any resulting historicism is undercut from the start. As Habermas notes, after all, modern modernity was itself "that radicalized consciousness . . . which freed itself from all specific historical ties."[26] In a debate where modern modernity and postmodernity are the only options, history-makers such as Jameson (as is sometimes averred) necessarily appear atavistic: a critical dinosaur. Yet, of course, Jameson is not the only atavism to stalk the Jurassic Park of the postmodern. One has only to review, for instance, such major, historicizing gambits as Lyotard's comparison of postmodernity to romantic sublimity or Habermas's contrast of the Enlightenment to the

Nietzschean "entry into postmodernity."[27] The general argument in the concluding paragraph of my essay above is that since historicism is demonstrably required by our ablest interpreters of postmodernism yet does not fit on the "modern versus postmodern" gameboard, then it is the gameboard itself that must be expanded to accommodate the risks and gains actually being contributed by historical understanding. The only solution to the historicism paradox, in other words, is to place postmodernism in a longer view: one that significantly deepens modernity beyond "modern modernity," embraces centuries rather than just one century, and differentiates discrete moments in the process of modernization: premodern, early modern, Enlightenment, Romantic, and so on.

My specific argument is then that while much can be gained by referring postmodernism to any past period of history, it is especially pertinent to initiate an interview between the postmodern and the Romantic. Contact between postmodernity and such older epochs as the classical, pre-Christian, or medieval is in essence exotic. When Gilles Deleuze and Félix Guattari investigate paradigms of nomadic life or medieval cathedral-building in *A Thousand Plateaus*, for example, they produce within our contemporary sensibility an effect akin to what Foucault, at the beginning of *The Order of Things*, calls "the exotic charm of another system of thought[,] . . . the stark impossibility of thinking *that*."[28] The emphasis is on a delicious frisson of momentary contact between modernity and the (pre)historical other: other than Western modernity, subjectivity, mentality, and so on. But when Lyotard and Habermas link postmodernism to Romanticism in the latter's complex emergence from the Enlightenment, then a different theater of hermeneutics opens in which it is not the charm of the exotic but the uncanny compulsion of the familiar that dominates interpretation. The difficult relation of similarity and otherness characterizing the birth of Romanticism from the Enlightenment is itself—to the second power—the progenitor of the equally complex relation of similarity and otherness characterizing the breach of postmodernism from modernism. The track that Romanticism made as it broke out of the furrow of Reason was the antecedent of the unfurrowing, the delirium, of postmodernism.

After all, it was Romanticism (or "romantic modernity," as Habermas calls it)[29] that first confronted the historicism paradox ("I am 'new' or 'original,'" it said, but also: "Let us remember origins"). It was Romanticism that thus constructed what might be called an oxymoronic "history of the new"

(Wordsworth: "I would enshrine the spirit of the past / For future restoration").[30] And it was thus Romanticism that precipitated nineteenth-century historicism and so helped establish the very primacy of historical understanding whose paradox has now returned to haunt us. If at the "end of history" we are once more perplexed by the historicism paradox, then it is not surprising that such interpreters as Habermas or Lyotard implicitly recommend measuring the history of the new that is postmodernism against the history of the new that was Romanticism.

The list of themes that Romanticism and postmodernism share is surprisingly replete: the sublime, subjectivity, simulation ("imagination"), reproduction (the status of copies relative to auratic naturals), mass culture, political revolution (July 1789; May 1968), industrial and technological revolution, the aestheticization of cognition (as "feelings" or "intensities"), organicism and antiorganicism, neoconservatism, aesthetic improvisation, fragmentary artistic forms, and many more. So many and so important are these shared problems, and so often do interpreters of postmodernism allude to Romanticism, that there is every reason to think the two epochs intersect in more than an accidental way. More than other periods, perhaps, Romanticism and postmodernism are not just part of the centuries-long process of modernization but the stages in that process wherein modernity reflects self-consciously on the historical bounds of its freedom to be "new." The two periods may differ in the answers they offer, but their question is the same: what does it mean to be historically determined to be indeterminate, to be conditioned to be free?

Notes

This essay was first presented in preliminary form in 1992 at a session of the Modern Language Association convention (one of a pair of sessions entitled "Romanticism and Postmodernism" that I organized for the MLA's Division on the English Romantic Period). My focus in this essay on "postmodernism" is a symptom of that moment, when it seemed important to make a connection between the Romantic field's recent experimentation with "new historicism" and late-twentieth-century aesthetic and cultural concerns as they appeared in that same decade under the banner of postmodernism. Now another decade on, I would want to position "postmodernism" in retrospect as just one element in the larger formation of a postindustrial "now" into which all historical awareness is vanishing. My forthcoming book, *The Laws of Cool: The Culture of Information* (Chicago: University of Chicago Press) takes a postmillennial perspective on information culture (and the associated postindustrial ethos of "workplace 2000") as the epitome of an endless, benighted, postindustrial "now." The only true Romantics today are those who are "cool."

1   Jean Baudrillard, *Selected Writings*, ed. Mark Poster (Stanford: Stanford University Press, 1988), 171–72; Fredric Jameson, *Postmodernism; or, The Cultural Logic of Late Capitalism* (Durham: Duke University Press, 1991), 38–45; Jean-François Lyotard, *Pacific Wall*, trans. Bruce Boone (Venice, CA: Lapis, 1990); Paul Virilio and Sylvère Lotringer, *Pure War*, trans. Mark Polizzotti (New York: Semiotext(e), 1983), 71–75.

2   Jameson in Anders Stephanson, "Regarding Postmodernism: A Conversation with Fredric Jameson," in *Universal Abandon: The Politics of Postmodernism*, ed. Andrew Ross (Minneapolis: University of Minnesota Press, 1988), 18. See also Terry Eagleton on the topic of postmodernism and history in his *Ideology of the Aesthetic* (Cambridge: Blackwell, 1990), 377–78.

3   Baudrillard, "The Year 2000 Has Already Happened," in *Body Invaders: Panic Sex in America*, ed. Arthur Kroker and Marilouise Kroker (New York: St. Martin's Press, 1987), 41. The classic paradigm of such historicity is the nostalgia-film as studied by Jameson (*Postmodernism*, 19–21).

4   Jean-François Lyotard, *The Postmodern Condition: A Report on Knowledge*, trans. Geoff Bennington and Brian Massumi (Minneapolis: University of Minnesota Press, 1984); Jürgen Habermas, *The Theory of Communicative Action*, trans. Thomas McCarthy, 2 vols. (Boston: Beacon, 1984, 1987).

5   Walter Benjamin, "The Work of Art in the Age of Mechanical Reproduction," in *Illuminations*, ed. Hannah Arendt (New York: Schocken, 1969), 240. On postmodern distraction, see Jameson, *Postmodernism*, 117. See also Margaret Morse, who has recently said in her study of the postmodern "non-space" of the freeway, the mall, and television that we know in the agora today only an "ontology of everyday distraction" ("An Ontology of Everyday Distraction: The Freeway, the Mall, and Television," in *Logics of Television: Essays in Cultural Criticism*, ed. Patricia Mellencamp [Bloomington: Indiana University Press, 1990], 193–221).

6   Lyotard, *Postmodern Condition*, 79–81 (on the "feeling" of the unpresentable, which Lyotard associates with what he calls the "differend," see also his *The Differend: Phrases in Dispute*, trans. Georges Van Den Abbeele [Minneapolis: University of Minnesota Press, 1988], 13); Gilles Deleuze and Félix Guattari, *A Thousand Plateaus: Capitalism and Schizophrenia*, trans. Brian Massumi (Minneapolis: University of Minnesota Press, 1987), esp. 4; Baudrillard, *The Ecstasy of Communication*, trans. Bernard Schutze and Caroline Schutze, ed. Sylvère Lotringer (New York: Semiotext(e), 1988); Donna J. Haraway, "A Cyborg Manifesto: Science, Technology, and Socialist-Feminism in the Late Twentieth Century," in *Simians, Cyborgs, and Women: The Reinvention of Nature* (New York: Routledge, 1991), 150; Michel de Certeau, *The Practice of Everyday Life*, trans. Steven Rendall (Berkeley: University of California Press, 1984), xxiv (Certeau is here quoting Witold Gombrowicz); Jameson, *Postmodernism*, 71, 34, 72. I leave aside here "ethics" as the third player in the Weberian/Habermasian thesis that meaningful cognition split apart into specialized realms of instrumental rationality, morality, and aesthetics. As in such works as Lyotard's *Just Gaming*, however, it is clear that while the postmodern celebration of aesthetics may not require a classical metaphysical foundation (the "truth" or "nature" that once grounded the "beautiful"), it does search for a grounding in ethics (the "good"). Jean-

François Lyotard and Jean-Loup Thébaud, *Just Gaming*, trans. Wlad Godzich (Minneapolis: University of Minnesota Press, 1985).

7   Susan Buck-Morss, "Aesthetics and Anesthetics: Walter Benjamin's Artwork Essay Reconsidered," *October* 62 (Fall 1992): 3–41.

8   This is one way to express the main argument of my *Wordsworth: The Sense of History* (Stanford: Stanford University Press, 1989).

9   Eagleton, *Ideology of the Aesthetic*.

10   The italicized excerpts in this essay are based on notes, tape recordings, and photos of a visit to the Spruce Goose dome in Long Beach, California, on July 2, 1992 (the second of two visits that year). Shortly afterward, the Disney-owned exhibit was shut down and the plane (owned by Aero Club of Southern California/Aero Exhibits, Inc.) was transported in disassembled sections to Oregon beginning in October 1992 to await the building of a new exhibition facility at the Evergreen Aviation Museum in McMinnville, Oregon. See the Web site of the Evergreen Aviation Museum for the recent history of the Spruce Goose: *http://www.sprucegoose.org/*; accessed May 13, 2002.

11   Benjamin, "The Work of Art in the Age of Mechanical Reproduction," 222–23.

12   See Miles Orvell's *The Real Thing: Imitation and Authenticity in American Culture, 1880–1940* (Chapel Hill: University of North Carolina Press, 1989) on the modern obsession with fabricating the "real thing."

13   Relevant here is Deleuze and Guattari's slogan against uniqueness: "Subtract the unique from the multiplicity to be constituted; write at $n - 1$ dimensions" (*A Thousand Plateaus*, 6). Or as Jameson puts it, postmodernism is the blank parody, the pastiche, of modernist "uniqueness" (*Postmodernism*, 17).

14   Morse, "An Ontology of Everyday Distraction," 203.

15   See, for example, Jan Tschichold's 1928 *The New Typography: A Handbook for Modern Designers*, trans. Ruari McLean (reprint, Berkeley: University of California Press, 1995). In speaking of "hyperspace," I am beholden to Jameson, *Postmodernism*, 38–39, 44.

16   This is an allusion to a photograph I took that I have not been able to reproduce in this article. The photograph shows one of the potted trees in the Spruce Goose dome discarded outdoors in a large trash bin labeled "Art," the name (one presumes) of the proprietor of a local garbage company.

17   Hughes and his engineers designed a cantilevered bra to show off Russell's breasts in the 1943 film *The Outlaw*.

18   On Foucault's laugh, see *The Order of Things: An Archaeology of the Human Sciences* (New York: Vintage, 1973), xv–xvii.

19   Baudrillard, *Selected Writings*, 213.

20   In the "history of distraction" I call for here, the emphasis is on "history," as opposed — for example — to the emphasis on "practice" in Michel de Certeau's project of recovering the many ways of practical reason.

21   See my "Local Transcendence: Cultural Criticism, Postmodernism, and the Romanticism of Detail," *Representations* 32 (Fall 1990): 75–113; and "The New Historicism and the Work of Mourning," *Studies in Romanticism* 35 (1996): 553–62.

22   See note 16 above.

23 Habermas, "The Entry into Postmodernity: Nietzsche As a Turning Point," in *The Philosophical Discourse of Modernity: Twelve Lectures*, trans. Frederick G. Lawrence (Cambridge: MIT Press, 1990).

24 Jameson, *Postmodernism* (especially the sections on architecture); David Harvey, *The Condition of Postmodernity: An Enquiry into the Origins of Cultural Change* (Oxford: Basil Blackwell, 1989); Edward W. Soja, *Postmodern Geographies: The Reassertion of Space in Critical Social Theory* (London: Verso, 1989).

25 Jameson, *Postmodernism*, 3.

26 Habermas, "Modernity: An Incomplete Project," in *The Anti-Aesthetic: Essays on Postmodern Culture*, ed. Hal Foster (Port Townsend, WA: Bay Press, 1983), 4.

27 Lyotard, "Answering the Question: What Is Postmodernism?" trans. Régis Durand, in *The Postmodern Condition*; Habermas, "Entry into Postmodernity."

28 Foucault, *The Order of Things*, xv.

29 See Habermas, "Modernity," 4, on "the romantic modernist."

30 William Wordsworth, *The Prelude* (1805), bk. 11, ll. 341–42.

Notes on Contributors

SRINIVAS ARAVAMUDAN is associate professor of English at Duke University. He specializes in eighteenth-century British and French literature. He is the author of *Tropicopolitans: Colonialism and Agency, 1688–1804* (1999; MLA prize for best first book, 2000) and the editor of *Fiction*, volume 6 of *Slavery, Abolition, and Emancipation: Writings of the British Romantic Period* (1999). He has completed a book on South Asian Anglophone religion entitled *Guru English* (forthcoming in 2004). He is writing a book on Orientalism and is editing for classroom use William Earle's antislavery romance, *Obi: or, the History of Three-Fingered Jack* (1800).

IAN BAUCOM is associate professor of English at Duke University. He is the author of *Out of Place: Englishness, Empire, and the Locations of Identity* (1999) and is currently completing a manuscript provisionally titled *Specters of the Atlantic: Finance Capital, Melancholy, and the Philosophy of History*.

JAMES CHANDLER, the Barbara E. and Richard J. Franke Professor in English Language and Literature at the University of Chicago, is the director of the Franke Institute for the Humanities. He has published *England in 1819: The Politics of Literary Culture and the Case of Romantic Historicism* (1998) and *Wordsworth's Second Nature: A Study of Poetry and Politics* (1984). Together with Arnold Davidson and Harry Harootunian, Chandler coedited *Questions of Evidence* (1994), and with Kevin Gilmartin, *Romance Metropolis* (forthcoming, 2004). He is now completing work on the new *Cambridge History of English Romantic Literature* (forthcoming, 2005).

WAI CHEE DIMOCK is William Lampson Professor of American Literature at Yale University. She is the author of *Empire for Liberty: Melville and the Poetics of Individualism* (1989); *Residues of Justice: Literature, Law, Philosophy* (1996); and coeditor of two collections of essays, *Rethinking Class* (1994) and *Literature and Science: Cultural Forms, Conceptual Exchanges*, a special issue of *American Literature* (December 2002). She is now at work on two book projects, *Literature for the Planet: Global Readers of Dante* and *American Literature and Planetary Time*.

IAN DUNCAN is professor of English at the University of California, Berkeley. He is the author of *Modern Romance and Transformations of the Novel* (1992). Forthcoming publications include articles on Adam Smith and Ossian, Victorian regional and provincial fiction, and Edinburgh as Romantic metropolis; an edition of James Hogg's *Winter Evening Tales* (2002); and a new book, *Scott's Shadow: The Novel in Romantic Edinburgh* (2003).

FRANCES FERGUSON is Mary Elizabeth Garrett Professor of Arts and Sciences at Johns Hopkins University and director of the Center for Research on Culture and Literature. She has published essays on eighteenth- and nineteenth-century literature, and is the author of *Wordsworth: Language As Counter-Spirit* (1977), *Solitude and the Sublime: Romanticism and the Aesthetics of Individuation* (1992), and the forthcoming *Pornography: The Theory*.

KEVIS GOODMAN is assistant professor of English at the University of California, Berkeley. Her contribution to this issue comes from her book, *Georgic Modernity and British Romanticism: Poetry and the Mediation of History* (forthcoming in 2003), which studies the early history of concerns about media (or "mediums") in new anxieties surrounding the expansion and inundation of the senses during the eighteenth century and Romantic periods. She has also published articles on Milton in *ELH*, and on Wordsworth and the new historicism in *Studies in Romanticism*.

JENNIFER KENNEDY is an independent scholar who received her Ph.D. in English from Yale University in 2000. She has published essays in *PMLA*, *Early American Literature*, *American Literature*, and *Modernism/Modernity*.

CELESTE LANGAN is associate professor of English at the University of California, Berkeley. She is the author of *Romantic Vagrancy* (1995) and essays on Scott and Byron. Her current book project, *Post-Napoleonism*, is an examination of cognitive autonomy and political sovereignty after Eighteenth Brumaire.

ALAN LIU is professor of English at the University of California, Santa Barbara, where he works in the fields of Romanticism, new media studies, and theory. He is the author of *Wordsworth: The Sense of History* (1989) and *The Laws of Cool: The Culture of Information* (forthcoming). He is the editor of Voice of the Shuttle, the Web site for Humanities Research and also directs a research and curricular-development project titled *Transcriptions: Literary History and the Culture of Information*. His current research focuses on the place of literature amid the information streams native to postindustrial society.

A native of Germany, THOMAS PFAU obtained degrees in English and Comparative Literature from the University of Constance, the University of California, Irvine, and the State University of New York at Buffalo. A member of the Duke English Department since 1991 with a joint appointment in German Studies, he has translated and edited theoretical writings by Friedrich Hölderlin (1987) and F. W. J. Schelling (1994). He has also edited two essay collections on English Romanticism—one being a special issue of *SAQ* (1996) and the other an anthology, *Lessons of Romanticism* (1998). Following his 1997 book, *Wordsworth's Profession*, he completed a study on the historicity and construction of Romantic emotion.

THE VELVET LIGHT TRAP
A CRITICAL JOURNAL OF FILM AND TELEVISION

The **Velvet Light Trap** offers critical essays on significant issues in film studies while expanding its commitment to television as well as film research. Each issue provokes debate about critical, theoretical, and historical topics relating to a particular theme.

■■

The **Velvet Light Trap** is published biannually in Spring and Fall.
Single copy rates: Individual $15, Institution $30
Canada/Mexico, add $3.50; other foreign(airmail), add $7.

Yearly subscription rates: Individual $26, Institution $50
Canada/Mexico, add $7; other foreign(airmail), add $14.

University of Texas Press Journals,P. O. Box 7819, Austin, Texas 78713-7819
Phone # 512-232-7621, Fax # 512-232-7178, journals@uts.cc.utexas.edu

Graduate Faculty
Philosophy Journal

The **Graduate Faculty Philosophy Journal** is published in association with the Department of Philosophy, the New School for Social Research. The **Journal** is a forum for the communication of ideas concerning continental philosophy and its tradition.

VOL. 23 NO. 2

All communications should be addressed to the Editor, **Graduate Faculty Philosophy Journal**, Department of Philosophy, New School for Social Research, 65 Fifth Avenue, New York, NY 10003. The Journal is biannual. Domestic rates: Individuals: $20.00/year; Students: $12.00/year; Institutions: $45.00/year.

DUKE

Duke University Press is pleased to announce that current subscribers will receive free electronic access through Ingenta Select in 2003!

Duke University Press titles available online through Ingenta Select in 2003

American Literary Scholarship
American Literature
American Speech
boundary 2
Camera Obscura
Common Knowledge
differences: A Journal of Feminist Cultural Studies
Eighteenth-Century Life
Ethnohistory
French Historical Studies
GLQ: A Journal of Lesbian and Gay Studies
Hispanic American Historical Review
History of Political Economy
Journal of Health Politics, Policy and Law
Journal of Medieval and Early Modern Studies
Mediterranean Quarterly
Modern Language Quarterly
Nepantla
Neuro-Oncology
Pedagogy
Poetics Today
positions: east asia cultures critique
Public Culture
Radical History Review
SAQ: South Atlantic Quarterly
Social Science History
Social Text
Theater

Beginning in January 2003, selected Duke University Press journals will be available electronically through Ingenta Select—free with a current print subscription. Institutional subscribers will be able to access current 2003 titles as well as back volumes from 2000–2002.

For information regarding registration, please call us at 919-687-3602 or visit our Web site—**www.dukeupress.edu/journals**.